Between Feminism and
Psychoanalysis

Between Feminism and Psychoanalysis

Edited by Teresa Brennan

Routledge

London and New York

First published 1989
by Routledge
11 New Fetter Lane, London EC4P 4EE
29 West 35th Street, New York NY 10001

Typeset by LaserScript Limited, Mitcham, Surrey
Printed in Great Britain by Richard Clay Ltd Bungay, Suffolk

British Library Cataloguing in Publication Data

Between feminism and psychoanalysis.
  1. Psychoanalysis related to feminism.
  2. Feminism related to psychoanalysis
I. Brennan, Teresa
305.4'2

ISBN 0-415-01489-1
ISBN 0-415-01490-5 Pbk

Library of Congress Cataloging in Publication Data

Between feminism and psychoanalysis/[edited by] Teresa Brennan.
p. cm.
Based on a series of talks given at Cambridge University in King's College from Jan.
to July 1987.
Includes index.
ISBN 0-415-01489-1. — ISBN 0-415-01490-5 (pbk.)
1. Feminist therapy—Congress. 2. Psychoanalysis—Congresses.
3. Feminism—Congresses. I. Brennan, Teresa, 1955- . II. King's College
(University of Cambridge)
[DNLM: 1. Psychoanalysis—essays. 2. Women—psychology—essays.
WM 460.5.W6 B565]
RC489.F45B47 1989
616.89'17—dc19
DNLM/DLC
 for Library of Congress 88-38894

Contents

Preface

Between Feminism and Psychoanalysis is based on a series of fifteen seminars given at Cambridge University in King's College and the Social and Political Sciences Faculty from January to July 1987. The series was organized in an attempt to explore the often intense debates that have arisen around psychoanalysis, especially of the Lacanian type, and feminism.

The women who presented the seminars are identified with different, sometimes opposing theoretical positions in these debates. Mainly, the debates concern essentialism, the kind of symbolic law culture requires, sexual difference, how far knowledge is inherently patriarchal, and the practical and political use of psychoanalysis for feminism. Those key debates in the series also structure this book. My first thanks go to the women, key protagonists in these debates, who came to Cambridge from India, the United States, France, and elsewhere in Britain, often interrupting their own busy schedules to do so.

In so far as debates on psychoanalysis and feminism have a common point of departure, it is feminism's concern with social transformation: a political question, nominally appropriate to a Faculty of Social and Political Sciences. But the contributors are mainly literary theorists; only two of us, Parveen Adams and myself, have social science backgrounds. And the audience came not just from sociology and politics, but from modern and medieval languages, English, classics, and so on across the disciplinary board. The interdisciplinary compass and appeal of feminism is established; evidently, it is not limited when feminism is tied to psychoanalysis.

It is not possible to thank all the women and men who came every second week to listen, question, argue, and amplify. The following are mentioned both for their informed questions, and especially for a variety of helpful, practical acts: Malcolm Bowie, Ann Caesar, Stephen Coles, Silvana Dean, Ben K. Fred-Mensah, Helena Gaunt, Helen Gibson, Anthony Giddens, Simon Goldhill, David Good, Felicia Gordon, Sarah Greaves, Elizabeth Guild, Stephen Heath, John Henderson, Pam Hirsch, Sarah Kay, Michael Moriarty, Christopher Prendergast, Suzanne Raitt, Morag Shiach, Naomi Segal, Patricia Touton-Victor, Janet Todd, Phyllis Tralka, Cathy Urwin, Margaret Whitford, and Alison Young. Special thanks to Elizabeth Guild, who did most of the interpreting during Luce Irigaray's stay in Cambridge, as well as translating her paper. Cathy Urwin also presented a paper in the series. Unfortunately, it was not available for publication here.

The series was mainly supported by King's College and the Social and Political Sciences Faculty; further assistance was provided by the French Cultural Delegation in Cambridge, and by Clare Hall. It was conceived in discussions with Jennifer Jarman and Ingrid Scheibler, who helped me to arrange it, and whose enthusiasm, labour, and skill made it an adventure and a pleasure. Without them there would have been no seminars, nor, consequently, this book. In the production of the book itself, thanks to Janice Price of Routledge for excellent advice and constant encouragement throughout the project; to Lisa Jardine, for providing me with the institutional context to do it in; and to Susan James. I am also grateful to Anne Marie Goetz, and have a deep debt to Kwok Wei Leng, for ongoing theoretical discussion, assistance in preparing typescripts, careful observations on the works of Sigmund Freud, and a great deal more.

TMB

Introduction

Teresa Brennan

This introduction and to some extent this book is preoccupied with four stagnant issues in feminist, psychoanalytic thinking, and how to move beyond them. The issues are: the status of the Lacanian 'symbolic', sexual difference and knowledge, the bearing of essentialism on feminist politics, and the relation between psychical reality and the social. If this introduction has a thesis, it is that thinking about these issues is deadlocked, of late, because their specific political *or* psychoanalytic contexts have been neglected. At the same time, residues of the initial contexts survive in exegetical clichés and stock phrases that make it more difficult to rethink the issues.

By tracing out some of the background to the issues, it is possible to see where political and psychoanalytic problematics have been confused in feminist writing. Of course any notion of opposition between psychoanalysis and politics has to be qualified: psychoanalysis is a thoroughly political entity. The question here is one of context and emphasis. If psychical processes are emphasized, as they are in the context of Lacan's theory of the symbolic, this contextual emphasis needs to be taken into account before a political critique can be fully elaborated, before politics can figure in a productive way, taking account of psychical issues, rather than closing its eyes to them. With these matters in view, the first section sets out a brief summary of Lacan's theory of the symbolic, some feminist responses to it, and the related issue of sexual difference. But while the specific psychical concerns of the symbolic may have been played down in some feminist writing, political issues have been played down (and deeply confused with psychical ones) in recent critiques of essentialism. This, and the respective claims of psychical and social reality, are discussed in the second section.

While putting forward the view that political and psychoanalytic contexts have been unproductively entangled, the first two sections are also expository, intended to provide some background to issues discussed in this book. The third section is more reflective. It reflects on the psychical function of the stock phrases, the stereotypes and credos that contribute to deadlocked and stagnant thinking, that are repeated in one psychoanalytic feminist exegesis after another.[1] My argument is that such stereotypes reconcile conflicting identifications, with feminism, psychoanalysis, and the academy. They also provide guarantees in what Gayatri Spivak calls the 'scramble for legitimation in the house of theory',[2] and assuage the ego's social anxiety about 'expulsion from the horde'.[3] I had intended to write a separate paper on this theme. But as I worked on that paper and the introduction together, they became intertwined: the argument of the paper drew more and more on the contributions to this collection. In the end, I made the paper into this introduction's third section. If the reader wants to do so, she can miss this section without it affecting the sense of the introduction, and turn to the description of the papers on pp.14–20.

From the symbolic to sexual difference

In what was a useful way in, and is now an exegetical cliché, feminist debate is often cast in terms of the difference between Anglo-American and French perspectives. French feminism is meant to be about the insistence that women are different, and a challenge to phallogocentric thinking and patriarchal structures of language. Its Anglo-American counterpart is characterized by the insistence that women are equal, and its concern with the real world.[4] Yet this division is occludent. It hides substantial differences between the 'Anglo' and the 'American', as well as the French, on the question of the Lacanian symbolic.

There differences are plain enough if one reflects on the different positions that have emerged, mainly but not exclusively, in Britain on the one hand, and France and the United States on the other, around Lacan and his reading of Freud.[5] Very roughly, one, associated with British feminists and especially Juliet Mitchell, has defended Lacan and Freud. The second, associated with the work of French women theorists/psychoanalysts (Luce Irigaray chiefly, Hélène Cixous, and others), has tried to find ways around the male dominance implied by Lacan's 'symbolic' law. On the face of it, this project has won more sympathy in the US, where it has been creatively developed, than it has in Britain.[6]

The thing is, the challenge to Lacan is often read as, or reduced to, the challenge to patriarchal structures of language and phallogocentrism, which of course in part it is. But Lacan's theory is not only about a patriarchal order of language. It is also about psychical organization; it is an argument that the symbolic is the condition of sanity. It should become evident that this aspect of Lacan's theory has also received attention in French difference feminisms, especially from Irigaray. Moreover, it is only when this aspect of Lacan's theory is taken into account that the British feminist defence of him makes any sense.

For Mitchell the problem with the attempts to undercut the symbolic is that without *a* symbolic law human beings cannot function. Briefly, and I will unpack this definition in a moment, the symbolic places human beings in relation to others, and gives them a sense of their place in their world, and the ability to speak and be understood by others. It does this by enabling them to distinguish themselves from others, and through establishing a relation to language. Outside the symbolic law, there is psychosis. Mitchell, a practising analyst, shares this view with Julia Kristeva.[7] On this issue, their views owe little to geographical affiliations. Where terrain has some relevance is that Mitchell, and some other British feminists, are more closely identified with a *defence* of Lacan, with an expository, critical style that supports the man, rather than the propositional eclecticism of some of the French, Kristeva included. For the latter, Lacan's theory counts for a lot, but not all.[8]

Assuming that it is true that psychosis is the alternative to the symbolic, this need not of itself be an unsurpassable obstacle, providing one can conceive of a symbolic that is not patriarchal. The real problem is that Lacan's symbolic makes patriarchy seem inevitable. I will indicate his argument to this effect.

The symbolic's patriarchal nature relies on the interlocking functions of the symbolic father, which I will discuss first, and the notorious phallus. Lacan says the symbolic father intervenes in the imaginary ties between mother and child. For Lacan the actual father matters infinitely less than his structural, symbolic position as an intervening third party. In the imagination, the father's position is the same as that occupied by language, in that language intervenes in the imaginary dyad as the symbolic words that rupture the threads of phantasy that hold lack at bay and the illusion of union in place. To borrow the vocabulary of mainstream psychoanalysis for a moment, this intervention is critical to the process of psychical differentiation, to the subject's differentiating itself from others; and this is one reason why sanity relies on the symbolic. How changing the sex of either the intervening third party or the primary care-giver, or the actual father's social position, would affect the process of differentiation is another matter; but real changes in either parenting patterns or the social position of women and men must have consequences for the symbolic.

In short, the symbolic's patriarchal nature relies in part on the coincident meeting of two intervening 'third terms': language, and the structural position of third party, currently occupied by a man. The man occupies this position in an arrangement where women take primary care of children. But he also occupies it in a social context where men are valorized. Generally, Lacanians insist that the symbolic is patriarchal because the woman is the primary care-giver, the man the intervening third party, occupying the position co-incident with language. Whether this coincidence could be separated, whether there would still be a symbolic if it were, is debated. Moustafa Safoun thinks the separation would be catastrophic. Ellie Ragland-Sullivan puts forward a subtle and I think convincing alternative view, that the key to the patriarchal problem is the fact that men are socially valorized. At the least, whether the symbolic is inherently patriarchal because women take primary care of children, or because of the coincident intervention of a socially privileged father and language, is a wide open question.[9] But the patriarchal symbolic has another anchor in the form of the phallus; or more precisely, in a tie between sexual difference and phallic dominance. It is this tie that seems harder to break.

It is a tie that depends on the visually significant penis. While Lacanians never tire of insisting that the penis and the phallus are not the same thing, and they are right, this visual significance is none the less a point at which penis and phallus converge. Let us consider first the phallus, then its visual tie to the penis.

The phallus is the mark of lack, and difference in general and sexual difference in particular. As the mark of lack, it refers to the fact that the subject is not complete unto itself. It is here that the symbolic father and phallus connect; the former breaks up the illusion of unity, the latter represents that break. As the mark of difference in general, the phallus is allied with the logos, with the principle that the recognition of difference is the condition of logic and language alike. That is to say, thinking as such requires difference. This brings us to a critical Lacanian claim that sexual difference is the crucial one in being able to speak, thus think; and, *mutatis mutandis*, that speaking is critical to sexual difference. The visual recognition of sexual difference is a channel connecting the heterogeneous experience of the feeling, sensing body to something that is alien to it: the differential structure of language; in turn, that language lets it name the difference.

Here comes the twist in the argument. By the fact that it appears more visible, and because it can represent lack, the penis stands in for the would-be neutral phallus. In other words, at a *non-visual* level, the phallus is meant to be no more than a neutral signpost: a signifier representing nothing, or nothing more than that lack propels us into speaking, and that in doing so, we differentiate. Yet in connecting the body to this thoughtful process, we rely on the visual representation of sexual difference. Hence the ideally neutral phallus is represented in a one-sided masculine way. Not only this, but the feminine position, as opposed to the masculine phallic one, is meant to have no content, to be nothing more than difference from the masculine. Feminists influenced by Lacan have stressed that both sexes can take up the masculine and feminine places; these shift and slide – no one has the phallus. Yet the tie between phallus and penis exists, and persists.

There is something here that needs to be highlighted. In the Lacanian account two distinct processes are merged. On the one hand, there is recognizing difference, the rudiments of logical differentiation. On the other, there is the subject's psychical differentiation. Not only do the father and language alike figure as third terms in the subject's psychical differentiation, but the phallus figures in the recognition, and use, of the differential structure of language and logic.[10] It may be objected that the distinction between these two processes is unwarranted: are they not both processes of differentiation? Yes, and they overlap, *but one pertains more to the subject's identity, the other to the subject's reason*. This distinction will become significant when this discussion returns to the question of exegetical stereotypes, and the difficulty of going beyond them. Meantime, it should be stressed that Lacan draws both forms of differentiation together under the same phallic name. Often in fact

Lacan falls back on a net of interconnecting, closely-related meanings, not all of which have been discussed here.[11] I have emphasized those aspects of his theory that make the psychical significance of the symbolic plainer.

More precisely, the emphasis has been on those things that show why sanity is a stake in the arguments for the symbolic. When Mitchell defends Lacan, the context is in some sense clinical; the cost of defaulting on the symbolic is psychosis. In this context, to criticize Mitchell, yet again, on *prima facie* political grounds for relying on a phallocentric theory is to beg the psycho-analytic question.[12] The criticism of itself does not dispose of an argument for the symbolic as a psychical necessity. Of course the issue cannot be left there. Rather, the question becomes: what would a non-patriarchal symbolic entail? With this question, the political factor re-enters, but at a different level. When I wrote at the outset that psychical factors had to be considered in their psych-ical context before an informed political critique could be mounted, this is what I had in mind. Moreover, once the symbolic's bearing on psychical organ-ization and sanity is taken into account, the work of French difference theorists, especially Irigaray, appears in a more complex light. For instance, Irigaray's renowned explicit attention to the female body can be read, not as a celebration of the body for its own sake, but as a psychoanalytically informed argument, intended to counter the centrality of the penis in psychical differentiation.[13]

In short, I am suggesting that Irigaray, like Mitchell, may have a clinical issue in mind: the idea that the phallus is represented by the penis implies, according to some thoroughly criticized Lacanian accounts, that men are more capable of differentiating themselves. For those same Lacanians, this explains the empirically greater incidence of psychoses amongst women: women are more likely to be undifferentiated, goes this reasoning, thus psychotic.[14] Hence a paradox. The patriarchal symbolic is a condition of sanity for both sexes, women excepted. If this Lacanian muddle is the context for much of Irigaray's work – and Margaret Whitford's remarkable rereading, in this collection, of Irigaray on differentiation suggests that it is – then when Irigaray draws attention to the difference of the sexes, and dissects the privilege accorded the visual, she is not only a 'French difference theorist' concerned with the countering of patriarchal language and modes of thought; she is also intervening *qua* analyst in a psychoanalytic debate over the symbolic, ad-dressing the specific problem of psychical organization, of sanity.

Having said that, it should be stressed that this psychical concern is not the only one motivating Irigaray, let alone Cixous. When I alluded to the stylization of French feminism in terms of its concern with difference, language, and the critique of phallogocentrism, I was not denying the significance of these concerns for French women writers. One of the problems in emphasizing issues that have been neglected is not to undervalue the concerns that have received more widespread recognition. I may have undervalued the critique of phallogocentrism and, if so, want to remedy that now, albeit briefly, before closing this section.

Irigaray, like Cixous and others, is also partaking of the broad Derridean critique of metaphysics. For one can criticize Lacan on the grounds of his metaphysics alone, as Derrida does when he argues that Lacan privileges sexual difference and ties sexuality to a knowledge dependent on binary oppositions, where masculinity dominates by presence, and rationality is established through the exclusion of the feminine (or so it appears). Lacan's explanation of phallic dominance partakes of the logic of presence; indeed it is a prime exemplar of it. The fact that one sex appears more visible than the other will confer privilege in a world where presence itself is privilege.[15]

At the same time, Derrida's and related critiques raise another set of problems. It can seem that the choice is between being rational or logical, and being feminist, that the choice is between reason and revolution. These considerations take us into debates on epistemology, the dependence of western metaphysics on presence and on the exclusion or absence of woman; debates that are crucial both in terms of their own trajectory, and in their relation to psychoanalysis. They are one way of dealing with the notion that femininity has no content, that it is the negative term; that sexual difference is difference *from* the phallus.

But given that, for Lacan, the negativity of the feminine is a symbolic psychical necessity, the question remains: can a reformulation of the terms of sexual difference take account of the issue of psychical organization: can this issue, and that of the metaphysical critique, the knowledge issue, be brought together?

From sexual difference to essentialism, and a debate about psychical reality

Thus far, the emphasis has been on the psychical problems the Lacanian symbolic poses, and on how psychical issues figure in sexual difference. In this section I turn to another area where political and psychoanalytic propositions need to be disentangled before they can be reconsidered: the escalating debate over essentialism. This debate intertwines with that over the symbolic. In fact it is this entanglement that makes the threads in the dispute over essentialism difficult to unravel.

To begin drawing the political problems out of the psychoanalytic ones, it is necessary to restate why essentialism came into disrepute. Initially in Britain, essentialist theories were criticized from a Marxist theoretical standpoint. Essentialist theories are those that believe in some essential aspect of 'human nature'; in something pre-given, innate, natural, biological; in something which cannot be changed. This critique of essentialism was elaborated in the context of early 1970s shifts within received views on Marxism: a shift away from a 'humanist' reading of Marx's theory of ideology towards the structuralist interpretation that criticized the early Marx on epistemological and related political grounds for his tacit reliance on the notion of a 'human essence'.[16]

This took Marx outside the parameters of historical materialism, beyond the territory shaped entirely by history, and therefore, supposedly, entirely open to change. Where Marxism was allied with feminism, the critique of essentialism carried over. Its focus became sharper: essentialist theories are those which appeal to sexual biology. The early condemnations of essentialism, in feminist literature in the late 1970s, usually have the question of change as their context.[17] As much as it was an argument against natural rather than historical, materialist explanation, this was an argument for a logical principle. If it was allowed in any context that there was something fixed in sexual identity, then that argument was open to abuse: if women were naturally more nurturant, then by the same logic, women could be naturally incompetent. To admit even a positive argument from nature was to foreclose (too soon?) on the belief in an ultimately social account of sexual difference; to rule out strategies for change directed against the social order as it stands.[18]

From the early 1980s on, leading British feminists have endorsed Lacan's theory as a non-essentialist one: non-essentialist because it theorized femininity as a non-biological construction; because it claimed that femininity had no content, and because it made the feminine position available to both sexes, although in a highly qualified sense. Why Lacan's theory was endorsed in the feminist context is another question, one that Jane Gallop asks in a subtle argument that bears on the one I am making here. For Lacanian non-essentialism had little to do with the political rationale of the 'critique of essentialism': its relation to change was unpromising; the femininity it theorized was not 'biological', but nor was it historical.[19] And, as numerous critics have said, this account of femininity still implicates biology: femininity, as the negative term in sexual difference is constructed in relation to the phallus; and the thoroughly natural, essentialist penis lends itself to the representation of the phallus. The symbolic depends on this construction, and the symbolic is a universal, structural event. Despite this, it seemed to be enough to say, and it was mainly feminists sympathetic to Lacan and also to a socialist tradition who said it, that Irigaray was essentialist and therefore wrong because she called on the female body, and that by contrast Lacan's theory of femininity was non-essentialist.[20] That this critique took no account of Irigaray's own concern for the symbolic is ironic. Moreover it contributes to another occluding dyadic division: on the one hand there are those who recognize the symbolic law and oppose essentialism; on the other, there are the essentialists. I will return to this issue in a moment.

The immediate issue is the words, essentialist, non-essentialist. These words helped bridge a Marxist theory and a Lacanian one. By the shaky bridge they built, these words provided a means for reconciling political and psycho-analytic standpoints which might otherwise be in conflict. While the 'differ-ence'/equality dyad obscures the significance of the symbolic for psychical organization in much French work on difference, the critique of essentialism has a similar obscurantist function where politics are concerned. This does not mean that all contemporary opponents of essentialism leave the political context of their opposition vague.[21] The concern here is precisely with 'non-essentialism' as a supposed virtue regardless of whether the context is a (Lacanian) psychoanalytic or a political one. As Braidotti argues in this collection, they cannot be the same.

The description 'non-essentialist' functions as a kind of sclerosis in the system of feminist enquiry. It lets a potentially productive conflict between psychoanalysis and politics lie quiescent; it smooths things over by presenting the theories as compatible. What is more the concern with change that the critique of essentialism initially encapsulated is displaced; it becomes oddly inexpressible, in that Lacan's non-essentialist theory (and all it implies, the necessity for a symbolic) is not a theory of historical mutability.

Despite the way the critique of essentialism smooths over a potential conflict between a feminist politics founded on change, and the implications of the Lacanian symbolic, that conflict re-emerges, symptom-like. It does so in Lacanian-influenced criticisms of Nancy Chodorow, criticisms which rely on the Lacanian symbolic.[22] The arguments against Chodorow come to this: to see the nature of masculinity and femininity as the result of the internalization of the social relations governing parenthood is to reduce psychical reality to social reality. It is to make sexual difference the result of the social order rather than the foundation of the symbolic order; the symbolic is the means for taking in information about gender stereotypes. In other words, sexual difference is not only the result of socialization but its condition.

The Lacanian account is very different from that tradition of sociological appropriations of psychoanalysis (including Chodorow's) which focuses on how social relations and sexual stereotypes are internalized. It has to be added here that these sociological arguments are highly compatible with the feminist reasoning which assumes that socialization or social history shapes sexual identity. It also has to be said that this sociological argument has close affinities with the Marxist argument against essentialism, in that it points to a social rather than a natural, biological foundation for sexual identity.

The difficulty with the sociological argument is that it really cannot explain the exceptions to gender stereotypes, and because of this it becomes what Toril Moi calls 'culturally essentialist'. The essence of the female or male human being is nurtured in the culture, and planted within that being as securely as if it had been born there. But to acknowledge the argument is weak is not to say that its motivation was misplaced. In the first instance psychoanalysis was harnessed to the feminist project to comprehend how patriarchal sexual identities go as deep as they do, why the masquerade of femininity is such a strong act: Mitchell's enquiry in *Psychoanalysis and Feminism* was governed by the quest for knowledge about precisely that. In that work, which came well before her espousal of the theory of the symbolic, her social terms were those of the Marxist theory of ideology. These terms were more sophisticated and more wide-ranging than Chodorow's, but to some extent they embody a similar difficulty: they neglect the tension between psychical and social realities. In this, they may be missing exactly what is needed to push the feminist appropriation of psychoanalysis beyond its impasse. Both Parveen Adams and Joan Copjec suggest that the very difficulties Freud and Lacan pose can be turned into a feminist advantage.[23]

In short, if the terms under which Mitchell's project could be conducted have changed utterly in the last ten poststructuralist years, if assumptions about a direct line between social cause and psychical effect are in doubt, this does not mean that there is no connection between psychical and social reality, or that the questions that inspired the original project should be repressed. It means the terms of the project have to be rethought.

Returning to the symbolic

The distinctions which now lend themselves to ill-fitting clichés and stereo-types, the oppositions 'Anglo-American' and 'French', 'essentialist' or 'non-essentialist', were not introduced mindlessly. When they were introduced, they carried debates forward. They are only a problem when they gloss over differences, hold up thinking, lead to stagnation on certain key issues. The question becomes, why or how are ideas used this way? Why do they persist, when their political and intellectual use is unclear?

These questions have been addressed by Barthes, and by Bourdieu at more length. I will not attempt even a brief summary of their arguments on the meaning of history, signification, and the related role of academic institutions in featuring certain ideas at different times.[24] Rather, I will assume that their arguments on the relations between 'history' and 'leading ideas' are known, and explore some psychical mechanisms by which the subject is tied to, identified with, ideas.

In *Group Psychology and the Analysis of the Ego* Freud suggests that ideas and individuals alike can constitute a prestigous other with whom the subject identifies. They do so in a process whereby the subject identifies its ego ideal with that other. On this basis, I am going to suggest that certain theories prevalent within feminism as a movement, other theories within the university field, and some of the individuals and institutions that constitute these respective fields serve as various, frequently conflicting, ego ideals. As such they become identification points for the ego, and their power lies precisely in their being means of identification, and often, legitimation. I then want to suggest (and for this suggestion, Lacan will be necessary) that one function of stereotypes and credos within feminism is to reconcile conflicting ident-ifications. But first more needs to be said about Freud's theory of the ego-ideal identifications with others and ideas. In saying it, I want to distinguish between the nature of the social identifications involved in this theory, and reductive social readings of psychoanalysis.

In discussing identifications with others in *Group Psychology*, Freud makes a very interesting distinction, between the ego's identification with the object, where the ego takes into itself the object or its characteristic(s), and its identification of its own ego-ideal with another, where that other comes to stand for the ego-ideal. The former mode of identification is far better known; the notion of the ego as the precipitate of abandoned object-cathexes is a cornerstone for the reductions of object-relations psychology. The latter is more complex: although the ego-ideal, by Freud's account, is formed out of identifications,[25] it can be identified with others in an ongoing social process, whenever the subject puts another person, an object, or an idea, in the place of its ego-ideal.

Still, it may be objected here that this is making a social matter out of a psychical affair (sociologizing); especially by Lacan's account the ego-ideal is a primary structure, constituted at the mirror-stage, and basic to the imaginary. At the same time, by Freud's account, through the ego-ideal, the individual makes social identifications that I will call transitory, rather than formative.[26] The identifications of the ego-ideal drag the subject into diverse social currents. Freud makes a related distinction between psychically basic and socially flexible aspects of the super-ego (for which the ego-ideal was of course the prototype) in another context, which I quoted from at the outset. The general context is *Inhibitions Symptoms and Anxiety*, the particular context is social anxiety, to which the formula, 'separation and expulsion from the horde' applies, but it 'only applies to that later portion of the super-ego which has been formed on the basis of social prototypes, not to the nucleus of the super-ego, which corresponds to the introjected parental agency'.[27]

This distinction raises significant possibilities, *some* of them more positive than the mindless behaviour Freud analyses in *Group Psychology*. A contemporary social identification of the ego-ideal with another could offset the more traditional super-ego; which might help explain how it was ever possible to think outside patriarchy, if it was as thoroughly internalized as Nancy Chodorow believes.[28] We can postulate that an ego-ideal identification with feminism, in the form of a person, people, or a body of writing, suspends the ego-ideal's existing prohibitions, that it *permits* different thinking. For when the ego identifies its ego-ideal with a social other, it is permeable to the wish, will, or ideas of that other. It does not simply displace the ego-ideal onto someone who mirrors the attributes of the existing ego-ideal (although it certainly can do). On this reading of Freud, by the very fact of displacing the ego-ideal onto another, the subject leaves itself open to new influences. At the same time, it is in the nature of any ego-ideal to lay down another set of prohibitions (for instance, the prohibition on essentialism).

There is another aspect to the social identifications of the ego-ideal. By Freud's account, these identifications are multiple:

> Each individual ... is bound by ties of identification in many directions, and
> he has built up his ego ideal upon the most various models. Each individual

But how did feminism begin?

therefore has a share in numerous group minds – those of his race, of his class, of his creed, of his nationality, etc. – and he can also raise himself above them to the extent of having a scrap of independence and originality.[29]

The fact of multiple identifications is another reason this theory lends itself to a non-reductionist account of the relation between psychical and social reality. Which identifications will adhere is not pre-ordained. They are flexible, as well as predictable. This might be evident after considering how multiple identifications cohere. Lacan thinks that they cohere at the level of the imaginary, in fixed ideas which smooth over difference. To amplify, I will exemplify.

In suggesting that the stereotypic adjective 'non- essentialist' smoothed over potential conflicts between psychoanalytic and political affiliations, I could have said that it and similar formulae allow a temporary harmony of being to the woman who, in Alice Jardine's terms, is in the impossible position of trying to be a feminist, psychoanalytic, and an academic. For tensions are created when points of identification come into conflict. Continuing with this line of thinking for a moment, we might consider how certain feminist positions deal with a more thoroughgoing conflict, between an unavoidable, unconscious, patriarchal identification and a feminist one. The feminist defence of Freud may belong here. Loyal to father and feminism alike, this defence – whatever its intellectual merits – may reconcile an atavistic, patriarchal super-ego and a feminist ego-ideal.

But I am straying too far from the workings of stereotypes. The term 'non-essentialist', to persist with that paradigmatic example, also functions as a division, it establishes an opposition. At this point it should be stressed that identifications are not coterminous with identity. Because identification forges a unity with another, it also poses an imaginary threat. To maintain a separate identity, one has to define oneself against the other: this is the origin, for Lacan, of that aggression towards the other who threatens separateness, and thereby threatens identity. That one is not what the other is, is critical in defining who one is. Thus the truism, that one is most likely to define oneself against who or what one is most like. The divisions within a psychoanalytic feminist discourse define one thing against another. To the extent that they function as points of identification, these divisions can figure in psychical differentiation ('*I* am *not* a French essentialist'). Of course, and this has not been stressed enough, these divisions are also the product of thoughtful differentiation. They cease to be signs of a thought-through difference only when there is an unwillingness to relinquish them in the face of further thought, when or as they become points of identification. This introduces a digression, but one worth including. In the first section on the symbolic I wrote that the phallus is the crucial point of convergence between difference as the condition of language and logic, and the subject's psychical differentiation. By the Derridean name, phallogocentrism, and also by Lacan's logic, phallus and logos are firmly tied together, through a specular identification. The discussion in this section suggests that divisions in and as thought (roughly and occasionally equivalent to logic) and the identification points for psychical differentiation are tied, but also that they move apart from time to time. If they did not, there could be no shifts in patterns of ideas, nor critical innovations. The very act of thinking past fixed ideas shows that differentiation in thought is not indissolubly tied to psychical differentiation, and the identification points the latter embodies. It follows that to the extent that the logos is a name for the former process and the phallus the mark of the latter, there is a level at which the phallus and the logos embody antagonistic principles. For the phallus marks a fixed identification, and any fixed identification between subject and idea runs, at a certain level, against the logic of the analytic process. From this perspective, it is not so much the sign itself that is the problem, as for instance the later Barthes argues; it is more the nature of the identification with the sign, and the way signs are fixed together, forming stagnant blocks of identification.[30]

When ideas are fixed side by side, as they are when the words 'essentialist, against-the-symbolic' are run together, their fixity makes it difficult to divorce questions about the symbolic or essentialism from the associations they have accrued. To think fluidly about associated terms, and their difference rather than their similarity, they have to be unfixed; the grounds for their association re-examined. This re-examination is always in some measure historical. To say this much is to assume only that the recovery of the course of the debates and issues that compose the historical context leads to another perspective; it is not a claim that a finding on a context is ever final, merely that the process of trying for it is a corrective. It is exactly the business of tracing and retracing contexts that puts things in a different light. When it works, this process helps to pinpoint the blocks in understanding. In this, it is akin to what Lacan describes as the historical work of analysis:[31] going back, suspending the habitual, reconstructing the story from its premises to see if things look different. Proust, advocating a somewhat similar process, said it requires 'giving up one's belief in the objectivity of what one had oneself elaborated': instead of reassuring screenish memories, familiar categories which one believes to be accurate, one is obliged to go back as far as possible to first premises. Proust gives this example, immediately following the sentence quoted: 'instead of soothing oneself for the hundredth time with the words: "She was very sweet," one would have to transpose the phrase so that it read: "I experienced pleasure when I kissed her.".'[32] Reconstruction is not only remembering what one would rather forget, but calling on Spivak again, 'actively forgetting' what one would rather remember.

This analytic historical work is a vehicle for the symbolic's intervention in the clinical situation. It is a manifestation of the unimpeded differentiation necessary for logic. For it deconstructs the misleading identifications that constitute the imaginary blocks on understanding, and as indicated, reconstructs another story. In thinking about this I am influenced by Toril Moi, and her reading of Freud in this volume.[33] But there are two qualifications that need to be placed on this notion of historical, analytic work in our context. I mention them partly, and paradoxically, because they also illuminate its relevance to a feminist, or any other curious enquiry.

First, for Lacan one's history can only be approached from the standpoint of the future; from what one is in the process of becoming. Yet this cannot be known in advance. In a personal analysis, to anticipate particular goals may be, probably would be, to block the unconscious unfolding of a 'destiny' (his term). In a political movement, there is something of the same, which Rosi Braidotti alludes to in her preference for the 'conditional present' when 'thinking as a feminist'. How can one know where feminism is going from the standpoint of all our fixities? At the same time, where the desire to do or know something is forgotten, when for instance a particular feminist question disappears from the literature, this, from a psychoanalytic standpoint, could mark the presence of an opposition to that given wish or desire to know. An opposition that may be grounded in imaginary identifications with institutions, disciplines, vogues. In which case remembering that wish becomes crucial to the process of what one is becoming. Wishes can be replaced or given up, but the conscious supersession of old desires is altogether different from forgetting that they were there. In some cases of course those desires should be retained, maybe modified, maybe realigned, but recognized as wishes worth having. The wish to know femininity, or the wish to understand what the lived experience of sexuality is about, are surely in this class.

Second, if it is the case that it is through historical contextual work that imaginary associations can be undone, or actively forgotten, and a continuity of memory restored, it is also the case that this undoing involves often radical shifts in perspective. It involves new ideas, as well as, or as part of, the recollection of old ones. In this process, the extent to which associations can be divorced is affected by the fact that one's ego needs its fix: it is fixed in relation to given points of identification, tied up in associations. When – if – these associations are undone in analysis they are undone in a dialogic process: the emergence of a chain of *free* associations requires an interlocutor. It also requires a break with the mirroring that characterizes most personal, social relations. The analytic interlocutor is precisely not a mirror of this sort,[34] but is none the less a point of identification, one that I think sustains some sense of coherence while one comes to terms with a dependence on the images one receives from others, and an identification with them and their ideas; or, to say the same thing differently, while the symbolic breaks up the imaginary.

Here, then, is the paradox. If fixed associations forge an illusory but utterly necessary sense of coherence, by bringing together identifications with political movements, theories, institutions (not to mention friends, families, and other entities I am obliged to bracket) how does one move beyond them outside the analytic situation? It is not enough to say that in everyday life, as well as analysis, the symbolic breaks up the imaginary. Even in the analytic situation, the symbolic does not effect the break without the aid of an interlocutor.

The fact is, of course, we move. But how? Interlocution, from what has been said so far, is as much the problem as the cure; as a way out, it is a necessary condition, but not a sufficient one. To understand what makes for more sufficiency, we might consider Naomi Segal's stress on the damage done by the wrong mirroring process, and Morag Shiach's stress on the importance to Cixous of Clarice Lispector, who ended Cixous' wandering for ten years in over-published solitude without seeing a single woman's face.[35] Perhaps Cixous sought, and found, a point of identification for what she was trying to say, and which existing words left half-said. To suggest this is too summary, but for now I will have to leave it.

The papers

In various ways the contributors to this collection argue for a rethinking of fixed associations. If they all have some thing in common, it is that. They also represent different sides of the debates that frame this book. Very broadly, some are grounded in the critiques of Freud and Lacan developed by Irigaray especially, and also Cixous. Others try to use Freud and Lacan for the benefit of feminism. Others work through internal critiques. But none are confined to the existing terms of debate. They go beyond them, do more than restate current positions within (or on) psychoanalysis and feminism. Some change the existing terms of debate by a direct focus on the disagreements discussed here. Others have little or nothing to do with those disagreements, only a tangential relation to them. Yet their very tangentiality points to other perspectives, the reflections they prompt lead to other ways for thinking about 'feminism and psychoanalysis'. Perhaps it is unnecessary to add that the articles collected here are not confined by the thematic issues discussed in this introduction. The fact that these papers are about much more, and that they resist and spill outside thematic or familiar categories, will speak for itself to readers whose preoccupations are different.

In the first section, 'The story so far', Jane Gallop and Rachel Bowlby recover histories. Some of the significance of Gallop's paper was indicated earlier. From her analysis, one can see how a word can give the appearance of compatibility between theories that are actually in conflict. She focuses on Mitchell's use of the terms 'historical' and 'biological', showing how the historical of Mitchell's psychoanalytic work is not quite the same as the historical of her Marxist work. This is the pivot for a broader re-evaluation of the union of Lacanian psychoanalysis and feminism; a union Gallop once advocated, and whose sense she now queries. Emphasizing that Lacan's symbolic castration, as the break between the human and the natural, is paralleled by the cut between the human and natural sciences, Gallop asks how far this disciplinary division suits feminism, or psychoanalysis, which resists the attempts to cleanse it of biology. An exploration that began with the politics of Lacan and feminism ends at the border of the human and natural sciences.

Bowlby also reflects on the marriage (or misalliance) of psychoanalysis and feminism. She picks up the archaeological metaphor that framed Freud's difficulties in digging out the facts on women and departs on a genealogical journey, an exploration of the term 'repudiation'. Psychoanalysis writes of the repudiation of femininity; feminists of the repudiation of psychoanalysis by feminism. Is psychoanalysis then in the despised feminine position where it is cast aside, together with the femininity it theorizes? Bowlby's skilled investigation of what repudiation means suggests we know even less than we thought about femininity.

In 'The story framed by an institutional context' Lisa Jardine and Alice Jardine take up different aspects of the contradictions between psychoanalysis, feminism, and the institution. Both women agree that real institutional power and its radically different effects on men and women should never be neglected. But their approaches to psychoanalytic theory and the tertiary institution are very different. Lisa Jardine concentrates on the material, historical determinations within the university as a place where women fare badly (in Britain especially); and the relation between the exclusion of women in the institution, and their exclusion by psychoanalytic theory. Her question is: why are seminars on psychoanalytic and feminist theory well attended in Cambridge, when there is no change in the real power relations between women and men in this institution? Ironically, while the history and materiality of male/female relations is neglected in some psychoanalytic feminism, there is none the less an awareness of it: Lisa Jardine suggests that the awareness of the fact that our subjective histories place us in or outside power in the institution is evident in the way women tell personal stories, often bodily stories, after seminars on feminism and psychoanalysis. Aware that the institution excludes them because of their history, they attempt to tell it.

Alice Jardine writes that the different generations of feminists in the university have been brutally stylized as 'history-minded mothers and theory-minded daughters'. Given this, it is worth stressing that the two papers in this section were written completely independently, in a transatlantic coincidence. This is worth stressing, as Lisa Jardine might be identified with the case for history, Alice Jardine with the case for theory, in a dichotomy both women find too crude.

Alice Jardine ties the differences between the generations of feminist women active in university institutions to debates on the weight to be given deconstructive and psychoanalytic theories on the one hand, and political action on the other. She interprets these differences with the aid of writings by the two generations of women reflecting on their own psychoanalyses. From here it is possible to take advantage of psychoanalytic insights in accounting for the blind spots that afflict either generation's perspective on the other; that which is criticized in the one is the projected, thereby disowned, failing of the other.

What both papers bring sharply into focus is the shift away from the historical materialist context of the initial recuperation of psychoanalysis for feminism. A context shaped by the concern for change.

In the leading paper in the first section on the symbolic, 'The essential thing', Rosi Braidotti argues that the strategic politics of essentialism are now the politics of change. In this brilliant reversal of the terms structuring debates on essentialism, Braidotti suggests that the denial of any essential bond is a simultaneous assertion that women have nothing in common other than oppression. This chapter continues and elaborates on Braidotti's longstanding concern with the ethics of feminism. Her sophisticated discussion of essentialism refers both to the history of metaphysics and the metaphysical nature of philosophy. It makes clear distinctions about the implications of sexual difference and essentialism in the political context, which is Braidotti's concern, and their implications in the psychoanalytic context.

These themes carry over to the next paper, where Margaret Whitford rereads Irigaray. In this major reinterpretation Whitford argues against the received views on Irigaray, especially the stereotype of her as a crude biological essentialist who takes no account of the psychoanalytic significance of the symbolic. On the contrary, interprets Whitford, for Irigaray the symbolic is critical. The cultural failure to symbolize women's relation to their maternal origins means that both the mother–daughter relation (and by extension relations between women overall) is unmediated or fused, and will remain so if the mother's body and the relation to it is left as the place of lack.

In short, Irigaray's argument goes in the opposite direction to that which has been attributed to her. She is not advocating an unmediated relation to the mother's body, or saying that women have specifically female biological drives that should be celebrated. If she was, she would indeed be ignoring the need for mediation and for symbolization. But she is fully aware of where the failure to symbolize leads (to psychosis, among other things).

In the next paper in this section, Luce Irigaray argues for a rethinking of women's relation to language through an analysis of two gestures: that of lying down on the analytic couch, and the famous gesture of Freud's grandson Ernst in the *fort/da* game.[36] Irigaray argues that these gestures are never neutral, and that only the boy's gesture is symbolized in this culture. In arguing this, she concentrates on the spatial, gestural aspects of the *fort/da*, in an analysis that comes close to and reflects on Derrida's reading of that game.[37]

The second section in 'Towards another symbolic' takes its subtitle from a suggestion of Lacan's ('*Beyond the Phallus* – a good book title, the next one in the Galilée series?'). Any direct indebtedness to Lacan in this section is largely confined to this titular irony. In two out of the three articles, Derrida is more of a presence. The three articles are by Elizabeth Wright, Morag Shiach, and Naomi Segal. Their common but certainly not their only interest is in the relation between the symbolic, the phallus, and difference.

Elizabeth Wright has provided an introduction to trends and directions in the psychoanalytic, feminist literary criticism that frames much of the discussion of this section. Wright argues that a psychoanalysis for feminism has flourished in the context of literary criticism, where it can detach itself from the ideologies of institutionalized psychoanalysis. She discusses the convergence between psychoanalysis, feminism, and postmodernism, a convergence anchored in the rejection of the dichotomy of masculine and feminine as metaphysical. For Wright, this rejection is best exemplified in the work of Julia Kristeva.

Morag Shiach begins with Hélène Cixous's use of the feminine, and her critique of binary oppositions. The writing and thought which exceed binary oppositions is named feminine, and is practised by women and men. But there is a complicating reality. It is historical women who, for a variety of oppressive sociohistorical reasons, have a vested interest in disrupting fixed categories of thought, in writing the feminine, in disrupting the sociality of the masculine Same. Cixous turns to Clarice Lispector to illustrate the connection between writing the feminine and social transformation.

The problem remains: how to think difference, without thinking it in terms of dual hierarchized oppositions? At this point Cixous brings Derrida's concept of *différance* into play, literally. Shiach develops the fascinating thesis that Cixous's writing on theatre is a means for reconciling the temporal and spatial aspects of *différance*, in Derrida's sense. The visual dimension of theatre also realigns Derridean and psychoanalytic thinking. For, given the significance of the visual in constituting sexual difference in psychoanalytic theory, theatre may challenge that visual constitution on its own terms, but by a different living vision, acting out alternatives. Thus in Cixous's play about Oedipus, Jocasta's suicide leaves the king uncertain of his identity, bereft of 'the comforting mirror of devoted love'.

This mirror theme is developed by Naomi Segal. She reads French *récits* for the psychical dynamics they reveal to the unintended reader. In her set of texts, the male narrator, a 'son', tells his story to some sort of father. In most cases, that story involves the death or disappearance of a loved woman, who substitutes for the mother, as all loved women do, according to Freud. This woman-mother's death leads to an identity crisis: he is listless, almost lifeless, until he recovers through the act of telling his tale. Segal argues that the dynamics involved are best understood through the myth of Narcissus and Echo, that imaginary myth that preceded Oedipus. Echo (the woman) validates the image which Narcissus (the man) receives from the pool (also the woman as mother).

In these *récits*, the price of entry into the symbolic of the father is castration: the break with the imaginary, phantasized union with the mother's body. In drawing this out, Segal's interpretation validates Lacan's theory rather well. However it also shows Lacan's explanation to be insufficient. If castration involves not just a severance from the 'mother' but her metaphorical death, then this too needs a theoretical account.

The second half of this book is gathered together under the name of sexual difference. Gayatri Spivak begins the section on 'Reason and revolution' with a reassessment of her previous position on the name of 'woman'. The paper has two points of departure. One is Jacqueline Rose's critique of Derrida. The other is contextual. Spivak wrote this important position paper immediately after six months in India. She rethinks the relation between politically disenfranchised women, and theories of difference and 'woman'. She writes against dominant readings of 'deconstruction', emphasizing that 'logocentrism is not a pathology', or a prison from which the new, fully decentred, dispersed subject should burst forth. This dominant reading, and the related claim that there is nothing fixed about 'woman', removes theory ever further away from the disenfranchised women confined by fixed political boundaries. Paradoxically, even though Rose criticizes Derrida, she is affected by the institutionally prevalent, and by Spivak's account inaccurate reading of 'deconstruction': this reading is motivated by a desire to find nothing fixed in the name 'woman'.

Toril Moi's article begins with one of the issues Jane Gallop mentioned in concluding hers: the relation between feminism, science, and the philosophy of science. Moi's focus is on psychoanalytic theories of knowledge, sexuality, and sexual identity. She argues against the feminist use of object-relations theory in the philosophy of science, on the grounds that it cannot logically escape from its equation of masculinity, objectivity, and rationality. Moi turns to feminist theorists who have attempted to deconstruct binary oppositions, then to philosopher Michèle le Doueff, who argues that philosophy needs to exclude something, to regard this excluded other as lacking knowledge, in order to define itself as knowledge. Classically, the locus of lack is woman. 'The idea of "woman" as defective becomes a defence against the thinking male subject's potentially devastating insight into his own lack.' Lack returns us to Lacan. Moi turns to his theory of the dialogic knowledge of analysis. The structure of psychoanalytic dialogue, the interplay of transference and countertransference, means that we have to reflect on the things we otherwise exclude from thought. Through this process, secure positions constantly break down. Finally, Moi turns to Freud's theory of the drive for knowledge. Drives are in no sense reducible to biology, but they are constructed in relation to it. Reason is permeated with the emotion and energy of the drives; an idea which of itself challenges the binary opposition between reason and emotion.

In the next section, 'The psychical in the social', Copjec's paper also returns us to the matter of Freudian drives. This time, it is not the drive for knowledge, but the death drive. For the main part, this important, original article does not directly address feminist, psychoanalytic issues. Rather, with these issues constantly in mind, it rethinks some standard philosophical assumptions about Aristotle and causality, assumptions which infect feminism. If a given effect is already contained in a cause, there is no escaping that effect. The implications for feminism of this view of cause and effect are dire. If the effects of sexual oppression are contained in the cause (and if the cause is fixed) then that, so to speak, is that.

These assumptions about cause and effect are built in to those views (Foucault is implied, not named) which see the psychical subject as a social effect, whose pleasure is socially produced. For psychoanalysis, the relation between the psychical and the social is complicated: Freud saw the social order as, in part, an enactment of the pleasure principle, the wish-fulfilment of fantasies. Yet even from the psychoanalytic standpoint, there is no accounting for tension between psyche and social order without the death drive. Copjec argues that Lacan's rereading of Freud's death drive embodies an understanding of causality that is radically different from some standard ones. Not only does this lead to a different understanding of causality. It also provides an account of why the subject is other than the bundle of phantasies and positions that are socially available to it.

The last paper is a path-breaking one by Parveen Adams. It takes the question of the psychical and the social by surprise, ending, not starting there, on the principle that an understanding of the relation between psychical and social effects is better grasped through studying a 'new sexuality'. Adams studies a new perversion, lesbian sadomasochism. She argues that it disrupts the normative psychoanalytic coupling of perversion and pathology, and that some of its clinical features are inconsistent with received psychoanalytic views on the nature of masochism. Does one look for an explanation of the inconsistency in psychoanalysis or reality?

The full significance of this paper becomes apparent when one remembers that psychoanalysis is not just about sexual identity, it is also about actual sexual practices, which is often forgotten. I add here that the neglect of sexual practices has not been helped by a normative shift within psychoanalytic practice and theory. In some quarters (American ego psychology and British Kleinian schools), heterosexuality, potency, monogamy, and the absence of perversion are listed as desirable outcomes of psychoanalysis. This would have been foreign to Freud, who recognized the force of social sanctions in causing unhappiness, but did not think it was the analyst's job to induce conformity. His criterion for health, 'the ability to love and work' depended on a different model. Repression, energy, sublimation, sexuality were the factors that mattered in it. Social values mattered far less as ends in themselves than as things which increased repression or impeded sublimation.[38]

Significantly, sexual practices have been neglected in feminist appropriations of psychoanalysis. One reason for this could be, as Adams argues, that the categories of a biological sex and a social gender organize thinking about femininity. The psychoanalytic concept of sexuality is about neither sex nor gender; it is a construction that cuts across both categories. In stressing this, Adams is challenging the familiar opposition between biological and social determination.

The relation of psychical structures to the political realities of women's social conditions is unsettled by this collection. Many arguments in it undermine one of the founding assumptions in the appropriation of psychoanalysis for feminism; namely, that psychoanalysis is about the ephemera or ideology, and materialism the core, of women's oppression. They do so by crossing the borders, to borrow Gallop's metaphor, on which this assumption relies. Borders between biology and history, mind and body, subject and object, cause and effect. To this extent, feminist psychoanalytic writing bears on more than psychical structure. It adds up to a strong case for rethinking the assumptions used in studying the social parameters of women's lot. Between psychoanalysis and feminism, there is an open space without anachronistic boundaries, where basic premises are being rethought.

Notes

1 The use of the term stereotype has to evoke Barthes, and in fact his analysis of stereotypes figures in the section on 'Returning to the symbolic' on p. 9. I am juxtaposing 'stereotype' and 'cliché' here to indicate the particular sense of stereotype (Barthes has more than one) I have in mind.

2 Gayatri C. Spivak in this volume. Unless otherwise stated, references to the contributors are to their papers in this collection.

3 Sigmund Freud, *Inhibitions, Symptoms and Anxiety*, in *The Standard Edition of The Complete Psychological Works of Sigmund Freud* (hereafter *SE*), ed. James Strachey, trans. James Strachey *et al.*, 24 vols (London: Hogarth Press and the Institute of Psychoanalysis, 1978), 20, p. 139.

4 This is not to suggest that the Anglo-American/French distinction was introduced, nor that it is always used, without disclaimers. Those who introduced it are usually careful about stressing that Anglo-American concerns are also present in France, and vice-versa. For a representative and influential account of the distinction, see the introductions to E. Marks and I. de Courtivron, *New French Feminisms* (Brighton: Harvester, 1981). Having noted that, I want to qualify the term 'British'. It is no more accurate than the terms 'American' and 'French' when it comes to identifying a distinctive feminist theoretical position. First, a lot of the 'British' are from Norway, New Zealand, and other parts of the world. Second, writers in the United States, notably Shoshana Felman, also take Lacan's law relatively seriously.

5 These differences are also reflected in a dispute between some British and American feminists over a specific, appropriation of psychoanalysis for feminism, exemplified by but not confined to Nancy Chodorow's *The Reproduction of Mothering*. This appropriation of psychoanalysis is not represented in this book, but some of the disputation it led to is discussed in the next section.

6 Jane Gallop's *The Daughter's Seduction* (London: Macmillan, 1982) is one example. Other names that come to mind here are Naomi Schor, Peggy Kamuf, Nancy Miller, and Susan Suleiman.

7 Kristeva, like Mitchell, is also an analyst. However, Kristeva's views on the symbolic and psychosis as its unattractivea lternative antedate her becoming an analyst; they figure in *La Révolution du langue poétique* (Paris: Seuil, 1974), *Revolution in Poetic Language*, trans. M. Waller (New York: Columbia University Press, 1984). Mitchell has a different rajectory. Her concern with the symbolic comes later and in some sense marks a reversal on her position in *Psychoanalysis and Feminism*. See pp. 8–9.

8 In her recent work Kristeva continues to call on a variety of analytic

sources, including the Kleinians Segal, Bion, and Rosenfeld (although she does not always identify them as Kleinians). There is an excellent overview of Kristeva's theoretical shifts in Jacqueline Rose, *Sexuality in the Field of Vision* (London: Verso, 1986).

9 M. Safoun, 'Is the Oedipus complex universal?' *m/f* 5 and 6; E. Ragland-Sullivan, *Jacques Lacan and the Philosophy of Psychoanalysis*, (London and Canberra: Croom Helm, 1986). Ragland-Sullivan's argument hinges on a distinction between primary castration (infant and mother) and secondary castration (femininity, in Freud's sense).

10 I am aware that differentiating between these two types of differentiation may be controversial, given that logic seems to be everywhere guilty by association with the phallus, and it may be a mistake to introduce the distinction in a context where its justification has to be limited. In fact the distinction is implicit in a lot of Lacanian commentary, where different sides of the differentiation question are highlighted by different people. There is an exemplary discussion of psychical differentiation in John P. Muller's 'Language, psychosis and the subject in Lacan', in Joseph H. Smith and William Kerrigan (eds), *Interpreting Lacan* (New Haven, Conn.: Yale University Press, 1983).

11 For an introduction to Lacan that complements this one, emphasizing the significance for Lacan of the mother's desire, see Elizabeth Wright, this collection.

12 There is a style of *prima facie* criticism that seizes on use of the wrong term, or the wrong use of any term, at the expense of what the writer is trying to do. Critiques of Mitchell's phallocentrism, of which there are a great many, exemplify this style of ... stereotypic criticism.

13 For relevant rereadings, see Margaret Whitford 'Luce Irigaray: speaking as a woman', *Radical Philosophy*, Summer 1986; also Jane Gallop *'Quand nos lèvres s'écrivant*: Irigaray's body politic', *Romanic Review*, January 1983, as well as Whitford, this volume.

14 Especially E. Lemoine-Luccioni, *Partage des femmes* (Paris: Seuil, 1974). For a recent discussion of this particular Lacanian line, see Alice Jardine, *Gynesis* (Ithaca, NY: Cornell University Press, 1985).

15 Juliet MacCannell, in *Figuring Lacan*, (London and Sydney: Croom Helm, 1986) argues that Lacan is more conscious and critical of this logic than most Derridean readings suppose. To the complex relations between Lacan and Derrida, Barbara Johnson remains an excellent guide: 'The frame of reference: Poe, Lacan, Derrida', *Yale French Studies*, 55/6 (1977).

16 The classic work here is L. Althusser and E. Balibar, *Reading Capital*, trans. Ben Brewster (London: New Left Books, 1974).

17 The early issues of the British journals *m/f* and *Ideology and Consciousness* are particularly representative; thus P. Adams, *m/f* 1 (1978) and 3 (1979), M. Page, *m/f* 2 (1978). For a well-received formulation of a Marxist-feminist position arising out of second-wave feminism, relevant to the essentialist issue, see Michèle Barrett, *Women's Oppression Today* (London: Verso, 1980).

18 In a forthcoming article ('This essentialism which is not one' *Differences*, 1, 2 (1989)), which I read as this book was going to press, Naomi Schor delineates different uses of essentialism, pointing to an anti-essentialist feminist debt to Beauvoir, and Beauvoir's Marxism. The fact that Beauvoir is rarely referred to in early feminist formulations on essentialism in Britain is, I think, probably due to the extent that Althusserian Marxism defined

itself against existentialist and humanist Marxisms, including Beauvoir's.

19 Jane Gallop, 'Moving backwards or forwards' this collection. On the difference between Lacanian and Althusserian views on essentialism see also my 'Impasse in psychoanalysis and feminism', forthcoming in S. Gunew (ed.) *Feminist Knowledge: Critique and Construct* (London: Routledge, 1989). (For more information on the relation between feminism, marxist feminism, and the New Left, see Lisa Jardine and Julia Swindells, *What's Left?* (London: Routledge, 1989).

20 For instance J. Rose, 'Introduction II', *Feminine Sexuality: Jacques Lacan and the Ecole Freudienne*, ed. J. Mitchell and J. Rose (London: Macmillan, 1982).

21 Toril Moi especially is explicit about the politics of essentialism: *Sexual/Textual Politics* (London: Methuen, 1985).

22 Rose, op. cit., p. 37, also interview with J. Rose and J. Mitchell, *m/f* 9 (1983).

23 P. Adams and J. Copjec, this volume.

24 For Bourdieu, see P. Bourdieu, 'Champ intellectuel et projet createur', *Les Temps modernes* (November 1966). Similar themes are found throughout Bourdieu's very extensive *oeuvre*, but are developed particularly in *Homo Academicus* (Paris: Minuit, 1984).

Barthes's more recent views on signification and 'history' are outlined in R. Barthes, 'La Mythologie aujourd'hui, in *Le Bruissement de la langue*. This essay is translated variously as 'Change the object itself' (trans. S. Heath, in *Image Music Text*) and 'Mythology today' (trans. R. Howard, in *The Rustle of Language* (Oxford: Blackwell, 1986). There is an excellent discussion of Barthes on stereotypes and codes, Michael Moriarty, 'Barthes: ideology, culture, subjectivity', *Paragraph* 11, 3 (November 1988). For the problems with Barthes's complex relation to the subject's historical context, see C. Prendergast, *The Order of Mimesis* (Cambridge: Cambridge University Press, 1986). This remarkable book actually sustains an argument on developments in poststructuralist and postmodernist thinking and the question of referential relations to the real world.

25 On the relation between ego-ideal and identification, see Kristeva, 'L'abject d'amour', *Tel Quel* 91, pp. 17–32.

26 Cf. a pertinent observation of Malcolm Bowie's, on the relation between the imaginary, the specular ego and the external world. The imaginary 'grows from the infant's experience' of its 'specular ego' but 'extends far into the individual's experience of others and of the external world: wherever a false identification is to be found – within the subject, or between one subject and another, or between subject and thing – then the Imaginary holds sway': *Freud, Proust and Lacan: Theory as Fiction* (Cambridge: Cambridge University Press, 1987), p. 115.

27 Freud, *Inhibitions, Symptoms and Anxiety, SE* 20, p.139.

28 The key word here is 'help'. I stress again that this discussion of psychical identifications is intended as a supplement rather than any kind of critique of explanations directed to broader social forces.

29 Freud, *Group Psychology and the Analysis of the Ego, SE* 18, p.129.

30 There is an important discussion of the relation between the ego, identification, and signification in C. Chase, 'Transference as trope and persuasion', in S. Rimon-Kennan (ed.), *Discourse in Psychoanalysis and Literature* (London: Methuen, 1987).

31 J. Lacan, 'Function and field of language and speech in psychoanalysis',

Ecrits: *A Selection*, trans. A. Sheridan (London: Tavistock, 1977).

32 This reference to *Le Temps retrouvé* is to T. Kilmartin's translation, *Time Regained in The Remembrance of Things Past*, 3 vols (Harmondsworth: Penguin, 1985), vol. 3, pp. 932–3.

33 Toril Moi, this collection; Shoshana Felman, *Jacques Lacan and the Adventure of Insight* (Cambridge, Mass.: Harvard University Press, 1987).

34 The analyst can however be a different kind of mirror – revealing those *mechanisms* by which the ego seeks confirmation, rather than a confirming, engaged mirroring for the ego as it is.

35 Naomi Segal, 'Echo and Narcissus', this collection; Morag Shiach, 'Their symbolic exists. . . ', this collection.

36 Freud, *Beyond the Pleasure Principle SE* 20.

37 Irigaray, like Derrida, focuses on the spatial aspects of the *fort/da*. She also appears to follow Derrida in a rather unusual translation from the German, rendering *da* as near (rather than 'here') and *fort* as far (rather than 'gone', or 'it has gone'). J. Derrida, *La Carte postale* (Paris: Flammarion, 1980), pp. 331–6. As elsewhere Derrida uses the conventional translation of *fort/da*, I assume that the 'spatial' translation is in some sense contextually evocative. Irigaray makes it clear that her analysis of the *fort/da* is a response to Derrida's in 'La croyance même', the paper immediately preceding the one translated in this collection in her *Sexes et parentés* (Paris: Minuit, 1987).

38 There has been an extensive feminist debate over the politics of lesbian sadomasochism (as distinct from the psychoanalysis of it). This debate is discussed by Rosi Braidotti, '"Vanilla Sex" et sadomasochisme', *Les Cahiers du grif* 26 (1983).

The story so far

Moving backwards or forwards

Jane Gallop

Lacan and feminism: strange bedfellows?

There never was an alliance between the person Lacan and feminism. What there has been is an alliance some feminists have made with Lacanian thought. When I say 'Lacan and feminism' that does not mean Lacan the person but Lacan the body of writing. Ten years ago I was advocating bringing Lacan and feminism together. The phrase 'strange bedfellows' popped into my mind as a critique of this idea that you could put Lacan and feminism together. The phrase comes from the cliché 'politics makes strange bedfellows'. Feminism is, of course, a political movement and a way of thinking. Although the cliché is explicitly about politics, it sounds like it is about sex, about people sleeping together. If you put sex and politics together and start talking about the politics of sex, you are talking feminism. We all know the phrase 'sexual politics' as the name of an early book of feminist literary criticism. I guess 'strange bedfellows' came to me as some sort of joke feminist question about the politics of coupling Lacan and feminism.[1]

In considering, at this point in time, the relationship between Lacan and feminism, it no longer seemed appropriate to think about it in the abstract: to think about Lacan, think about feminism, think about what they would have in common. So I sought a text in which I could find that relation already consummated. What proposed itself to me was a text by Juliet Mitchell, the best-known feminist thinker who has been involved with Lacanian thought.

In 1974, Mitchell published a book called *Psychoanalysis and Feminism.*[2] What is extremely interesting about Mitchell's book is that it is probably the most widely-read book in English that actually mentions Lacan. It is the place that many English-speaking people encountered the name Lacan for the first time. One of the political aspects of 'Lacan and feminism' is the surprising fact that, at a moment when he was not becoming known through psychoanalysis, Lacan came to be known to a lot of Americans through feminism.

Taking for granted that people recognize Mitchell as a kind of feminist, the question is: what about her relation with Lacan? In 1982 a book was published entitled *Feminine Sexuality*; Mitchell and Jacqueline Rose were listed as its 'editors'.[3] The identity of the *author* of that book is somewhat problematic. If you look at the book, it is not clear whether 'Jacques Lacan and the *école freudienne*' are the authors of the book or its subtitle. In bibliographical references it shows up as both. When Lacan shows up in the subtitle, the book gets attributed (in the absence of an author) to the editors. At stake here is the question of the editors' relation to Lacan. If he (and his nameless disciples) is (are) the author(s), then the editors are serving him. If he is what 'their' book is about (the subtitle), then the editors are in a more masterful position. A certain difficulty in determining the editors' relation to Lacan (using him or used by him) also manifests itself as a problem in correctly reading the phrase 'Jacques Lacan and the *école freudienne*' on the cover and title page of the book. In any case, *Feminine Sexuality* is a collection of translations of Lacan's texts about sexual difference, feminine sexuality, and femininity, along with two texts that issue from Lacan's school; and Mitchell is one of the editors of that book.

Directly after that book was published in 1982, the two editors – Mitchell and Rose – were interviewed by two editors of the British feminist journal *m/f*. Asked why they edited this book of Lacan's texts, Rose replied: 'Your book, Juliet, on *Psychoanalysis and Feminism* had just come out and there was a whole atmosphere which had in part at least been produced by that book, which could be called "a return to Freud for women around questions of sexuality". Now, insofar as that return to Freud on the question of sexuality had gone hand in hand, had been informed by Lacan's rereading of Freud, it made a lot of sense to get back, or rather go on, to look at exactly what it was Lacan himself had to say about women.'[4]

In her statement, Rose puts the phrase 'a return to Freud for women around questions of sexuality' in quotation marks, not because somebody else said it, but because she says 'a whole atmosphere which could be called'. In other words, she is naming something, and making her naming explicit. The name she chooses, 'a return to Freud', has been intimately associated with Lacan and his project. Rose, here, is using that resonant phrase to talk not about Lacan's 'return' but about the return of women to Freud. In England around 1974, women within the feminist movement who presumably had not been reading Freud, had been turned off Freud because of his patriarchal attitudes, turned to Freud as part of the feminist project of theorizing the construction of sexuality. I might add that, as far as I know, no one else has ever named what these women did with the exact phrase 'a return to Freud'. The use of the phrase 'return to Freud' marries 'women' to Lacan by giving them his 'name'.

She then repeats the phrase: 'now, insofar as *that* return to Freud'. In saying 'that return to Freud', Rose is of course referring to what she has just called 'a return to Freud', but it also implies that there is another return to Freud, one she is in fact about to mention although she does not call it 'a return to Freud'. 'That return to Freud on the question of sexuality had gone hand in hand', had been informed by Lacan's rereading of Freud'. Rather than Lacan's 'return to Freud', she says 'Lacan's rereading of Freud', so that her use of Lacan's identity to name the women is not as patent in the text. The relation that subsumes what the women are doing under a Lacanian identity is latent at the very moment Rose is explicitly articulating a somewhat different relation between Lacan and the women. The women who are going back to Freud are 'hand in hand' with Lacan who is also going back to Freud. Less compromising than bedfellowship, holding hands is sexual yet seems innocent of the power politics inevitable in taking on someone's name.

That return, the women's return, had not only 'gone hand in hand', but also 'been informed by Lacan's rereading'. This sentence has a problem deciding between two versions of the relationship between Lacan and women. The two relations 'hand in hand' and 'informed by' are not articulated but simply (comma-)spliced together. Yet as different sorts of relations the two phrases necessitate different prepositions: 'informed *by*' and 'hand in hand *with*'. The incompatibility of these two different relationships remains marked by the absence of the preposition necessary to make 'hand in hand' grammatically link with Lacan. This ambiguity recalls the problem of deciding whether Lacan is the author or subject matter of *Feminine Sexuality*. The question of the relation between these women (the editors, the feminists) and Lacan seems to generate these ambiguities.

'Insofar as that return to Freud had gone hand in hand, had been informed by Lacan's rereading of Freud, it made a lot of sense to go back, or rather to go on.' There is some hesitation as to whether we are moving backward or forward, whether going to Lacan for women who have gone (back) to Freud represents progress or regress. In the context of a 'return', however, progress, in some way, is regress. If our goal is to get back, then each step forward takes us backward. This idea of returning (and not just to Freud) is absolutely central to Lacan's work.[5] One of Lacan's most important contributions to Freudian theory is his notion of retroaction as the temporality and the logic of psychoanalysis and of the subject.

I say 'contribution to Freudian theory' because in proposing this idea Lacan is supposedly only 'returning to Freud'; Lacan proposes this idea as Freud's. In her editor's introduction to *Feminine Sexuality*, Mitchell writes: 'For Freud, history and the psychoanalytic experience is always a reconstruction, a retrospective account: the human subject is part of such a history.'[6] Mitchell unambiguously attributes this to Freud. Yet I would contend that it can only be read in Freud after Lacan finds it there. Such a retroactive history means that events only take on their meaning 'after the fact'; so what comes second in some significant way necessarily precedes (the full realization of) what was first. Thus, for example, although chronologically Freud indubitably preceded Lacan, one could also say that Lacan comes first because only after reading Lacan can one read Freud, truly understand what Freud was saying (if we are to believe Lacan).

So with Lacan and feminism walking hand in hand, walking back to Freud, the question of back or forth begins to nag. The politics of sex might lead us also to hear this as a recurrent conjugal argument: these strange bedfellows trying to decide who comes first.

Women: The Longest Revolution

The text which I in fact chose for observing the relations between Lacan and feminism is actually neither *Psychoanalysis and Feminism* nor *Feminine Sexuality*. In 1984, Juliet Mitchell published a collection of her essays, dating from 1966 to 1983, under the title *Women: The Longest Revolution*. Right now in 1987 I find it extraordinary that a book with a lot of discussion of the psychoanalysis of Jacques Lacan should have such a title. That is what I set out as my problem for this chapter: what is the connection between Lacan and the sort of Marxist feminism which is embodied in such a title? Or, more simply, why is anybody talking about Lacan in a book called *Women: The Longest Revolution*?

At only one place in the book does Mitchell provide anything like an answer to that question. Each essay in the book is preceded by a page or so situating the text in the collection and for the reader. In the prefatory remarks to the text, which was originally published as her editor's introduction to *Feminine Sexuality*, Mitchell says something which relates directly to my question.

> Lacan's work interested me for many reasons. Feminism discovered women as a distinct social group – a group whose identity was as women. But there is another side to that description, there is the point where femininity disappears, where it is nothing other – neither more nor less – than the various places where it is constructed. In a very different idiom and speaking to very different questions, the interest in Lacan in this essay has some echoes of my interest in Althusser in 'Women: The Longest Revolution.' There women were nothing other than the different social and economic structures in which they were created; there was no essential category: 'women.' Lacan's work sets up that realisation at the heart of the question of the construction of femininity.[7]

This paragraph is really the only place in the book where Mitchell tries to articulate the relation between Lacan and the phrase 'women: the longest revolution'. In this quotation, 'Women: the longest revolution' is not the title of the book but of an essay, the very first essay in this book which dates from 1966. One of the first things Mitchell ever published, 'Women: the longest revolution' is a brilliant, lucid piece of analysis of the problems involved in Marxist interpretation of the status of women. The second wave of feminism really caught on around 1968; so 1966 is very early for this sort of analysis. Originally appearing in the *New Left Review*, frequently reprinted, it established her reputation as a feminist theorist. One of the things that really interests me about Mitchell's 1984 book is why she chose to call the whole collection by the name of the earliest essay.

In the quotation above, Mitchell is preparing the inclusion of an essay which originally served to introduce Lacan's writing in a book called *Women: The Longest Revolution* by connecting it to the 1966 piece of Marxist analysis by the same name. She connects thus: 'in very different idiom, speaking to very different questions, the interest in Lacan in this essay has some echoes of my interest in Althusser in "Women: The Longest Revolution".' Here is the very primal scene I've been trying to trace. Yet if this is Mitchell's most direct response to my question (and it is), it is a singularly evasive answer. Yes, there is a connection. But what are the details? How do they couple? 'Very different ... very different ... some echoes.' Pressed for detailed evidence of a connection, the text yields little of substance, except one concrete clue: a name, Althusser. Althusser is mentioned only twice in the book *Women: The Longest Revolution*: once in the preface to the 1966 essay and again, over 200 pages later, in the preface to the introduction to *Feminine Sexuality*. Never named within an actual essay, Althusser inhabits the connective tissue, the joints which allow Mitchell to smooth over the 'very different ... very different' with 'some echoes'.

In the mid- and late 1960s British Marxists got very interested in the work of Althusser. Around the same time, or a little bit earlier, Althusser had been promoting Lacan, demonstrating that there was some kind of solidarity between what Lacan was doing and the kind of Marxism Althusser was trying to do. So a lot of British Marxists, including a good number of feminists who came out of a Marxist tradition, were reading Althusser. Then the feminists, in particular, went to Lacan because feminists were interested not just in politics but in sexual politics, which is to say 'questions of sexuality', as Rose puts it. Althusser was not answering the questions of sexuality, but he was pointing to Lacan who seemed to have something to say about them. So if one wanted to give a simple derivation answer to the question of why at least this group of feminists was reading Lacan, one might say they were reading Althusser and Althusser suggested that they read Lacan.

When Mitchell republished her introduction to *Feminine Sexuality* in the 1984 collection, she retitled it 'Freud and Lacan: psychoanalytic theories of sexual difference'. That title has a resonant connective function since Althusser wrote a text called 'Freud and Lacan'.[8] Althusser's 'Freud and Lacan' was originally published in 1964 in the French Communist Party journal *La Nouvelle Critique*. The English translation first appeared in 1969 in the *New Left Review*, the British Marxist journal where Mitchell published 'Women: the longest revolution'. With the title 'Freud and Lacan: psychoanalytic theories of sexual difference', Mitchell implicitly reinscribed her introduction of Lacan in a feminist context as a repetition of Althusser's introduction of him in a Marxist context.

So we have 'some echoes' and the name of a go-between. We have dates and names and a 'whole atmosphere': Marxist thought around the *New Left*

Review in the late 1960s and early 1970s as the setting for the meeting of Lacan and feminism. We have the history behind the conjunction, the answer to the question of how they met, a story Mitchell vaguely hints at but does not tell, a narrative behind but not to be read in the book *Women: The Longest Revolution*.

I want to know more than names and dates and local colour, more than anecdote, more than how they met. I want to observe the ongoing relations between Lacan and feminism as they are embodied in Mitchell's 1984 book. The book begins with an intricate study of Marxist theory and its discussions of women whereas the last third of the book is strictly about psychoanalysis. I want to know how this is still one book. What are the themes or images that are the same between this 1966 article for the *New Left Review* and the texts from the 1980s in which she is talking in detail about certain psychoanalytic questions and about Lacan?

In the process of talking about Marxist feminism, Mitchell is constantly defining the word 'human'; its meaning is not taken for granted. In the process of discussing Lacanian psychoanalysis, she is also constantly defining the word 'human'. In both cases the word is linked to something she calls 'humanisation', some sort of process of becoming human. In considering the book as a whole, I find that what Mitchell's Marxism and Mitchell's Lacanianism have in common turns out to be this term 'humanisation'.

Women: the longest evolution

In 'Women: the longest revolution' Mitchell talks about what the emancipation of women meant to Marx: 'The emancipation of women [for Marx] would ... be ... an index of humanisation ... in the more fundamental sense of the progress of the human over the animal, the cultural over the natural.'[9] For Marx (or at least for Mitchell's Marx), humanization has to do with this progress of history. One could almost say evolution except that for Marx it is not evolution, is not an inevitable, natural progression; it is man-made; it is history. She uses the word 'progress' . We might want to ask about what kind of nineteenth-century ideologies are involved in this notion that we are making progress from the animal to the human. Later, when she is talking in Lacanian rather than Marxist terms, she will be very suspicious of words like 'progress' or 'development', and will propose 'history' as having a meaning that is in some way in opposition to 'progress' or at least different from this idea of progress. In her Lacanian period, 'history' will come to mean (as we saw above) reconstruction, retrospection, and retroaction, the intrication of progress with regress. But when she is talking within Marxist feminism, humanization has to do with this progress of the human over the animal, and the cultural over the natural. The emancipation of women for Mitchell and for Mitchell's Marx is tied up with some way in which the human will triumph over the animal and culture will triumph over nature.

Juliet Mitchell and the human sciences

There is a paper in Mitchell's collection entitled 'Psychoanalysis: a humanist humanity or a linguistic science?' which was originally delivered at the Rockefeller Conference on the Humanities in Bellaggio, Italy, in 1977. In that context of a conference on the humanities, Mitchell contrasts Lacanian psychoanalysis with American and English strains in terms of whether psychoanalysis is a science or a humanity. In the English-speaking academies, we speak of three divisions: the humanities, the social sciences, and the natural sciences. The social sciences have the word 'science' and the humanities do not; so the fundamental divide falls between the humanities and the sciences (social and natural). The French phrase 'the human sciences' displaces that split. Whereas in English the major break occurs between the humanities and the social sciences, in French it is located between the social and natural sciences.

In her paper at the Conference on the Humanities, Mitchell puzzles for a long time over whether psychoanalysis is a humanity or a science. In a French context that conflict could be avoided by saying it's a 'human science'. That phrase would have sutured the very divide her talk would consider. I think her question – 'humanity or science?' – remains pertinent in our context. Although we might import the phrase 'the human sciences' from France, the institutions where most of us operate devalue the humanities precisely because they are not considered to be science.

In her paper Mitchell says:

> Whatever the criticisms of its humane and humanist practice, and whatever may be the validity of its own claim to be a science, in one limited sense, psychoanalysis will always be a 'humanity.' It is about the human being within human culture. In attempting to reconstruct the history of the individual, the point to which psychoanalysis returns is to the inception of the human animal as a social being – to the origin and source of its humanity. Beneath that is what Freud called the 'biological bedrock,' ever-present but impenetrable by psychoanalysis. The human being of psychoanalytic inquiry is the individual within culture. He is not, nor can he be, an isolate or 'natural' man.[10]

She is arguing that although psychoanalysis may be a science, it will always be a humanity in one sense and that is, of course, the sense in which it is a human science, which is to say, it is about 'the human'. But in this passage, we not only read that argument, we can also read an insistent repetition of the word 'human'. For example, in the phrase 'it is about the *human* being within *human* culture', it seems odd to repeat the word 'human', rather than simply saying 'it is about the human being within culture'. By emphasizing it, she is setting off and valorizing the human *per se*. This insistence on the human has a lot to do with the break between the human and the natural sciences, with establishing a break between the human and the natural.

She then goes on to explain how psychoanalysis is about the human, and as she begins that explanation, the word 'history' appears. The word 'history' is rampant in Mitchell's discussions of psychoanalysis. It is not common in every discussion of psychoanalysis; it is not present in every discussion of Lacan. In fact both Lacan specifically and psychoanalysis generally have frequently been accused of ahistoricism. Mitchell has an idiosyncratic reading of Lacan which construes Lacan as reinforcing the historical side of psychoanalysis. By saying that her reading is idiosyncratic, I do not mean I disagree with her. The gesture makes lots and lots of sense, particularly in the context of a Lacan introduced through Marxism. It is just her constant use of the word 'history' that seems idiosyncratic, that bespeaks her subjectivity. For example, giving an overview of Lacan's theory in the introduction to *Feminine Sexuality*, she says: 'the question of castration, of sexual difference as the product of a division, and the concept of an historical and symbolic order, all begin, tentatively, to come together.'[11] Note the phrase 'an historical and symbolic order'. It is far from universal practice to couple the central Lacanian concept of 'the symbolic order' with the word 'historical', but Mitchell repeatedly does that. She repeatedly characterizes 'the symbolic' as 'historical'; she insistently uses the word 'history'.

History has a particular place among academic disciplines. In some universities it is considered one of the humanities; in others it is classed as a social science. Thus history is located precisely at the division between the humanities and the sciences; like psychoanalysis in Mitchell's paper's title, we need to ask of history – and cannot easily decide – is it a humanity or a science? Locating psychoanalysis and her own subjectivity emphatically with 'history' or the historical, Mitchell challenges the divide between humanities and science. Located somewhere between the humanities and the social sciences history is squarely in the center of the human sciences, or even, we might say, squarely in the center of the 'human', that other word that Mitchell insists on.

Returning to the long quotation from her 1977 paper for the Conference on the Humanities, we read: 'the point to which psychoanalysis returns is the inception of the human animal as a social being – to the origin and source of its humanity.' For Mitchell, psychoanalysis is about some sort of return to a point where something begins ('inception', 'origin', 'source') and something else ends. That point functions as a division, a kind of break, a *coupure*, between a social being and something else, between what is human and what is not. In 1966 humanization is a kind of continual progress, but when she moves into Lacan, although still very interested in humanization, she seems to mean by it some sort of absolute division between the human and the non-human, the social and the animal.

On the other side of that divide is 'what Freud called the "biological bedrock"'. The most frequently used words for what is across the divide are 'nature' and 'biology'. For Mitchell, Lacanian psychoanalysis is all about the line between the human and the natural and so also implicitly about the division between the human sciences and the natural sciences. The academic discipline of biology is located right on that line, at that point of division. Although clearly one of the natural sciences, biology includes the study of human beings, or rather we might say 'human animals'. In biology one can study the human as part of nature. The discipline of biology challenges the split between the human and the natural sciences.

In the introduction to *Feminine Sexuality*, Mitchell uses the same Freud quotation twice. It serves as the epigraph, and then it is repeated in the middle of the essay. The quotation is from a 1935 letter Freud wrote to Carl Muller-Braunschweig, where Freud says: 'I would only like to emphasize that we must keep psychoanalysis separate from biology.'[12] There are, in fact, lots of places where Freud does not respect the separation between psychoanalysis and biology. In that wonderfully confused text *Beyond the Pleasure Principle*, for example, the real locus of confusion is the slippage back and forth between the biological and the psychological. If Mitchell emphasizes this little-known statement from one of Freud's letters it is because she wants the Freud who is trying to establish a division, to make a clean cut between psychoanalysis and biology. At stake in that division is precisely the borderline between the human and the natural sciences. She is interested in a psychoanalysis that can and will patrol that border.

In the paper on whether psychoanalysis is a humanity or a science, Mitchell says: 'I am suggesting that just as it is at this moment of separation from biology that the human animal becomes a human being, so also it is at this moment that the natural object becomes (in its absence) a human object.'[13] Separation from biology and from nature for her is synonymous with the idea of humanization. To be human, for Mitchell, is finally to be separate from biology.

A few pages earlier, in the same paper: 'The thrust of Lacan's attack is against the biologism of prevalent psychoanalytic theories .... For the French psychoanalyst of the Lacanian school, the human being is human precisely at those points where he is severed from his biology.'[14] Both the theory and the subject must separate from biology. What is good for the human science is good for the human. For both the theory and the human subject separation from biology is violent ('thrust', 'attack', 'severed'), a kind of radical *coupure*. If I use the word 'coupure', the French word for the sort of clean-break, absolute divide I have been discussing, it is also to be taken literally. The word 'coupure' literally means 'cut'.

In the introduction to *Feminine Sexuality*, Mitchell writes: 'To Freud the castration complex divided the sexes and thus made the human being, human'.[15] Castration is what makes us human; humanization is severance from biology, for the human subject *and the human science*. Mitchell ultimately redefines the psychoanalytic term 'castration' to mean separation from biology so that this whole question of the division between the human and the natural

35

sciences and the investment in that split is all bound up with castration and the castration complex.

Feminism and the 'human'

What is at stake for women in Mitchell's idea of humanization as the break between the natural and the cultural, the cut from biology? In the 1966 article in the *New Left Review* she wrote: 'Marx sees history as the development of man's transformation of nature, thereby of himself – of human nature – in different modes of production. Today there are the technical possibilities for the humanisation of the most natural part of human culture. This is what a change in the mode of reproduction could mean.'[16] The phrase 'the humanisation of the most natural part of human culture' takes us very much to that border between culture and nature. 'The most natural part of human culture' is what, in colloquial rather than Marxian usage, we call 'reproduction': pregnancy, birth, maternity. 'Today there are the technical possibilities for the humanisation of [that] part of culture': in 1966 Mitchell, like many people, thought the pill was going to make an enormous amount of difference. That specific bit of technology was going to make it possible to humanize something at the furthest outpost of human culture. At stake here is the way that women have been relegated to the outskirts of culture, kept close to nature, in biology, trapped in unwitting reproduction.

A half-page earlier she says: 'Reproduction ... is a seemingly constant atemporal phenomenon – part of biology rather than history.'[17] For Mitchell it is repeatedly and finally a conflict between biology and history. Are women going to be part of biology or part of history? Is psychoanalysis going to be part of biology *or* is it going to be historical?

> Reproduction ... is a seemingly constant atemporal phenomenon ... In fact, this is an allusion ... [the 'mode of reproduction'] has been defined till now, by its uncontrollable natural character. To this extent, it has been an unmodified biological fact. As long as reproduction remained a natural phenomenon, of course, women were effectively doomed to social exploitation. In a sense, they were not masters of a large part of their lives ... their existence was essentially subject to biological processes outside their control.[18]

It is patriarchal ideology rather than any 'unmodified biological fact' that construes reproduction as atemporal. Mitchell clearly asserts that with her phrase 'in fact, this is an illusion'. There is none the less some confusion in her text as to whether it has never been atemporal or whether it has seemed atemporal until the present when it is beginning to look historical. When she says 'today there are the possibilities for the humanisation of the most natural part of human culture', she seems to be implying that heretofore it was not human. Of course it always not only has been human but has never been atemporal. Throughout history and across cultures the modes of reproduction have differed. One can do a history of mothering in our culture and in other cultures, a history of birthing, of lactating, of all those 'natural' things whose meaning and mode are very cultural and have never been simply natural. There is a slight contradiction in what Mitchell is saying. She asserts that reproduction was never atemporal but she also implies that right now it is going to stop being atemporal.

This contradiction should be considered a mark of Mitchell's vantage point as a subject in history. Phrases like '*today* there are the possibilities for the humanisation' of that part of culture and the mode of reproduction 'has been defined *till now*' bespeak a moment. Mitchell writes of a historic change in ideology, in the ideological conception of reproductive biology, but since she writes at the moment when ideology is changing, at the moment when an illusion is being uncovered, she necessarily writes both from within and without that ideology.

Mitchell's position would seem typical of the 1960s. Since the 1970s there has been so much feminist work on the history and institution of motherhood one could say that feminist scholars have actually accomplished the historicization of reproduction, of female biology. In the mid-1980s feminists can be quite certain that reproduction is neither atemporal nor 'an unmodified biological fact'. Biology no longer threatens to exist outside history.

The patriarchal ideology of industrial capitalism views sexual reproduction as part of unchanging nature, outside history and culture. Mitchell is not sure whether reproduction might not in fact be outside of culture. I think she is afraid it actually could be outside of culture. She is very much trying to pull it into culture, make sure it does not fall out into nature. Because what she calls 'the most natural part of human culture' is seen as at the edge, she tries to insure it a firm foothold in culture, in history, a well-fortified beachhead to make sure it does not float off into the sea of biology.

At certain moments Mitchell seems to suggest that it is biology itself or nature itself, rather than an ideological use of biology, rather than biologism, that oppresses women. I think that idea of biology as the enemy of women feeds her investment in the idea of a psychoanalysis as separate from biology, not only a psychoanalysis but more importantly a psychoanalytic concept of the human being as severed from biology.

Whether with Marx or Lacan, Mitchell is basically interested in women becoming fully human, which for her means being severed from their biology. In 1966, in her Marxist article, that means liberation from 'subject[ion] to biological processes outside their control'. Later with Lacan, you get these same themes: an insistence on history and humanization as separation from nature. In the early piece, the explicitly feminist piece, the reason to be severed from biology or rather the reason to give it up is in order to be 'master' of one's own life, in order to be in control. Yet the Lacanian human being severed from his biology is 'castrated', that is, never master and never in control. When

Mitchell's attack on biologism allies itself with Lacan, what happens to the feminist goal of women being freed from biology, entering into culture, in order to have more control of our lives?

Feminism and the human sciences

Having spent a lot of time lately teaching women's studies and reading feminist theory, I find myself feeling especially distant from one particular aspect of Lacanian doctrine: this whole insistence on the split. I certainly do not want a kind of lovely utopic continuum where we are all happy in nature; I remain suspicious of that. But recurring across the range of feminist studies and theory is an understanding that what Europeans call 'western culture' is based on this kind of violent split from biology, on a certain heavily-policed border with nature, which has had everything to do with the domination and exploitation of women. I thus find myself of late questioning the Lacanian insistence on the split. I find myself playing with models of another relation to the unconscious which would not be this kind of split, fundamental-division model. There are certain moments in Freud (for example, in *The Psychopathology of Everyday Life*) where he sees the unconscious as a wondrous ally, as one of our great resources. The split, the division model is always fundamentally defensive, always an adversarial position. I think there are models in Freud of other relations to the unconscious that are less adversarial. I think that the antagonistic model is coming from a certain masculinist ideology in which Freud and Lacan are thinking.[19]

I wonder if feminism is a science and what its place is on the academic map. Feminist studies or women's studies or gender studies are interdisciplinary; they span the humanities and the social sciences and cross into the natural sciences where they go as far as biology. Both feminist studies and the human sciences traverse the humanities and social science. The difference between them has to do with crossing the line and including biology. Whereas humanism constructs a notion of humanity that must continually defend against the incursions of biology, feminism includes biology in its vision of the human. The match between feminism and humanism is marred by a conflict over the border of the human sciences.

Notes

This paper is a revised version of 'Juliet Mitchell and the "human" sciences' which will appear in a forthcoming volume, *Lacan and the Human Sciences*, edited by J. J. Humphries and A. Leupin.

1 I have elsewhere used the metaphor of marriage to question the relation between psychoanalysis and feminism. See Jane Gallop, 'Reading the mother tongue', *Critical Inquiry* 13, no. 2 (1987), pp. 314–29.

2 Juliet Mitchell, *Psychoanalysis and feminism: Freud, Reich, Laing and Women* (New York: Pantheon, 1974). I wrote about this book over a decade ago, at

that time proposing the marriage between Lacan and feminism. See Jane Gallop, 'Psychoanalysis and Feminism', in *The Daughter's Seduction: Feminism and Psychoanalysis* (Ithaca and London: Cornell University Press and Macmillan, 1982).

3 Jacques Lacan and the *école freudienne*, *Feminine Sexuality*, ed. Juliet Mitchell and Jacqueline Rose (New York: Pantheon, 1982).

4 'Feminine sexuality: interview with Juliet Mitchell and Jacqueline Rose', *m/f* 8 (1982). Headnote to interview: 'Interviewed by Parveen Adams and Elizabeth Cowie on the publication of *Feminine Sexuality – Jacques Lacan and the Ecole Freudienne* [note the subtitle] translated by Jacqueline Rose, ed by Juliet Mitchell and Jacqueline Rose Macmillan September 1982.'

5 Or so at least I found. See Jane Gallop, *Reading Lacan* (Ithaca: Cornell University Press, 1985) chs 3 and 4.

6 *Feminine Sexuality*, p. 19.

7 Juliet Mitchell, *Women: The Longest Revolution: On Feminism, Literature and Psychoanalysis* (New York, Pantheon, 1984), p. 249.

8 Louis Althusser, 'Freud and Lacan', in *Lenin and Philosophy and Other Essays*, trans. Ben Brewster (New York: Monthly Review Press, 1971).

9 Mitchell, *Women: The Longest Revolution*, p. 21.

10 ibid., p. 237.

11 ibid., p. 265.

12 ibid., pp. 249, 272.

13 ibid., pp. 243–4.

14 ibid., pp. 239–40.

15 ibid., p. 269.

16 ibid., p. 32.

17 ibid., pp. 31–2.

18 ibid.

19 For an excellent analysis of that masculinist ideology and how it shapes science, see Evelyn Fox Keller, *Reflections on Gender and Science* (New Haven: Yale University Press, 1985). In many ways, this book was behind my thinking throughout the present paper.

Chapter Two

Still crazy after all these years

Rachel Bowlby

Blind dates

Not so long ago, I was looking around in the attic and came across some documents written in a script that was virtually indecipherable to me, and thoroughly enigmatic. I was interested and not a little perplexed by them, and devoted some time to trying to puzzle out their meaning. Eventually, I felt I had succeeded in breaking the code – though the documents came from a bygone civilization of which I know nothing, and I may have gone off on the wrong track altogether. They seemed to feature the same two personages (if that is the proper term) again and again; but I think they were written by diverse hands, so I cannot be sure if what I thought I was putting together was a simple story, stage by stage, or whether it was the same event – if there was an event – told from different and conflicting perspectives. I will provide a few examples to show you what I mean:

ξ, highly intelligent, discontented, 29, wishing to settle down, seeks ψ in hope of further developments ... ψ, prepossessing
in appearance, late 30s, flourishing legal practice, seeks ξ for
enlightening conversation ... ξ, still looking, seeks theory of why she is so unhappy. ψ Gkpsi welcome.
ξ still discontented, seeks theory of why she is so unhappy. ψ need not apply ... ψ met his friend ψ_2 in the bar. He said to him: What the hell *do* they want? And the consequence was that they both had a good laugh at her expense....

ξ met her friend ξ_2 at a conference. She said to ξ_2:
I get nothing out of my
$\psi\psi$ is the cause of all our problems. ξ_2 said to ξ: ψ is the answer to all our problems. There were more
conferences [consequences?] ... ψ, qualities as ever, still interested in ξ, but asks sincerely: What do you want?
ξ, not what you think, wants ... [there may be a gap here; or there may not]

I was puzzled by these various stories and their various outcomes (and I have only given you a fraction of the material at my disposal). They seemed to offer no definite conclusion, and might have been written by many different authors. Who were these characters ξ and ψ, and were they the same in each of the little samples? Why did they keep coming back to each other after the end of the story; or why could they never seem to get it together? My material was so fragmentary and blurred that it was difficult to know how to date it – whether all the pieces came from the same period, or whether they were scattered over a very long time. Nor was it possible to know whether the 'dates' they seemed to be setting up had ever moved from possibility to reality. Was I just dealing with the coy imaginings of some cosy Victorian parlour game, or was this the record of buried events of burning and hitherto unrecognized importance? I decided, at any rate, to devote such investigative powers as I could muster to examining this mystery – a mystery which, as I was fully aware, might well turn out to lead me, to coin a phrase, up the garden path, if not on the road to wilderness. For it might turn out that the mystery was in fact nothing other than the pretence of one: the solution would be that there had been no mystery after all. Yet how could I ever establish this? If the fragments held no secret, this could never be proved conclusively, once and for all: there would always be the chance that there was a further layer to uncover, something that I could never fathom. These reflections, however, were not conducive to sanity: that way, I said to myself with firmness, madness lies (or tells the truth, perhaps). So I decided to proceed along the path I had set for myself, without looking back.

I only wish that what I am about to tell you could be presented in the form of a coherent, linear narrative, leading inexorably from its starting point to its conclusion. But what I found was that the peculiar and piecemeal quality of the raw material kept coming back, if I may say so, to 'unstructure' my own account of how I tried to discover its source. I dare say I was led off along many false tracks – how could it be otherwise, when I did not know where I was going, or even whether there was a destination at the end? Given the strange character of my material, I encountered many problems of translation, and if my solution of these language difficulties seems at times tendentious or impudent, I can only protest that I was of course speaking 'tongue' in 'cheek'. No doubt I trailed too many wild geese, was led astray by a succession of shaggy dogs, flogged not a few dead mares. I can honestly say, though, that whenever I saw a cat I took no further steps and merely called it a cat, *mutatis mutandis*, or even *per os*.

But inevitably, then, I am going to tell some tall stories and some small stories – many pre-modern. If I did not find the solution to the enigma, I may at least have stumbled on some of the reasons for why it remained one. To put it another way, I think I found the key to the door, but not whether anything lay on the other side of it.[1]

Till death do drive us apart

To begin at the end, then, an excessively clear and schematic summary of the current state of play (or the permanent state of play) for the two protagonists. Psychoanalysis and feminism, it seems, have been together for a long time now, fixed into what seems to have become a virtually interminable relationship, marked repeatedly by expressions of violent feeling on both sides. Passionate declarations are followed by calm periods and then by the breaking out or resurgence of desperate denunciations and pleas once again. Past periods or episodes – Freud and the hysterics, the 'great debate' of the 1920s and 1930s – are dimly glimpsed or resuscitated, long-forgotten dates, taking on renewed if not new meanings from the perspective of contemporary interests. Vehement denials and vehement advocacy characterize the proposals of both parties. 'We were made for each other', says one partner in the first flush of rapture; only to be followed at a later, more bitter stage by a transformed insistence that 'the relationship was doomed from the start'. The one constant seems to be that neither side ever lets go: even when far apart, between their scattered blind dates – the 1890s, the 1920s and 1930s, the 1970s and 1980s – they have always somewhere been on each other's mind.

Both sides accuse the other of conforming to cultural edicts which they should rather be challenging. For the anti-psychoanalysts, an awesome 'Freudianism' represents the reimposition of the law of patriarchy by which women have always been oppressed, and so is detrimental to the cause of women's emancipation. These feminists see in psychoanalysis an endorsement, rather than a critique, of just what makes patriarchal society unbearable for women. For the pro-psychoanalytic feminists, the problem lies rather with (the rest of) feminism's assumption that the identity of women as women (and men as men, for that matter) is unproblematically given, or that difficulties of sexuality and conflicts of subjectivity are no more than the effect of contingent social oppression. Psychoanalytic feminism takes non-psychoanalytic feminism to be too simple in its notion of subjectivity for it to be capable of achieving the very political goals it sets itself; while anti-psychoanalytic feminism sees in the psychoanalytic stress on subjectivity a needless detour from feminism's real concerns, if not a pernicious undermining of the tough, coherent agents needed to carry through political action with a subjectivity united at both the individual and the collective level.[2]

It is thus not only that feminisms for and against psychoanalysis have trouble in knowing how they feel about each other, but that these difficulties come to be related to problems of how they identify each other's position. The psychoanalysis that one side sees as the cure, or at least as an account of the workings of the disease, is seen by the other as just another instance of the same infection, all the more insidious for being misrecognized as its mitigation. Psychoanalytic feminism claims that feminism needs an extra edge of questioning that only psychoanalysis can supply, while non-psychoanalytic feminism argues in its turn that feminism is quite radical enough on its own and would only fall back into the very traps from which it is trying to free women by taking up with a psychoanalysis irretrievably tainted with conservative, masculine norms.

The issue, repeatedly, revolves around deciding what is to be considered truly political for feminism: one of the baselines of the argument is the implied legitimation in terms of the gesture of 'more political than thou'. And it is in relation to this that the double question of origins and ends arises: Where are women's difficulties supposed to have started; and where does feminism think it is going? Is psychoanalysis a time-wasting diversion from the principal goal; or (from the other side) has the feminism that ignores psychoanalysis taken a short cut that will only return it to the same questions in the long run?

But we have so much in common

If psychoanalysis and feminism seem to be locked into combat or copulation unto the death – and the choice of which one depends entirely on the viewpoint of the spectator – then it may come as less of a surprise that they could be said to have been together all along. The *Oxford English Dictionary*, completed in 1933, has no entry for psychoanalysis. Feminism is listed, but with just one citation, from 1851, meaning 'the qualities of females', together with the curtly italicized information: '*rare*'. If feminism were a naturally female quality perhaps it would never have had to be invented; at any rate, in the first *OED Supplement* – which in fact appeared in the same year as the dictionary was completed – both psychoanalysis and feminism are allotted a place, and in recognizable guises, with detailed entries both for themselves and for their loyal practitioners, the feminist and the psychoanalyst. Psychoanalysis, for which the first English usage is recorded in 1906, is supplied at the start with an author and a geographical location – it is 'a therapeutic method for treating certain disorders elaborated by Dr. S. Freud of Vienna' – and there follow some further details. Feminism is defined cumbrously and perhaps undecidedly as 'the opinions and principles of the advocates of the extended recognition of the achievements and claims of women; the advocacy of women's rights'. But the entry begins emphatically: 'Delete *rare* and add.'

In the *OED* context – English at its purest – it is significant that both words are presented as foreign imports. Psychoanalysis is said to be taken from the German as well as invented by the named Viennese doctor; feminism is attributed to the French *féminisme* (though more specific filiations lie behind that, as we shall see).[3] It is as though English, if not England, stands in need of additions which will complete it, become part of its own language and culture, but which can only be thought from abroad. And this is paralleled by the specific logic of the *Supplement*: part of the dictionary but yet an extra, an addition; something in which it has been found to be lacking, and which it cannot do without in order to complete itself, but which is none the less situated as external and separate. Psychoanalysis and feminism share the same relationship to the legitimating English dictionary as one of those advocated as the relationship linking psychoanalysis to feminism: feminism cannot do without a psychoanalysis which is yet something other than it (and the same would be true the other way around).

Not only, then, are psychoanalysis and feminism joined together until death, but the pair apparently have in common the same moment of birth, like twins destined for endless love and rivalry from the very beginning. Sharing a kind of quasi-legitimacy, neither fully integrated nor unequivocally cast out, they both owe their official introduction to the anglophone world to the *OED Supplement*. It is as if they were both fated to be marginal to official Englishness, placed off-centre (but placed none the less) and deriving their critical force (or perhaps their ineffectiveness) from just such a doubtful position, not quite inside and yet not absolutely excluded or ignored.

Trivial pursuits

The possibility, or inevitability, of mistaken identification – each side seeing in the other what it longs for or what it dreads – seems to be built in to the structure of this case. Perhaps there is no relationship between psychoanalysis and feminism. Or perhaps the blind dates that seemed to be suggested in the historical fragments with which we began will offer some further insights. If the couple are unknown to each other, there is first the possibility for boundless expectations in the imagining of what the other party may have to offer. Disappointment gives place to disillusionment; but then, after a period of temporary forgetting, the whole thing can start up again, with both partners blind to the fact that they have ever met before. What becomes more disturbing in this perpetual restaging of the same passionate drama, the same old serial, is that it might be quite literally a programmed repeat, with no differences at all. If every move, every question, and every answer is entirely given in advance, a perfect copy of an unchanging script, then the joke of the blind date is not only on the hapless participants, but on the spectators trying in vain to maintain their belief in the 'live' spontaneity of the proceedings – or perhaps, finally, not caring one way or the other. An allusion to Cilla Black's infamous television show, where the jokes are all pre-written and the blind dates are spectacularly predictable, may seem out of place in the serious context of the dates, or rather debates, between psychoanalysis and feminism. I bring her on stage, or onto the screen, provocatively, as the doubtful *dea ex machina* who will guide me to what I want to suggest is a serious question about triviality.[4]

Both psychoanalysis and feminism throw into confusion ordinary conceptions of what is to be considered as 'merely' trivial; and not least – though not necessarily from the same angle – in terms of what constitutes the basis for the 'obvious', everyday distinction between the sexes. Freud says towards the beginning of his 'Introductory lecture' on 'Femininity': 'When you meet someone, the first distinction you make is "male or female?" and you are accustomed to make this distinction with unhesitating certainty.'[5] This is the distinction which is so automatic, so 'unhesitating', as to go without saying; and for that very reason, as he will go on to suggest, all the more liable to question. The triviality of the example – any everyday encounter with an unknown person – reverses the implications of the 'accustomed' grid, the habit becoming suspect precisely because it is habitual.

But there is more to triviality than this. The word is derived not from a binary but from a triple distinction: the Latin 'trivium', *tris viae*, 'three ways'. In the context of psychoanalytic stories, this indicates a further step back, from Latin into Greek and Sophocles' play about Oedipus, where the event that may or may not have taken place when the hero, travelling many years before, killed an old man at the intersection of a 'triple way', Τριπλης δη, becomes a question of the utmost importance.[6]

There is another point at which psychoanalysis comes upon a crossroads at which three ways, three roads, lead off. This is none other than the crucial original encounter with that other person as 'male or female': the mythical moment of 'fright' at first sight when the meaning of sexual difference impinges upon the child.[7] And at this juncture, each of the two trivially obvious sides of the distinction turns out to be broken down into three different possible ways. For the boy, the realization of the girl's lack sends him off along one of three lines – homosexuality, fetishism, or 'normality' – which respond to his newfound vulnerability. Feminist priorities mean that we do not have time to follow the boy's adventures further. For the girl, there are also three possible 'lines of development' – to neurosis, to the 'masculine protest', or to 'normal' femininity – and we shall have occasion to return to them later on.[8]

Boy meets girl?

One of the difficulties in bringing about or rejecting the desirability of a final union between psychoanalysis and feminism has been precisely that of identifying the sexes of the two parties. From the point of view of anti-psychoanalytic feminism, the person of Freud as a Victorian patriarch is usually taken as the ground for assuming an inescapably anti-feminist stance built into the texts and the practice of psychoanalysis ever since. 'Dora', who walked out before the conclusion of her analysis by a Freud who had not recognized his own interest in seeing her desire as simply heterosexual, can be regarded from this point of view as the first heroine of feminist protest against a psychoanalysis which was doing no more than reconfirming the prevailing sexual norms. From the other side, that of pro-psychoanalytic feminism, Freud's early researches into hysteria mark the starting point of what was to be an undoing of every bourgeois or patriarchal assumption as to the biological naturalness of heterosexual attraction, or the masculinity and femininity predicated of men and women.

The first *OED Supplement* example for the word 'feminism' may possibly be enlightening here. It dates from 1895, and reads: 'Her intellectual evolution and her coquettings with the doctrines of "feminism" are traced with real humour.' This might alert the reader to a possible danger in assuming too easily a convenient equality or symmetry in the origins of psychoanalysis and feminism in Britain. Here, as the inaugurating example, the 'very first' instance which will set the terms for the established meanings of the word, we have something that appears to be just the same old misogynist bar-room joke. Not only is feminism in quotation marks, but it is something merely to flirt with – temporarily, perhaps, on the way to a womanhood that would have nothing to do with 'feminism'. The relation between the 'intellectual evolution' and the 'coquettings with "feminism"' is not specified. They might be complementary, reinforcing each other as reason and emotion. They might both be taken as delaying the arrival at normal femininity, but only in the sense of predictable 'phases' to be treated with indulgent paternal 'humour'. Or feminism might be considered the principal deviant: all intellectually evolved women are likely to go through a feminist 'phase'. As a last possibility, the two might be antagonistic, the feminism militating against the intellectual development or the 'coquettings' distracting the brain.

The exemplary first occurrence of feminism (or rather 'feminism') begins, on closer scrutiny, to look more and more like a miniature illustration of the questions surrounding the psychoanalytic account of femininity. Does this vignette postulate the implied relationship between intellect, feminism, coquetting, and the acquisition of a 'normal' femininity as something that calls for explanation, or rather as a matter of course, obvious as the difference of the sexes? Is the choice of a first citation for feminism in which these moments are said to be treated with 'real humour' an exposé of the standard smutty jokes at women's expense whose structure Freud lays bare, or is it just one more example of them?[9]

Oddly or inevitably enough, 1895 is also the date of the publication of Freud's and Breuer's *Studies in Hysteria*, in which the 'cases' analysed raise all the same questions as does this questionable 'case' of feminism as to the pertinence of the psychoanalytic account of feminine development. Either the hysterical women analysed by Freud and Breuer open the way to a general understanding of the typical structures which make femininity difficult for women, or they inaugurate an ineradicable complicity of psychoanalysis with the same notions that make all women into aberrant 'cases' for masculine correction or contempt, and make feminism into a permanent joke between men.

It is perhaps quite appropriate that the English girl should be 'coquetting' with feminism, the word carrying with it all the quintessentially English connotations of its Frenchness. 'Feminism' is French too, according to the dictionary; the pair seem to be well-matched, and heterosexually, since it is with men that girls are supposed to coquette. And further investigations with the French dictionary reveal that feminism is in fact ultimately a masculine word – not only by grammatical gender, but in that Fourier is specifically named as its (male) inventor: 'Le mot "féminisme" fut créé par Fourier.'[10] This makes feminism's kinship with Dr Freud's personalized psychoanalysis take on different implications. In its origin, as in Freud's interpretation of it, it apparently represents a 'masculine' line of development. Or, like psycho-analysis, its beginnings seem to have the form of the father's kindly inter-vention to set the dissatisfied girl to rights. An investigation of the source of the coquetting quotation makes things no simpler; but we will not allow ourselves to be waylaid by this here.[11]

The question of the relationship between intellectual evolution and fem-ininity is one that is broached by Freud, too, quite soon after this, for instance in a footnote to the 'Dora' case, where he refers to 'her declaration that she had been able to keep abreast with her brother up to the time of her first illness, but that after that she had fallen behind him in her studies'. He goes on:

> It was as though she had been a boy up till that moment, and had then become girlish for the first time. She had in truth been a wild creature; but after the 'asthma' she became quiet and well-behaved. That illness formed the boundary between two phases of her sexual life, of which the first was masculine in character, and the second feminine.[12]

It is also significant that at the time when Dora was presented to Freud for analysis, she 'employed herself ... with attending lectures for women and with carrying on more or less serious studies'.[13] Read with hindsight, the passage can be seen as foreshadowing what will later become the definitive Freudian account of femininity as predicated on the giving up of what is first of all, but equally with hindsight, a masculinity shared by children of both sexes. In the meantime, the structures of castration and the Oedipus complex have been fully installed in Freud's theory, to make the 'boundary' between the 'two phases' of the girl's life acquire all the sharper a distinction.

Your place or mine?

There is a famous passage at the end of one of Freud's last essays, 'Analysis terminable and interminable' (1937), which is partly about the difficulty of bringing a long relationship to an end, and which throws some more light on this difficult passage or connection between masculinity and femininity. Freud writes:

> We often have the impression that with the wish for a penis and the masculine protest we have penetrated through all the psychological strata and have reached bedrock and that thus our activities are at an end. This is probably true, since, in the psychical field, the biological field does in fact play the part of the underlying bedrock. The repudiation of femininity can be nothing else than a biological fact, a part of the great riddle of sex.[14]

This is one of those places where Freud seems most open to the charge of biological reductiveness, on the grounds – the 'bedrock', no less – that he makes of an untenable femininity, femininity as by definition to be repudiated, femininity as the point below which analysis can go no further, the bottom line which cannot itself be further broken up into component or underlying parts. The monumental impenetrability of a geological formation seems to be set irrefutably as the natural base for sexual difference.

But, as with all such pronouncements in Freud's texts, it turns out that the conclusion can be turned on its head. For Freud is using what he calls 'the biological factor' as his foundation for making a statement which in fact removes masculinity and femininity from the order of direct relationship to male and female bodies. Rather than their being natural outgrowths or symmetrical identities, the man's identity as a man is founded, as a footnote makes clear, on the fear of castration, on the denial of being a woman.

But this departure from the biological 'bedrock' still leaves us back where Dora started – merely transposing the problem to another level or layer. The form of the asymmetry or discontinuity of masculinity and femininity remains a problem. There is no equivalent insistence for the woman that she is not a man – no repudiation of masculinity – and to the extent that there can be said to be a first, more natural identity, it is masculine, not feminine:

> In females also the striving after masculinity is ego-syntonic at a certain period, namely in the phallic phase, before the development to femininity has set in... A great deal depends upon whether a sufficient amount of her masculinity-complex escapes repression and exercises a permanent influence on her character.[15]

Femininity is thus the place where no man – male or female – wants to be, and its repudiation is the attitude that characterizes both the 'normal' man and the woman who has remained masculine, refusing or failing to change her first, masculine nature for femininity. Even though Freud characterizes the repudiation of femininity as an immutable, quasi-biological given in this essay, he does not appear to be treating it as necessarily a universal attribute of women. Instead, it would seem to apply only to the 'masculine' line of development and not to the 'normal' feminine woman whose masculinity has been adequately repressed.

Now this quotation is the best-known, but not the only Freudian occurrence of 'repudiation' in relation to femininity. In 'The psychogenesis of a case of female homosexuality' (1920), we read: 'After her disappointment, therefore [in relation to her father], this girl had entirely repudiated her wish for a child, her love of man, and the feminine role in general.'[16] This description would fit with the later essay, in that repudiation goes together with the adoption of a masculine attitude (here related to the woman's 'masculine' adoration of a woman).

But there is a further instance which complicates this relatively straightforward paradigm. In the 1933 lecture on femininity, published four years before 'Analysis terminable and interminable', in the same year as the *OED Supplement*, repudiation turns up in the summary of the 'three possible lines of development' that lead off for the girl following 'the discovery that she is castrated':

> Her self-love is mortified by the comparison with the boy's far superior equipment and in consequence she renounces her masturbatory satisfaction from her clitoris, repudiates her love for her mother and at the same time not infrequently represses a good part of her sexual trends in general.[17]

Here, repudiation is explicitly linked to the two changes – in relation to the chief place of her erotic arousal, and to the sex of the one she loves – which the girl, who now turns out to have been 'masculine' up to this point, has to make in order to become a woman. The recognition of sexual difference in the form of her own lack brings with it the recognition that the formerly phallic mother is no better off, and therefore to be 'debased in value', as Freud puts it at the end of the paragraph. The repudiation of the mother, which goes along with the general depreciation and devaluation of 'the woman', by women as well as by men, is the repudiation of her as feminine.

Freud has enumerated the three possible 'lines of development' for the girl as being to sexual inhibition or neurosis; to the masculinity complex; or to normal femininity. The context does not make it clear which of them is being described at this point. Freud begins the paragraph by announcing it as referring to the line to sexual inhibition or neurosis. The line of masculine protest is subsequently given a separate exposition, but the third line, to normality, effectively blurs into the neurotic line, so that it is justifiable to see the passage above as covering both where they deal with renunciation and repudiation: it is the degree of sexual repression that distinguishes the two. And here we seem to have come upon an unexpected turn of events. In the other two examples, the repudiation of femininity was symptomatic of neither of these, but of the third line, that of the masculinity complex. Now, far from being confined to one of the three 'lines', the masculine one that ought to be furthest from normal femininity, the repudiation of femininity has come to characterize all three, including that of femininity itself.[18]

A little later in the 'Femininity' lecture, Freud refers to 'the wish for a penis being *par excellence* a feminine one'.[19] This might seem to be logical on the grounds that if anyone is going to wish for the thing, it will be the woman, who does not have it. But previously, femininity has been characterized as the end-point which implies the woman's coming to terms with the fact of her castration, rather than continuing to resent or seek to remedy it, in contrast to the still protesting woman who is hopelessly wanting what she can never have. Freud says this explicitly in another of the *New Introductory Lectures*: 'It is also easy to follow the way in which in girls what is an entirely *unfeminine* wish to possess a penis is normally transformed into a wish for a baby.'[20] There seems to be something of a contradiction here, and stated in exaggerated form: the wish for a penis is 'entirely unfeminine', and it is *'par excellence'* feminine. A longer version of the second passage may perhaps make matters clearer, since it too is concerned with the achievement of femininity through a baby. The passage states:

> Often enough in her combined picture of 'a baby from her father' the emphasis is laid on the baby and her father left unstressed. In this way the ancient masculine wish for the possession of a penis is still faintly visible through the femininity now achieved. But perhaps we ought rather to recognize this wish for a penis as being *par excellence* a feminine one.[21]

The second passage reinterprets the first, which insists that femininity is precisely not the wish for a penis – 'entirely unfeminine' – by emphasizing instead the continuity, given that the baby-wish simply takes the place of the penis-wish: it is its substitute and it is also what hides its continuing existence. But removing a contradiction has only produced the scandal. There is no place of femininity at all: femininity itself is still 'the masculine wish for the possession of a penis'. Even the properly feminine woman is still caught up in the masculinity complex, still hankering after a penis, even if this is covered over by the wish for a baby, and still repudiating the femininity she is said to have attained. If it seemed at first that there were three roads, of which only one led to the 'final' destination of femininity, it now seems that all roads lead to the same destination, or rather to the same non-destination, the same repudiation.

A thicker entanglement

In view of this loaded background in the texts of Freud, it is intriguing that 'repudiation' is a word which has often appeared or recurred in arguments over the proper relationship between psychoanalysis and feminism. To begin with the opening page of Juliet Mitchell's *Psychoanalysis and Feminism*, the book which launched the present engagement: 'It seems to me that we have turned things on their head by accepting Reich's and Laing's analyses and repudiating Freud's.'[22] Then Jane Gallop, analysing Mitchell's criticisms of those who criticize Freud on biographical grounds declares: 'Interestingly, the repudiation of the trivial *ad hominem* argument returns continually.'[23] In Jacqueline Rose's fine reply to Elizabeth Wilson's criticisms of psychoanalysis, the word occurs a few times in relation to both the British left and British feminism, in their joint or separate 'repudiation' of psychoanalysis. What Rose calls 'a fairly consistent repudiation of Freud' is also a fairly consistent application of the term 'repudiation' by those who are for psychoanalysis to those who are not.[24]

Given the cluster of associations which link repudiation and femininity in the Standard Edition, it may well be worth examining the implications of this recurrent charge in some detail. For 'repudiation', even aside from its Freudian uses, is not, after all, just any old word. It is strong language, and seems to imply not just rejection or refusal, but also that what is rejected is somehow a part of the repudiator: that it is illegitimately cast off. Repudiation's five emphatic syllables seem to proclaim their refusal a little too loudly. There is the implication that what you repudiate really belongs to you, stays behind to haunt you, however hard you try to get rid of it. Repudiation carries the suggestion of an arbitrary gesture which is not concerned with arguing in terms of moral rights or logic. In this respect, the word is precisely differentiated from its near homonymic neighbour 'refutation', which has – or had, until it began recently to be used as synonymous with 'disagree' – just that dispassionate reason which repudiation lacks. Or put the other way round, repudiation has all the emotional conviction to which refutation is indifferent.

Returning to the *OED* for more rational or impartial enlightenment, we find that there are further layers to be uncovered. The primary meaning, now defunct, of the verb 'repudiate' is specific and revealing. It is 'to divorce', and it was used in English of a man in relation to a woman but not the other way around. In the expansion that follows the initial definition, we have first: 'Of a husband: To put away or cast off (his wife): to divorce, dismiss'; and then 'cast off, disown (a person or thing)'. If we put this piece of information back into the context of the relation between psychoanalysis and feminism, the situation seems all the more confusing. To say that feminism repudiates psychoanalysis is to put feminism in the position of a man rejecting his wife, in a gesture that could not be reciprocated. It means that the feminist rejection of psychoanalysis is equivalent to an exemplary instance of the exercise of patriarchal power; it means also that there is no position other than that of an identification with patriarchal authority from which it can be done. And if repudiation connotes the putting asunder, at the instigation of one of them, of two 'persons or things' which were to have been joined together for life, it suggests a newly literal side to what are claimed as the 'fatal' consequences that would ensue on feminism's refusal to couple itself with psychoanalysis.[25]

The use of the term 'repudiation' by advocates of psychoanalysis seems then to have the effect of a double bind – or rather, a forced marriage. It accuses feminism of acting with the arbitrary prerogatives of a representative of patriarchy, of inserting itself into precisely the paradigm from which it wants to free women, and on the side of masculine power. If feminism accuses psychoanalysis of merely validating the established forms whereby women are supposed to find their fulfilment as wives and mothers, psychoanalysis turns this back on feminism by declaring it already married to a psychoanalysis from which it can only be separated by itself re-enacting or reinstalling those structures of patriarchal authority: repudiation is just one of the lesser known and more patriarchal of the fifty accredited ways to leave your lover.

Bearing in mind all these complexities, some old-fashioned 'feminine' sympathy is perhaps not out of place for the heroine or victim of one of the dictionary's examples of the word, taken from the *Edinburgh Review* of 1803: 'She does not appear even to have understood what they meant by repudiation.' Now this poor lady so patronizingly chided is in fact none other than Madame Suzanne Necker, the mother of Madame de Staël and the wife of Louis XVI's minister, Jacques Necker. In 1794 she published from exile in Switzerland a book on divorce. But we don't have time to pursue this lead any further...[26]

There are still further layers to be uncovered: we have not reached 'bedrock' yet. The English 'repudiation' is a direct import from the Latin *repudium*, which is in turn cognate with *pudor*, meaning 'shame', whence in English the (still Latin, euphemistic) *pudenda*. Literally, the *pudenda* are simply 'parts for which shame should be felt'; the use of the word (in Latin as later in English) to refer only to the female genitals is an interesting case of the figure of part for whole (or rather hole for whole). A single instance of nebulous neuter 'things for which shame is appropriate' comes to take the place of the entire class. Both the euphemistic equivocation and the generality of the *pudenda* serve as a thin veil for the word which in practice can mean only one thing. It is the female genitals, in their lack by comparison with those of the man, which figure as the ultimate cause in Freud for the disparagement of femininity, for the determination on the part of protesting men and women to be exempt from such a meagre and shameful endowment.[27]

All this leaves us with some contradictory consequences. In psychoanalytic theory, supported by linguistic fossils if not by human anatomy, there is apparently no case of repudiation which is not, at bottom, at rock-bottom, a repudiation of femininity. There is further no attitude to femininity which is not that of repudiation: thus no place, once past the crossroads where the question 'male or female?' is first posed or imposed, no place that does not imply the repudiation of femininity, including the place of femininity itself, which is *repudianda*, to be repudiated, for feminine women and feminists alike. And this merely repeats the fate of the *pudenda*, themselves concealed inside the word: there are no shameful parts other than the parts which are those which distinguish, or rather diminish, the woman. Repudiation implies the taking of a masculine position and the rejection of a feminine one; at the same time there is no escape from that femininity which is everyone's cast-off or ex-wife, be they man, feminist, or lady.

So where does this leave psychoanalysis and feminism? If repudiation is always the repudiation of femininity, then in its own terms psychoanalysis can hardly blame feminism for an attitude which it has identified as inevitable. This is perhaps just a different inflection of that old psychoanalytic saw about Dostoevsky's 'knife that cuts both ways', to which Freud alludes in a footnote about nothing other than feminist objections to psychoanalysis: any objection to psychoanalysis can always be interpreted psychoanalytically, as can the psychoanalytic account of femininity, which then leads to 'no decision'.[28]

Psychonalytically, it is impossible to adopt psychoanalysis (which is what the sceptics are being urged to do): it cannot but be repudiated. To put it bluntly, the knife that cuts both ways is also the three ways that fork only one way. You can't refute it; to which we may now add: you can only repudiate it.

All this may provide some kind of explanation for the interminability of the courtship of psychoanalysis and feminism. Psychoanalysis is certainly accusing feminism of taking a masculine stance. But even more significantly, it is putting itself in the impossible place of the woman. For just as they are locked into a state of mutual denunciation, each accusing the other of acting like a man, so they come straight back together in their joint claim that something should speak from the position of the cast-off woman.

Three words in a boat

But further discoveries await us. So far we have been assuming that there is some kind of textual justification for the connection we have been making between the various Freudian feminine repudiations. But if we go back behind the familiar words of the Strachey translation to take a look at the original language of psychoanalysis, a startling revelation awaits us. For it turns out that the German word translated by 'repudiation' is different in each of the three cases noted above. In the 'Femininity' lecture, it is *verwerfen*, meaning 'to throw away' or 'discard'. In the 'Analysis' essay, 'repudiation' translates *ablehnen*: 'to decline, refuse, remove'. And in the 'Female homosexuality' text, it is *weisen*, in a construction where it means 'to exile, expel, or banish'. These words are not identical in meaning or in force.[29] In fact, the mildest word, *ablehnen*, is the one which occurs in the most intractable, most often cited passage, the one which makes the repudiation of femininity into the 'biological "bedrock"'. In view of the fact that 'the repudiation of femininity' has become one of the most familiar phrases in anglophone discussions of Freud and femininity, this assimilation on the part of the translator, deliberate or not, seems to be worth some attention. 'Repudiation' covers three different German words in the same context of an attitude to femininity; the three words are themselves used elsewhere in Freud without being translated by 'repudiation'.

Just as in Freudian theory the obviousness of 'male or female?' must be broken down to show the three ways offered to each sex at the point of that initial separation, so the 'repudiation' of femininity which has turned out to dominate, even to block, all the possible paths seems now to be itself made up of three different words, hitherto unsuspected beneath the familiar, unified cover. Arguably, then, the decision can be seen retrospectively to have marked a turning point in the future possibilities for discussions of psychoanalysis and feminism. Perhaps, indeed, it may have inaugurated a distinctively English, or anglophone, 'line of development': 'No femininity please, we're British.'

We could then carry this to the limit, and ask what it would mean if 'the repudiation of femininity' were nothing but an error of translation, a bad

English dream that has been marring the fates of femininity and feminism ever since. What a momentous difference would then turn out to have ensued when psychoanalysis crossed the Channel and arrived in Britain: at one stroke, we might then have found the answer to why psychoanalysis has never made its way into British culture, or why English-speaking feminists have been reluctant to adopt it as a theory. What a relief, or a shock, after all these years, if the trouble could all be blamed on an idiosyncratic predilection, say, for that satisfying and rare five-syllable word – or else just on the slightest assimilating slip of the Strachey pen. Legend has it – and I have not been able, despite earnest researches, to find the source[30] – that when Freud arrived in the United States to deliver a series of lectures in 1909, he said of his new science and its new destination: 'We are bringing them the plague.' It would be a nice irony if the plague with which the Standard Edition infected the English-speaking world was not Freud's psychoanalysis at all.

But the problem cannot be put in quite such clear-cut terms – all the more so since the clearness of the cut is precisely what is at issue. Instead, the multiple origin of 'repudiation' raises more general questions about the necessary interpretation and distortion that accompany the translating and the transporting of theories from one language and culture to another. There are also the issues surrounding the gesture of a 'return' to the texts of Freud – questions which are particularly risky at this point because one of the German words translated as 'repudiation', *verwerfen,* is also the word from one of whose uses in Freud Lacan extracts the concept of foreclosure associated with psychosis.[31] It might be argued that there is a crucial difference in the two moves: Lacan is openly admitting that he is drawing out implications which are not thematized in the master text, whereas Strachey, who says nothing about what he is up to, is smuggling in his plague upon women by the back port, in the guise of a direct rendering. But the moral terms of this could just as easily be put the other way round: Strachey is the simple man who does not realize the significance of what he is doing, while Lacan is claiming as faithfully Freudian something which is actually not there in the original. Putting the issue like this sets up dividing lines which only send the question back to the problem of the master text: to distinguish between the honest importer and the pirate, between the judicious and the blind interpretation, involves just the same appeal to the initial text as the rock which harbours the pure ore of indisputable meaning. The straight and the stray translation are indistinguishable: the 'Strachey' translation. Even if it could somehow be demonstrated that 'the repudiation of femininity' did not correspond to 'what Freud really said' or 'really meant', this would not cancel out all the arguments about psychoanalysis in English that have been carried on in the meantime: it would simply be the vehicle of a further stage in them.

Now that the rock of repudiation has been shattered, or at least its impenetrability put in question, do the three German words that lie beneath it offer us any potential way out of the impasse of femininity? One meaning of *die Verwerfung* is that of a geological fault: using the translator's licence in reverse, we could put this back into the passage from 'Analysis terminable and interminable'. In this sense, it would seem that 'the biological "bedrock"' was not the repudiation of femininity but the faulting of femininity, leaving open, in the slide between the strata, the possibility that there might be further to go after all, a still more 'basic fault' that had previously not been seen.

The gap between German and English takes us back to the meaning of *weisen von sich*, 'to exile or banish', in the passage from the 'Female homosexuality' case. The word 'repudiation' has itself exiled, repudiated, the femininity that might not have been so utterly ruled out in the German original. This story of a forced exile is also, of course, that of the girl's sudden and shattering realization of the significance of her sex and her doomed departure on a one-way ticket to the far land of femininity that never comes, or at which she never arrives.

And what of the time before that? For Freud uses the motif of feminine exile in an explicit and famous simile: 'Our insight into this early, pre-Oedipus, phase in girls comes to us as a surprise, like the discovery, in another field, of the Minoan–Mycenaean civilization behind the civilization of Greece.'[32] Let us pause for a moment with this Minoan–Mycenaean civilization that was producing such archaeological excitement in Freud's time, the layers of an even more ancient Greece below the one that had previously been thought to be the bedrock, the furthest back or down that there could be. It is generally dated about 1400–1100 BC, and has been the source of much evidence for the society from which the Homeric poems and the legends of Greek tragedy then turned out originally – in their first, orally transmitted, form – to derive. It had been thought that this society was non-literate; then came the discoveries of tablets with writing, and the eventual deciphering after many years of the script known as Linear B. Here are some Linear B ideograms:[33]

It is from this other Greece that Freud takes his analogy for the world of the girl before the discovery of her castration.

Imagine, then, lovely Rita, the psychoanalytic girl, her illusions ruined, forced to emigrate from the world of Mycenae into civilization, having to make that choice between three journeys that is no choice after all. The travel agent, who has seen it all before, demands the usual excessive price and explains the various options. 'It will be the trip of a lifetime.' He hands her the standard brochure. It is in twenty-four blue volumes, very heavy for travelling. She takes one look and casts it back in disgust: 'It's all English to me.' But it is too late – the ship is already pulling away and her mother is bidding her goodbye with a repressive wave from the quayside.

Now imagine, several millennia later, the psychoanalytic girl, still travelling. She has been to Phrygia, to Protest City. She has been to Vienna, to Berlin, to Paris; she has crossed the sea to London and sailed across the ocean to New York. Then she was in France again, and lately she has been attending many international gatherings. Never has she come anywhere near to the promised destination of Normal, in the state of Femininity, and in any case she has never been able to avoid the feeling that it does not sound like a place where she would like to end up. She is tired out and disappointed with the trip that cost her so much, longing for home in spite of it all; she is inclined to think that the agent ripped her off. With great difficulty, she procures a passage back to Mycenae, telling herself that she might have been mistaken in the reasons for leaving which seemed so pressing at the time.

She travels for many miles, and eventually the landscape starts to seem familiar. The old town looks the same as she steps down from the train, except that the station seems to have been modernized. There is no more grass, but there is a big tree, to which some zealous bureaucrat has pointlessly attached a label bearing the word 'tree'. And what do those signs mean on the doors over there? She never saw them (were they there?) when she was a girl, but now in a flash it hits her that they must be the same as the ones she has seen at every stop on her journey. Just in time, with a well-trained feminist instinct, she jumps back into the compartment, and away she goes again.

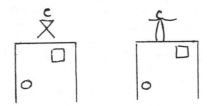

She thought she loved, she thought she was full of love. This was her idea of herself. But the strange brightness of her presence, a marvellous radiance of intrinsic vitality, was a luminousness of supreme repudiation, repudiation, nothing but repudiation.

Yet ... this state of constant unfailing repudiation, was a strain, a suffering also ...

... why need she trouble, why repudiate any further. She was free of it all, she could seek a new union elsewhere.[34]

Notes

1 For (possibly misleading) clues to these extracts, the reader is referred not to the door (which will be tried again in the course of this investigation), but to Freud's 'Dora': 'Fragment of an analysis of a case of hysteria' (1905), Pelican Freud Library (hereafter PFL), 8 (Harmondsworth: Penguin, 1977), p. 119. Also in *The Standard Edition of the Complete Psychological Works* (hereafter *SE*) (London: Hogarth Press and the Institute of Psychoanalysis), 7, p. 82.

2 On this point see Angela Weir and Elizabeth Wilson, 'The British Women's Movement', *New Left Review* 148 (November/December 1984), pp. 74–103.

3 For another deployment of English and French dictionary examples and definitions of feminism, see Alice Jardine, 'Men in feminism: odor di uomo or compagnons de route?', in Alice Jardine and Paul Smith (eds), *Men in Feminism* (London: Methuen, 1987), pp. 54–5.

4 For the uninitiated: Cilla Black, 1960s Liverpool pop star, has acquired a second wave of fame as the presenter of a British TV show called *Blind Date*, which is loosely modelled on the American *Dating Game*.

5 Freud, *New Introductory Lectures on Psychoanalysis* (1933), PFL, 2 (Harmondsworth: Penguin, 1973), p. 146; in *SE*, 22, p. 113.

6 Sophocles, *Oedipus Tyrannos*, 800f.

7 'Probably no man is spared the fright of castration at the sight of a female genital', 'Fetishism' (1927); 'The little girl, frightened by the comparison with boys, grows dissatisfied with her clitoris', 'Female sexuality' (1931), PFL, 7 (Harmondsworth: Penguin, 1977), pp. 354, 376; *SE*, 21, pp. 154, 229.

8 Parveen Adams's piece in this collection analyses the three lines of sexual development further.

9 For Freud's analysis of the structure of the dirty joke, see *Jokes and their Relation to the Unconscious*, PFL, 6 (Harmondsworth: Penguin, 1976), pp. 140–6. Also *SE*, 8, pp. 97–102.

10 'The word "feminism" was created by Fourier.' The Robert dictionary is here quoting Braunschwig's *Notre littérature étudiée dans les textes*; the date of Fourier's invention is given as 1837.

11 Just a little here, though. It is an anonymous review in the *Athenaeum* 3522 (27 April 1895, p. 533), of a novel called *The Grasshoppers*, written by Mrs Andrew Dean. 'Mrs Andrew Dean' is of course a pseudonym, for the much more plausibly named Mrs Alfred Sidgwick, who wrote some thirty-five novels spanning a period from the 1890s to the mid-1930s. The short *Athenaeum* account does not shed much light on the precise configurations of femininity in *The Grasshoppers*; the sentence informing us that 'the most elaborate portrait ... is of the terrible German aunt – a vicious semi-lunatic of the most deadly kind' may tell us more about the contents of the reviewer's late-Victorian mental attic than about Mrs Sidgwick's novel itself. The titles of her other works are in fact tantalizingly suggestive in matters of feminine psychology and feminist argument: they include *Below Stairs, The Bride's Prelude, Law and Outlaw, Maid and Minx, Masquerade*, and *A Woman With a Future*. It is perhaps not purely a flight of fanciful speculation to wonder about the themes they seem to share with the writings of Mrs Alfred Sidgwick's exact authorial contemporary, Dr Sigmund Freud, especially since another of her novels was called *The Professor's Legacy*. Closer to home, and bearing in mind Mrs Sidgwick's evident achievements in her feminine, if not her 'feminist', line, we scan with some interest the much shorter list of publications by Mr Alfred Sidgwick. And it is rather difficult to resist the suspicion that he might have felt he had

something to prove or disprove when we note, in addition to the relative smallness of their number, the fact that one of his books was entitled, firmly and laconically, *Fallacies*.

12 'Dora', PFL, 8, p. 119; *SE*, 7, p. 82.
13 ibid., p. 53; p. 23.
14 'Analysis terminable and interminable' (1937), *SE*, 23, p. 252.
15 ibid., p. 251.
16 'The psychogenesis of a case of female homosexuality' (1920), PFL, 9 (Harmondsworth: Penguin, 1979), p. 384; *SE*, 18, p. 158.
17 *New Introductory Lectures*, p. 160; *SE*, 22, p. 126.
18 ibid., p. 162; p. 129.
19 On the convergence of the three lines, see further the first chapter of Luce Irigaray, *Speculum: Of the Other Woman*, 1974, trans. Gillian C. Gill (Ithaca: Cornell University Press, 1985).
20 'Anxiety and instinctual life', ibid., p. 134; italics mine.
21 'Femininity', ibid., p. 162.
22 Juliet Mitchell, *Psychoanalysis and Feminism* (1974; rpt Harmondsworth: Penguin, 1975), p. xv.
23 Jane Gallop, *The Daughter's Seduction: Feminism and Psychoanalysis* (Ithaca: Cornell University Press 1982), p. 5.
24 Jacqueline Rose, 'Femininity and its discontents', 1983, in *Feminist Review* (ed.), *Sexuality: A Reader* (London: Virago, 1987), p. 177 *et passim*.
25 For the 'fatal' quality of this relationship, see Juliet Mitchell, *Psychoanalysis and Feminism*: 'The argument of this book is that a rejection of psychoanalysis and Freud's works is fatal for feminism' (p. xv). If this feminism here says to psychoanalysis, 'I cannot live without you', or (to the rest of feminism), 'Without it, we will die', then just as forcefully, those on the other side proclaim that it is precisely psychoanalysis that is or would be 'fatal' to feminism. Elizabeth Wilson declares: 'In the Freudian or more fatally in the Lacanian account, the organization of difference not only does but *must* occur around the dominant symbol of the Phallus' ('Psychoanalysis: psychic law and order', in *Feminist Review* (ed.), op. cit., p. 179).
   For a different exploration of the 'marriage' of psychoanalysis and feminism, see Jane Gallop's chapter in this collection.
26 Or just a little perhaps: see further the *Edinburgh Review* 1 (January 1803), pp. 486–93. The article's running head, 'Mad. Necker, *Reflexions sur le Divorce*', referring to the new edition of the book in question, is indicative of the writer's attitude to the question of the intellectual development of women which was raised in relation to Dora: 'Though we are not disposed to assign any limits to female acquisitions in literature or erudition, the display of them ought to be attended with some caution.... She may be a sort of prodigy in her own circle, without having acquisitions beyond those of a boy of sixteen' (p. 493).
27 This might also suggest some underground connections – not etymologically founded, this time – between 'repudiation' and another of its close neighbours, 'reputation'. For just as surely as a woman is subject to repudiation so she is awkwardly situated with respect – or with disrespect – to the notion of reputation. Reputation's basic meaning, according to Webster's dictionary, is that of 'the state of being well reported of, credit, distinction, respectability'. But 'a woman with a reputation' is a woman without a reputation – she has lost it or she never had it in the first place. 'A woman of good repute' has to be differentially marked by the positive term: she is guilty until proved innocent, and, as with repudiation, ordinary justice does not apply. If she is to

be granted a reputation for something other than sexual virtue or immorality, then it will not be a woman's reputation. In the same way that repudiation comes down to repudiation of the woman, and repudiation of the woman comes down to that of her genitals, so a woman who gets herself a reputation is always tainted with a specifically sexual shame. And just as the initial disparagement is what pushes her from one extreme to the other, to take on the perfect reputation of the chaste goddess or guardian of morality, so 'prudery', another near homonym, is in effect the sexual shame of femininity taken too literally, to the point where it veers over into caricature.

28 Freud, 'Female sexuality', PFL, 7, p. 377; SE, 21, p. 230.
29 I thank Ulrike Meinhof for her help with the linguistic aspects of this section.
30 This footnote is left blank for the insertion of that source.
31 See further the entry under 'foreclusion' in J. Laplanche and J.-B. Pontalis, Vocabulaire de la psychanalyse (Paris: Presses Universitaires de France, 1967), pp. 163–76.
32 Freud, 'Female sexuality', p. 372; SE, 21, p. 226.
33 These examples are taken from Lilian H. Jeffery's article on 'Writing' in Alan J. B. Wace and Frank H. Stubbings (eds), A Companion to Homer (London: Macmillan, 1963), p. 550. They show man, woman, and olive tree.
34 D. H. Lawrence, Women in Love (1921), ch. 19, 'Moony'.

Trivial allusions

As well as those directly footnoted, quotations or near quotations from the following works (among others) have been used: Michael Balint, The Basic Fault; The Beatles, 'Lovely Rita'; David Bowie, 'Suffragette City'; Sigmund Freud, Fragment of an Analysis of a Case of Hysteria ('Dora'); Tom Jones, 'The Green, Green Grass of Home'; Jacques Lacan, 'The agency of the letter in the unconscious', and Encore; No Sex Please We're British, the title of a long-running London show; Elvis Presley (and later The Pet Shop Boys), 'Always on My Mind'; Ferdinand de Saussure, Course in General Linguistics; Paul Simon, 'Still Crazy After All These Years' and 'Fifty Ways to Leave Your Lover'; Oscar Wilde, 'The sphinx without a secret'.

Part Two

The story framed by an institutional context

Chapter Three

The politics of impenetrability

Lisa Jardine

I start with the proposition that the series of seminars (on which this volume is based) is a landmark in the history of feminism within Cambridge. We have mastered the discourse of sexuality, we are on familiar terms with the language of sexual difference. And if we don't actually enjoy it, at least we can fake it. What I want to give serious attention to today is the institutional politics of this acceptance of feminist psychoanalytical theory – this having made it, if not yet into the curriculum, then at least into well-attended departmental seminars – an acceptance which is *not accompanied by* any alteration in the power relations between women and men – their relative employment and promotion prospects, their access to the machinery of university government, their access to the means of production of something more material than discourse. And then I want to talk about inevitable appropriation, and what that is going to mean (or perhaps means already).

We can usefully retrace our steps, and go back to Lacan and the *Encore* seminar. That allows us, importantly, to retrieve the original institutional context of Lacan's symbolic construction of the subject, in particular, the female subject.[1] In the first paper in the present series Alice Jardine offered us the position of theorists in the institution; in the second Rosi Braidotti gave us current theory.[2] In *Le Séminaire* they are there together: the Master and his classroom practice; the theory in the process of being produced:

> There is no woman except as excluded by the nature of things, which is the nature of words, and it has to be said that if there is one thing women themselves are complaining about quite enough, it is certainly that – only they don't know what they are saying: that is all the difference between them and me.
> It is none the less the case that if she is excluded by the nature of things, it follows precisely from that that in being not-all [*pas toute*] she has a supplementary *jouissance*[3] in relation to what the phallic function designates of *jouissance*.
> You notice that I said *supplementary*. Had I said *complementary*, where would we be! We'd fall right back into the *all*.

Women content themselves with this [phallic] *jouissance* we're talking about [*dont il s'agit*][4] – not that any of them content themselves with being not-all – and my God, it would be a mistake not to recognise in general that (contrary to what is said) it is women, nonetheless, who possess men.

Working-class men – I know a few, they're obviously not here but I do know quite a few – call women *la bourgeoise*. That is what that means. That it is he who does the sucking up, and not her. Ever since Rabelais we have known that the phallus, her man as she calls it, is not a matter of indifference to her. Only, and this is the whole issue, she has various ways of taking it on, this phallus, and of keeping it for herself. Her being not-all in the phallic function does not mean that she is not in it at all. She is in it *not* not at all. She is right in it But there is something more [*extra*]. That 'something more', mind, be careful not to read too much into it too quickly. I can't find a better way of putting it, because I am having to cut and to go quickly.

There is a *jouissance*, since we are sticking to *jouissance*, a *jouissance* of the body which is, if you will allow me the expression, *beyond the phallus*. Why not make a book title out of that – the next one in the Galilée series? That would be great [*mignon*]. It would give a new lease of life to the Women's Liberation Movement [*Mouvement de libération des femmes*]. A *jouissance* beyond the phallus ...

You may have noticed – and naturally I am speaking here to the few seeming men that I can see here and there, luckily for the most part I don't know them, that way I'm not prejudging the rest – you may have noticed how occasionally it can happen that women fall between two stools: that something rouses them [*secouer*], or it relieves them [*secourir*]. If you look up the etymology of these two words in Block and Von Wartburg's *Dictionary*, which is one of my favourite books, although I am sure none of you even have it in your libraries, you will see the relationship between them. And it's not accidental.

There is a *jouissance* proper to her, to this 'her' which does not exist and which signifies nothing. There is a *jouissance* proper to her and of which she herself perhaps knows nothing, except that she feels it – that much she does know. She knows it, of course, when it happens. It does not happen to all of them....

What gives what I am arguing some likelihood (that is, that the woman knows nothing of this *jouissance*) is that for as long as we've been begging them, begging them on our knees – I spoke previously of women analysts [*je parlais la dernière fois des psychanalystes femmes*] – to try to tell us about it, well, not a word! We have never managed to get anything out of them.[5]

Within the symbolic discourse, Lacan explains to his seminar, woman (as

Cixous and others put it) lacks lack – fails even to establish the symbolic relationship of aspiring to the phallus.

There is a *jouissance* proper to her, to this 'her' which does not exist and which signifies nothing. There is a *jouissance* proper to her and of which she herself perhaps knows nothing, except that she feels it – that much she does know.

But in Lacan's pedagogic discourse (the discourse of authority, the hierarchy of the academic institution) 'it is women, all the same, who possess men' ('it would be a mistake not to recognise that, contrary to what is said'). *That* insight comes from 'everyday life' (introduced textually with 'rough talk', Rabelais, and lewdness). The move *across* to this other site of discourse (the pedagogic, hierarchical) takes place, it might be argued, *in spite of* Lacan: the construction '*s'en tenir à*' (to stick to, to be satisfied with, to content oneself with) is innocuous (perhaps) in the psychoanalytic symbolic – the production of the subject in terms of desire and *jouissance* – but it strikes discordantly in relation to woman's being 'not-all'. Slide to the intimacy of 'what we know about women' *outside* the symbolic, *inside* the history of rankings, status, and hierarchy; and thence to what it would be a mistake not to recognize (in spite of what is said to the contrary).

At the same time Lacan 'can't get anything' out of his (middle-class) female analysts on the subject of *jouissance* – where '*la bourgeoise*' was 'boss' in the working-class sexual partnership, the professional woman suggests frigidity, and Lacan 'can't get anything out of them' (a feature, you recall, of middle-class women in Freud's Dora case-history also).[6]

Class and gender politics and the politics of the institution are crucially the site of this discourse. Hierarchy, who speaks, where deference is owed (and, just as crucially, where it is not), who is addressed ('seeming men who I can see here and there'), who remains silent ('We have never managed to get anything out of them'). The exploration of the male and female unconscious as interelated trajectories of desire ('the phallus as privileged signifier, the constant and final meaning of symbolic exchange, for men and for women')[7] is itself embedded in a gendered classroom practice which reproduces the sex and class history of Lacan, the *maître d'équipe*.

By publishing *Speculum, de l'autre femme*,[8] Luce Irigaray quit on Lacan (he, however, thought he dismissed her), just as Dora gave notice to Freud.[9] But this glimpse of the supposedly historyless discourse of theory (the unconscious crucially the solution to a production of the subject outside history)[10] as it is hemmed in by discourses *with* a history in the seminar room is surely something we cannot ignore. It is particularly disturbing since Lacan himself persistently denied the hierarchy of teacher/student (even) as operating in his seminar:

A principle much stressed by Lacan is that 'the analyst is authorised from himself or herself', psychoanalysis exists and is learned, that is, in the analytic situation, cannot be contained, at best approached, in theoretical constructions (the unconscious is *radically* another scene), cannot be authorised by master or institution (the analyst is not the possessor of a diploma but the site of a listening attention in which he or she is constantly surprised, reimplicated).[11]

That's not what I hear in 'Dieu et la jouissance de la femme'.

The female analyst leaves the Master's seminar and begins to produce a theoretical model of an alternative female imaginary.[12] Irigaray's second psychoanalytically 'badly behaved' book includes a critique of the text we have just been looking at.[13] She too picks up a way in which that linguistic construction of 'sticking to/being content with' phallic *jouissance* (which I maintained provided a bridge for Lacan from psychoanalytical to pedagogic discourse) is not innocuous:

> Thus Psychoanalytic theory enunciates the truth about the status of female sexuality, and of the sexual relationship. But it is content with that [*Mais elle s'y tient*]. Refusing to interpret the historical determinations of its [or his?] discourse – 'if there's one thing I detest, for very good reasons, it's History' – and notably refusing to consider what the implications are of the fact that so far the applications of the laws of psychoanalysis have produced an exclusively masculine sexualization [*la sexuation*], psychoanalysis remains trapped in phallo-centrism, from which it claims to construct universal and eternal values.[14]

Her strategy (a strategy *within* psychoanalytic theory and the sphere of the symbolic) is to speak otherwise, to produce female discourse as the trajectory of a peculiarly female desire which resists the categories of non-existence, of 'not-all', and the 'supplementary'. Continuously speaking, she is *impenetrable*.[15]

Rosi Braidotti has described Irigaray's intervention into the Lacanian production of the symbolic, her insertion of a claim for a female imaginary, a peculiarly female consciousness, silenced and mute under the terms of phallocentric discourse. Here is Irigaray, speaking the female imaginary, leaving the (male) imaginary to his own devices (or is she, but we'll return to that):

> Perhaps we should return to the repressed female imaginary? Thus woman does not have a sex. She has at least two of them, but they cannot be identified as ones. Indeed she has many more of them than that. Her sexuality, always at least double, is in fact *plural*. Plural as culture now wishes to be plural? Plural as the manner in which current texts are written, with very little knowledge of the censorship from which they arise? Indeed, woman's pleasure does not have to choose between clitoral activity and vaginal passivity, for example. The pleasure of the vaginal caress does not have to substitute itself for the pleasure

of the clitoral caress. Both contribute irreplaceably to woman's pleasure but they are only two caresses among many to do so.... [So] *woman has sex organs just about everywhere*. She experiences pleasure almost everywhere. Even without speaking of the hysterization of her entire body, one can say that the geography of her pleasure is much more diversified, more multiple in its differences, more complex, more subtle, than is imagined – in an imaginary centred a bit too much on one and the same.[16]

I have left out a sentence or two, about female parts and specifically female pleasures (and I'll come back to that also).

We can now, I think, recognize that that move by French feminists within psychoanalytic theory was both a move *within* theory and (but still within the confines of the theoretical space) a *political* move – a move to shift the balance of power *within* the set of linguistic exchanges which psychoanalytic theory takes as its specific subject. By claiming the female body as the site of an alternative symbolic (impossible in the terms of phallocentric discourse, hence literally unthinkable), a kind of essentialist strategy, as Braidotti, like Spivak, provocatively insists, Irigaray claims a voice which is not susceptible to the Master's imperial command: he had claimed to speak for her – the phallus as privileged signifier ('the variety of mental structures that overrun the anatomical difference of the sexes has nevertheless a fixed reference, phallic sexual difference').[17] She, perversely, transgressively, speaks the vagina, the multiplicity of female desire, the 'alternative female unconscious'.

But it is a strategy which has its problems. If it deliberately discountenances the men, we too have always felt a certain uncomfortableness with it (that's why I left a bit of the last passage out). And many women (including myself) have reacted with irritation at this reintroduction of female biology into the picture. And then again, there are many women for whom the impenetrability of the discourse Irigaray produces is as alienating as it was intended to be for the men. We have managed to get a hearing (here we are), but it is at the expense of the immediate recognition (dare I say it, the *interpellation*) which in many other contexts bonds women as women, indicating (perhaps) that at a crucial level their ideological formation is shared.[18] So was the hearing worth getting, does it get *us* anywhere?

What I want now to argue is that both the indignation at the *difficulty* (as it appears) of the discourse, and the anxiety about the body in the institutional context, while they undoubtedly fail to do justice to the subtlety of a good deal of feminist psychoanalytic theory, are nevertheless symptoms of a 'real' problem concerning the production of that particular theoretical discourse (and above all its reproduction) in academic institutions. They point, I now think, to the specific problem that we have failed to notice a set of imperatives (social, cultural, historical) to which the discourse of female sexuality harks back *at the same time* as it productively challenges the phallocentricity of Lacanian psychoanalysis (and succeeds in getting a hearing, a space for that challenge).

The intellectual elegance of Luce Irigaray's intervention as a woman into Lacanian psychoanalysis lies in her 'performing' precisely as the theory requires her to perform, but to excess. 'We've been begging them, begging them on our knees' (these woman analysts), and Irigaray takes that up (most notoriously in 'Quand nos lèvres se parlent' [When our lips speak to one another], and surely that's 'behaving badly' in relation to Lacan's 'Une lettre d'âmour'?),[19] as a *mimesis* (an imitation and intensification), which will 'de-anchor' male discourse.[20] On the face of it, this commitment to discourse, to woman's ability to unsettle, de-anchor, through discourse is particularly attractive within the academic institution.

In academic institutions what, above all, is at stake is the production of oneself in discourse. In so far as there is 'struggle', discourse itself is ostensibly the site of that struggle (we are competing lecturers, with competing publications, that's how we get jobs, isn't it?).[21] Remembering to recognize this (that speech and writing are the battleground, and promotion the prize) is, of course, a recurrent problem for so-called 'radical' theory:[22] critics (for instance) talking of 'subversion' or 'power over', when all that is being subverted, or dominated, is a text.

Hence the lure of the difficulty, the very impenetrability, of feminist psychoanalytic theory, for the men as well as for the women. And for the men there is also a spectacle which causes a *frisson* – inversion/misrule. Woman (for the time being) is the source of the authoritative discourse, the one they need to hear, need to listen to. The *frisson* of feeling (for the time being) is marginal, on the edge. But only (and I think this is all I shall say about appropriation) until they have it. Until it is a body of text they can return to and subject (victim again) to its own discourse analysis (there is an outbreak of footnote references to Irigaray in Shakespeare criticism wherever a male critic encounters a female figure speaking – Irigaray has given him the model for analysis and application of 'peculiarly female discourse').

It is inversion, misrule, he is only temporarily on the margins, because the appeal to the *body* of feminist psychoanalytical theory announces that very thing. Historically, women have been identified with the body, and feminism has identified the body (at least at points) with women's oppression. While Irigaray's *mimesis* has its strategic significance in relation to Lacan's seminar discourse, outside that seminar, in another seminar, this seminar, it keeps women in place, in so far as it reidentifies us with/as body. And here, I think, we come to the crux. It has been clear for some time that, illusion of equal discourses antagonistically engaged or no, different subjects have different histories, and those histories *do* (like the pedagogic cat-and-mouse of Lacan's *séminaire*) produce differential power relations among participants – power relations which include a built-in domination of the female by the male. Because of *that*, the drawing attention to the female body which is an essential (sometimes even an essentialist) part of the strategy is a catastrophe as far as destabilizing existing classroom power-relations is concerned. It doesn't.

Discourse, for a moment, has to be separated from the power relations of the seminar (this seminar) where women speak. For discourse of the body reinforces all that has been oppressively said about women *as* body. And, in fact, compared with occasional temporary *invisibilities* of the female body in institutional polemic, it restabilizes them. For within the academic institution female is subsumed under male, the female professional is there in so far as she attains to the standards/categories of the male (hence, that impenetrability can become victimization).

The most disturbing feature of this is that the domination of the female by the male is, therefore, at one level *greater* in these present seminars than in (let us say) a weekly seminar on 'Communication and the media' in which the maleness and femaleness of discourse is not itself explicitly an issue. It is greater at the level of a particular theoretical *content*, not at the level of the structure of the seminar situation itself. Here we come back to the homology between Lacan's structural seminarial authority, and the theoretical content of his discourse. In *his* situation they went hand in hand – Master in the middle, women on the outskirts, in the theory and the classroom. In *this* situation they conflict to some temporary extent – woman in the middle, standing here, Master(s) on the margins, seated there. Yet in some of the theory that is being discussed here, in these seminars, as in Lacan's, women are still the body.

Paradoxically, we can replicate the identification of women with the body yet again when we talk of personal histories, as is done frequently in the discussions after the seminars, which implicate us as bodies. But, something else, none the less, is going on here. What gives the Master in the middle his power is his history. We identify power with history, given that powerful institutional places are occupied by men *because* of history. Thus in the act of pointing to personal history, we are pointing to a source and place of power's reproduction.

And, by the way, women are *not* getting promotion on the strength of their production of peculiarly female discourse, or even on the strength of their theoretical disquisitions on the subject.[23] Even so, the illusion of equal discourses antagonistically engaged is currently allowing some men plausibly to produce statements like: 'feminists have got to give *us* some space' (uttered from that illusory position of discourse marginality).[24]

For my final point I return to the question of history. The psychoanalytic discourse asks incessantly for a familial history to ground itself in – a history which is at once *personal* and *outside* History with a capital H.[25] But the only history the academic institution regards is the history of domination, hierarchy, and status (the history which validates each speaker's claim to a position in the pecking order). The answer to the speaking voice of authority is for the speaker from the floor to cite other (authoritative) sources, to consolidate his own position (I think we would all recognize that as a technique for asking questions in seminars). But in the context of seminars like the present ones, when the authoritative voice (the voice of the *analyste femme*) stops, some women (entirely appropriately in terms of the psychoanalytic frame) respond by offering their personal histories, their autobiographies, as privileged case-histories. But in terms of the institutional frame, that politics of the classroom, they are the *wrong* history; her story not his.

Notes

1 Accordingly, given the institutional context of my discussion, I shall largely restrict myself to the *Encore* seminar itself, and two influential 'feminist' (or so-called 'feminist') discussions of it: Luce Irigaray, 'Cosi fan tutti', in *Ce Sexe qui n'en est pas un* (Paris: Minuit, 1977), pp. 85–101, and S. Heath, 'Difference', *Screen* 19 (1978), pp. 51–112.

2 Lisa Jardine was the third speaker in the series on which this collection is based; Alice Jardine's paper was not the one included in this collection ('Notes for an analysis') but another paper which also discusses theory in the institution (D'apres *Gynesis*').

3 I have followed the by now well-established tradition of not translating *jouissance* on the grounds that it is untranslatable (see e.g. Roland Barthes, *Image Music Text* (London: Fontana 1977), trans. S. Heath, translator's note, 9: '*Plaisir/jouissance* – English lacks a word able to carry the range of meaning in the term *jouissance* which includes enjoyment in the sense of a legal or social possession (enjoying certain rights, enjoy a privilege), pleasure, and crucially, the pleasure of sexual climax.' In fact, however, I find the spurious *weightiness* of the untranslated word oppressive. If we were to substitute 'enjoyment' throughout the present passage, it would not only convey pretty accurately the sense of the original, but at certain points, e.g. the next note below, it would be quite revealing in relation to the classroom/theory binary production of discourses to which I am drawing attention.

4 This is the sentence which I think is most altered if we substitute 'enjoyment' for '*jouissance*': 'Women content themselves with this [phallic] enjoyment we're talking about.' At this crucial point in Lacan's discourse 'enjoyment' seems pretty clearly to me to mean that the man does the enjoying, and the woman enjoys his enjoying (as classic formulation of men's and women's sexual pleasure with a long History); we don't get that from that reified '*jouissance*'.

5 Jacques Lacan, *Le Séminaire livre XX* (Paris, 1975), pp. 68–9; my translation. For another translation see Jacqueline Rose and Juliet Mitchell, *Feminine Sexuality: Jacques Lacan and the Ecole Freudienne* (London: Macmillan, 1982), pp. 144–6.

6 Heath does admit that the tone of 'Dieu et la jouissance de la femme' is offensive; but Jane Gallop is right in seeing that Heath (I not-a-woman = man, as she says) cannot help being implicated in Lacan's classroom practice (J. Gallop, *The Daughter's Seduction: Feminism and Psychoanalysis* (Ithaca and London: Cornell University Press and Macmillan, 1982), pp. 50–1.

7 Heath, 'Difference', p. 67.

8 Luce Irigaray, *Speculum, de l'autre femme.* (Paris: Minuit, 1974).

9 For the key feminist articles on Freud's Dora case-history see C. Bernheimer and C. Kahane (eds), *In Dora's Case: Freud – Hysteria – Feminism* (London: Virago, 1985). On Dora's 'giving notice', in particular, see Gallop, 'Keys to Dora', op. cit., pp. 132–50.

10 This implication of the theoretical novelty of Lacan's unconscious is brought out

strongly in Louis Althusser, 'Freud and Lacan', *New Left Review* 55 (1968), pp. 48–65. 'History, "sociology" or anthropology have no business here, and this is no surprise! For they deal with society and therefore with culture, i.e. with what is no longer this small animal – which only becomes human-sexual by crossing the infinite divide that separates life from humanity, the biological from the historical, 'nature' from 'culture'....We need only recognize this specificity and hence the distinctness of the object that it derives from, in order to recognize the radical right of psychoanalysis to a specificity of its concepts in line with the specificity of its object: the unconscious and its effects' (pp. 57–8).

11 Heath, 'Difference', p. 52.

12 I am reminded irresistibly of Hannah Cullwick and her 'Massa'. See Julia Swindells, 'Liberating the subject? Autobiography and "women's history": a reading of *The Diaries of Hannah Cullwick*', (*Interpreting Women's Lives: Feminist Theory and Personal Narratives*, Bloomington: Indiana University Press, in press).

13 'Cosi fan tutti', op. cit.

14 'Cosi fan tutti', op. cit., p. 99 (my translation).

15 It is not an accident, either, that once we are in the discourse of psychoanalysis, the sexual puns in the language we produce open up as wit *and* (in this case) resistance. But according to its own rules, the permanent dominance of the male (less 'lacking' under the phallic order) means that resistance is the resistance of the *victim*. See Susanne Kappeler, *The Pornography of Representation* (Oxford: Polity, 1986).

16 Luce Irigaray, *Ce Sexe qui n'en est pas un* (Paris: Minuit, 1977), pp. 25–6; trans. in E. Marks and I. de Courtivron, *New French Feminisms* (Brighton: Harvester, 1981), pp. 102–3.

17 Heath, 'Difference', p. 65.

18 See Althusser, 'Ideology and ideological state apparatuses', in *On Ideology*, pp. 127–86.

19 'Cosi fan tutti', op. cit. 88–9.

20 See Gallop, *Feminism and Psychoanalysis*.

21 This being the case, the academic context compares interestingly with the one discarded as politically vacuous by Michèle Barrett, 'Ideology and the cultural production of gender', in *Feminist Criticism and Social Change* (London: Methuen, 1985), pp. 65–85: 'There is the world of difference between assigning some weight to ideological struggle and concluding that no other struggle is relevant or important. The relief with which the intellectual left has seized upon these ideas as a justification and political legitimation of any form of academic work is in itself suspicious and alarming. For although I would not dispute the political significance of such activity, a distinction must be retained between this form of struggle and the more terrestrial kind. Are we really to see the Peterloo massacre, the storming of the Winter Palace in Petrograd, the Long March, the Grunwick picket as the struggle of discourses?' (p. 72).

22 Feminists like Michèle Barrett and Deborah Cameron have begun to point out the way in which 'struggles' in language (a necessary part of combating oppression) have come to stand, within academic institutions, for the struggle itself: 'The original question put to this panel was: "is gender implicated in the struggle for the sign?" Let me therefore begin by saying that in my view, that question is somewhat misleadingly framed. If there is indeed a struggle for the sign – or, as I prefer to put it, a struggle for meaning – it is not propelled by its own linguistic momentum, but by wider social and political forces. Hence my insistence on a two-sided project, directed to oppression and not just to

language. It is idle, I believe, to address questions of sexual *difference* in isolation from the issues of *dominance*, and my argument is constructed with that point in mind. The struggle for meaning which concerns me here, then, is a more or less conscious part of the political struggle against women's oppression. And in this feminist struggle gender is not merely *implicated*, it actually is the disputed territory' (D. Cameron, 'What is the nature of women's oppression in language?', *Oxford Literary Review* 8 (Sexual Difference Issue) 1986, p. 79).

23 Indeed, it is striking how men avowedly committed to feminist theory fail entirely to support such work in 'open' academic competition. It would be interesting to produce a checklist of the comparative institutional statuses of the women who are giving the present seminars, and their male counterparts (the ones they challenge, the ones they are supposed to have silenced).

24 The image that comes to my mind at this point is the following: we women are in the cupboard, and these men are hammering on the door saying, 'let us in, give us some space' – trying to join us in the cupboard.

25 Althusser insists particularly strongly on this inherent need of a familial history as base for the discourse of the unconscious. Ultimately he cannot find it in Freud or Lacan. See Althusser, 'Freud and Lacan', p. 53.

Chapter Four

Notes for an analysis

Alice Jardine

'Writing *on* psychoanalysis always runs the risk of reducing the efficacity of its scene.'

Luce Irigaray[1]

Imagine the scene. For just a while you do not have to fight to stand up on your own two feet. You are lying down on your back. Now 'say – and only say – everything that comes into your head. As it comes to you, there, now. Don't leave anything out. Don't worry about contradictions, conventions. Don't organize what you say ...'[2] Say everything now, here. *Silence.* 'What are you thinking about?'/'How much I hate this! How frightening it is!' There is a voice – *double* – it floats towards the ceiling where there is nothing to see, fading, halting, unsure. 'The *impossibility* of the fundamental rule is to *say now, that.*'[3] Nothing but the accent, the inflexion, the intensity, the volume, the duration. 'The beginning [is] before you, the goal and end behind you.'[4] You are not the subject-source. There is someone in back of you, behind you; the couch is behind your back. (Is someone under the bed? Old terrors.) Right is left, left is right. Her right is your right, left your left – as if you were looking in the same mirror. When you are standing on your own two feet, 'in representation', you have a front and a back, an up and a down. Now you are dizzy, the cardinal points of your being in sway. The only support: two voices, double-voiced, your object *behind* you. In front of you: profusion, excess, where do *I* begin? Who 'I'? Who 'you'?/But I want an author, an agent, an object, a mirror – a theory, a pedagogue, a magician, a master, a slave, a guarantee!/Silence. Try again. Cross over, diversely, inside, outside, enter, leave, weave, *knit* your way in and out. Luce Irigaray has taught us that this '*praticable*', of this scene, is not just 'one empirical element among others, one form of application of psychic logic among others, one experience among others. But ... [rather] a *praticable* which derails, disconcerts, deassures the scene of representation'[5] – which is always based on a kind of logo-phono-phallo-centrism privileging the being-up-front, so you can see it, be sure whether the 'I' has got one or not – for example, as in the university. Of course, that's true on the couch too. If you're on your back.

These are notes; that is, what follows. Fragments, footnotes, memoranda; mine, the analyst's, the analysand's, the woman writer's. A professor's notes. Student notes – their grades; and how much is the bill? Glyph notes ... Lou Andreas-Salomé was always the only woman present on those Wednesday nights in Vienna. 'Sometimes she and Freud would exchange notes when they sat side by side. She knit, but never spoke.'[6] Marie Bonaparte listened intently and noted all of Freud's words until he told her to write nothing more concerning her analysis because it would keep her from exploring the deepest layers of her-self. She later, as an analyst, took up knitting rather than noting behind the couch. And H. D., too, was forbidden to take notes. She did though. A Second Coming.

Notes – *tones* is its anagram. Tone of voice. Musical notes. In a note to Lou, Freud remarked on that which in Lou's writing he could not follow because 'not yet subordinated to speech' – always an octave above his melody, he said.[7] Bell tones – high octave notes. Class Bells. Doorbells. Regulating the two spaces – academic and psychoanalytic – that I am supposed to be addressing here; two spaces that I have in fact been addressing over the past few years, now in speech, now in writing, now lying down, now standing up ... running out-of-time.

If we bring these two spaces – academia *and* psychoanalysis – together as psychoanalysis *in* the university, we arrive at a place where something is happening that deserves our notice. And/In – no simple opposition or analogy. I hope you will grant me the benefit of the doubt, even if not demonstrated now, that I am conscious of the fact that there are no simple inside/outside dichotomies here: on this note, we could perhaps re-member and be guided by the ins and outs of transference between 'Literature' and 'Psychoanalysis' orchestrated so beautifully and influentially for us by Shoshana Felman over ten years ago.[8]

Also, we will not demonstrate here – even if we must never and can never leave behind – the macropolitics *organizing* the ins and outs, interior and exterior frontiers of these two mental institutions (psychoanalysis and the university): first, *money* of course; and second, an organization, conception of *the mental*, of the mental apparatus which psychoanalysis and the university mirror constantly in each other: a particular figuration of the highest faculties, constructed at the beginning of the nineteenth century in Berlin. And, of course, both psychoanalysis and the university are institutions *with schools*, and as David Carroll has pointed out recently and succinctly, 'Institutions and schools exist to occupy positions of power, to neutralize dissent, and to domesticate all oppositional forces and foreign bodies; their authority depends on it.'[9] How can we possibly forget that both of these institutions finally report to the state? Note Nietzsche on the professor's speaking mouth with many ears, the university culture machine, and so-called academic freedom – as in *On The Future of Our Educational Institutions*;[10] or, more visibly, let us not forget the collaboration of institutions of psychoanalysis with certain Latin American or Soviet states as noted, for example, in Derrida's 'Géopsychanalyse – "and all the rest of the world"'.[11]

For now, all of these difficult questions will simply have to underwrite what I want to voice here – haltingly, tentatively – about two *particular* political problems currently preoccupying me – and a few others I think.

The first problem is sometimes referred to in working shorthand as the dilemma of short-term vs. long-term political effects, of working *fast* vs. working *slow*. This debate, in literary critical circles, is most often articulated in traditional binary fashion as: (1) construction vs. deconstruction; (2) the drive to name vs. disarticulation; (3) unity vs. heterogeneity; (4) the Cartesian 'I' vs. complex subjectivity; (5) Anglo-American vs. French; and, increasingly, as (6) a return to literary history vs. literary theory – there is even the question of 'politically correct texts of pleasure' vs. 'politically wrong texts of jouissance'. The dis-ease associated with these ultimately epistemological battles currently continues to spread on the international scene in several different forms: for example, critical legal studies people are attacked because of anxieties about how endless deconstruction of the legal text leaves no room for legal definition; activists argue that the 'undecidable' – as the very definition of the political – evoked by Barbara Johnson's stunning essay on 'Apostrophe, animation, and abortion' probably did not, after all, get very many people out to vote no (which meant yes) in the Massachusetts Abortion Referendum in November 1986.[12] In a different scene, and in Richard Rorty's words, we see such twisted battles as where 'the French critics of Habermas [are] ready to abandon liberal politics in order to avoid a universalist philosophy, and ... Habermas [is] trying to cling to a universalist philosophy, with all the problems that involves, in order to prop up a liberal politics'.[13] Or, for example, we hear debates over whether in the United States we must take the time to think through the paleonomic and tropological implications of 'Apartheid' and 'Solidarity' or rather, go out and do/write/say whatever is necessary to provoke immediate US divestment from South Africa.[14] That is, there seems to be growing political impatience with the debate over how politically patient one should be. And the solution of 'one always does both anyway' – i.e., act conservatively and radically at the same time – seems to be wearing thin, when it's not wrapped up in pluralist giftwrap and handed over to the powers that be. I am particularly concerned in this context by what I have analysed elsewhere as a kind of territorializing of more specifically feminist versions of these questions by *paranoia* and *fetishism*.[15] While both participate in what I call 'a demand for doubling', paranoia is about deciding, defining, making strong cases; fetishism about the both, neither/nor, refusal to decide, define, or go to court. I am referring here, for example, to the difference between asserting that 'women are different from men' (implying we *know* what women are) and saying (in the same breath) 'Women are different. No they are not' – implying we *do not* know what they are. I have suggested that the current period of tense coexistence of these two states is about living and thinking in a mode of *impossibility* sometimes referred to in other contexts as 'postmodernism', a state within which women are caught like everyone else.... But we will return to the impossible in a moment.

The second immediate political problem with which I am concerned as a feminist teaching in the university is with the problems and questions arising now that there are at least two generations of explicitly and politically feminist women professors in the academy: let us say those who received their Ph.D. between 1968 and 1978 and those who received it after 1978. Now I want to emphasize '*at least two* generations' and '*explicitly* and *politically* feminist' here for two reasons. First because, of course, there are technically three (soon to be four) generations of women professors in the United States today. Most significantly, there is an important generation of women who received their Ph.D. (often long) before 1968. Secondly, however, what is more important here than the question of 'generation' is the question of one's discursive, political positioning *vis-à-vis* the women's liberation movement. Before 1968 it was difficult, if not impossible, to be an explicitly political feminist scholar in the institution. And I think it is safe to say that the majority of those women who were allowed access, before the late 1960s, to full status as professors were not explicitly political feminists. Many were, in fact, resistent when not hostile to feminism even as they were fighting feminist battles every day of their lives. Those extraordinary few women full professors who were explicitly and politically feminist before 1968 were most extraordinary indeed and I would include them within the first post-1968 generation. (It is perhaps important to remember that these women often did not receive recognition for their (feminist) work until relatively late in their careers – that is to say, until *after 1968*.) Let us just say that it is the two generations of explicitly and politically feminist women who have come to intellectual/academic age since 1968 that will be of primary interest to me here.[16]

Now, first of all, there is the question of what the institution has done/is doing to all of these generations of women: that is a long story. What happens to women 'constrained to transport the discourse of men and the body of women',[17] has, of course, been analysed for a long while. Alternatives include: be alone, isolated, and asexual; get sick; at least act, look, and speak neuter; or leave. I am talking about the power of the desire of the homosocially patriarchal academy to force women to relinquish 'the feminine' – in the strong Irigarayan force of the term, what Juliet Mitchell describes as 'the Other' for both sexes[18] – so as to make them, first, 'undesirables' within dominant heterosexual ideology and, then, eventually, *ne-euter* (neither one nor the other) in the terms of male representations. This desire creates either (as Mary Ann Doane puts it) 'an asexual ... perfect and unthreatening mate for the "good old Americano"'[19] – or else has you kicked out. This situation has raised a lot of questions – especially on the part of an upcoming generation, the young women Ph.D. students I know – about what price they are willing to pay, how much they are willing to give up, for a place in the academy. That is, a lot of them – those who are politicized at least – do not want to live like the first generations of academic women have had to live.

But there is also the perhaps even more difficult question of the relationships *between* the two post-1968 generations of feminist women in the academy. I would like to avoid the mother/daughter paradigm here (so as not to succumb simply to miming the traditional father/son, master/disciple model), but it is difficult to avoid at this point being positioned by the institution as mothers and daughters.[20] Structures of debt/gift (mothers and increasingly daughters control a lot of money and prestige in the university), structures of our new institutional power over each other, desires and demands for recognition and love – all of these are falling into place in rather familiar ways. Accusations fly about on both sides as to who is really feminist or not; who has been recuperated or not; who is just miming the masters (is it the often more history-minded mothers or more theory-minded daughters?); whose fault is it that there is a general perception that feminism has become facile, tamed while, precisely, the humanities are being feminized? People are asking – or should be – how did we get to the intellectual and political point where one of the reigning topics of discussion among supposedly politicized women is often quite exclusively hiring/firing and chances for tenure? It sometimes sounds, as Patricia Baudoin has put it, as if the *political* has become the *personal* – as if our professional status has even become our personal status.[21] And throughout all of this, no one, neither mother nor daughter, can ever seem to accomplish enough....

At this point, I would like to suggest that, with a slight change of optic, it is in fact *feminist women*, of both of these post-1968 generations in the academy, who are in a special, strategic position as new kinds of subjects to think through and act upon these problems, together, in potentially new and radical ways. I think this potential exists because feminism, psychoanalysis, and the institution are, today, triply implicated in a major historical, archaeological, epistemological mutation: a mutation of the public and private spheres, a new kind of interference between the *polis* and *ta oikeia*.[22] *At the same time*, there is a massive *oedipalization* as privatization of the public sphere and a massive *publification* (in Latin, democritization) of the private sphere. More specifically (and narrowly given the contexts and texts which interest us here), there is a reconfiguration of public and private spaces throughout our institutions; in the university, for example, (a particular scene of representation), *concurrent with the entry of women into that scene*. Further, *both* women and psychoanalysis are entering that scene *together*, disrupting it – which is logical since women are psychoanalysis's reason for existence, its history and stories: we are its cases (as Mary Ann Doane reminds us: the text of the unconscious *is* the female hysteric).[23] In fact, many of the same women who are disrupting the institution work in psychoanalysis, a lot of them are even *in* analysis (usually with women). Even more specifically, this mutation of the public and private, the contamination of the classic scene of representation with and through 'the other scene' (scene of the other), has a lot to do (as you might guess) with writing and the voice: this is a dichotomy perhaps intellectually problematized years ago but which has continued to structure our energies and affects in specific ways. We have learned how writing and the voice weave together, overlap, are exchanged – through the voice's writing and writing's voice – always, but differently. At the same time, we have thought less perhaps about what this new kind of knowledge is doing to the patriarchal institution and its systems of representation: public writing (scientific, academic, and literary publishing) and the public voice (lecturing and teaching) have traditionally been gendered as male; private writing (diaries and letters) and private voice (intimacy; the analytic space) have been gendered as female. That has begun to change with women's history-making move from the private to the public (their massive publification) and the creation of certain chiasmatic and paradoxical situations such as writing being gendered as feminine in the male public sphere; or, as Juliet Mitchell has pointed out, the fact that feminism and psychoanalysis share a central paradox which is shaking up the pedagogue in all of us: they are both *humanist* (concerned with how the 'I' is constructed) and, at the same time, and often through the same moves, dramatically *counter-humanist* (decentering the Man in each of us).[24]

What I am trying to get to here is a new and different scene, at a new intersection of psychoanalysis, feminism, and the institution, where a radical deconstruction of the academic subject is taking place; where a radically new kind of knowledge is being produced; and where women are becoming radical agents of that new knowledge and of political change *if* and *when* they actualize freely the mutations and paradoxes I have been referring to. In order to think just a bit more about all of this – especially about the two specific problems I raised concerning (1) short-term and long-term political effects and (2) generations of women – I would like to suggest returning to this intersection briefly from two other, different directions: first, more 'abstractly', in terms of the radical differences between the 'analytic' and 'pedagogic' scenes (to which women have had special access) and secondly, more 'concretely', by thinking about two other generations of women – those at the beginning of this century and those at its end who have somehow, in some form, for some reason, *written* about their own psychoanalysis – a very odd thing to do.

Jane Gallop has come close to defining the institution as massive group transference.[25] I would add: if that institution is the university, it is the very site of the 'being-up-front' mentioned earlier on. The *traditional* institutional scene at least is anywhere the scene of representation is based on the mirror and where women's discourse is carefully controlled, sometimes by her own narration. It is a 'life-trap' (in Rilke's phrase), where there are 'practical demonstrations' of pre-packaged knowledge, the 'object of university diplomas'.[26] Again, without wanting to forget that there are no easy oppositions here, no pure spaces, I do think there is *another* scene, a scene of psychic logic tentatively evoked in my opening notes: an analytic scene between two, increasingly between two women. An entire issue of a feminist journal in Europe, *BIEF*, has recently been devoted to the twentieth-century analytic space as a *female* space to which women have increasingly turned in much larger numbers than men (especially with a certain democritization of analysis under the influence of feminism). Women have done this not *just* as (or not only just as) victims in search of an other private space because access to a public voice and public writing is still, historically, very difficult for women;[27] but they have turned to this other space also as *artists* and *agents of change* who can there let go of the all-powerful fantasmatic other holding them back.

The institutional scene is to the analytic scene as assurance is to the lack thereof; as self-mastery is to the relinquishing of control; as fast is to slow; as product is to process; certainty to doubt; as emphasis on success is to failure; gaining time to losing and wasting it; as project is to projection; reason to unreason; *la gestion* (bureaucracy) to gestation (nurturing); as solutions are to dissolutions; progressions to regressions; required good humor and social smiles to tantrums and tears; as consolidate is to *ana-lyein* (to break up or to loosen); as memorizing is to anamnesis; the voluntary to the involuntary; gain to loss; as that which has already been said is to that which language does not yet know how to say. In the institutional scene, what is important is the best possible performance. In the analytic scene, what is important is to dream. In the pedagogical scene, one must make known an object, make it universally knowable; whereas, of course, the dream is not reproducible, can never be made universally accessible.[28] In short, the bodies of teaching and bodies of the unconscious were never supposed to meet. But they have and it is women who know about that.

Especially women who have been in analysis. When I asked several analysts about the idea of women writing about their own analysis, many found it a contradiction in terms. As the blurb on Erika Kaufmann's book *Transfert* puts it: 'An analysis stays secret. It voices itself, it listens to itself, it does not write itself. What is voiced is drowned in silence, even if sometimes capitalized upon by the analyst.' But Kaufmann also continues: '[But then] the unconscious [is] once again chased away, there is loss of revolt. Of struggle. My unconscious was demanding speech, writing. [So] I wrote letters to my analyst.'[29]

And she is not the only one. Erika Kaufmann's book, published in France in 1975, is just one of many, many books, published by women in the 1970s and 1980s, devoted to analysis, often to their own analysis. In terms of psychoanalysis, this is a *second* generation of women crossing over from the private into the public, the voice into writing, in ways which fundamentally confuse the *genres*: in both senses, in terms of gender and in terms of the ways literary, autobiographical, autoanalytic, psychoanalytic narratives are being recombined to confound the boundaries between private and public discursive spaces.

As a kind of 'popularization' of psychoanalysis, this recent outpouring of texts would seem to send us back to the first wave of popularization of psychoanalysis in the 1910s and 1920s and on through the 1940s (especially through surrealism) and its attendant *first* generation of remarkable women. These women, born in the 1860s and 1880s, came to analysis primarily through Freud, and if their textual moves between the private and the public, voice and writing, often superficially resemble those of the second generation, there are great differences. Their steps toward public vulnerability are more measured and, for the moment, that measure and resistance to public vulnerability is what I am interested in. These extraordinary women were all caught in the passionate crosscurrents of Freudian transferences. For example, most women around Freud who eventually became analysts – such as Helene Deutsche or Marie Bonaparte – explicitly admit (or rather their dreams do) their desires to be, at the same time, the Father's 'most beautiful daughter and his most intelligent son'.[30] Of Deutsche's analysis with Freud in 1918, we learn very little from her own hand. She insists upon and defends in her autobiography, *Confrontations with Myself*, the difference between an autoanalysis and the memoires of an analyst, only once mentioning in passing one precious titbit: how she, having just given birth and while in analysis with Freud, provided his wife with milk. As Julia Kristeva suggests in her introduction to the French edition of Deutsche, we can only read such a woman's 'secret autobiography' as metamorphized in each of her interpretations.[31]

Marie Bonaparte's written records of her analysis with Freud, her steps from the private to the public, are also carefully guarded – but this time by her family: the notes she took during 1925–6 (in spite of Freud's admonishment) are hidden away in the archives of the Bibliothèque Nationale in Paris, not to be released until the year 2000. Her biographer, Celia Bertin, gives us a few notes nevertheless – for example, this passage from Bonaparte's analysis notebooks: 'This reflex to flee into writing has stayed with me: the chagrin, the pain, far from keeping me from writing, push me more immediately toward the refuge of literary and scientific creation.'[32]

It is, perhaps predictably, Lou Andreas-Salomé and H. D. who give us the most written access to (their own) analysis even if, again, fictional, theoretical, and biographical boundaries are often kept clear. From Lou, the first woman shrink, with regard to her autoanalysis of 1911 and work with Freud, we have little public voice but much private writing: especially her 1912–13 journal and, of course, her rich correspondence with Freud.[33]

H. D. followed a three-month cure with Freud in 1933 with two texts: one, her private daily notes (the 1933 'Advent') and one 'more destined for publication' as she put it (the 1944 'Writing on the wall').[34] These texts are goldmines for testing the limits in the beginning of this century between voice and writing, private and public, for women; the constructions of self and its demise. H. D., who was never satisfied by any of her books, whether published or not, sometimes lying on the couch in Freud's office or ten years later, sitting in her room in London, never shrank away from writing the entire difficult process: 'This writing is, in any case, coherent; it is the composition of one person; it is written, designed by the same hand. What remains to be known is whether this hand or this person is me.'[35]

Here I can only evoke the second generation of women writing in and through psychoanalysis, through different degrees of autobiographical fiction: Elizabeth Wilson's *Mirror Writing*, published in 1982, for example, where what she calls the 'identity split between public and private life' is written through the juxtaposition of an analytic experience ('the opposite of an explanatory, synthesising or theorising one') and the women's movement demanding an identity and a voice for women.[36] Or there are the immensely popular novels like *August* by Judith Rossner or *Other Women* by Lisa Alther; or, in France, one finds transcriptions of autoanalysis (Marie Bellour's *Le Jeu de l'Origine*), written letters (Kaufmann's *Transfert*), or fluid semi-auto-graphical reflections on analysis by analysts (like Jacqueline Rousseau-Dujardin's *Couché par écrit*). Maria Torok, in her introduction to Claudie Cachard's *L'Autre histoire*, even explicitly links this kind of work back to the early part of the century.[37]

In thinking here about these two psychoanalytic generations of women in relation to the two academic generations of women mentioned earlier, certain analogies come to mind.[38] I will mention here only those which will help me bring these notes to an end.

First, there is the privileged place of male mentors in the intellectual lives of both of the first generations: from Freud, Abraham, and Ferenzi to those male new critics, structuralists, etc., who served as male mentors and models to women over 40 in the academy. Whereas, for the women of the two second generations, while those male sources are obviously historically important, most often – either consciously or unconsciously – it is *women* who have been their most influential teachers, models and – yes – analysts. At least as they have written it down. Is it possible that the first generations idealized their intellectual fathers; the second, their intellectual mothers? Second, there would seem to be some correspondence between the ways in which our two first generations dealt with the challenges of the major new discoveries confronting them in their young intellectual lives (psychoanalysis for the first psychoanalytic generation; feminism for the first academic generation): there was a seduction, combined with a resistance to the full implications of those two discourses. Whereas our two second generations would seem to be in full transference with both discourses. Third, the two first generations would seem to correspond to some combination of Kristeva's first two generations of feminists evoked in her article 'Women's time': the first psychoanalytic and academic generations of women often fell either into the category of those women wanting a secure place in linear history or those women wanting to affirm a different, monumental time outside of men's history and story. Our two second generations would seem to want to correspond (at least some of the time) to Kristeva's third generation: those who want a place in male history and male stories but *only* in order to affirm their radical, singular differences.[39]

Finally, and this will bring me to the end of these notes: it seems to me that the two first generations are involved in a politics and an ethics of the *possible* (where the public and private are kept comparatively separate and transfers between the two are highly coded); whereas both of the second generations seem to be involved in a politics and ethics of the *impossible*, where they are attempting to confound and live the public and private differently, based, in large part, on the first generation's lives and work.

So now what scene are we left in? Is the only answer to these public and private, generational, short- and long-term dilemmas, to be an activist, analyst, professor, writer of both generations all at once!? Impossible for most of us. And that is the note upon which I would end: these notes were taken because it seems to me that feminism has not yet thought through what we shall call here the function of the *radical feminist intellectual, teacher, and writer* in the way other radical movements have at least tried to do. It seems to me that if we could do that by looking carefully at (instead of avoiding) the new and strong tensions between and within psychic and representational spaces – as well as between and within generations of women – then the radical political potentials located at the intersections we have been criss-crossing here could begin to be orchestrated in new ways. Feminist women could then assume together a renewed and privileged political position as the *agents* of radical change evoked earlier on.

I would just add a few measures to that note. First, I think that this new kind of feminist intellectual must fully inscribe herself within an ethics of impossibility. Second, she might do so through an acute attention to something other than past, present, or future: the *future anterior*, the privileged modality, as we know, of the psychic, the poetic, the feminist, and the postmodern. Lacan:

> What is realized in my history [my story] is not the past definite of what was, since it is no more, or even the present perfect of what has been in what I am, but the future anterior of what I shall have been for what I am in the process of becoming.[40]

Moving from an individual to a collective analytic perspective, the future anterior incorporates the possibility of understanding the history/story we are, through and from the perspective of the generation before us, in so far as that perspective becomes or is now our own – and is realized in the future. Further, to the extent that each generation is necessarily in a transferential relation to the other, what one generation criticizes in the other may (and probably must) echo the difficulties within itself. In other words, to place ourselves within a generation of women, while paying attention to the multiple projections inherent to the scene of psychoanalysis, might help us to identify our own blindspots. So that, finally, to place ourselves, *as feminist women* – across the generations – together, at the very place of the most chiasmatic, most paradoxical intersections of the future (*post*) anterior (*modo*) can allow us to do away with paranoia (and its publics); fetishism (and its privates); and the concept of 'generation' altogether.

But then perhaps you should just consider what I have been writing here as but some notes upon a mystic writing pad....

Notes

1 Luce Irigaray, 'Le praticable de la scène', in *Parler n'est jamais neutre* (Paris: Minuit, 1985), p. 240. This first double-voiced scene of my notes is obviously indebted to Irigaray's brilliant essay. See also her contribution to this volume.
2 Luce Irigaray, 'Le Sexe fait comme signe', in *Parler n'est jamais neutre*, p. 169.
3 ibid., p. 169.
4 'Le practicable de la scène', p. 240.
5 ibid., p. 239.
6 Wendy Deutelbaum, 'Disputes and truces: the correspondence of Lou Andreas-Salomé and Sigmund Freud', unpublished paper, p. 7.
7 Quoted by Marie Moscovici in her preface to Lou Andreas-Salomé, *L'Amour du narcissisme* (Paris: Gallimard, 1980), pp. 25–6.
8 Shoshana Felman (ed.), *Literature and Psychoanalysis*, special issue of *Yale French Studies* 55/6 (1977). Reissued by Johns Hopkins University Press, 1982.
9 David Carroll, 'Institutional authority vs. critical power, or the uneasy relations of psychoanalysis and literature', in Joseph H. Smith and William Kerrigan (eds), *Taking Chances: Derrida, Psychoanalysis and Literature* (Baltimore: Johns Hopkins University Press, 1984), p. 129.
10 Cf. Jacques Derrida, 'Otobiographies', in *The Ear of the Other* (New York: Schocken, 1985), pp. 3–38.
11 Jacques Derrida, 'Géopsychanalyse – "and all the rest of the world"', in *Géopsychanalyse: Les souterains de l'institution* (Paris: Confrontation, 1981).
12 Barbara Johnson, 'Apostrophe, animation, and abortion', in *A World of Difference* (Baltimore: Johns Hopkins University Press, 1987). (First published in *Diacritics* Spring 1986.)
13 Richard Rorty, 'Habermas, Lyotard et la postmodernité', *Critique* 442 (March 1984), p. 182. Quoted and translated by Meaghan Morris, 'Postmodernity and Lyotard's sublime', in *Art and Text* 16 (1984), p. 53.
14 Cf. Jacques Derrida, 'Le dernier mot du racisme', in *Critical Inquiry* 12 (Fall 1985), pp. 290–9; the response by Anne McClintock and Rob Nixon, 'No names apart: the separation of word and history in Derrida's "Le dernier mot du racisme"', and Derrida's response in turn, 'But, beyond ... (Open letter to Anne McClintock and Rob Nixon)', in *Critical Inquiry* 13 (Fall 1986), pp. 140–70.
15 Cf. my 'In praise of impossibility', a response to Jane Gallop's 'The problem of definition', SCMLA, New Orleans, October 1986.

16 For the sake of clarity, from here on in I shall refer to these two post-1968 generations as generations one (Ph.D. 1968–78) and two (Ph.D. 1978–88). Obviously, the notion of 'generation' is ultimately a very frustrating one (biological age does not always correspond to academic age, etc.) and is used here only as a tentatively useful, almost hypothetical device for raising certain issues. Given this, it is especially important not to bracket the word 'political'. There are today, for example, women across all the generations in the academy who do 'feminist this and that' but maintain no historical or current political relationship to the women's movement.

17 Cf. Isabelle Lasvergnas, 'La trace du féminin dans la pensée?' in a special issue of *BIEF*, 'Des femmes, et la psychanalyse' 18 (June 1986), p. 90.

18 Juliet Mitchell, 'Psychoanalysis and the humanities: old endings or new beginnings?', in the *Dalhousie Review* 64, 2 (Summer 1984), p. 221.

19 Mary Ann Doane, 'The clinical eye: medical discourses in the "woman's film" of the 1940s', in Susan Suleiman (ed.), *The Female Body in Western Culture* (Cambridge Mass.: Harvard University Press, 1985), p. 163.

20 Even those in the same academic generation are more and more positioned this way. Since writing these notes, an essay written in a different vein but very much concerned with these questions has appeared. See Evelyn Fox Keller and Helene Moglen, 'Competition and feminism: conflicts for academic women', in *Signs* 12, 3 (1987).

21 This was discussed during a personal conversation following a feminist seminar at Harvard University in Fall 1986.

22 My thanks to Otto Steinmayer for this formulation.

23 Mary Ann Doane, op. cit., p. 152.

24 Juliet Mitchell, op. cit., p. 222.

25 Jane Gallop, in the 'Prefatory material' to *Reading Lacan* (Ithaca: Cornell University Press, 1985), especially p. 28.

26 Cf. Luce Irigaray's discussion of the dangers of reducing the analytic process to this state as well: 'Misère de la psychanalyse', in *Parler n'est jamais neutre*, pp. 257–8.

27 Cf. Marie-Claire Boons, 'La psychanalyse et une femme', in *BIEF*, op. cit., p. 27.

28 Jean-François Lyotard, *Le Postmoderne expliqué aux enfants* (Paris: Galilée, 1986), p. 98. I am indebted to this little book for helping me make many of the initial connections between these two scenes.

29 Blurb on back cover of Erika Kaufmann, *Transfert* (Paris: des Femmes, 1975). Translated from the Italian (Milan: Giangiacomo Feltrinelli Editore, 1974).

30 For example, see Helene Deutsch's chapter entitled 'Freud' in *Confrontations with Myself* (New York: Norton, 1973).

31 Julia Kristeva, 'Les secrets d'une analyste', Preface to Helene Deutsch, *Autobiographie* (Paris: Mercure de France, 1986), p. 11.

32 Celia Bertin, *Marie Bonaparte* (Paris: Librairie Académique Perrin, 1982), p. 385.

33 Lou Andreas-Salomé, *Correspondance avec Sigmund Freud suivie du journal d'un année (1912–1913)* (Paris: Gallimard, 1970).

34 Collected in H. D., *Tribute to Freud* (New York: Pantheon, 1956).

35 H. D., The beginning of Section 33 of 'Writing on the Wall', ibid.

36 Elizabeth Wilson, *Mirror Writing* (London: Virago, 1982).

37 Judith Rossner, *August* (New York: Warner, 1983); Lisa Alther, *Other Women* (New York: Penguin, 1985); Marie Bellour, *Le Jeu de l'origine* (Paris: des Femmes, 1985); Jacqueline Rousseau-Dujardin, *Couché par écrit* (Paris: Galilée, 1980); Claudie Cachard, *L'Autre histoire* (Paris: des Femmes, 1986).

38 Analogies are always problematic as we know. For example, to analyse thoroughly the following ones, it would be necessary to bring in *biology*: for the most part, the second psychoanalytic generation to which I have been referring (born in the 1920s–1940s, publishing in the 1970s–1980s) corresponds in terms of *age*, roughly to the 'biologically' first (Ph.D. pre-1968) *and* second (Ph.D. 1968–78) academic generations. This leaves the 'biologically' third academic generation (Ph.D. 1978–88) – and the fourth (Ph.D. 1988–98) – without analogies....

39 Cf. Julia Kristeva, 'Women's time', trans. Alice Jardine and Harry Blake, *Signs* 7, 1 (1981).

40 Jacques Lacan, 'The function and field of speech and language in psychoanalysis', in *Ecrits: A Selection* (New York: Norton, 1977), p. 86.

Part Three

Towards another symbolic (1): the essential thing

Chapter Five

The politics of ontological difference

Rosi Braidotti

Genealogical perspectives

A culture has the truths it deserves; it is therefore significant that the notion
of 'difference' has been on the western theoretical agenda for over a century.
Since Freud and Nietzsche it has emerged as one of the main vehicles of
critique of the metaphysical, idealist, Hegelian vision of 'the knowing subject'
cast in the image of 'the man of reason'. [1] As a sign of western culture's
will-to-know, the overriding importance granted to 'difference' in the age of
modernity marks a double shift, away from the belief-like notion that the
subject coincides with his conscious, rational self but also away from the
overwhelming masculinity of such notions as subjectivity and consciousness.

Psychoanalysis as theory and practice is highly representative of this
historical double shift, which opens the age of modernity simultaneously onto
the crisis of the classical vision of the subject and the proliferation of images
of the 'other' as sign of 'difference'. The signifiers 'woman ' and 'the
feminine' are privileged metaphors for the crisis of rational and masculine
values. Recent developments of continental, especially French thought have
added a new chapter to this on-going metaphorization of woman/the feminine
as signs of difference. From the 'becoming-woman' of Derrida and Deleuze
to Freudo-Marxist defences of the feminization of values (Marcuse) the notion
of 'sexual difference' has been subjected to such an inflationary value that it
has led to a paradoxical new uniformity of thought. 'Postmodern' (Lyotard),
'deconstructive' (Derrida), 'microphysical' (Foucault), 'critical' (Deleuze), and
other kinds of philosophers have first of all sexualized as 'feminine' the
question of difference and secondly have turned it into a generalized
philosophical item. As such it is clearly connected to the critique of classical
dualism and of its binary oppositions, in the context of the dislocation of the
subject. Yet it is not directly related to either the discursivity or the historical
presence of real-life women.

It seems to me therefore that the specific orientations that mark the
formulation of the question of sexual difference in feminist theory are being
systematically blurred in mainstream postmodern or deconstructive thought

about sexual difference. Far from being a reactive movement of critical opposition, the feminism of sexual difference is also the active gesture of affirmation of women's ontological desire, of our political determination as well as our subjective wish to posit ourselves as female subjects, that is to say not as disembodied entities but rather as corporeal and consequently sexed beings. The sexualization and the embodiment of the subject are the key notions in what I would call 'feminist epistemology' in that they provide the conceptual tools and the gender-specific perceptions that govern the production of feminist thought.

Feminist theory and practice at the end of this century is a double-edged project involving both the critique of existing definitions, representations, and theorizations of women and also the creation of new images for female subjectivity and suitable social representations of it. Historians of feminist thought[2] have pointed to the shift in focus away from the early woman-centred analysis of the female condition, which took as its starting point women as empirical subjects, to a gender-centred type of analysis. The early 'materialism' of the radical feminist approach, along the line of de Beauvoir's famous formula 'one is not born, one becomes a woman', is being replaced by a new emphasis on the 'materiality' of the female subject as a bio-cultural entity. The impact of psychoanalytic theories, especially of the French Lacanian brand, is often quoted as having played a major role in the reorientation of priorities in the feminist theoretical agenda. I will return to this point.

In order to make sexual difference operative within feminist theory I want to argue that one should start politically with the assertion of the need for the presence of real-life women in positions of discursive subjecthood, and theoretically with the recognition of the primacy of the bodily roots of subjectivity, rejecting both the traditional vision of the subject as universal, neutral, or gender-free and the binary logic that sustains it. In upholding such a view, I do not mean to make feminist theory sound more monolithic than it actually is. Whereas the rejection of the pseudo-universalist stance that takes the masculine as the norm is a point of consensus among feminist theoreticians, the positions on sexual difference are very wide-ranging. As Catharine Stimpson put it[3] they range from the wild maximalists who believe in radical differences between the sexes to the wimpy minimalists who are prepared to negotiate around common margins of humaneness. Suffice it to say, however, that several major political issues in the feminist movement today, such as the prostitution debate; the various schools of feminist theology and their definition of the sacred; questions surrounding women's relationship to the state and women's reaction to totalitarian practices of all sorts; lesbian theories; the work of women from ethnic minorities and the developing world; the debate on the new reproductive technologies and artificial procreation – all bring out the significance as well as the complexity of the notion of sexual difference.

In my understanding of the term, what distinguishes *feminist* theories of sexual difference is the need to recognize as a factual and historical reality that there is no symmetry between the sexes and that this symmetry has been organized hierarchically. Recognizing that difference has been turned into a mark of pejoration, the feminist project attempts to redefine it. The starting point, however, remains the political will to assert the specificity of the lived, female bodily experience, the refusal to disembody sexual difference into a new allegedly postmodern anti-essentialist subject, and the will to re-connect the whole debate on difference to the bodily existence and experience of women.

Politically, the project amounts to the rejection of homologation, that is to say the assimilation into masculine modes of thought and practice and consequently sets of values. Recent socio-economic developments in the status of women in western, post-industrial societies have in fact shown – besides the persistence of classical forms of discrimination leading to the feminization of poverty – that female emancipation can easily turn into a one-way street into a man's world.

Far from separating the struggle for equality from the affirmation of difference I see them as complementary and part of a continuous historical evolution. The women's movement is the space where sexual difference becomes operational, through the strategy of fighting for the equality of the sexes in a cultural and economic order dominated by the masculine homo-social bond. What is at stake is the definition of woman as other-than a non-man.

Another important factor that brought about this shift in feminist theory towards difference is the passing of time which has created age differences or generation gaps among the women of the movement. A generation is measured not chronologically but discursively: women like myself aged 35 and under, have grown up with and within feminism; we have inherited both benefits and disadvantages from the struggle for emancipation carried out by those whom in Europe we call 'historical feminists'. In stressing the significance of discursive generation gaps I do not mean to flaunt the arrogant superiority of 'youth' but rather to state my historical debt towards women who came before me and whose efforts have brought about an enlarged and more equitable definition of what it means to be a woman. It is just that each generation must reckon with its own problematics and, in my perspective, the priority issue seems to be how to struggle for the achievement of equality in the assertion of difference.

The theoretical edge of the debate between notions of difference in feminist as opposed to mainstream theory seems to me to be the following: how can 'we feminists' affirm the positivity of female subjectivity at a time in history and in the philosophy of the west where our acquired perceptions of the subject are being radically questioned? How can 'we feminists' reconcile the recognition of the problematic nature and the process of construction of the subject with the political necessity to posit woman as the subject of another history? In other words: how far can 'we feminists' push the sexualization of the crisis of modernity and of the subject of discourse? How can we go on arguing that sexual difference is ontological, that is to say constitutive of the subject? Should the issue of sexual difference be sexualized? For me, 'being in the world' means always already 'being sexed', so that if 'I' am not sexed, 'I' am not at all.

What is at stake conceptually is one of the most complex questions for both feminism and contemporary philosophy: how to go about rethinking the *unity* of the thinking being at a time in history when the rationalistic naturalistic divine paradigm has been lost? Is a radically materialistic post-Marxist reading of the subject as discontinuous unity of body and mind possible? How can one argue both for the loss of the classical paradigm and the need to reintegrate the bodily unity of the subject? And given that feminism is eminently modern as a theory and practice, in that the very conditions that make it possible as a discourse and as a social movement are structurally co-extensive with modernity itself, how can 'we feminists' uphold both the need to assert the sexual-specificity of the female subject and the deconstruction of traditional notions of the subject, which are based on phallocentric premises? If 'we feminists' posit the contemporary subject as a dazzling collection of integrated fragments, what sense, place, and status can 'we feminists' give to his/her sexed nature? What is *her* specificity as a conceptual, libidinal, and empirical subject? And, above all, what political stand can we develop that would respect the theoretical complexity of the view of the subject that we share with contemporary philosophy, while maintaining our commitment to the women's struggle? What are the politics of the female split-subject?

Arguing that the question of sexual difference is the fundamental theoretical problem of our century,[4] and that it calls for the elaboration of a political stance, I would like to try and spell out in this paper the theoretical steps connecting the main points of reference of the feminist debate on sexual difference, namely: 'thinking as a feminist', 'being-a-woman', and 'essentialism'. More specifically, I am concerned about the argumentative lines and the polemical targets that have led the debate on sexual difference towards the murky depths where 'essentialism' means fixed masculine and feminine essences. I am wondering why sexual difference became assimilated to essentialism and acquired such negative political implications. As Naomi Schor rightly put it: 'Essentialism in modern-day feminism is anathema.'[5] Teresa Brennan has argued that its original meaning has been lost. Essentialism used to refer to something beyond the reaches of historical change, something immutable and consequently outside the field of political intervention. Often reduced to mere biological determinism, the term 'essentialism' is more important as a negative critical pole than as anything else: what is being conveyed in the name of anti-essentialism is, indeed, the key question.

Resisting the reduction of essentialism to determinism or to ahistorical essences I will challenge the view that the essentialist feminist position is apolitical or even potentially reactionary. On the contrary, I am in profound agreement with Gayatri Spivak that essentialism may be a necessary strategy.

I will also assert that a feminist woman theoretician who is interested in thinking about sexual difference and the feminine today cannot afford not to be essentialist. My defence of essentialism rests on three basic premises. First, that in order to make sexual difference operative as a political option, feminist theoreticians should re-connect the feminine to the bodily sexed reality of the female, refusing the separation of the empirical from the symbolic, or of the material from the discursive, or of sex from gender. Secondly, that this project is important as both the epistemological basis for feminist theory and the grounds of political legitimation for feminist politics in the social, economic, political, and theoretical context of the postmodern and the postindustrial condition. Thirdly, that in thinking about sexual difference one is led, by the very structure of the problem, to the metaphysical question of essence. Ontology being the branch of metaphysics that deals with the structure of that which essentially *is*, or that which is implied in the very definition of an entity, I will argue for the ontological basis of sexual difference. I will add that the project of going beyond metaphysics, that is to say, of redefining ontology, is an open-ended one which neither feminist nor contemporary philosophers have managed to solve as yet. Thus, unless we want to give in to the facile anti-intellectualism of those who see metaphysics as 'woolly-thinking' or to the easy way out of those who reduce it to an ideologically incorrect option, I think we should indeed take seriously the critique of discourse about essences as the historical task of modernity.

'I', this other

Although the notion of 'difference' thus presented refers primarily to differences *between* men and women, this heterosexist frame of reference is not exhaustive. 'Difference' refers much more importantly to differences *among* women: differences of class, race, and sexual preferences for which the signifier 'woman' is inadequate as a blanket term. Furthermore, the problematic of 'difference' points to another layer of related issues: the differences *within* each single woman, meant as the complex interplay of differing levels of experience, which defer indefinitely any fixed notion of identity.

This last point is especially important: my discursive strategy cannot be dissociated from the place of enunciation and the enunciative, textual game in which I am involved. The thinking/speaking 'I' which signs this paper is neither the owner nor the king of the complex network of meanings that constitute the text.[6] The power of synthesis of the 'I' is a grammatical necessity, a theoretical fiction that holds together the collection of differing layers, the integrated fragments of the ever-receding horizon of my identity. The idea of 'differences within' each subject is tributary to psychoanalytic theory and practice in that it envisages the subject as the crossroads of different registers of speech, calling upon different layers of lived experience.

To translate this standpoint back into the debate on the politics of subjectivity within the feminist practice of sexual difference I would ask the following questions: how does the 'woman-in-me' relate to the 'feminist-in-me'? What are the links and the possible tensions between my 'being-a-feminist' and 'being-a woman', between politics and the sense of self, between subjectivity and identity, between sexuality as an institution and also as one of the pillars for one's own sense of self? In other words, what are the devices that make sexual difference operational as a place of enunciation? What is the technology of the self at work in the expression of sexual difference?[7]

This question is political in both an explicit and an implicit way. Explicitly, the political implications are far-reaching in that they call into question the very grounds of legitimation of feminism as a political movement. The crucial question is: where does political belief come from? What founds the legitimacy of the feminist political subject? What gives it its validity? Where does political authenticity come from? From the refusal of oppression? As an act of solidarity with fellow-sufferers: 'sisterhood is powerful'? As an act of pure, that is to say gratuitous, rebellion? Or does it spring from the wish to exorcise our worst paranoid nightmares, or alternatively our most secret power-fantasies?

In a more implicit way, the question of sexual difference is political in that it focuses the debate on how to achieve transformation of self, other, and society. It thus emphasizes the ethical passions underlying feminist politics. Furthermore, by raising the paradox of the female condition not merely in terms of oppression but rather as both implication and exteriority *vis-à-vis* the patriarchal, phallo-logocentric system, it reformulates the complex issue of women's involvement – some would say complicity – with a system which actively discriminates against and disqualifies us. It finally helps us to redefine the question: what does it mean to think and speak 'as a feminist woman'?

Speaking 'as a feminist woman' does not refer to one dogmatic framework but rather to a knot of interrelated questions that play on different layers, registers, and levels of the self. Feminism as a speaking stance and consequently as a theory of the subject is less of an ideological than of an epistemological position, to use Teresa de Lauretis' formulation. By providing the linkages between different 'plateaux'[8] of experience, the feminist thinker connects, for instance, the institutions where knowledge is formalized and transmitted (universities and schools) to the spaces outside the official gaze, which act as generating and relay points for forms of knowledge as resistance (the women's movement).

The feminist woman thinker, however, has other types of linkages to worry about; what is significant about thinking 'as a feminist woman', regardless of what one is actually thinking about, is the extreme proximity of the thinking process to existential reality and lived experience. Feminist theory is a mode of relating thought to life.[9] As such not only does it provide a critical standpoint to deconstruct established forms of knowledge, drawing feminism close to critical theory; it also establishes a new order of values within the thinking process itself, giving to the lived experience priority. First and foremost in the revaluation of experience is the notion of the bodily self: the personal is not only the political, it is also the theoretical. In redefining the self as an embodied entity, affectivity and sexuality play a dominant role, particularly in relation to what makes a subject *want* to think: the desire to know. The 'epistemo-philic' tension that makes the deployment of the knowing process possible is the first premise in the redefinition of 'thinking as a feminist woman'.

Finally, the woman who thinks in the sense outlined above knows that thinking has something to do not only with the light of reason but also with shadowy regions of the mind where anger and rebellion about socio-political realities related to the status of women combine with the intense desire to achieve change. Thus, something in the feminist frame resists mainstream discourse, but something in the fact of 'being-a-woman' is in excess of the feminist identity. The project of giving a structure, to this 'excess', which (much to the delight of Lacanian psychoanalysts) is also constitutive of 'feminine identity' in our – ever so phallocentric – culture, becomes, within feminist theory, a project aiming to redefine female subjectivity.

Hence a related set of questions: how does a collective movement re-invent the definition of the subjective self? Where does that sort of transformation come from? How does one invent new structures of thought? Where does one find the words to express adequately that which cannot be said within the parameters of the phallo-logocentric discourse of which we are all part-time members, even the most radically feminist among us? I will argue later that what is needed is a notion of community[10] as a legitimating agent.

Impressed as I may be by the argumentation of Lacanian critics of the logic of phallo-logocentrism[11] I am nevertheless convinced that the conceptual challenge of feminism is radically other than the project of psychoanalysis. It has to do with the epistemological dimension mentioned above: how to connect the 'differences within' each woman to political practice which requires mediation of the 'differences among' women, so as to enact and implement sexual difference. Within feminism, the politico-epistemological question of achieving structural transformations of the subject cannot be dissociated from the need to effect changes in the socio-material frames of reference, which is one of the points of divergence between the feminist and the psychoanalytic 'scenes'.

The body, encore

In lots of ways, the body is the dark continent of feminist thought; early radical feminist theory inherited from Marxism a perfectly binary distinction between the 'biological' and the 'social', modelled along the lines of the 'private' and 'public' distinction.[12] The idea of the social construction of gender dominated the approach to questions related to biology, or to the body, which were more often than not read as the sign and the site of oppression. Feminists called upon 'history' and social conditioning to explain the representations and the images attached to the corporeal reality of the female. The emphasis was shifted, however, by the thought and the practice of sexual difference.

In this regard it is significant that one of the most common images in the feminist debate over difference is the one about 'mothers and daughters'. Its recurrence expresses the political urgency of thinking about the formalization and the transmission of the feminist heritage; but over and above the elementary vicissitudes of the feminist generation gap, the 'mother–daughter' metaphor expresses the need to formulate what Irigaray aptly calls a 'theoretical genealogy of women' or 'a feminine symbolic system'. This project rests on the notion of sexual difference as its working hypothesis; the sudden eruption of the Oedipal plot within feminist theory, however, also means that the thorny knots surrounding the maternal body as the site of origin has reinvested the women's movement, inevitably intersecting the winding roads of psychoanalytic theory. The 'mother–daughter' debate is thus both a symptom and a privileged form of enactment of sexual difference within feminism (see Alice Jardine, this collection).

One of the most accurate ways of measuring the progress accomplished by feminist thought on biology and the female body is to take up this 'mother' metaphor. Whereas in earlier feminist analyses the 'mother' and the 'maternal function' were seen as potentially conflicting with the interests of the 'woman' in so far as compulsory heterosexuality had made them the social destiny of all women, more recent feminist readings of the maternal function[13] have stressed the double bind of the maternal issue. Motherhood is seen as both one of the pillars of patriarchal domination of women and one of the strongholds of female identity.

Accordingly, the 'mother–daughter' image has changed considerably and, particularly in the work of Irigaray[14] it has emerged as a new paradigm. It is an imaginary couple that enacts the politics of female subjectivity, the relationship to the other woman and consequently the structures of female homosexuality as well as the possibility of a woman-identified redefinition of the subject. In Irigaray's thought, this couple is endowed with symbolic significance in that it embodies a new vision of female inter-subjectivity which is presented as a viable political option. In a phallo-logocentric system where the Name-of-the-Father provides the operative metaphor for the constitution of the subject, the idea of 'a feminine symbolic function' amounts to the revendication of the structuring function for the mother. It attempts to invest the maternal site with affirmative, positive force.

As opposed to the early, dichotomized readings of the relationship between body and society, the hypothesis of sexual difference has broken down the polarized oppositions between the public and the private, society and the self, language and the materiality of the body. Over and beyond dualism, it puts forth as the ruling notion the inextricable *unity* of the subject as a bio-psychic entity. There are obvious Nietzschean undertones in this project of reintegrating the constitutive elements of the human being.

As a consequence the body meant as the bodily roots of subjectivity becomes a problematic notion, not a prescriptive or pre-defined one. The 'body' in question is the threshold of subjectivity: as such it is neither the sum of its organs – a fixed biological essence – nor the result of social conditioning – a historical entity. The 'body' is rather to be thought of as the point of intersection, as the interface between the biological and the social, that is to say between the socio-political field of the microphysics of power and the subjective dimension (see Adams, this collection). This vision implies that the subject is subjected to her/his unconscious; the driving notion of 'desire' is precisely that which relays the self to the many 'others' that constitute her/his 'external' reality.

The problem of the articulation of the empirical with the symbolic, the material with the spiritual and the libidinal, the political with the subjective, is common to both feminist theory and practice and to psychoanalysis. They both posit as a central axiom the non-coincidence of anatomical differences with the psychic representations of sexual difference. In other words, there is a fundamental qualitative distinction to be made between anatomy and sexuality as such; sexuality is de-naturalized by psychoanalysis through the hypothesis of the unconscious, to which feminism adds the political insight about the socio-historical construction of sexual identities.

In the feminist perspective, patriarchy defined as the actualization of the masculine homo-social bond can be seen as a monumental denial of the axiom expressed above, in so far as it has been haunted by the political necessity to make biology coincide with subjectivity, the anatomical with the psycho-sexual, and therefore reproduction with sexuality. This forced unification of nature with culture has been played out mostly on woman's body, upon which patriarchal discourse and practice has built one of its most powerful institutions: the family. A related aspect of this power strategy, perverse in its structure, is the enforcement of the myth of the complementarity of the two sexes which is socially coded as the practice of heterosexism, or compulsory hetero-sexuality.

Both feminism and psychoanalysis provide an in-depth critique of the perversion that animates patriarchy and its masculine homosexual symbolic; they both stress the toll that each subject pays for belonging to such a system and, by splitting open the false symmetries and fake coincidences, they assert the highly fictional and constructed nature of human sexuality, denouncing the imposture of identity. But although psychoanalytic theory has done a great deal to improve our understanding of sexual difference, it has done little or nothing to change the concrete social conditions of sex-relations and of gender-stratification. The latter is precisely the target of feminist practice; feminism is neither about feminine sexuality, nor about desire – it has to do with change. This is the single most important difference between the psychoanalytic and the feminist movements: the definition of change and how to go about achieving it. Psychoanalysis and feminism seem to tackle the issue of political transformation from radically different and ultimately incompatible angles.

Furthermore, this divergence on the political issue may well be due to a very different perception of the ethics of inter-subjectivity. Another vital insight that feminism shares with psychoanalysis, in fact, is in recognizing the importance of the relation to the other. Both practices are about relating to and learning from and within the relationship to the other, asserting that at some vital level 'I' rest on the presence of an-other.[15] The assertion of the primacy of the bond, the relation, however, leads the two to draw different conclusions.

The psychoanalytic situation brings out, among other things, the fundamental dissymmetry between self and other, that is constitutive of the subject; this is related to the non-interchangeability of positions between analyst and patient, to the irrevocable anteriority of the former, that is to say, ultimately, to time. Time, the great master, calling upon each individual to take her/his place in the game of generations, is the inevitable, the inescapable horizon. One of the ethical aims of the psychoanalytic situation is to lead the subject to accept this inscription into time, the passing of generations and the dissymmetries it entails, so as to accept the radical otherness of the self.

Feminist practice, on the other hand, having stressed from the start the lack of symmetry between the sexes, posits the necessity of the relation to the other woman[16] as the privileged interlocutor, the witness, the legitimator of the self. The feminist subject, as Adrienne Rich put it, fastens on to the presence of the other woman, of *the other as woman*. It even posits the recognition of the otherness of the other woman as the first step towards redefining our common sameness, our 'being-a-woman'.

In pointing out that the sexualization of the other, and of the subject, is a point on which psychoanalysis and feminism seem to part, I do not wish to suggest any incompatibilities between them. In the experience of many feminist women the feminist and the psychoanalytic patient/practitioner coexist successfully, although the political revendications of an-other feminine identity and the expressions of the unconscious have to get adjusted to each other. Once again, the game of modulations or of variations on a tune is very important: recognizing the different registers, layers, and levels of experience and speech is in my opinion the most ethical way of reconciling the divergences between the feminist and the psychoanalytic situations. Any attempt at a synthesis between the two can only lead to the ideological or sociological distortion of the latter and to a loss of political focus for the former.

One central point remains, however, as the stumbling block for this whole debate: how to rethink the body in terms that are neither biological nor sociological. How to reformulate the bodily roots of subjectivity in such a way as to incorporate the insight of the body as libidinal surface, field of forces, threshold of transcendence.[17] As a notion the body is related to the onto-theological debate about the overcoming of metaphysics and the quest for a new definition of the human as an integrated unity of material and symbolic elements. Stressing the metaphysical dimension of the question of the body is a way of shifting the debate away from the false dichotomy of the biological vs. the political. And if we do situate the problematic of the bodily roots of subjectivity back into the structure of metaphysical thought where it belongs, the whole question of essences becomes both crucial and inevitable.

It is precisely this notion of the body that is at work, with varying degrees of coherence, in Luce Irigaray's texts. In her deconstruction of sexual polarization in the discourse of classical ontology, Irigaray mimes perfectly the conceptual operation of essentialist logic as the key of phallo-logocentric discourse. In other words, Irigaray takes quite literally the position to which 'the feminine' has been assigned by centuries of patriarchal thought – as the eternal other of the system. Irigaray's strategy consists in refusing to separate the symbolic, discursive dimension from the empirical, material, or historical one. She refuses to dissociate questions of the feminine from the presence of real-life women and in so doing she may appear to repeat the binary perversion of phallo-centrism, by equating the feminine with women and the masculine with men. But the apparent mimesis is tactical and it aims at *producing* difference for, Irigaray argues, there is no symmetry between the sexes, and therefore attributing to women the right – and the political imperative – of voicing their 'feminine' amounts to deconstructing any naturalistic notion of a female 'nature'. Encouraging women to think, say, and write the feminine is a gesture of self-legitimation that breaks away from centuries of phallo-logocentric thought which had silenced women.

Classical, ontological visions of the subject are indeed essentialist in that they deal with the complex problem of the unity of the human in terms of binary oppositions. They distribute the basic elements (fire, earth, air, water), the fundamental principles (active/passive; attraction/repulsion, etc., etc.), and the passions along dualistic lines which postulate one of the poles of the opposition as the norm and the other as a deviation. Essentialism meant as the substantive opposition of related contraries is a constant not only in classical thought but also, by negation, in contemporary attempts to deconstruct the edifice of metaphysics. With a few notable exceptions[18] little feminist criticism has been devoted to the essentialization of the feminine as a sign of becoming in the work of such masters of deconstruction as Derrida. On the other hand, Irigaray's essentialist side has been the object of intense criticism.[19]

It is important[20] to make a distinction between the inevitability of essentialism in the critique of metaphysics and the mimetic strategy that feminist theoreticians such as Irigaray adopt in order to work out and on sexual difference. This point is not only methodological but also ethical: unless 'we feminists' are happy to go on giving political answers to theoretical questions, in fact, we need to face up to the theoretical complexities that we have helped to create. The problem of 'essence' is one such problem, and in order to deal with it properly 'we feminists' cannot do without the in-depth analysis of the very conceptual structures which have governed the production of the theoretical schemes in which, even today, is caught the representation of women. Feminism has an ethical obligation to think rigorously about the historical and discursive conditions of our enunciation: we must *work through* the knot of interrelated questions about sexual difference. And in arguing for difference to be embodied by female bodily subjects we simply cannot avoid the essentialist edge of the structure of human subjectivity. Taking *a priori* an anti-essentialist stand may be politically right, but remains nevertheless conceptually short-sighted. The real question is strategic, namely: where is this long journey through essentialist, differential logic going to take us? What is the philosophy of sexual difference moving towards? What is the politics of it?

Essentialism with a difference

In my reading, the thought of sexual difference argues the following:[21] it is historically and politically urgent, in the *here and now* of the common world of women[22] to bring about and act upon sexual difference. 'We' women, acting as members of the feminist community, as a political movement, act upon the enunciation of a common epistemological and ethical bond among us: a feminist cogito. 'We' women, the movement of liberation of the 'I' of each and every women, assert the following: 'I, woman, think and therefore I say that I, woman, am.' I am sexed female, my subjectivity is sexed female. As to *what* my 'self' or my 'I' actually is, that is a whole new question, dealing with identity. The affirmation of my subjectivity need not give a propositional content to my sense of identity: I do not have to define the signifier woman in order to assert it as the speaking subject of my discourse. The speaking 'I' is not neutral or gender-free, but sexed.

It is on this point that a political and epistemological consensus can be reached among women: the affirmation of the *differences within* joins up with the assertion of a collective recognition of the *differences between* all of us and the male subject, as well as the *differences* which exist *among* us female subjects. The recognition of the sameness of our gender, all other differences taken into account, is a sufficient and necessary condition to make explicit a bond among women that is more than the ethics of solidarity and altogether other than the sharing of common interests.[23] Once this bond is established and the epistemological common grounds of the feminist community are recognized, the basis is set for the elaboration of other values, of different representations of our common difference.

There is nothing deterministic about the assertion of a feminist cogito as a sexed subject of enunciation ('I, woman, think and therefore I say that I, woman, am'). Being-a-woman is not the predication of a prescriptive essence, it is not a causal proposition capable of predetermining the outcome of the becoming of each individual identity. It pertains rather to the facticity of my being, it is a fact, it is like *that*: 'I' am sexed. 'I' have been a woman – socially and anatomically – for as long as 'I' have existed, that is to say, in the limited scale of my temporality, forever. 'I', woman, am the female sexed subject who is mortal and endowed with language. My 'being-a-woman', just like my 'being-in-language' and 'being-mortal' is one of the constitutive elements of my subjectivity. Sexual difference is ontological, not accidental, peripheral, or contingent upon socio-economic conditions; that one be socially constructed as a female is an evidence, that the recognition of the fact may take place in language is clear, but that the process of construction of femininity fastens and builds upon anatomical realities is equally true. One is both born and constructed as a woman, the fact of being a woman is neither merely biological nor solely historical and the polemical edge of the debate should not, in my opinion, go on being polarized in either of these ways. Sexual difference is a *fact*, it is also a *sign* of a long history that conceptualized difference as pejoration or lack. What is at stake in the debate is not the causality, the chicken-and-the-egg argument, but rather the positive project of turning difference into a strength, of affirming its positivity.

'Being-a-woman', as the result of a construction of femininity in history and language, is to be taking as the starting point for the assertion of the female as subject. 'We' feminists can therefore adopt the strategy of defining as 'woman' the stock of cumulated knowledge, the theories and representations of the female subject. This is no gratuitous appropriation, for 'I, woman' am the direct empirical referent of all that has been theorized about femininity, the female subject, and the feminine. 'I, woman' am affected directly and in my everyday life by what has been made of the subject of woman; I have paid in my very body for all the metaphors and images that our culture has deemed fit to produce of woman. The metaphorization feeds upon my bodily self, in a process of 'metaphysical cannibalism'[24] that feminist theory helps to explain.

This is why 'I woman' shall not relinquish easily the game of representation of woman, not shall I loosen the tie between the symbolic or discursive and the bodily or material. I take it upon myself to recognize the totality of definitions that have been made of women as being my *historical essence*. On the basis of the responsibility I thus take for my gender, I can start changing the rules of the game by making the discursive order *accountable* for them. The factual element that founds the project of sexual difference, and which is also a sign is not biological, it is bio-cultural, historical. Its importance lies in the fact that it allows me, and many like me in the sameness of our gender – all differences taken into account – to state that 'we' women find these representations and images of us highly insufficient and inadequate to express our experience. Before any such assertion is being made, however, the consensus point needs to be cleared, that 'being a woman is always already there as the ontological pre-condition for my existential becoming as a subject'.[25] The same could and indeed should be said about 'being-a-man', but the male subject has historically chosen to conjugate his being in the universalistic logocentric mode. Even that may change, though.

As a consequence, there is no need to justify or legitimate the definition and representation of woman by appealing to a history of oppression or, even worse, of alienation. Let us take, instead, the fact of being a woman as the essential, i.e. origin-al, premise for the redefinition of the female subject. The starting point is the recognition of both the sameness and the otherness of the other woman, her symbolic function as agent of change. In other words, the affirmation of sexual difference becomes a political strategy which assigns to women as a collective movement the right and the competence to define our vision, perception, and assessment of ourselves. Thus, the 'feminine', to take up Irigaray's problematic again, would cease to be the effect of male fantasies – of myths and representations created by men; it would not be reducible to the mere impact of socio-economic conditions either. The 'feminine' is that which 'I, woman' invent, enact, and empower in 'our' speech, our practice, our collective quest for a redefinition of the status of all women. It is up to us, gathered in the feminist movement, to redefine this signifier in terms of how 'I, woman' fasten on the presence of other female subjects. So long as other women are here and now sustaining this discursive power game, so long as a community legitimates it, a politically redefined collective subject – a female symbolic system – can indeed empower the subjective becoming of each one of us.

This does not aim at glorifying an archaic definition of female 'power',[26] nor does it wish to recover a lost origin – it is rather a tactic which legitimates our demand for the recognition of ways of knowing, modes of thinking, forms of representation that would take sexual difference as the starting point. It is an act of self-legitimation which asserts as the collective will-to-be the ontological desire of being-a-woman. It is also a clear discursive strategy which turns feminism into a critical speaking stance, a very privileged angle through which to change the reality of theoretical practice. Far from being prescriptive in an essentialist-deterministic way, it opens up a field of possible 'becoming', providing the foundation for a new alliance among women, a symbolic bond among woman *qua* female sexed beings.

In this sense, and in this sense only, do I think that 'a feminist woman theoretician who is interested in thinking about sexual difference and the feminine today cannot afford not to be essentialist'. Let me add, however, that I would not want this double negative to amount to a self-assertive imperative: 'thou shalt be essentialist'. A double negative need not add up to a single meaning; I would like us to respect the double shift of the statement – 'cannot afford not to be' and to resist the temptation to reach an essentialist synthesis. Not only because, as Naomi Schor points out: 'essentialism is not one', but also because the shift must be accompanied by an enunciative nuance. I would like us to adopt a special mode of thinking, trying to leave behind the centuries-old habit that consists of thinking in terms of identity and oppositions, thesis and antithesis. Let us think differently about this, in a mode that I would call, following Irigaray, the conditional present.

If you think back to the early feminist theory of the 1960s and 1970s you could say that it is written in the simple future tense, expressing a deep sense of determination, of certainty about the course of history and the irresistible emancipation of women. The future is the mode of expressing an open-ended game of possibilities: half prophecy and half utopia and, above all, blueprint for action. The conditional present mode, however, goes beyond the logic of ideology and of teleological progress. More akin to dreamtime, it is the tense of open potentiality and consequently of desire in the sense of a web of interconnected conditions of possibility. The conditional present posits the continuity of desire as the only unifying agent between self and other, subject and history. Desire determines the ontological plane on which the subject defines her-/him-self. Therefore the conditional is the mode of inscription of desire in the present, in the here and now of our speaking stance. It is also the poetic time of fiction.[27]

It is the 'philosophy of *as if*': in order to enunciate a feminist epistemological position the feminist woman must proceed as if a common ground of enunciation existed among women. As if the subjectivity of all was at stake in the enunciative patterns of each one. In this respect, feminist theory rests on another double negative: it proceeds as if it were possible to negate a history of negation, to reverse through collective practice a centuries-old history of disqualification and exclusion of women. To deny a centuries-old denigration so as to move onto the threshold of a redefinition of woman is the discursive leap forward of feminism as a movement of thought and action.

The project of redefining 'being-a-woman alongside other women in the world', so as to disengage the female 'I' from the trappings of a 'feminine' defined as the dark continent, or of 'femininity' as the eternal masquerade, is the fundamental ethico-political question of our century. In arguing that 'I, woman' involved in this process cannot afford not to be essentialist I am also expressing my wanting feminism to matter because it carries ethical and theoretical values that cannot be reduced to yet another ideology or doxa. Feminism is the conscious revendication of representations of the feminine and women by and of women themselves. To make any sense at all, it requires a political practice, and has to be acted out, collectively.

Theoretically, the paradox of implication and exteriority which feminist women embody reveals a profound truth about the structures of human subjectivity. Truth is of this world and so are women: beings of flesh and bones, we are condemned to the spiralling staircase of ordinary language; beings of language (Lacan's 'parlêtre'), like all beings, women are both the effect and the manipulators of linguistic signs. There is no outside, no easy way out of the social and symbolic system for which the male sex has provided the basic parameters of reference: no real 'ideological purity' as such. As women we are firmly attached to a culture and to a logic of discourse which has historically defined woman, and the feminine, in a pejorative sense. The conscious political realization of our being already present, however, in a system that has turned a blind eye/I to the fact of what we are and that we are, instead of becoming a statement of defeat, could pave the way for a new ethical and political project aimed at affirming the positivity of the difference we embody. Beyond the fantasy of feminine power and the illusion of a pure female species, the project of sexual difference and the ethical passion that sustains it may well be the last utopia of our dying century.

Notes

I would like to thank the following people for their useful comments in the drafting of this paper: Teresa Brennan, Naomi Schor, and Anneke Smelik. My thanks are also due to the members of the Women's Studies Programme of the University of Utrecht in the Netherlands, and in particular to Angela Grooten.

1 G. Lloyd, *The Man of Reason* (London: Methuen, 1986).
2 H. Eisenstein, *Contemporary Feminist Thought* (London and Sydney: Allen & Unwin, 1983).
3 K. Stimpson, 'Women's Studies in the US today', unpublished seminar paper, 1988.
4 L. Irigaray, *L'Ethique de la différence sexuelle* (Paris: Minuit, 1984).
5 N. Schor, 'This essentialism which is not one', (forthcoming, *Differences, 1, 2*).
6 M. Foucault, *Surveiller et punir* (Paris: Gallimard, 1977). *La Volonté de savoir* (Paris: Gallimard, 1978).
7 M. Foucault, *L'Usage des plaisirs* (Paris: Gallimard, 1984); T. de Lauretis, *Feminist Studies, Critical Studies* (Bloomington: Indiana University Press, 1987).
8 G. Deleuze, *Mille plateaux* (Paris: Minuit, 1980).
9 E. Fox Keller, *A Feeling for the Organism* (San Fransisco: Freeman, 1983); *Reflections on Gender and Science* (New Haven, Conn.: Yale University Press, 1984).
10 T. Kuhn, *The Structure of Scientific Revolutions*, 2nd edn (Chicago: University of Chicago Press, 1970).
11 J. Mitchell and J. Rose, *Feminine Sexuality* (New York: Norton, 1982).
12 T. Brennan, 'Impasse in psychoanalysis and feminism', in S. Gunew (ed.), *Feminist Knowledge: Critique and Construct* (London: Routledge, forthcoming).
13 A. Rich, *Of Woman Born: Motherhood as Experience and Institution* (London: Virago, 1977).
14 See Margaret Whitford, 'Rereading Irigaray', in this collection.
15 F. Molfino, 'Feminismo e psicoanalisi' in C. Marcuzzo and A. Rossi-Doria (eds) *La ricerca delle donne* (Torino: Rosenberg & Sellier, 1986).
16 Irigaray, *L'Ethique de la différence sexuelle*.
17 G. Deleuze, *Anti-Oedipe* (Paris: Minuit, 1972), p. 80.
18 G. Spivak, 'Displacement and the discourse of women' in Mark Krupnick (ed.), *Displacement: Derrida and After* (Bloomington: Indiana University Press, 1983), but see also her paper in this collection.

19 T. Moi, *Sexual/Textual Politics* (London: Methuen, 1985).
20 M. Whitford, 'L. Irigaray and the female imaginary', *Radical Philosophy 43 (Summer 1986), pp. 3–8.*
21 Irigaray, *L'Ethique de la différence sexuelle*; A. Cavarero 'Il pensiero della differenza sessuale', *La ricerca delle donne.*
22 Rich, *Of Women Born.*
23 A. Muraro, 'Piu Donne che uomini', in A. Cavarero (ed.), *Libraria delle donne* (Milan: Libreria delle donne, 1983).
24 Ti-G. Atkinson, *Amazon Odyssey* (New York: Link, 1974).
25 R. Braidotti, 'Envy', in *Men in Feminism* (New York: Methuen, 1987).
26 M. Daly, *Gyn/Ecology: The Meta-ethics of Radical Feminism* (Boston: Beacon, 1978).
27 N. Miller, *The Poetics of Gender* (New York: Columbia University Press, 1986); 'Changing the subject' in T. de Lauretis (ed.), *Feminist Studies, Critical Studies* (Bloomington: Indiana University Press, 1987).

Chapter Six

Rereading Irigaray

Margaret Whitford

What I want to argue in this paper is that Irigaray's project is an attempt to effect change in the symbolic order, and that what she has been interpreted as advocating or positing in fact resembles more closely her diagnosis of what is wrong with the symbolic order.

It is probably always and inevitably the case that a work of any theoretical complexity contains within itself aspects which may be heterogeneous and are not necessarily reconcilable. Irigaray's work is controversial, both in that it is not yet entirely clear how it should be read, and also in that, whatever reading one adopts, her analysis and strategy are not of the kind which impose themselves without discussion.

Her work is not, in my opinion, as accessible as some of her critics would have us believe. I'm thinking particularly of some Anglo-American criticism which assimilates her, along with Cixous and Kristeva, under the heading of *écriture féminine* (women's writing or writing the body), and makes her work sound like little more than a heroic and inspiring, but ultimately rather utopian, manifesto. In fact, her work is steeped in the history of philosophy from the pre-Socratics to the poststructuralists. To read *Speculum*, for example, we really need to know not only Freud but also, among others, Plato, Aristotle, Kant, Hegel, Derrida. To read *Ethique de la différence sexuelle*, one needs to know the Greeks, Descartes, Spinoza, Kant, Hegel. She has written a whole book as a dialogue with Nietzsche, another one as a dialogue with Heidegger, and has also engaged with contemporaries: Lacan of course, but also Merleau-Ponty and Levinas. She is working primarily in philosophy, but she is also a psychoanalyst, and has also done research in linguistics: her first book was a study of the language of the mentally-ill,[1] and her work at the Centre National de Recherches Scientifiques in Paris has been linguistic research. Ironically, some of those who do recognize this erudite background reproach her for it, as Eléanor Kuykendall points out:

> The first question for a political analysis of Irigaray's psychologic and mythic proposals for matriarchy is whether it is elitist, hence in its very form an undercutting of a feminist politics, separating women from one

another by class.... Simone de Beauvoir, for example ... has suggested that *écriture féminine* is an inappropriate way to do feminist political work, which would be more effectively accomplished by using everyone's language, ordinary language.... I found no one, up until a year after its publication, who had been able to read *Amante marine* with its complex literary allusions.... What, then, is the political force of a writing style inaccessible to all but those highly trained academically?[2]

I do not intend here to either justify or attack her project; my more limited aim is to attempt to clarify what that project is. And in order to do this, I want to defend her against certain readings which have become prevalent in Britain and the States, and to suggest that these are misreadings.

There have been many readings of Irigaray, for example, which interpret her as an essentialist of one kind or another, and some of these readings I discuss below. Although I am arguing, broadly speaking, that these readings are misconceived, I do none the less recognize that they are not total fabrications, and that they *are* constructed from textual evidence, albeit incomplete. In this paper, I wish to foreground another aspect of Irigaray which has on the whole received little consideration, but which is none the less *also* quite evidently present in her work. For the moment, and at this relatively exploratory stage of interpretation, the question of the possible articulation of these different aspects can perhaps be left to one side.

There are two main readings of Irigaray current in this country. One is that she is a biological essentialist, that she is proclaiming a biologically-given femininity in which biology in some unclear fashion simply 'constitutes' femininity.[3] The other is the Lacanian reading of Irigaray as a 'psychic essentialist', a term coined by Lynne Segal.[4] This reading argues that Irigaray has misunderstood or misrepresented the implications of Lacan's theories,[5] that she takes the feminine to be a pre-given libido, prior to language, in which specific female drives are grounded, thus positing two distinct libidos – a masculine and a feminine. Against this pseudo-Irigaray, it is then argued that Lacan has shown that 'there is no feminine outside language'[6] and that Irigaray has not grasped the Lacanian Symbolic dimension and what it means for the construction of sexual difference. There is a third reading, which seems to be mostly found in North American feminism, according to which Irigaray is celebrating relationships between women in which identities are merged and indistinct.[7]

I am not going to attempt to deal here with the charge of biological essentialism. I have indicated elsewhere[8] why this dismissive reading is unsatisfactory, though I think that the essentialist/anti-essentialist issue is one which needs to be re-examined, and not reduced, as it often now is, to a battle of epithets.[9] Very briefly, it assumes that Irigaray posits an unmediated causal relation between biological sex and sexual identity, leaving out completely the imaginary dimension, in which sexual identity may be related in an unstable and shifting way to the anatomical body, or the symbolic, linguistic dimension, in which sexual identity may be constructed. Secondly, biological essentialism (in the form in which it is usually attributed to Irigaray) is a deterministic and often simplistic thesis which makes change impossible to explain, whereas in my view Irigaray is a theorist of change. I do not wish to deny that there are problems and contradictions in Irigaray's text, but I do wish to reject the implicit presupposition that she takes no account of the linguistic, social, or cultural determinants of the meaning and construction of gender; that is to say, the presupposition that she takes no account of the symbolic. Both the second and third readings confuse description with prescription. They do not recognize that Irigaray is not a pre-Lacanian but a post-Lacanian, who is confronting the implications of Lacan's work, while seeking to expose its patriarchal bias.

So whether she is celebrated for her new vision of the feminine, or attacked for it, both readings miss an essential dimension of her work – the stress on the determining power of the symbolic order. As a general statement of my position, I shall summarize it by suggesting that one reason why she has been dismissed so summarily by the Lacanians is that they take her to be doing no more than providing an alternative account of female psycho-sexual development. For example, she is coupled with Michèle Montrelay, who is writing something far more limited in scope. In fact, Irigaray has a highly ambitious project: she is attempting to begin to dismantle from within the foundations of western metaphysics.

A note on terminology. I shall be referring on several occasions to the unsymbolized mother/daughter relationship. By describing this relationship as unsymbolized, Irigaray means that there is an absence of linguistic, social, cultural, iconic, theoretical, mythical, religious, or any other representations of that relationship. One can readily think of examples of the mother/son relationship, enshrined in Christian doctrine. Irigaray argues that we have to go back to Greek mythology – Demeter and Persephone, for example – to find available, culturally embodied representations of the mother/daughter relationship. This does not mean that there are none – the feminist movement has been resuscitating and/or creating literary and artistic representations of relations between women, and one can certainly find denigratory versions (such as the wicked stepmother) – but they are not adequate: they afford women 'too few figurations, images, or representations by which to represent herself'.[10]

The mother/daughter relationship

Irigaray claims explicitly that the unsymbolized relationship between mother and daughter constitutes a threat to the patriarchal symbolic order as we know it: 'The mother–daughter relationship is the *dark continent* of the *dark continent*.'[11] 'The relationship between mother/daughter, daughter/mother constitutes an extremely explosive kernel in our societies. To think it, to change it, amounts to undermining [*ébranler*] the patriarchal order.'[12] Why should this be so? Because an unsymbolized mother/daughter relationship hinders women from having an identity in the symbolic order that is distinct from the maternal function, and thus prevents them from constituting any real threat to the order of western metaphysics, described by Irigaray as the metaphysics of the Same. They remain 'residual', 'defective men', 'objects of exchange', and so on. So Irigaray insists that:

> from a feminine locus nothing can be articulated without a questioning of the symbolic itself.[13]

> For, without the exploitation of the body-matter of women, what would become of the symbolic process that governs society?[14]

> The culture, the language, the imaginary and the mythology in which we live at present ... let us look at what foundation this edifice is built on....
>   This underpinning is woman reproducer of the social order, acting as the infrastructure of that order; all of western culture rests upon the murder of the mother.... And if we make the foundation of the social order shift, then everything shifts.[15]

The alternative to not threatening the patriarchal symbolic order is for women to remain, in the absence of symbolization, in a state of *déréliction*: this term, which is much stronger in French than in English, connotes for example the state of being abandoned by God[16] or, in mythology, the state of an Ariadne, abandoned on Naxos, left without hope, without help, without refuge. Women are abandoned outside the symbolic order; they lack mediation in the symbolic for the operations of sublimation.[17] Irigaray explains clearly in *Speculum*, using Freud's lecture on femininity as an exemplary text, why the difficulty for women of performing the operations of sublimation arises precisely from the unsymbolized relation between mother and daughter.

Now the practical question for feminism, as Irigaray sees it, is how to construct a female sociality (*les femmes entre-elles*), a female symbolic, and a female social contract: a horizontal relation *between* women,[18] so that women are no longer left in this state of dereliction. Attempts to do so have revealed the discrepancy between the idealization of women's nature found in some radical feminist writing and the actual hostilities and dissensions engendered *within* the women's movement itself. Irigaray suggests that it may be impossible to negotiate the problems thrown up by the horizontal relationship without attending to the vertical relationship, that prototypical relationship between mother and daughter. And it may be impossible to do the latter – collectively at any rate – within the present symbolic order. I will return to this point later.

Here first are some of the features which Irigaray enumerates of the problems which women face in attempting to create a female social and symbolic order. It will be seen that she does not, unlike certain radical feminist accounts, attribute any special 'natural' virtues to women, and that there is no suggestion that communities of women – at least within the present order and before any changes are made – will automatically be idyllic or irenical spaces from which conflict, aggression, or destruction have been excluded. So women are prey to:

- interminable rivalry between women (even if undeclared). This is because: 'since the place of the mother is unique, to become a mother would mean occupying this place, but without a relation *with her in this place.*'[19] 'Love for the mother, for women, perhaps must only or could only exist in the form of a *substitution*? Of a taking her place? Which is unconsciously suffused with hate?'[20]
- permanent risk of destruction in the absence of a female symbolic[21]
- the cruelty which takes place when relations are not mediated by anything, whether by rites, by exchanges or by an economy,[22] so women often become the agents of their own oppression and mutual self-destruction [*anéantissement*][23]
- various forms of pathology: flight, explosion, implosion (all forms of immediacy)[24]
- murder: 'Thus a sort of international vendetta is set up, present more or less everywhere, which disorientates the female populace, the groups and micro-societies which are in the process of being formed. Real murders take place as a part of it, but also (insofar as they can be distinguished), cultural murders, murders of minds, emotions and intelligence, which women perpetuate amongst themselves.'[25]

To summarize all this, one could say that women suffer from 'drives without any possible representatives or representations',[26] which, for Irigaray, is another way of saying that the relation between mother and daughter is unsymbolized. The problems do not arise from immutable characteristics of women's 'nature', but are an effect of women's position relative to the symbolic order as its 'residue',[27] or its 'waste'.[28] A picture which superficially resembles a stereotypically misogynistic version of women's psychology is in fact attempting to state the conditions under which, say, hate or envy or rivalry might be both operative and inescapable in relations between women – because a way of negotiating them symbolically was not available – and to attribute such unmediated feelings directly to the way in which 'woman' figures in the discourses of metaphysics and society.

A more familiar way of putting the issue would be so say that women suffer from inability to individuate themselves, from 'confusion of identity between them',[29] from lack of respect for, or more often lack of perception of, the other woman as different.[30] The problem of individuation for women is a theme known to us from Nancy Chodorow's work on object-relations theory in relation to women, so it might seem as though we are here on familiar ground. However, the aims and presuppositions of Chodorow and Irigaray are quite different.

Chodorow explains that, at an unconscious level, women often never separate sufficiently from their mother; their identity never becomes distinct from that of their mother, and they remain, unconsciously, in a state of merging or fusion in which it is impossible for them to distinguish between their own feelings and those of their mother:

> Mothers tend to experience their daughters as more like, and continuous with, themselves. Correspondingly, girls tend to remain part of the dyadic primary mother–child relationship itself. This means that a girl continues to experience herself as involved in issues of merging and separation, and in an attachment characterized by primary identification and the fusion of identification and object choice. By contrast, mothers experience their sons as a male opposite. Boys are more likely to have been pushed out of the preoedipal relationship, and to have had to curtail their primary love and sense of empathic tie with their mother. A boy has engaged, and been required to engage, in a more emphatic individuation and a more defensive firming of experienced ego boundaries. Issues of differentiation have become intertwined with sexual issues.[31]

> As long as women mother, we can expect that a girl's preoedipal period will be longer than that of a boy and that women, more than men, will be open to and preoccupied with those very relational issues that go into mothering – feelings of primary identification, lack of separateness or differentiation, ego and body-ego boundary issues.[32]

As a phenomenological description, Chodorow's account is most persuasive.[33] However, from the standpoint which Irigaray adopts, there would be a number of problems with her theory. First, Chodorow does not present the construction of sexual identity as a problem; she does not deal with the unstable nature of sexual identity in the unconscious, and so tends to equate sexual with biological or social identity.[34] Second, because she is uncritical of the discourse of psychoanalysis, she is unable to confront the way in which psychoanalytic theory itself reproduces the structure of sexual difference as it is deployed in western thought. Third, when envisaging possible ways in which the situation of women could be changed, she makes only a token gesture in the direction of the collectivity; her solution of shared parenting is a familial rather than a social solution, because she is offering a predominantly descriptive account of how individual women acquire the ability to mother. And there is in her picture, implicitly at any rate, a certain inevitability or static quality about the way mothers and daughters relate to each other, as though the *only* way to stave off the suffocating merging of identities were for the father to become involved in parenting too.

Now, Irigaray accepts the clinical view that women have difficulty in separating from their mothers, that they tend to form relationships in which identity is merged, and in which the boundaries between self and other are not clear. However, she presents this psychoanalytic data as a symptom or result of women's position in the symbolic order, and it is this order which she is primarily concerned to expose. She argues for example that the clinical picture also applies to metaphysics; in metaphysics, too, women are not individuated: there is only *the place of the mother*, or the *maternal function*.

Whereas the fundamental ontological category for men is *habiter* (dwelling), whether in a literal or figurative sense: men live in 'grottoes, huts, women, towns, language, concepts, theories, etc.',[35] women's ontological status in this culture is *déréliction*, the state of abandonment, described significantly in the same terms (*un fusionnel*) as the psychoanalytic term for women's failure to individuate and differentiate themselves from their mother. Dereliction is defined as 'a state of fusion [*un fusionnel*] which does not succeed in emerging as a subject'.[36] So, Irigaray explains:

If women don't have access to society and to culture:
– they remain in a state of dereliction in which they neither recognise or love themselves/each other;
– they lack mediation for the operations of sublimation;
– love is impossible for them.[37]

It is necessary for a symbolism to be created among women in order for there to be love between them. This love is in any case only possible at the moment between women who can speak to each other. Without that interval of *exchange*, or of words, or of gestures, passions between women manifest themselves in a ... rather cruel way.[38]

they need language, a language. That house of language which for men even constitutes a substitute for his home in a body, ... woman is used to construct it, but (as a result?) it is not available to her.[39]

It is *confusion of identity*, then, that leads to pathological phenomena in relations between women. And fusional, non-individuated relationships are a symptom of dereliction. So one must be wary of how one describes what 'feminine' it is that Irigaray is celebrating. When Irigaray describes the female imaginary in *This Sex* as plural, non-identical, multiple, '*neither one nor two*', this is not a recommendation that relationships between women in the real world should be of the kind described by Chodorow as fusional or merged. The imaginary is plural because it is fragmented, in bits and pieces: 'scraps, uncollected debris.'[40] The following remarks from Irigaray's 1975 seminar at Toulouse University should help to clarify this point:

In this connection, I would like to raise another ... question: do women rediscover their pleasure in this 'economy' of the multiple? When I ask what may be happening on the women's side, I am certainly not seeking to wipe out multiplicity, since women's pleasure does not occur without that. But isn't *a multiplicity that does not entail a rearticulation of the difference between the sexes* bound to block or take away something of women's pleasure? In other words, is the feminine capable, at present, of attaining this desire, which is *neutral* precisely from the viewpoint of sexual difference? Except by miming masculine desire once again. And doesn't the 'desiring machine' still partly take the place of woman and the feminine? Isn't it a sort of metaphor for her/it, that men can use? Especially in terms of their relation to the techno-cratic?[41]

To turn the 'body without organs' into a 'cause' of sexual pleasure, isn't it necessary to have had a relation to language and to sex – to the organs – that women have never had?[42]

This warning about the interpretation of multiplicity is echoed in the following remarks on the mother/daughter relationship, where the 'neither one nor two' of an earlier essay is shown to be, not a desirable and delightful state of fluid identity, but a pathological symptom of a cultural discourse in which the relation between mother and daughter cannot be adequately articulated:

But there is no possibility whatsoever, within the current logic of sociocultural operations, for a daughter to situate herself with respect to her mother: because, strictly speaking, they make neither one nor two, neither has a name, meaning, sex of her own, neither can be 'identified' with respect to the other.... How can the relationship between these two women be articulated? Here 'for example' is one place where the need for another 'syntax', another 'grammar' of culture is crucial.[43]

I think therefore it is necessary to insist that statements about the female imaginary be looked at again and reread in the light of Irigaray's critique of metaphysics and its discourse.[44] I shall indicate in the final section some of the reasons why I think that the female imaginary is a concept which is both labile and refractory, liable to twist and turn in the hands, or theory, of the user.

Women's relation to origin: *Speculum*

I turn now to the Lacanian interpretation. One of the central claims made, for example, is that according to Irigaray women have specific feminine drives which return them to the real of the maternal body.[45] Now the real of the maternal body, in Lacanian terminology, means psychosis or foreclosure. So Laplanche and Pontalis, glossing Lacan, define foreclosure as follows: 'Foreclosure consists in not symbolising what should have been symbolised.'[46] What is odd about such an interpretation of Irigaray is that it is raising against her as an objection the very point that she makes herself.[47] Irigaray writes repeatedly and consistently that the problem for women lies in the *non-symbolization* of the relation to the mother and to the mother's body, and that this threatens women with psychosis.[48] The Lacanians take Irigaray to be talking about feminine specificity at the level of the drives, whereas I take her to be talking about feminine specificity at the level of the symbolic, or representation. Although some of her formulations could readily be taken to support the Lacanian interpretation, my view is that, in everything she has written, she has been addressing herself to the symbolic and not to the innate. So I want now to look at the analysis of the conceptualization of the mother/daughter relationship in *Speculum* to illustrate this point, and in particular to look at the question of the desire for, and relation to origin, and the loss of origin inherent in becoming a subject.

Jacqueline Rose states that, for Irigaray, 'Women are *returned*, therefore, in the account and to each other – against the phallic term but also against the loss of origin which Lacan's account is seen to imply.'[49] Now look at the way Irigaray discusses the question of the loss of origin. Discussing Freud's essay on 'Femininity' in his *New Introductory Lectures on Psychoanalysis*, Irigaray makes a point about Freud's interpretation of clinical evidence. When the small girl's playing with dolls can be seen as evidence of a desire for a penis, this is interpreted as a manifestation of femininity. When playing with dolls is clearly the child representing to herself her relation to her mother, this is interpreted by Freud as *phallic*.[50] So that for the girl to represent to herself her relation to her mother is not a manifestation of her femininity.[51] Now, it is obviously not a matter of deciding whether Freud's interpretation is correct. How would one decide what constituted a manifestation of femininity, unless one believed one already knew what femininity was? Irigaray comments that it is rather the case that the girl-child 'exiles herself from, or is banned from a *primary metaphorization* of her, female, desire in order to inscribe herself in that of the boy-child, which is phallic'.[52] I think one can see how comments of this kind *could* be taken to imply the two-libido thesis, and lead to the interpretation of essentialism. The vital point, however, seems to me to be the impossibility of a *primary metaphorization*, that is, the language in which one represents desire to oneself. Unless one accepts the need for women to be able to represent their relation to the mother, and so to origin, in a specific way, i.e. not according to a masculine model, then women will always find themselves devalued. Neutral/universal/single-sex models always turn out to be implicitly male ones. So I interpret statements about female desire or female specificity as statements about *representation*.

Irigaray again:

In fact this desire for re-presentation, for re-presenting oneself in desire is in some ways *taken away from woman at the outset* as a result of the radical devalorization of her 'beginning' that she is inculcated with, subjected to – and to which she subjects herself: is she not born of a castrated mother who could only give birth to a castrated child, even though she prefers (to herself) those who bear the penis? This shameful beginning must therefore be forgotten, 'repressed' – but can one speak at this stage of repression when the processes that make it possible have not yet come into being? Even if woman is sexually repressed, this does not mean that she actively achieved this repression – in order to defer to a valid [*valeureuse*] representation of origin.[53]

The girl, indeed, has nothing more to fear since she has *nothing* to lose. Since she has no representation of what she might fear to lose. Since what she might, potentially, lose, has no value.[54]

Irigaray points out that if one reads in tandem Freud's description of the girl's psychic development after her discovery that she is 'castrated' and that her mother is also 'castrated', with the account of the difference between mourning and melancholia, one discovers that many of the characteristics of melancholia can be mapped on to Freud's description of the state of the little girl. The girl-child in certain respects remains in a state of melancholia; she can never accomplish the work of mourning the loss of the object, because she has *no representation of what has been lost*. As a result, 'the little girl's separation from her mother, and from her sex,[55] cannot be worked through by mourning'.[56] Irigaray insists on the fact that the impossibility of mourning arises from the fact that the girl-child cannot grasp consciously what it is that has been lost, so she cannot mourn it: 'In more ways than one, it is really a question for her of a "loss" that radically escapes any representation.'[57] In this process, the little girl may identify with the lost object that can never be found.[58] (Identification with a lost or abandoned object that cannot even be represented is then another form of women's dereliction.) Freud states that in melancholia, the work of mourning is hindered by the (unconscious) ambivalence, both love and hate, which the person feels for the lost object. Connecting this with the description of the little girl in Freud's account, Irigaray writes:

Now, the relation of the daughter to her mother is not without ambivalence, and becomes even more complicated when the little girl realises that her mother is castrated, while the person to whom her love was addressed was – according to Freud – a phallic mother. This devalorisation of the mother accompanies or follows, for the little girl, that of her sexual organs. As a result, 'the relation to the (lost) object is no simple one in her case; it is complicated by the conflict due to ambivalence', 'which remains withdrawn from consciousness'. To which it should be added that no language, no system of representations, will be available to replace, or stand in for [*suppléer, assister*] the 'unconsciousness' in which the conflictual relations which the daughter has with her mother and with her sexual organs, remain. As a result we get the 'reminiscences' in the form of somatic complaints that are characteristic of melancholia? Of hysteria as well, of course....[59]

It is not simply, as a psychoanalyst might say, that because women lack a penis it is more difficult for them to symbolize lack. The boy-child, with his penis *but also* with a system of representations which is phallic, can more readily symbolize the loss of origin. The girl-child has available to her no adequate representations of 'what she might fear to lose', since 'what she might ... lose, has no value'. So Irigaray sums up:

> This 'effective castration' [*castration réalisée*] that Freud accounts for in terms of 'nature', 'anatomy', could equally well, or rather, be interpreted as the impossibility, the prohibition that prevents women ... from ever imagining, conceiving of, representing, or symbolizing ... her own relationship to beginning.[60]

Irigaray goes on to say that these terms – imagining, conceiving, and so on, are all inadequate, because they are part and parcel of the same system of discourse which creates this impossibility, a system in which 'within discourse, the feminine finds itself defined as lack, deficiency, or as imitation and negative image of the subject'.[61]

For what reason does Freud choose to conceptualize the girl's relationship to her mother as phallic rather than as feminine? The reasons Irigaray suggests are twofold. Firstly, at the local level, she suggests that Freud's imaginary (which is also the imaginary of western representation) is anal, that is to say, it does not recognize sexual difference: for Freud, the little girl is a little man, as in the sexual theories or fantasies of children.[62] At a more global level she suggests that Freud's thought is governed by the terms of classical philosophy,[63] what Derrida refers to as the metaphysics of presence.[64] Western representation privileges *seeing*: what you can see (presence) is privileged over what cannot be seen (absence) and guarantees Being, hence the privilege of the penis which is elevated to a phallus: '*Nothing to be seen is equivalent to having no thing. No being and no truth.*'[65] In other words, Irigaray's explanation here is situating itself at the level of ontology: the ontological status assigned to women in western metaphysics is equivalent to the status assigned to them by an imaginary that does not recognize sexual difference. Again:

> No attempt will be made by the little girl – nor by the mother? nor by the woman? – to symbolise the status of [*ce qu'il en serait de*] this 'nothing' to be seen, to defend what is at stake, to claim its value/worth. Here again, there seems to be no possible economy whereby her sexual reality could be represented by/for the woman.[66]

Irigaray is not the only person to point to the primacy of *seeing* in Freud's account of the castration complex, but the problems with this have been identified by many others: it seems to make the castration complex dependent upon a contingency (whether or not one happens to see); and second, as Lacan points out, there can be nothing 'missing' in the real.[67] For Irigaray it is indicative of a metaphysics, in which the symbolic representations, which might enable women to perform certain symbolic operations of sublimation, are absent. For this reason, Irigaray makes the claim that what is needed is a female symbolic. What would this mean? In the first place, it would imply an interpretation which symbolizes the relation between the girl-child and her mother in a way which allows the mother to be both a mother *and* a woman, so that women are not forever competing for the unique *place* occupied by the mother, so that women can differentiate themselves from their mother, and so that women are not reduced to the maternal function. But on a collective, as opposed to an individual level, this is not so straightforward as it sounds, for if the present symbolic order is bound up with a complete metaphysical structure, as Irigaray suggests in *Speculum*, then collectively it would mean an attempt to turn the symbolic order inside out. Irigaray herself says that women need a religion, a language, and a currency of exchange or a non-market economy of their own.[68] It is not an agenda that could conceivably be implemented by any one individual.

The imaginary and the symbolic

In this final section, I wish to raise some of the problems I've come up against in trying to elucidate what we are to understand by the ideas of a female imaginary, female symbolic, female language, female rationality, and so on.

I will begin with the imaginary. The problem can be stated as follows: if identity is imaginary, and if identity – as Irigaray insists – is male,[69] then either the idea of a female imaginary is self-contradictory, or else the female imaginary in so far as it attributes identity to the female side of sexual difference, would still fall within the parameters of male thought, i.e. would be a male definition of the female. As I argued in the first section, some writers on Irigaray have tried to deal with this difficulty too summarily, by a precipitate celebration of the female imaginary, which bypasses the problem of its existence (whether it exists and what kind of existence it might have) within the present symbolic order. The imaginary can be described in more than one way. (a) The female imaginary can be seen as the unconscious of western (male) thought – the unsymbolized, repressed underside of western philosophy. In this sense, it falls under the description in *This Sex*: it is plural, because it is 'scraps, uncollected debris',[70] an imaginary which consists of the residues or remnants left over by the structuration of the imaginary by a dominant symbolic order. It may make its presence felt in the form of 'somatic complaints'. (b) But there is another sense in which the female imaginary could be understood as something which does not yet exist, which still has to be created.[71] This would be a non-essentialist thesis; the female imaginary would be, not something lurking in the depths of women's unconscious, but a possible restructuring of the imaginary by the symbolic which would make a difference to women. We have the problem here of stating what it is that women need which would not leave them in dereliction – unsymbolized – but which would not be thought of either simply in terms of identity, since an identity that is equivalent to sameness is an integral part of the metaphysics which represses the female. For this reason, I think that one cannot think the female imaginary without thinking the female symbolic. Irigaray has been criticized for failing to make a clear distinction between the two, but this may be because the two go hand in hand. (c) It is clear then that it is difficult to limit the term 'imaginary' to the unconscious phantasy of any one individual, though the term is used in this way in *Speculum*. But as soon as Irigaray begins to use the term more extensively, in *This Sex*, and *Ethique*, it is applied to a social, cultural, and philosophical fantasy, implied by the symbolic order in which we live: the unconscious phantasies of the dominant discourse and their concrete embodiments. One should conceive of the creation of a female imaginary, then, as a collective process.

The symbolic can also be interpreted in more than one way. First, it can be taken in a more or less developmental sense (though with qualifications): it is the order of discourse and meaning, the order into which all human beings have to insert themselves and which therefore precedes and exceeds individual subjectivity; it is what enables the subject to break out of the imaginary mother–child unity and become a social being. But more importantly, it can be interpreted in a structural sense, as that which enables the break from the imaginary to be made at all, at any time. It is clear that the social human being continues to function for most of the time in an imaginary register, locked into various unconscious phantasies, which may or may not find support in one's social or interpersonal world. Irigaray makes this point when she writes for example that the present symbolic order is completely imaginary: 'The symbolic that you impose as a universal, free of all empirical or historical contingency, is *your* imaginary transformed into an order, a social order.'[72] (The 'you' she is addressing is 'Messieurs les psychanalystes'.) She makes a similar point when she writes that the 'subject of science', the epistemological subject, has not made the break, but is still dominated by a *male* imaginary. Or again, when she explains that western metaphysics is governed by an anal imaginary. The crucial problem then becomes: how to effect the break from the imaginary. Teresa Brennan points out that is can be effected in two ways; either external reality obstinately refuses to match the phantasy, or, in psychoanalysis, the analyst refuses the imaginary projections of the analysand.[73] It is relatively easy to see how this function might be carried out by the analyst. It is rather more difficult to see how a female symbolic might be created which would serve the function of 'break' to the male imaginary in external reality. I will return to this question in a moment.

It looks, then, as though one needs to think two things simultaneously. The first is that the female symbolic depends upon a female imaginary. If one attempts to bypass the question of the female at the level of the imaginary, by moving directly into the symbolic – stating for example that women are capable of reason too, or pointing out that the fact that the phallus is the signifier of difference does not imply any inevitable oppression of women within the symbolic and social order[74] – then one is relying upon a most precarious position; the break from the imaginary, which is the structural sense of the symbolic, may not have any support in the social; social institutions continue to support the phantasies of the male imaginary. If one abandons the imaginary to the male, women will still be left without *representations* or *images* or, one might add, institutions, to serve as identificatory support.[75] But if a female symbolic depends upon a female imaginary, it is also the case that a female imaginary depends upon a female symbolic. The imaginary is an *effect* of the symbolic; it is the symbolic which structures the imaginary, so that there is a sense in which the imaginary does not exist if it is unsymbolized – one may not even be able to say that it is repressed: 'can one speak at this stage of repression when the processes that make it possible have not yet come into being?'[76]

Now this idea of a female symbolic is obviously problematic, even if it is put in social and philosophical rather than psychoanalytic terms; some people would say it is not even coherent. One thing I would suggest is that for Irigaray, *the* symbolic, that is to say, that break with the imaginary in which one is capable of thinking *about* one's own imaginary instead of being thought *by* it, is unlikely to take a social form so long as there is no real *other*. At the moment, according to Irigaray, what we have is an economy of the Same, exchange between men – the same, male imaginary with nothing to act as the 'break', *except women*. In other words, for men to make the break with *their* imaginary, another term would be needed women as symbolic. So long as women continue to be *objects of exchange* within that imaginary, they cannot be the term that effects the break. There is a symbolic castration which men have yet to effect: cutting the umbilical cord which links them to the mother. And they will only be able to do this when it becomes possible to distinguish between the mother and the woman, when the relation between mother and daughter is symbolized.

Another way of understanding this might be through the idea, developed by Teresa Brennan, that 'social relations can either oppose or reinforce psychical products'.[77] Let us assume, for the sake of argument, that the male imaginary, or what Lacan calls the 'psychical fantasy of women', or the child's belief that there is only one sex, that all these are transhistorical factors. Then one direction for action would have to be the construction of social relations which *oppose* this imaginary, for instance the construction of a women's sociality, or representations of women which directly counter it. There is no reason why the social should automatically be no more nor less than the psyche writ large, and to assume so would be to collapse the social into the psychic.[78] The crucial question, of course, and one which can *only* be addressed collectively, is that of how to make changes in the symbolic.

So the question of the imaginary and its relation to the symbolic, however one interprets these terms, directly raises the question of change, and how it might be brought about. For Irigaray, I believe it is not a question of *knowledge* (a new 'theory of women'),[79] but, above all, a question of change. The 'subject of science' is male, meaning that male language, the epistemology of the sciences, knowledge which leads to control, mastery, and domination, are all subtended by the male imaginary, whatever the actual sex of the knower. Female language on the other hand, like the language of the psychoanalyst, should be language *which has an effect*: 'to reintroduce the values of desire, pain, joy, the body. Living values. Not discourses of mastery.'[80] Women are being asked to refuse, like the psychoanalyst, the imaginary constructions of the 'male' subject. Irigaray is attempting to restore the link between knowledge and its origins in the passions, raising the question: 'What is knowledge for?' Her project, then, which she defines in very broad terms as 'psychoanalysing the philosophers'[81] is to use the methods of the psychoanalyst as a heuristic and epistemological instrument, in an attempt to change the social imaginary of the west by dismantling the defences, undoing the work of repression, splitting and disavowal, restoring links and connections, and putting the 'subject of science' in touch with the unacknowledged mother.

Without doubt, there are problems with the attempt to use the psychoanalytic conceptual framework to make cultural diagnoses – and this is one area that further discussion of Irigaray's work could well focus on, bearing in mind that, whatever the status of psychoanalytic theories, psychoanalysis as *therapy* works to bring about change in the unconscious itself. But for the moment, I'd just like to conclude by summarizing again what seems to me to be central to Irigaray's diagnosis: in psychoanalysing the philosophers, she claims to have discovered that the order of discourse in the west, its rationality and epistemology, are supported by an imaginary that is in effect governed unconsciously by one of the 'sexual theories of children', the phantasy that there is only one sex, that that sex is male, and that therefore women are really men, in a defective, 'castrated' version. In this imaginary, the mother is at best only a function. Irigaray suggests that symbolizing the mother/daughter relationship, creating *externally located* and *durable* representations of this prototypical relation between women, is an urgent necessity, if women are ever to achieve ontological status in this society. As Lucienne Serrano and Elaine Hoffman Baruch put it in 1983, 'While many feminists are minimalists, denying sexual differences beyond the purely reproductive, Irigaray might be called a maximalist.'[82] She wants to give sexual difference an ethical and ontological status. To aim for a state 'beyond sexual difference' could only maintain the 'neutral' or 'universal' that conceals the male, and the status of women in our society would continue to be secondary, she argues. The feminine should have a transcendental status too. Rather than minimizing sexual difference, she thinks the only way forward is to assert it; and that the only way in which the status of women could be fundamentally altered is by the creation of a powerful female symbolic to represent the *other* against the omnipresent effects of the male imaginary.

Notes

1 Luce Irigaray, *Le Langage des déments* (The Hague: Mouton, 1973).
2 Kuykendall, Eléanor, 'Toward an ethic of nurturance: Luce Irigaray on Mothering and Power', in Joyce Trebilcot (ed.), *Mothering: Essays in Feminist Theory* (Totowa, NJ: Rowman & Allanheld, 1984), pp. 269–70.
3 See Janet Sayers, *Biological Politics: Feminist and Anti-Feminist Perspectives* (London: Tavistock, 1982), p. 131; Janet Sayers, *Sexual Contradictions: Psychology, Psychoanalysis, and Feminism* (London: Tavistock, 1986). pp. 42–8. Janet Sayers claims that for Irigaray 'Femininity ... is essentially constituted by female biology, by the "two lips" of the female sex' (*Biological Politics*, p,131), and assimilates Irigaray to Adrienne Rich (1986, pp. 42 and 47) in a startling but not unusual example of complete theoretical decontextualization. The problem of the over-literalist reading of Irigaray is exemplified by Kate McLuskie, who stands Irigaray on her head and suggests that she is putting forward an 'anatomical determinism' which rules out the need for language (in fact the *reverse* of Irigaray's main thesis, as I hope to show in this paper): '[Irigaray] is able to deny the need for language ... there is no need for the symbolic substitution which language provides', expostulating that 'To relinquish that function of language would be to return to the ghetto of inarticulate female intuition' (Kate McLuskie, 'Women's language and literature: a problem in women's studies', *Feminist Review* 14 (Summer 1983) pp. 57–8). Like Sayers, McLuskie focuses on the 'two lips' which seem to prove a stumbling block for many readers. For counter-readings of the 'two lips', see Jane Gallop, *'Quand nos lèvres s'écrivent*: Irigaray's body politic', *Romanic Review* 74 (1983), pp. 77–83, and Jan Montefiore, *Feminism and Poetry: Language, Experience, Identity in Women's Writing* (London: Pandora, 1987).The latter points out that 'This metaphor of "two lips" is *not* a definition of women's identity in biological terms: the statement that they are "continually interchanging" must make it clear that Irigaray is not talking about literal biology' (p. 149). Gallop argues that just as the phallus is a symbolic term, with a reference to the body admittedly, but without having itself a biological referent, so Irigaray is using the two lips as an alternative symbolic term. It is perhaps helpful to bear in mind Irigaray's self-proclaimed stance as a 'poetic' writer, and her desire to reject a hard and fast distinction between 'theory' and 'fiction' (see *Le Corps-à-corps avec la mère* (Montreal: Editions de la pleine lune, 1981), p. 45). Biological essentialism, as I understand it, is a critique made primarily from a socialist–feminist or Marxist–feminist position. It is the fear that Irigaray is basing her work on a definition of feminine specificity and thereby positing a femininity which is not constructed by society and which would therefore fall outside the realm in which one may work for change – in particular, changes in the status or position of women in society. It is the fear that, as Lynne Segal puts it in a recent state-of-feminism book: 'The writings of Irigaray are most readily interpreted as strengthening and celebrating traditional gender ideologies of fundamental biological difference between women and men' (Lynne Segal, *Is the Future Female? Troubled Thoughts on Contemporary Feminism* (London: Virago, 1987), p. 133). Feminists who take this position are usually arguing for us to work towards a society in which sexual and sexist stereotypes will disappear.

The emphasis is placed on the social practices which create masculinity and femininity. I shall be arguing in this paper that Irigaray is *also* addressing herself to the construction of femininity by the symbolic. For me, the main difference between the socialist–feminist position and Irigaray's is located in the area of strategy and is to do with how change is effected. Very broadly, the socialist–feminist position would argue that changes in the symbolic follow from changes in the material; if you work to bring about changes in women's social status and social institutions, then masculinity and femininity will come to have quite different meanings, or perhaps will disappear altogether as sexual stereotypes. Irigaray's position is that one cannot alter women's symbolic status in this way. One cannot so easily change symbolic meanings, because they have an imaginary foundation which persists despite material changes. Instead of working towards undermining the masculine/feminine distinction, she wants to strengthen the feminine side of the pair through the creation of a female 'world', a female symbolic which would act as a counterweight to the male one. She would argue that if the feminine is not supported by specifically feminine social institutions, then it will always be swallowed up again by the masculine. Women need to be able to *represent* their difference, whether in language or in another social form (such as an economy or a religion). It is not so much a question of strengthening 'traditional gender ideologies of fundamental biological differences between women and men'; on the contrary, Irigaray argues for the difference between masculine and feminine to be reartic- ulated since, for her too, the problem is what is *built on* those biological differences.

4 Segal, op. cit., p. 132.
5 See, for example, Ellie Ragland-Sullivan, *Jacques Lacan and the Philosophy of Psychoanalysis* (Urbana and Chicago: University of Illinois Press, 1986), p. 273.
6 Jacqueline Rose, *Sexuality in the Field of Vision* (London: Verso, 1986), p. 80.
7 See, for example, Kuykendall, op. cit.
8 Margaret Whitford, 'Luce Irigaray and the female imaginary: speaking as a woman', *Radical Philosophy* 43 (Summer 1986), pp. 3–8; Margaret Whitford, 'Luce Irigaray's critique of rationality', in Morwenna Griffiths and Margaret Whitford (eds), *Feminist Perspectives in Philosophy* (London: Macmillan, 1988).
9 See Rosi Braidotti in this volume for one attempt to grapple seriously with the question of essentialism and feminism.
10 Luce Irigaray, *Speculum: Of the Other Women*, trans. Gillian C. Gill (Ithaca and New York: Cornell University Press, 1985), p. 71. (French edn, *Speculum, de l'autre femme* (Paris: Minuit), p. 85.)
11 *Le Corps-à-corps*, p. 61.
12 ibid., p. 86.
13 Luce Irigaray, *This Sex Which Is Not One*, trans. Catherine Porter with Carolyn Burke (Ithaca and New York: Cornell University Press, 1985), p,162. (French edn, *Ce Sexe qui n'en est pas un* (Paris: Minuit, 1977), p,157.)
14 ibid., p. 85, Fr. p. 81.
15 *Le Corps-à-corps*, p. 81.
16 On the implications for women of the absence of a female divinity, see Luce Irigaray, 'Femmes divines', *Critique* 454 (March 1985), pp. 294–308.
17 Luce Irigaray, *Ethique de la différence sexuelle* (Paris: Minuit, 1984), p. 70.
18 ibid., p. 106.
19 ibid., p. 102; my italics.
20 ibid., p. 100.
21 Luce Irigaray, 'Créer un entre-femmes', interview in *Paris-Feministe* 31/2 (September 1986), p. 38. (First published in *Rinascità*, 28 September 1985).

22 *Ethique*, p. 103.
23 ibid., p. 102.
24 ibid., p. 111.
25 Luce Irigaray, 'Woman, the sacred and money', trans. Diana Knight and Margaret Whitford, *Paragraph* 8 (October 1986), p. 14.
26 *This Sex*, p. 189, Fr. p. 183.
27 ibid., p. 114, Fr. p. 112.
28 ibid., p. 30, Fr. p. 29.
29 *Ethique*, p. 66.
30 ibid.
31 Nancy Chodorow, *The Reproduction of Mothering: Psychoanalysis and the Sociology of Gender* (Berkeley: University of California Press, 1978), pp. 166–7.
32 ibid., p. 110.
33 Other feminist accounts which stress women's difficulty in effecting separation can be found in Luise Eichenbaum and Susie Orbach, *Outside In ... Inside Out. Women's Psychology: A Feminist Psychoanalytic Approach* (Harmondsworth: Penguin, 1982), and Sheila Ernst and Marie Maguire (eds), *Living With the Sphinx: Papers From the Women's Therapy Centre* (London: The Women's Press, 1987)). (See also Julia Kristeva, *Soleil Noir: Dépression et mélancolie* (Paris: Gallimard, 1987). But the fact that they agree on the symptom should not mislead one into concluding that there is any similarity between Irigaray and object-relations theory in their theoretical presuppositions.
34 And see Rose, op. cit., p. 60 n.28.
35 *Ethique*, p. 133.
36 ibid., p. 72.
37 ibid., p. 70.
38 ibid., p. 103.
39 ibid., p. 105.
40 *This Sex*, p. 30 Fr. p. 29.
41 ibid., p. 140–1, Fr. p. 138; first italics mine
42 ibid, p. 141, Fr. p. 139.
43 ibid., p. 143, Fr. p. 140–1.
44 Look for example at the following statements by Kuykendall, op. cit.: 'we can see that an ethic which Irigaray can develop from her perception of women as experiencing ourselves as paralyzed, unable to act, must begin by healing what she believes is a life-destroying breach between mother and daughter' (p. 267). 'The ethical imperative that Irigaray would draw ... is to cease to pursue the psychic separation between mother and daughter required by patriarchy' (p. 267). 'Suppose, then, that we consider the possibility of a matriarchal ethic to replace that patriarchal imperative to separate mother from daughter' (p. 267). These statements are correct, provided that one does not equate the 'patriarchal imperative to separate' with the psychic separation essential for separate identity; what Irigaray regards as life-destroying is the *failure to separate* and the consequent lack of distinction between the identity of the mother and that of the daughter. But in that case, how is one to interpret Kuykendall's statements that 'Recent feminist arguments emphasize recognition rather than equality as a mark of mutuality, and some, like Luce Irigaray's, verge on a conception of mutuality as identity, as in the identity of mother with daughter' (pp. 264–5); or 'But it is not clear, either, what more general interpretation can be offered to support a psychological interpretation of that relationship [between women] as conducive of fusion, rather than separation with the ensuing mutuality and empowerment' (p. 269) which, by taking fusion to be empowerment, simply

claim the opposite of what Irigaray is actually writing? Such imprecision in terminology can only perpetuate misreading. But in more general terms, it is difficult, I think, for the Anglo-American reader familiar with feminist psychoanalytic theory through the work of Chodorow and object-relations theory, to understand what is different in Irigaray's theory unless considerably more theoretical context is supplied. (Cf. Alice Jardine, *Gynesis: Configurations of Woman and Modernity* (Ithaca and London: Cornell University Press, 1985), on the problems of reading French theory out of context.)

See also Susan Rubin Suleiman '(Re)writing the body: the politics and poetics of female eroticism', in Susan Rubin Suleiman (ed.), *The Female Body in Western Culture: Contemporary Perspectives* (Cambridge, Mass.: Harvard University Press, 1986), pp. 7–29. She may not be wrong to write that: '"When Our Lips Speak Together" is a text that celebrates love between women. What is most specific about such a love? ... In the perfect reciprocity of this relation, there is no place for an economy of exchange, or of opposition between contraries. The lovers are neither two nor one, neither different nor the same, but un-different (indifférentes)' (p. 13). But without further explanation, it is difficult for the reader to know exactly what is being celebrated; Suleiman's description could easily be read as an account of what for Irigaray is the *symptom.*

45 Rose, op. cit., p. 79.

46 'Foreclosure', in Jean Laplanche and J.-B. Pontalis, *Vocabulaire de la psychanalyse* (Paris: Presses Universitaires de France, 1967), p. 166. (English edn, *The Language of Psychoanalysis*, trans. David Nicholson-Smith (London: Hogarth Press, 1973).) I have also found André Green, 'The borderline concept', *On Private Madness* (London: Hogarth, 1986), pp. 60–83, helpful as a non-Lacanian discussion of the different mechanisms which might be involved. In particular, Green distinguishes between repression and splitting, and between splitting in psychosis and splitting in borderline disorders. However one conceptualizes the process of non-symbolization which Irigaray discusses in *Speculum* (and which I refer to below), it is clear that it is not repression; as Irigaray points out, 'can one speak at this stage of repression when the processes that make it possible have not yet come into being?' (*Speculum*, p. 84, Fr. p. 101). Some more radical inaccessibility of representation is at work here. What is original about Irigaray's analysis is that she locates it primarily not in the individual psyche but in the symbolic order itself.

47 For example, Ragland-Sullivan, op. cit., writes, against Irigaray:

The particular tragedy, however, for daughters who identify with their mothers along traditional gender and role lines is that they refuse a complete primary Castration (that is, an adequate difference or psychic separation) and thereby accept secondary Castration! By refusing an Oedipal resolution, they value themselves essentially as adjuncts, wives and mothers ... Females ... are doubly castrated: first, by identification with the mother's gender and, second, by deferring to the myths that link that gender with loss. It is hardly surprising, then, that sons feel less ambiguity toward their mothers than do daughters. Male difficulties with the internal (m)Other, on the other hand, are displaced onto other women.

Since Irigaray sees woman as the victim of male mediation, she misses the greater tragedy: that her gender identification with the traditional mother limits her sphere of influence to Imaginary politics and primary (body) narcissism. (p. 302)

Ragland-Sullivan does not recognize that in *Speculum* Irigaray is precisely analysing *the reasons why* daughters 'refuse a complete primary Castration' and *the reasons for* their 'gender identification with the traditional mother'.

48 Cf. *Speculum*, p. 71, Fr. p. 85, and p. 43 n. 26, Fr. p. 47 n. 28.
49 Rose, op. cit., p. 79.
50 Sigmund Freud, *New Introductory Lectures on Psychoanalysis* (Harmondsworth: Penguin, 1973), p. 162.
51 *Speculum*, pp. 77–8, Fr. pp. 92–4.
52 ibid., p. 84, trans. adapted, Fr. p. 101.
53 ibid., pp. 83–4 Fr. p. 101.
54 ibid., p. 84, Fr. p. 102.
55 'sex' translating 'sexe' which can mean either 'sexual organs' or 'sex' as in 'the female sex'.
56 *Speculum*, p. 67, Fr. p. 80.
57 ibid., p. 68, Fr. p. 80.
58 ibid., p. 69, Fr. p. 81–2.
59 ibid., p. 68, trans. adapted, Fr. p. 81. The quotations are Irigaray's, from Freud's 'Mourning and melancholia'.
60 *Speculum*, p. 83, trans. adapted, Fr. pp. 100–1.
61 *The Sex*, p. 78, Fr. p. 76.
62 See Sigmund Freud, *On Sexuality* (Harmondsworth: Penguin, 1977), pp. 183–204. I discuss this in more detail in 'Luce Irigaray's critique of rationality', op. cit.
63 *Speculum*, p. 93, Fr. p. 113.
64 ibid., p. 83, Fr. p. 101.
65 ibid., p. 48, Fr. p. 54, Irigaray's italics.
66 ibid., p. 49, trans. adapted, Fr. p. 56.
67 Quoted in Rose, op. cit., p. 66.
68 'Women, the sacred and money', p. 9.
69 See Irigaray, *Ethique*, pp. 117ff., and Irigaray, *Parler n'est jamais neutre*, (Paris: Minuit, 1985)pp. 311–13.
70 *This Sex*, p. 30, Fr. p. 29.
71 This is the reading given by Montefiore, op. cit.
72 Luce Irigaray, *Parler n'est jamais neutre* p. 269.
73 Teresa Brennan, 'Impasse in psychoanalysis and feminism', in S. Gunew (ed.), *Feminist Knowledge: Critique and Construct* (London: Routledge, forthcoming).
74 This issue is discussed in Jane Gallop, *The Daughter's Seduction: Feminism and Psychoanalysis* (Ithaca and London: Cornell University Press and Macmillan, 1982), ch. 1; Rose, op. cit., pp. 49–81; Brennan, op. cit.
75 In this respect, one might see the work of Derrida, for example, as a cautionary tale. Rose, op. cit., pp. 18–23, points out that in Derrida's work, the woman returns in the classic position of otherness. This danger is also extensively discussed by Jardine, op. cit. See also Rosi Braidotti, 'Ethics revisited: women and/in philosophy', in Carole Pateman and Elizabeth Gross (eds), *Feminist Challenges: Social and Political Theory* (Sydney and London: Allen & Unwin, 1986), who points out that the contemporary male philosopher cannot have precisely the same place of enunciation as the feminist.
76 *Speculum*, p. 84, Fr. p. 101.
77 Brennan, op. cit.
78 On this point, see Rose, op. cit., pp. 1–23, and Brennan, op. cit.
79 Irigaray states that:

In other words, the issue is not one of elaborating a new theory of which women would be the *subject* or the *object*, but of jamming the theoretical machinery itself, of suspending its pretension to the production of a truth and of a meaning that are excessively univocal. Which presupposes that women ... do not claim to be rivalling men in constructing a logic of the feminine that would still take onto-theo-logic as its model, but that they are rather attempting to wrest this question away from the economy of the logos. (*This Sex*, p. 78, Fr. p. 75–6)

80 From the blurb on the cover of *Le Corps-à-corps*.
81 See *This Sex*, p. 75, Fr. p. 74.
82 In Janet Todd (ed.), *Women Writers Talking* (New York and London: Holmes & Meier, 1983), p. 232.

Chapter Seven

The gesture in psychoanalysis

Luce   Irigaray
(Translated by Elizabeth Guild)

Gesture is very rarely discussed in psychoanalytic theory, except by Freud and
the early analysts. Today, the question of gesture seems to be addressed only
by therapies treating psychotics, and children, or by therapeutic practices
derived from psychoanalysis. Yet gesture is an essential part of the conventions[1] of any psychoanalytic practice, as the following examples will show.

   1 In the scene of analysis there are arrangements and mechanisms which
are gestural and which are often neglected in favour of what is verbally
expressed. The patient lies on his back, immobile. According to Freud, the
analyst sits, and he too is immobile. From time to time, he will show signs
of slight activity. Sometimes the patient may too: he or she twists his or her
ring, moves feet or hands, adopts a stereotypical posture which is far from
irrelevant to what he or she is talking about. All of this forms a whole which
must be perceived and treated as such. Furthermore, all of this combines with
the psychoanalyst's gestures to constitute a whole where the gestures of the
one give the lead to the gestures of the other – and of course this dynamic
includes instances in which the analysand's gestures determine the analyst's.
Often it may be necessary for the psychoanalyst to invent gestures which
prevent the economies of the two subjects becoming intricated.

   At first I thought that I would concentrate exclusively on this issue. I imagined that I would explain to you why, for instance, the topology of knitting
or tapestry affords the analyst such intelligent and subtle opportunities both
for listening to a patient, whether male or female, and for preserving the liberty
of both partners in the scene. It has taken me years to discover this, and to
begin to interpret it. I had also envisaged that I would describe to you some
of my discoveries about gesture which have enabled me successfully to conclude the treatment in certain cases. It's fascinating! But wouldn't this put both
me and you, my readers, in an unethical position? For I would in effect be
playing the analyst *acting out,*[2] displaying to you things which must, in my
opinion, remain bound by the rules of professional confidentiality. It's a difficult
question. For years it has stopped me from writing a book on psychoanalytic
clinical practice. I have suggested to my patients, male and female, that they
work with me in the presentation of their analyses. Not a very fruitful

suggestion. Perhaps they wanted to keep their secrets? But they themselves have written about their treatment, elsewhere, more often than not without revealing the name of their analyst. It's true that I am a woman, which must count for something in their reticence. So as concerns psychoanalytic practice, I myself have only presented a few fragments with a view to studying their discursive structures and communicative schemata.[3] This mode of interpretation seems to me a way of making public certain mechanisms of transference, and also of undercutting the inflated power of psychoanalysis which results from the silence shrouding its practice, without however betraying the secret of the analysis. And I doubt that the patients will recognize themselves in the short extracts of their discourse I have used.

So, to respect the psychoanalytic ethic, and above all to respect my patients, I shall, rather, review those gestures which are present in any and every analysis, starting, again, with that gesture which is a necessary part of the analytic setting [*praticable*], and which has taken over from the hypnotic method: the one (originally female) lying on her back; the other seated; lying down, with the analyst sitting behind, back turned or at an angle, rather than fact-to-face. These two parameters: not facing, lying down, disturb not only social conventions but also the individual's relation to linguistic signs. For, habitually, the relation between the production of linguistic signs and the choice and constitution of their sense is orthogonal. The psychoanalytic posture prevents this type of production. What annoys or distresses the patient (male or female) who is lying down is, initially, the impossibility of producing a meaning, or even a word, which is exact, and which has meaning in and for the present. This scene is designed for *remembering*. The patient remembers, or rambles, or entrusts the truth of his utterance to the analyst, whose position is orthogonal to him.[4] Moreover the patient cannot send a *message* which is meaningful in the present either, because the identities of the speaker, the listener, the world – or , in other terms, of the subject, the addressee, the object – are not fixed. The economy of discourse and communication is thus disturbed. After hypnosis, Freud immersed the (originally female) patient in language and in the familiar relations of exchange. From the start of the session, or sessions, the patient was removed from his or her habits as a speaking subject, from his or her systems of representational, social, and familial relations. The patient is not really hypnotized, but, rather, immersed in language and in his or her history as though in another self and yet the same as himself or herself (a horizon, a territory, a veil, clouds, an ocean ...), in a self which he or she does not know. And it is not easy for him or her to build himself or herself gangways or bridges by which to escape, deprived as he or she is of the power *in the present* to produce *meaningful* discourse. Understandably enough, this position may be experienced as an aggression, for that is what it is. On the other hand, if the analyst is skilled, whilst this may be aggression it will not involve the same assumption of power as hypnosis. It is a necessary transition: the patient must make this journey back through his or her language. The patient has come to analysis because he or she is suffering. Here he or she is not allowed to simulate normal behaviour (in so far as any such thing exists). He or she is brought to a halt, in order to reconstitute his or her discourse differently. I mean discourse broadly speaking, including gesture. Clearly it is not a question of teaching the subject a new code, or a doctrine, for instance; rather, it is a question of helping him or her to, in Heidegger's words, build his or her house of language. Jacques Lacan probably owes his definition of the unconscious to just this conception of the link between the subject and language. The phrase: 'the unconscious is structured like a language' is very close to Heidegger's: 'Man acts as though he were the shaper and master of language, while in fact language remains the master of man'[5]

2 Thus the scene of psychoanalysis is defined by a configuration of gestures alien to any other situation. And are these gestural arrangements and mechanisms the same for men and women alike? Are they identical for different sexes? And identical whether the analyst is a member of the same sex as the patient or not? No. Why? For a very simple reason: the sexual connotations of lying down are different, depending on whether one is a man or a woman. In an erotic situation, it quite often happens that a man will say to a woman: 'Lie down', or else, he will make her lie down. This social convention, I might add, leads occasionally to cases of rape by analysts of their female analysands. Between women and men it is rare that the woman will make the 'man's' move, except for the gesture within therapeutic practice. Between members of the same sex, the connotations are more fluid.

Psychoanalytic practice is gesturally quite distinctive, in terms of discursive and communicative practice, in a way which is not neutral.[6] It will vary, its variants sexed according to the sex of the partners. The patients are sexed, they have a sexed past and present; likewise the analyst. It seems that sexologists still have a more unsexed than sexed mentality. I wonder where this so-called neutral mentality comes from. Is it a puritanism, religious in origin? Or does it come from lack of information? Thus for instance most do not know that men and women do not have the same number of corporeal orifices: for men the urinary canal and the seminal canal is one and the same, but not for women. The erotic consequences of this are many and serious: often a source of repression, but also of mistaken assumptions that self and other are sexually identical. It may also be a question of a lack of sexual imagination, or of misplaced idealism.

In my view, the current insistence on the notion of the neutral is an effect of cultural fashion and moment alike, linked to the pervasive authority of technology and to its concomitant, an appeal to a neutral energy – that is, an energy which vies with, or imitates, the machine. This energy resides most strikingly in God, despite the fact that God has never been neutral in any of our traditions since monotheism.

3 One of the arguments invoked to defend the thesis of the lack of sexual differentiation in analysis concerns the return to *enfantinage*.[7] I have coined,

or recoined the term. And with this, I shall move on to the third point I want to consider here: *is a child neutral*? Is it because – as I have heard it suggested – the word for child in German, Freud's language, is neuter in gender, that a child is considered sexually neutral? The argument seems very thin to me. But it is moreover tragic, tragic in the sense in which Hegel speaks of the tragic in the constitution of the ethical order, tragic in the sense the term assumes in the great tragedies which inaugurated our sociocultural order.

So, even the child, or already the child, is assumed to be neutral, neutralized before learning to talk. What a loss of liberty, of imaginary, symbolic, gestural freedom! Moreover, I wonder what the recourse of some analysts to bilingualism can possibly mean, in relation to the bilingual therapies which Anna O. invented for herself. Don't some of those who are unable to express themselves in their own language have recourse to another language in order to articulate themselves? It is a necessary recourse, in the place of their aphasia and paralysis. The problem is that in this instance, as in other similar instances, this symptom, which the patient produces in order to deal with their own illness, becomes a normative truth.

It is perhaps important to realize that this placing of the child under the sign of the neutral is also upheld by this technological era of ours, to which psychoanalysis belongs. If its practitioners do not give it enough thought, psychoanalysis becomes no more than a technocratic orthodoxy for schooling the unconscious. The machine aims to present itself as being more or less sexually neutral. Its truth is intended to be sexually neutral, as is that of money. Our technological world claims to be sexually neutral – which nature has never been. Nature is always sexed.

These two hypotheses are compatible. Aphasia or paralysis is replaced by a model which can function as a prosthesis, or artificial limb. This model is all the more rigid because it has been severed from the living symptomatology of the subject. The *one*, the *all*, the *everyone* of the model, its purported *truth*, are inevitably much more rigid than Anna O.'s symptoms: when I listen to *them*, I find that these symptoms have the greater energetic and theoretical potential, and that their hieroglyphs are far from having been deciphered.

4 But let us return to the child, and consider whether it is sexually neutral. I shall approach the question by returning to Freud's scene of entry into the symbolic order. His example is his grandson Ernst handling a reel on a string during his mother's absence. The child throws the reel away from him, hides it, and then draws it back towards him, saying *o-o-o-o* and *da*, meaning, according to Freud *fort–da*. He throws it away from him over the side of the cot, where it is hidden from him, then pulls it towards him, back from behind the cot, so that he can see it. *Fort* means far away [*veut dire loin*], *da* means near [*veut dire près*].[8] In the economy of consonants and vowels, *fort* (or *o-o-o-o* as it is in his discontinuous signal) plays on the far-and-near: it is articulated by the mouth's forming a little triangle, a triangle formed by lips and tongue: the *o* is inside it, but cannot be swallowed. The far away is not

introjected; it describes, in the mouth above all, a determinate space, a frame, framing, as it were, a space of departure and return, coming to a halt with the *t*, if the word is *fort*, or with the discontinuity of the sound if it is the *o-o-o-o*. Whereas the *da* can be swallowed, a sharp, dry mouthful, thus inverting the *fort*, unless it [*da*] stays in the back of the palate. So, everything also happens in the mouth, between the lips, the tongue, the palate, the teeth, the larynx, which may be confused with the oesophagus, both of which may in turn be confused with the pharynx, and so on. *Da* is not sung, in any case, it is swallowed. Near, it is introjected; far, it can be mastered: it stays in the mouth like a sweet difficult to suck, or else becomes a discontinuous signal, difficult to transform into a melody. It remains a sort of syncopated rhythm, lacking what is needed to form a closed object. In terms of gesture, this quasi-thing lies in readiness in the cot. It ought to wait there, hidden while he calls it. *Da* approaches abruptly, otherwise the reel will not come, and is either swallowed or is suspended at the back of the palate without there being any play to and fro. Whether it does go down or not, it is further inside you than *fort*, and is closed by being a dental consonant, closed by the teeth.

Both *fort* and *da* are closed up by the teeth. Whilst the reel comes and goes, and whilst the arm (probably the right arm) moves, breath and meaning are controlled by the teeth. The mother is held beyond the teeth. She cannot get out, at any rate. She is held on to so that she is available to become articulation (*fort*) or she is inside, swallowed or closing up the throat at the back of the palate (*da*). She can no longer leave the mouth. She is in the cot, and she is also in the mouth, behind the teeth. She is situated in two places, outside and inside. But inside she is already indefinitely divided by the teeth and by all the differences between the sounds.

This is the gesture of Ernst, of a small boy in the absence of his mother, mastering that absence – writes Freud. In *French* the syllables do not seem to be articulated in the same way; the outcome may be less happy, indeed, the position is reversed. Freud is writing in German; moreover, he is Jewish, which means that for him the opposition between vowels and consonants will be particularly important. We must bear in mind that such are his culture and language, we must understand this, and not blindly transpose a model constructed in one language onto another. What would be the corresponding model for a French-speaking small boy? Is there one? What syllables express it? Would the French child have said *ici* [here] and *là* [there]? The positions of these sounds in the mouth do not correspond. The German *fort* seems to be somewhere in between the French *ici* and *là*. And besides, the *a* occurs in the sound signifying outside, and it is the vowel *i* plus *s* which will express the *da*. *Ici* is pronounced right at the front of the mouth, lips open for the initial vowel *i*. The hypothesis that the gesture is one of appropriation is not invalidated with the change of language: but it is open to question.

What I think should be remembered with regard to the story of Ernst is that generally neither Freud's interpretation nor ours take into account that it is by a gesture of the hand and the arm, together with the pronunciation of some syllables, that the small boy enters the symbolic universe, by mastering the absence of his mother. What subsequently becomes of these meshed articulations of arm and phonatory apparatus? And another question: is Ernst walking or not at the time of the *fort–da*? Probably not. He does not use his legs to try to find his mother. Why? Why does he stay still, as though his legs were paralysed? Why does he speak, as it were instead of walking? He searches for his mother with his arms and his mouth. And with his ears perhaps? Sounds vibrate in his mouth and resonate in his ears. It is almost as though, in some way, he becomes speech, he speaks to himself. Certain sounds are spoken as though the mouth were pronouncing them towards the outside, others as sounds for oneself, vibrating in the inner ear. The *da* is said for the inside. It starts from outside, and is said inside. The *da* is said for the inside. It starts from outside, and is said inside. The *a* is also more maternal, more archaic, more enfolding. In listening to himself, it is possible that Ernst listens to his mother and drinks her in, in the *da*. At any rate, it is as though Ernst were driving a car or a cart. He is driving something with his mouth, his string, and his reel, something which has to do with his mother, his cot, his speech. It should be added that his second game, when his mother is away, is to make himself appear and disappear in a mirror.

Ernst is a boy. At a conference, when I addressed the question of the significance of his masculinity, someone objected that Ernst could have been a girl.[9] My response was: he was a boy. One must be faithful to the text. Substitution is not always possible, least of all as concerns sexual difference. So, in Freud's text, it is a boy. And Freud never wrote that it could be a girl. My hypothesis is that it cannot be a girl. Why?

In the absence of her mother, a girl's gestures are not the same. She does not play with a string and reel symbolizing her mother, for her mother's sex is the same as hers and the mother cannot have the objective status of a reel. The mother's identity as a subject is the same as hers.

So what will be a girl's reactions? 1) She is overcome by distress if she is deprived of her mother, she is lost, she cannot survive, and does not want to, she neither speaks nor eats, is anorexic in every way. 2) She plays with a doll, transferring the maternal affects to a quasi-subject, which allows her to organize a sort of symbolic space. This game is not just culturally imposed on girls; it also signifies a difference in the status as subject of boys and girls at the time of separation from the mother; for girls, the mother is a subject who cannot readily be reduced to an object, and a doll is not an object in the way that a reel, a toy car, a weapon, and so on, are objects and tools of symbolization. 3) She dances, thereby constructing for herself a vital subjective space, space which is open to the cosmic maternal world, to the gods, to the other who may be present. This dance is also a way of creating for herself her own territory in relation to the mother.

And does she speak? If she speaks, it is mostly in a playful way, without giving special importance to syllabic or phonemic oppositions. It may be bisyllabic, or like a litany, and rather singsong, modulated tonally. This language corresponds to a rhythm and also to a melody. Sometimes it takes the form of tender or angry words addressed to the doll, sometimes it takes the form of silence.

Women's relation to the 'same' between them, and the girl's relation to the mother, are not to be mastered by the *fort–da*. The mother always remains too familiar and too close. The girl has the mother, in some sense, in her skin, in the humidity of the mucous membranes, in the intimacy of her most intimate parts, in the mystery of her relation to gestation, birth, and to her sexual identity. Furthermore, the sexual movement fundamental to the feminine is much closer to gyration than to the gesture like little Ernst's of throwing away and drawing closer. The girl tries to reproduce around her or inside herself a movement whose energy is circular, and which protects her from dereliction,[10] from immediate effraction, from depression, from loss in itself. It is also, although this is in my opinion secondary, a means of seduction. The girl describes a circle, both inviting and refusing access to the territory thus inscribed. She plays with this gestural territory and its limits. There, there is no object, strictly speaking, nor a necessarily introjected, incorporated other. On the other hand, the construction of an initially defensive and subsequently creative territory is frequent among girls and women, particularly in analysis.

Graphic examples of the form of such territories are given by Jung. He compares them to Tibetan mandalas. In these drawings, it also seems that the girl or the woman does not call the other back, as does Ernst with his reel; rather, she calls the other and plays with the frontiers of access to a territory in which she stays.

If little girls are playing with a skipping rope, and if it is a question of their mothers, and of their relation to them, they turn round and round, spinning the rope around them. You have surely seen them playing like this in the play ground. They describe a circular territory around themselves, around their bodies. It is a completely different gesture to Ernst's. Often they do it in silence, or else they will be laughing, chattering, chanting nursery rhymes. Chanting is not quite the right word: they invent variations, phonic and syllabic games.

Girls do not enter language in the same way as boys. If they are too overcome by mourning, they do not enter language at all. Otherwise, they make their entry by producing a space, a track, a river, a dance, a rhythm, a song ... They describe a space around themselves and do not move a substitute object around, or from one place to another: visible in the hand, invisible in the cot, in the mouth in front of or behind the teeth, in the throat, and so on. Girls keep all or nothing. This is their mystery, their seductiveness. Doubtless they play with distance, but in other ways. They interiorize even great distances without dichotomic alternations, except for turning in different directions: outside, inside, at the frontier of the two. They turn not only towards or around an external sun but also around themselves and within themselves. The *fort–da* is not the gesture by which they enter language. It is too linear, too analogous with the in–out movement of the penis or of masturbation [*son substitut manuel*], or with the mastery of the other in the form of an object; also, too angular a movement. Girls enter language without taking in anything (except empty space). They do not speak around an introjected object, male or female, but rather *with* (sometimes in) a silence and with, in any case, the (m)other. They can find no replacement for her – unless it be nature as a whole, or appeal to the divine, or doing-the-same-as-her. Woman always speaks *with* the mother; man speaks in her absence. This *with her*, obviously, assumes different types of presence, and it must tend to put speech *between* (them), lest they remain woven together, in an indissociable fusion. This *with* must strive to become a *with oneself*. They turn around themselves, they rise and descend as they roll themselves around themselves but they also close up those parts of themselves which are two: the lips, the hands, the eyes.

The girl-subject does not master anything, except perhaps her own silence, her becoming, her excesses. Unlike the boy, she has no objects. She is split differently in two and the object or the aim is to reunite the two by a gesture, to make the two touch again, perhaps to *repeat*[11] the moment of birth, in order not to regress thoughtlessly, to remain whole, sometimes to stand upright. They do not want to master the other, but to create themselves. They only control the other (the other in the child, for instance, in so far as it is possible), if they fail to create their axis, fail to be free to create themselves. They move about an axis which also, besides, passes from between their feet, to the fontanelle, on this side and that. They have no absolute need for either the penis or the phallus, but rather, much more, a need to be born to themselves and to gain their autonomy themselves, not least the freedom to walk – that is, the freedom to go away and to draw close in all ways. The need for the phallus which is imputed to them is an *a posteriori* justification of the obligation placed on them to be mothers and legal wives. What they do need is to stand centred about their own axis, an axis which passes microcosmically from their feet to the top of their head, macrocosmically from the centre of the earth to the centre of the sky. This axis is present in the iconographic traces left by traditions in which women are visible. It is on this axis that women find the condition of their territory, of the autonomy of their body and their flesh, and the possibility of an expanding *jouissance*. Their *jouissance* does not require that they part with an arm or a hand to control the other; they keep all their limbs, their whole body, moving, and in particular their legs. It is significant that in the cases of paralysis in women described by Freud and Breuer it is the *legs* which are affected. Furthermore, the legs are affected differently, depending on whether the trauma is relatively recent or happened relatively long ago, and sometimes according to whether the trauma concerns a man or a woman. Such traumas are well described by Freud and Breuer;[12] even so, I do not agree with their interpretation. In my opinion, the suffering comes from the loss of, or the impossibility of access to, their auto-erotism;

as with the entry into language, so in auto-erotism, a woman's gesture differs from a man's. Not the same gestures, not the same words.

It may be that for girls to keep their *lips together* is a positive gesture. In the positive sense, closed lips do not exclude the possibility of either song or speech. This positive gesture expresses a difference. Daughters have less need to master the absence of the mother if they are (already) women. But they may also remain silent, and close their lips; in this case the lips, the labial consonants rather than the *dental consonants*, the lips as a whole, and not just the corners of the mouth, form the threshold of the mouth. If they sing, it is usually with all the lips, and not just the corners, unlike the *fort–da* or the *ici–là*. The importance of the lips may correspond with that of the generation of the universe, but already in silence, as certain traditions teach us, the tantric tradition in particular. These same traditions tell us that, in order to indicate that which is not yet manifest, one must say *m*, keeping the lips together. We often find the *m* in the word for mother. In French *maman* signifies, phonetically at least, that which remains unable to represent itself, speak itself, master itself, that which delays absorption but favours respiration, that which covers the whole of a black expanse expressed by the *m* and which is accompanied potentially by every possible colour thanks to the *a*. This name is one of the most perfect words possible.

I read in René Guénon's book, *Les Symboles de la science sacrée*,[13] that the etymology of the word labyrinth, *labrys*, is still unknown. Labyrinth may perhaps come from *lapis*, stone, or share the same origin. But my hypothesis is that the word has the same etymology as lips: *labra*, plural of *labrum*. The labyrinth – through which Ariadne, for example, would know the way – may thus be the labyrinth of her lips. The mystery of women's lips: their opening to create the universe, and their closing to touch each other again, so that the self-identity of the feminine individual may be perceived – this mystery may be the forgotten secret of the perception and creation of the world. Freud often situated feminine neurosis in, and confined it to, the oral (above all, labial) stage; and yet despite his vast cultural and archaeological knowledge, he makes no reference to the cultural tradition which has to do with lips. True, this tradition tends to be that of oriental religions and Christianity: the gestures of the Virgin closely resemble those of the oriental Yogi. But within the Jewish tradition, it happens that the lips figure as a reversed double Yod, a double reversed tongue.[14] The same motif is used for the Holy Spirit, when, in the form of a bird, it soars above the earth and its seas. At this point it signifies the creative spirit which moved over the waters when God spoke, and created heaven and earth.

The importance of the lips has been forgotten; this forgetting may have become both a labyrinth in which the quest to decipher the universe and language has lost its way, and also an enigma of sexual difference as yet beyond interpretation. The origins of this forgetting seem to be linked to traditions in which men take control of divine power, robbing women and the cosmos of this dimension of generative potential. Some of the male Gods, at least, and above all monotheism's male God, create the universe and all living things with the spoken word; to create man, God also uses his hands and breathes life into his creation. This world, their world, seems from the outset to be in a state of discontinuity, almost split in two. But the rhythm of the universe knows no intermittence; it is in continuous growth, opening out and returning to source, expanding and folding up again, flowering and taking root again.

So the enigma of the feminine seems, largely, to come down to that of her lips and to what she keeps hidden. This would explain the reaction of Dora – and many of her sisters – to Herr K.'s kiss. It seems to me that there is no need to find a pathological displacement mechanism. The lips as such represent an important enough place of investment for the imposition of a kiss to be an almost unbearable sort of violation. To take a woman's lips would be like taking the *fort–da* away from a man. Worse, in fact. The *fort–da* is already a substitution strategy, but the lips are the woman herself, the threshold of the woman, undistanciated by some object or other. To take a kiss from her, is to take what is most virginal in her, what is closest to her feminine identity. To make her pregnant is, possibly, another violation, crossing another threshold. To force a woman to speak, what is more, to force a woman lying down to open her lips, to come out of herself, may represent an analytic violation. The woman is not protected by the mechanism of the *fort–da*, by the way in which it is constituted by divisions of time, space, the other, the self, by its phonetic divisions. She is more often than not unable to express herself unless to start with, her lips touch each other again and she moves her whole body. A woman is more at a loss when she is immobile than when she is moving, for she is fixed in one position, exposed in her own territory.

5 The last aspect of gesture in the scene of psychoanalysis I want to consider here is the question of the opposition between the virgin woman and the paranoiac, between Dora and Schreber, the couple at the origins of analytic practice. Schreber constructs his persecution delusion around his status as virgin impregnated by the rays of God the father. But among men this delusion of virginity can only develop in the absence of his wife, or of women in general. On the other hand, he writes the account of this delusion for his wife. I interpret this as follows: unless women are allowed their gestures, their imaginary, their symbols, those symbols will be encysted in the verbal imaginary of men (verbal in the broad sense). Instead of a marriage, or weddings, both cultural events, there is on the one hand a virgin-become-real-mother, nothing else, and on the other, a man, a real father, whose delusion takes the form of a desire to be a virgin impregnated by God, in his wife's absence. The symbol of sexual difference and of its fecundity is lost. Unable to have become fruitful together through the spirit, man and woman lose their divinity, the realization of their humanity. The forms which the lips of the woman would have created, according to oriental traditions and still, also, Christian traditions, become the wounding rays which penetrate Schreber and 'bind him' to God.

I think that rather they bind him to the lost imaginary of his wife and to his own economy. What has not been engendered by the one, who is reduced to real maternity, becomes persecution delusion for the other. Schreber, like Ernst, played with gestures, with words, with his image in the mirror, to compensate for the absence of his mother. In these substitutions he wants to master the whole of her, including her feminine virginity, invisible but present above all in the specular processes of self-production and reproduction. It seems to me that before invoking God as cause, we must make ourselves be fully sexed, without misunderstanding the creative character of feminine sexuality in its biological forms and resources; these have not been neglected by other traditions. But Schreber, instead of becoming fully man, especially in his symbolic creativity, becomes woman, or tries to take on the virginal sex of his wife, distancing himself from her and putting himself in the hands of the medical profession.

This strange couple is still topical: this woman paralysed in her body and this man unable to realize his own male body and fantasizing the feminine imaginary instead. The violation of Dora and her resultant phobias, paralyses, and hysterias are the other side of Schreber's delusion. Woman's microcosmic and macrocosmic universe is often used in man's construction of deluded theory and practice, and of a system uprooted from its sources in the body, in its rhythms and its ruling cycles. Where once there were birth, growth, natural and plant cycles, is now the construction of artificial cultures with strange gods and heavenly bodies, labyrinthine laws and rules, founded in hidden mania [*cryptomaniques*], full of terrors, prohibitions, excessive, patho- genic, confused *jouissances*. Everything is on edge, becomes violent, needs medical men and medication. Internal and external perceptions seem to have been lost.

As some have said – Lacan, for example – the scene of analysis is constantly threatened by paranoia. My interpretation is that this threat comes from the lack of perception of, and lack of respect for, woman's virginal purity and from the resultant inflation of the world of the masculine imaginary, which appropriates this feminine mystery for itself, in its language and its mirror.[15] Self-deluding appropriation. In fact this mystery is a creative economy of the senses. If removed from its site and its style, this economy hardens, becomes rigid, becomes crypts and darts, painful rays and delirious parturitions. In the detail of their suffering, Dora and Schreber can indicate to us the reasons for their maladies and give us facts which may enable their recovery, and our own.

Notes

This essay first appeared under the title 'Le geste en Psychanalyse' in *Sexes et parentés* (Paris: Minuit, 1987).

1 Translator's note: the French is *praticable*, that is, the set of conventions which govern the psychoanalytic setting.
2 Translator's note: 'acting out' is in English in the original French text.
3 See 'L'Ordre sexuel du discours', *Langages*, 85 (March 1987), pp. 81–123.

4 On this topic see also Irigaray, 'Le praticable de la scène' in *Parler n'est jamais neutre* (Paris: Minuit, 1985), pp. 239–52.

5 See '...Poetically Man Dwells...', trans. A. Hofstadter, in Heidegger, *Poetry, Language, Thought* (New York: Harper & Row, 1971), pp. 213–29 (p. 215).

6 Translator's note: for most of this article, the French *neutre* has been translated as 'neutral'. *Neutre* can also be rendered as 'neuter', and Irigaray plays on both meanings.

7 'Regression to infancy.'

8 *Fort* usually translates in English as 'gone' or 'it has gone'; *da* translates as 'here' See Introduction, p. 23 n.37.

9 See Irigaray, *La Croyance même* (Paris: Galilée, 1983).

10 See Margaret Whitford, this collection 'Rereading Irigaray'.

11 Translator's note: emphasis added.

12 See *Studies in Hysteria, The Standard Edition of the Complete Psychological Works of Sigmund Freud* (London: Hogarth Press and the Institute of Psychoanalysis), 2. Also in the *Pelican Freud*, 3.

13 René Guénon, *Les Symboles de la science sacrée* (Paris: Gallimard, 1962).

14 See L. Charbonneau-Lassay, *Le Bestiaire du Christ*, 2nd edn. (Milan: Arche, 1975), p. 106.

15 See 'Femmes divines', in *Sexes et parentés* (Paris: Minuit, 1987), pp. 67–85.

Part Four

Towards another symbolic (2): beyond the phallus

Chapter Eight

Thoroughly postmodern feminist criticism

Elizabeth Wright

I propose to address a specific problem thrown up by the engagement of feminism with psychoanalysis, focusing on feminist criticism. The problem facing a feminist criticism is how to give woman access to discourse: the choice for her has been that of either submitting to the public language of patriarchy or of inventing a private language which keeps her marginalized and/or involves the risk of making her sound mystical. I write 'has been', for I shall argue that the current state of feminist criticism is such as to have created a space for her between these boundaries, a space more recognizable in the context of postmodernism.

In a recent critical assessment of the feminist struggle, Moi, following Kristeva,[1] marks out three main positions for women: 1) demanding 'equal access to the symbolic order', a battle for equal rights; 2) rejecting the 'male symbolic order in the name of difference', an assertion of the uniqueness of their femininity; and 3) rejecting 'the dichotomy between masculine and feminine as metaphysical', a deconstructed form of feminism, which Kristeva sees as her own position.[2] Moi would also like to take this position but points out that to adopt it prematurely runs the risk of making the feminist struggle redundant. You might say, if there were no enemies, who needs friends? A fully politicized feminist criticism, such as Moi clearly sets out, is rightly aware that to reject fixed gender definitions in theory is still to be stuck with them in practice, because at some point feminists may be forced, if only as a political strategy, to make the kind of bad choice that any logocentric system dictates. They can either fight patriarchy from within on a day-to-day practical basis (position 1), more usually associated with British and American feminists, or refute patriarchy from without by constructing alternative positions which stress the uniqueness of the feminine and fall into the danger of a new metaphysic (position 2, more often occupied by leading French feminists).

My aim in this paper is to investigate psychoanalytic feminist criticism under position 3, which takes (gender) identity as a cultural construct, in theory equally problematic for both sexes. In my critical investigation of psychoanalysis, feminism, and postmodernism I am particularly interested in revealing the uncertain foundation of any idealist system that considers itself based on ontological givens,[3] but at the same time I believe that feminist criticism is of specific relevance to that more general project, since it offers the clearest and the most visible instance of the difficulties of trying to subvert or re-form any system from within. The trajectory of the argument is informed throughout by the assumption that it is a positive advantage that all critical enquiry is itself open to such subversion, and this finally leads to the consideration of science as the most general instance of this principle.

With the help of feminism psychoanalysis has achieved prominence in the literary institution via a critique of the ideological usage within its own institution. Literary criticism is one field in which a psychoanalysis-for-feminism has flourished, for it has tackled orthodoxy in psychoanalysis, hard to combat in the psychoanalytic institution itself. It has taken on the fight against patriarchy and indeed against any oppressive system, considering in the process to what extent psychoanalysis might be 'refunctioned' (Bertolt Brecht's term for transforming ideologically-set material by recharging it with new critical potential) in order to become more political than it is claimed by some feminists to be already.[4] Literary criticism has given women access to discourse as both writers and critics, something they have not been able to have directly in psychoanalysis or in politics.

Psychoanalysis and gender

Psychoanalysis is a double-edged weapon (as the editor's introduction points out): on the one hand it enables feminists to demonstrate that gender is symbolic and not biological; on the other hand it constructs woman around the phallic sign. The mother's (unconscious) choice is not much of one: either she gives way to the Name of the Father and the Law, or she keeps her child with her in the imaginary at the level of an inadequate body unable to acquire the language of the Other.[5] Woman in patriarchy is condemned to occupy the place of signifier for the male other, who can give free reign to his fantasies and obsessions, and, what is more, implicate her in them.

It is for their theory and practice of the slippage of language caused by unconscious desire that feminists continue to embrace Freud and Lacan, even if somewhat coolly. It is a matter of continuing debate how far they may be said to serve the feminist cause. In the first instance women derived from them the proofs of their own oppression. They publicized by all the means at their disposal the extent to which the subjectivity of woman, what our culture calls femininity, has been and is determined by the discourse of patriarchy: in Freud's theory woman emerging as 'little man'-minus, in Lacan's as 'not-all'. In either case she is implicated in the ambivalence of 'the daughter's seduction'[6] as a precondition for moving from the mother's desire to that of the father. Gallop's book was the first full-length literary project which set out to challenge and subvert the psychoanalytic discourse from within its own feminist ranks, trying to create an intercourse between Lacanian psychoanalysis and feminism whereby each challenges the other's essentialism. What she has now come to reject in Lacan is, on the one hand, the facile equation of his concept of a castration that condemns the human being to absence of control with, on the other, a severance from a given biological stratum distinct from the human. A feminism which seeks to ally itself with Lacan is thus in danger of reifying both the 'human' and the 'natural' as exclusive values (see her paper in this book).

In her book *Figuring Lacan*,[7] MacCannell draws a useful comparison between Kant and Lacan. What must not be attributed to Lacan is the idea of the Symbolic Order as a categorical imperative. Lacan's Symbolic Order is a formula not for a realm of ideal judgements but for a mapping of mores that always remain adjustable. Like logic, it is the ghost of agreements, yet it must be applied to phenomena the whole time. The Symbolic Order is based on nothing but the principle of a splitting, a binary yes/no which any subject has to accept in order to emerge from the Real. The trouble comes when a binary content is allowed to become rigid, as though these oppositions had always existed. For it is not the structure in itself which is a threat to any freedom, but those who turn its presumed universality into a warrant for their own discourse of power. In that case human identity will be founded on false distinctions, such as those founded on racism or patriarchy. Under such circumstances language is no longer a proper game, with others having places equivalent to one's own, but a manipulation by others, whereby the subject is placed in a field of force within which it is compelled to adopt a false identity. This is what feminists are up against in the case of gender distinctions. There are those who accuse Lacan of merely shifting the cause of woman's oppression from 'men *per se*' to 'the structural organisation of society, language and exchange'[8] but others argue that it is his theory and praxis which enable feminists to see woman as a mythical construct and which can and must provoke alternative readings.[9] That is to say the old myths are to be abandoned and new ones to be invented. However, as Ragland-Sullivan points out, it is not at the Real level of primary castration (the separation from the mother's body) that the struggle for new forms of gender identity should be waged, but at the level of secondary castration, through the meanings attributed to the father's position in the triangle, for it is there that the masquerade begins.

> Woman's history will never appreciably change without a theoretical
> understanding of why there has ever been discrimination against women
> along gender lines. If Lacan's new epistemology is valid, however, the
> task placed before feminists is truly monumental, and, in part,
> impossible. The 'catch-22' lies in the circular nature of the dilemma
> itself. After Castration a mother's unconscious Desire is communicated
> to the infant, along with her attitudes toward the Phallus and messages
> about the infant's place within the symbolic, structural drama. To
> short-circuit the system, then, one must either change the gender of the

primary source of nurture and identification ... or change the unconscious Desire of mothers who, by accepting their femininity at all, support a system of phallic values.[10]

Those feminists who believe that Lacan's thought provides the basis for rewriting woman's and man's history are engaged in a criticism which does more than go to literature to find proof for the oppression of women. Neo-feminist criticism is rethinking the struggle of women for power and recognition because it sees the futility of perpetuating fixed binary oppositions. Instead of reading a text because it is written by a woman or considering the representation of woman, these feminist critics, taking up position 3, read texts for their hypothetical and marginal meanings, maintaining that it is these kinds of meaning which constitute a feminine subjectivity. They argue that a more radical kind of feminist criticism would be one which capitalizes on women's marginal position by refusing to make a clear distinction between subject and object.[11] In support of this they have interrogated the writings of Derrida as much as those of Lacan, finding that 'it is *woman* that must be released from her metaphysical bondage and it is writing, as "feminine operation", that can and does subvert the history of that metaphysics'.[12] Alice Jardine sees this 'anti-and/or post-feminism' of the French theorists as 'exemplary on modernity', in that their discourse systematically undermines all the categories we take to be natural ones.[13] There is an intrinsic undecidability in writing which is not ambiguity and which is beyond any fixed genderization. Yet it is to be called 'feminine', and therein lies the danger of a new metaphysics, despite the fact that men are not barred from this position.[14]

From the marginal to the maternal

The theorist who has done most to examine the marginal from a feminine if not a feminist perspective is Julia Kristeva. In her introduction of Kristeva's work, Moi sets out Kristeva's theory of a subject-in-process, based on a view of language as a mobile and provisional system of signification, its categorizations constantly disrupted by the resonating of early bodily drives.[15] Though this pre-oedipal sexuality returns in both sexes, it has led Kristeva and her followers to pay special attention to the mother's body, around which this early pre-self experience takes place, the mother being the primary object of love for the child's early spasmodic and uncoordinated sexual drives, satisfying its needs and coding its desires. But this focus on the space occupied by mother and child has now begun to shift to the focus on the mother herself as a devalued subject/object,[16] and on the attempt to find a positive sign for her to replace the various myths of the eternal feminine which idealized her out of corporeal existence in the past, yet at the same time helped to sustain her. Woman's continuing vulnerability in the symbolic order has raised new questions regarding the value of the maternal:

The desire to be a mother, considered alienating and even reactionary by the preceding generation of feminists, has obviously not become a standard for the present generation. But we have seen in the past few years an increasing number of women who do not only consider their maternity compatible with their professional life or their feminist involvement ... but also find it indispensable to their discovery, not of the plenitude, but of the complexity of the female experience, with all that this complexity comprises in joy and pain.[17]

The question of the continuing desire for motherhood can no longer be answered solely either in traditional terms or in psychoanalytic terms; so back to the literary text for its uncanny capacity to reveal the unsaid, this time to let the mother and the maternal speak.

A recent collection of essays[18] addresses itself to the feminist revision of the maternal narrative, centring particularly on the way psychoanalytic theory from Freud to Klein to Winnicott has constructed it. In psychoanalytic terms the mother's absence from her child indicates her presence not just elsewhere, but somehow attending to or being attended by the father. That is to say, she is always seen from the viewpoint of those who lay claim to her, whether it be the father or the child. To see the mother's need in relation to other women or to her work is not a view that psychoanalytic theory helps to promote.

In her illuminating essay in that collection Susan Rubin Suleiman argues that traditional psychoanalytic theory, being a theory of childhood, confines the mother to a purely sacrificial role, condemning her to a total selflessness. Suleiman points out that Melanie Klein speaks with great insight about the murderous impulses the child has towards the loved mother, but has nothing to say about the reverse. The notion that the mother may be in conflict regarding her child and her *work*, or the idea that the mother might be the subject of artistic creation rather than its object,[19] is a relatively new one: *'Mothers don't write, they are written* ... this is the underlying assumption of most psychoanalytic theories about writing and artistic creation in general.'[20] Suleiman calls for more information in the form of diaries, memoirs, essays by writing mothers. In the meantime she asks the question, 'Is there such a thing as the writing mother's fantasy?' and answers it by examining the 'fiction' of a mother. I shall briefly summarize her first example, a short story entitled 'Good housekeeping' by Rosellen Brown, herself the mother of two young children. A photographer-mother is going round the house with her camera, taking counter-domestic pictures (the title of the story is ironic). As her baby wakes, crying, she sees 'the baby's uvula quivering like an icicle about to drop'.[21] But as she points her camera at the baby, it stops crying and smiles, thus turning from object into subject. After a moment's pause the mother reaches out and pinches the child's thigh dispassionately, 'found the rosy tightness of it ... kept pinching hard, till she got that angry uvula again',[22] a uvula, described in a variety of metaphoric terms, far from the language of 'good housekeeping', as Suleiman points out. Suleiman writes: 'The power of the story for me, lies in the fantasy that I read in (or perhaps into) it: "With every word I write, with every metaphor, with every act of genuine creation, I hurt my child."' Hence for her the story is not just a story about what it feels like to be a mother, but 'a story about the *representation* of motherhood by a mother ... a story about the specular relation between mother-as-artist and her child',[23] a play of gazes in which the mother's aggression wins over her tenderness.

From feminism to postmodernism

Psychoanalytic criticism, unlike any other criticism, offers feminist critics a way of looking at sexually differentiated subjects, giving access to the subjectivity of women in writing and in all forms of discursive practice. But when feminism takes up psychoanalysis it also takes on postmodernism: like postmodernism, it is interested in the shifting of boundaries, the undoing of binary oppositions, but at the same time it offers postmodernism a politics to be conducted in the literary and artistic field. Without feminism, psychoanalysis and literature were locked into what has turned out to be a somewhat barren embrace: there has been little movement since Shoshana Felman's important advance in the 1970s, namely that literature and psychoanalysis were each to be the 'unthought' of the other: where psychoanalysis points to the unconscious of literature, literature points to the unconscious of psychoanalysis.[24] In other words, while literature was to be probed for its theories in fiction, psychoanalysis was to be investigated for its literariness, its slippages of meaning, which would reveal that there was fiction in theory.

Postmodernist theory provides feminism with an additional framework, enabling it to articulate the diversity and contradictions that spring up not only *between* various positions but also *within* various positions. In order to elaborate on the intersection of feminism and postmodernism I need to chart the main lines of the current debate. This seems to divide into a number of camps: 1) those who see postmodernism as a contamination of modernism, whose proponents (Bataille, Foucault, Derrida, are cited) 'claim as their own the revelations of a decentred subjectivity, emancipated from the imperatives of work and usefulness';[25] 2) those who similarly see it as negative, but for other reasons, namely, its reinforcement of 'the logic of consumer capitalism',[26] or its tendency to mime and parody 'the formal resolution of art and social life attempted by the avant garde, while remorselessly emptying it of its political content';[27] 3) those who see it as positive, welcoming the postmodern as a triumph of heterogeneity over consensus, artist and writer 'working without rules in order to formulate the rules for what *will have been done*' after the event has happened,[28] thereby able to resist capture by any form of ideology.

The notion of resistance to any form of reified meaning is central to the project of those who believe in the radical potential of postmodernism, but is this enough? Or is it not even counterproductive in that to lay stress on the marginal in experience undermines any sense of collectivity? The feminist critique of patriarchy and the postmodernist critique of representation intersect most fruitfully where the issue goes beyond a mere critique of representation. To stick within a particular problematic debating the pros and cons of representation has damaging consequences for a postmodern politics, 'where the power of representation is something sought, indeed passionately struggled for, by groups that consider themselves dominated by alien and alienating representations'.[29]

Feminism confronts this aporia by trying to do more than merely form a new alliance with theory. Feminists have taken up the struggle over the production, distribution, and transformation of meaning in a number of specific cultural practices as a focus of political intervention and opposition in order to challenge the forms of representation which constrain and oppress them. In this there is an analogy with the discourse of postmodernism as a discourse which attempts to conceive difference without opposition. The kind of simultaneous activity on many fronts (essentialist, culturalist, linguistic, psychoanalytic, anti-psychoanalytic) is already compatible with postmodern thought, as Owens[30] has pointed out. The fact that feminist artists are forging a new alliance with theory certainly has radical effects (some of which will be discussed below). Postmodernist feminist projects deliberately break across the boundaries of the discourses of art, criticism, and theory.[31] Owens maintains that both postmodernism and feminism challenge 'modernism's rigid opposition of artistic practice and theory'.[32] His intervention is to be welcomed in as much it points to the neglect among male postmodernist critics of the sexual politics inherent in women's postmodernist practice, particularly as regards the deconstruction of the male gaze. But are the politics inherent in these issues sufficiently positive?

One specific area where feminism and postmodernism engage in a mutual sexual politics is through their involvement with film theory, which enables them to challenge the way fantasy is put in the service of the oppressive ideology of capitalism. Film theory has certainly offered feminists a way of launching a substantial critique against the production and reproduction of fetishized images of women, constructed according to the male look. The postmodern has surrendered the belief in vision as a privileged mode of access to reality. Psychoanalysis has here enabled feminists to launch a critique on vision as sexually biased: in the Freudian scenario it is the look which determines the child's discovery of sexual difference and establishes the phallus as the privileged signifier of sexual identity. Film theory examines the cinematic manipulation of the gaze: the camera is conceptualized as an instrument of the gaze, which controls the spectator's eye. British and American feminist film theory has followed the control of the look in classical Hollywood films and shown how it is construed as a male patriarchal one and how it constitutes in turn the look of a spectator in the male field of vision.

147

Feminist film theory articulates ways of countermanding the patriarchal system of the look, where the woman is always in front of the camera and the man behind it. Mulvey proposes the destruction of narrative and visual pleasure as the foremost aim of women's cinema,[33] and Koch suggests a move not to a 'feminist aesthetic', but a 'feminist deaesthetic'.[34] This suggests that women's cinema, in common with postmodernism, has rejected an avant-garde aesthetic of subversion for a resistance to (filmic) representation, requiring the abandonment of traditional notions of the 'aesthetic'.[35]

This is certainly a different tactical move to that of feminist 'essentialism', yet it cannot be said to go beyond a politics of resistance. However, it would be wrong to define it, as Johnson does, as *mere* resistance:

> For postmodern feminists emancipation apparently means only a liberation from the normative privileging of any specific, culturally constructed mode or 'style' of human subjectivity. All that is proposed is an affirmation of the particularity of gender-based norms and the refusal of a repressive universalization of the standards of a peculiarly masculine, culturally constituted subjectivity.[36]

For Johnson, postmodernism cannot construct a positive model of the feminine, other than that which is already inscribed. Postmodernism is for her hopelessly relativist and quite unable to construct a positive difference. Johnson is here aligned with Habermas in her allegiance to the collective historical endeavour of the Enlightenment, and with Jameson in her (not uncritical) preference for modernism over postmodernism as a more coherent project which has not yet outlived its critical potential.

Breaking the boundaries of discourse

Yet what is most striking about the postmodernist feminist project is, as already mentioned, its transgression of the boundaries between art, criticism, and theory, an undertaking which modernism, with its stress on the autonomy of the aesthetic, would not have sanctioned. Lacanian-influenced feminist writers, such as Kristeva and Cixous, practise a postfeminist writing at the same time as they elaborate a theory; although this practice is not exclusive to feminist writing it is here that it is at its most overtly political. In her essay 'Stabat Mater'[37] Kristeva shows how the concept of the Virgin Mother is dependent on the discourse of the Church Fathers, mingling a historico-theoretical narrative with her own maternal discourse by placing vertical columns of each side by side, thus (typo)graphically demonstrating the political incongruity of the two discourses. In *The Newly Born Woman*,[38] Cixous would like to identify with the heroic woman in fiction but can only find male heroes, unlike Clément, the co-writer of the book, who feels that women must identify with the hysteric and the sorceress, who write from the knowledge of their own ideological repression. The book stages a dialectic between two feminisms, that of a poet-academic (Cixous) and a socialist intellectual (Clément) who comment self-reflexively on their kind of discourse and discuss which is more effective for feminism. Its general thesis, articulated in a style which deliberately conflates the theoretical and the lyrical, is that if women are going to partake in history they must write themselves into it, overcoming the obstacles of a dominant male culture, emerging in spite of it through their writing rather than by virtue of any biological essentialism. The route should be one of writing rebelliously (the hysteric), thereby bringing a feminine subject into existence and history, i.e. newly born: *La Jeune neé* means three things, 'newly born woman', ('Lá je une nais'), a pun referring to a 'feminine writing outlaw' (*la* Genet), and a non-existing feminine subject ('la je n'es').[39]

Monique Wittig also fights on the dual front of theory and fiction, though not necessarily conjointly. Her work is an example of a radical, partly reconstructive project, advocating a revolutionary politics. This is evident in her novel *Les Guérilliéres*,[40] where she uses the figure of the lesbian to deconstruct a feminine iconography, while launching a negative politics in her article 'The straight mind.'[41] One of her central targets is psychoanalysis, which she attacks for what she considers to be its bland assumptions regarding the construction of the subject: 'The discourses which particularly oppress all of us, lesbians, women, and homosexual men, are those discourses which take for granted that what founds society, any society, is heterosexuality.'[42] She believes that the existing system has interconnecting parts that support one another, with the effect of trivializing and oppressing those who attempt to define themselves in a mode not provided by the existing discourses. The article is a radical call to lesbians to refuse the heterosexual language, 'lesbians are not women',[43] returning again and again to the point that the differences established by the dominant patriarchal culture are such as to marginalize and render undefinable the radical categories incommensurable with a non-heterosexual order. 'The straight mind', as she calls it, in allusion to Lévi-Strauss's structural anthropology, conspires to define society according to a number of rigid concepts, such as '*the* exchange of women, *the* difference between the sexes, *the* symbolic order, *the* Unconscious, desire, *jouissance*, culture, history'.[44] She maintains 'that structuralism, psychoanalysis, and particularly Lacan have rigidly turned their concepts into myths', in that they have taken myths from the past and given them new interpretations which absorb them into the dominant ideology, thereby 'over-mythifying' them, making the interpretations myths in their turn.[45] In *Les Guérilliéres* Wittig produces a myth of her own in providing images of a Utopian society.

The problem, however, is that so far there has been no way of reconciling the notion of the feminine as a general issue for both sexes (linking up with the postmodernist critique of binarism and the need to rethink difference) with the historical need for women to find a collective voice in an oppressive phallocentric reality. Sandra Harding, writing a theoretical discourse, *The Science Question in Feminism*,[46] tentatively suggests that there can be a feminism which is both united in its universal commitment to the exploring and overthrowing of women's oppression under patriarchy, and polyvocal in its representation of a diversity of positive feminist movements, encompassing differences of race, colour, and class. By the same token she rejects the ideal of a value-free objective science, conducted from a spuriously neutral standpoint, preferring one that is critically aware of the inescapable bond between scientific and moral and political commitment, thus accepting the continual need for dialectical adjustments. In acknowledging the presence of dialectics within itself, science becomes postmodernist. Science has been *par excellence* the paradigm of a phallogocentric idealized system, and the challenge to it exemplifies feminism's project of the diversification of its modes of enquiry.

The feminist project entails that the worlds that have encoded projections of woman be subject to a general decipherment: feminism examines the processes whereby woman is given or refused access to discourse, and at the same time inaugurates a new way of thinking, writing, and speaking. There is now a plethora of women's writing springing up from all kinds of communities. In some areas, such as North America, women's studies are changing the face of university departments. What the diversity of feminist literary criticisms, backed by a rereading of psychoanalysis, shows, is that discourses are not merely about producing definitions but that they determine the 'nature' of the bodies and minds of the subjects they aim to govern. Thus feminist literary critics do not merely provide subversive readings of traditional and modern literary texts and modify the received images of femininity. They also offer a continual challenge to the prevailing power structure and its claims of impartiality, showing that there is nothing impartial under the sun, including the discourse of feminism itself, whose most vivid sign of life is its thriving on the difference within.

Notes

I should like to thank Dianne Chisholm for her fruitful suggestions and critical comments.

1 Julia Kristeva, 'Woman's time', in Toril Moi (ed.), *The Kristeva Reader* (Oxford: Blackwell, 1986).
2 Toril Moi, 'Feminist literary criticism', in Ann Jefferson and David Robey (eds), *Modern Literary Theory: A Comparative Introduction*, 2nd edn (London: Batsford, 1986), p. 124.
3 See, for example, Elizabeth Wright, *Psychoanalytic Criticism: Theory in Practice* (London and New York: Methuen, 1984).
4 Jacqueline Rose, *Sexuality in the Field of Vision* (London: Verso, 1986).
5 See Maud Mannoni, *The Child, His 'Illness', and the Others* (Harmondsworth: Penguin, 1973).
6 Jane Gallop, *The Daughter's Seduction: Feminism and Psychoanalysis* (London: Macmillan, 1982).
7 Juliet Flower MacCannell, *Figuring Lacan: Criticism and the Cultural*

Unconscious (London and Sydney: Croom Helm, 1986), pp. 139–51.

8 Elizabeth Gross, 'Love letters in the sand: reflections on *Feminine Sexuality: Jacques Lacan and the Ecole Freudienne*, ed. by Juliet Mitchell and Jacqueline Rose', *Critical Philosophy* 1, 2 (1984), p. 85; see also the questions raised in Gale Greene and Coppelia Kahn (eds), *Making a Difference: Feminist Literary Criticism* (London and New York: Methuen, 1985).

9 Juliet Mitchell and Jacqueline Rose, *Feminine Sexuality: Jacques Lacan and the Ecole Freudienne* (London: Macmillan, 1982); Jane Gallop, *Reading Lacan* (Ithaca and London: Cornell University Press, 1985); MacCannell, op. cit.; Ellie Ragland-Sullivan, *Jacques Lacan and the Philosophy of Psychoanalysis* (London and Canberra: Croom Helm, 1986).

10 Ragland-Sullivan, op. cit., pp. 298–9.

11 See Gallop, *Reading Lacan.*

12 Alice Jardine, *Gynesis: Configurations of Woman and Modernity* (Ithaca and London: Cornell University Press, 1985), p. 183.

13 ibid., pp. 21–5.

14 See Shiach and Spivak, this volume.

15 T. Moi (ed.), *The Kristeva Reader* (Oxford: Blackwells, 1986).

16 Julia Kristeva, *Powers of Horror* (New York: Columbia University Press, 1982).

17 'Women's time', in Moi, *Kristeva Reader*, p. 205.

18 Shirley Nelson Garner, Clare Kahane, and Madelon Sprengnether (eds), *The M(other) Tongue: Essays in Feminist Psychoanalytic Interpretation* (Ithaca and London: Cornell University Press, 1985).

19 See my *Psychoanalytic Criticism* for the various child-centred theories of creativity from Freud through to Winnicott.

20 Susan Rubin Suleiman, 'Writing and motherhood', in Garner, Kahane, and Sprengnether (eds), op. cit., p. 356.

21 ibid., p. 373, quoting Brown.

22 ibid.

23 ibid., p. 374.

24 Shoshana Felman, 'To open the question', *Literature and Psychoanalysis. The Question of Reading: Otherwise, Yale French Studies* 55/6 (1977), pp. 5–10.

25 Jürgen Habermas, 'Modernity – an incomplete project', in Hal Foster (ed.), *Postmodern Culture* (London and Sydney: Pluto, 1985), pp. 3–15 (p. 14).

26 Frederic Jameson, 'Postmodernism and consumer society', in Foster (ed.), op. cit., pp. 111–25 (p. 125).

27 Terry Eagleton, 'Capitalism, modernism and post-modernism', *New Left Review* 152 (1985), pp. 60–73. (p. 61)

28 Jean-François Lyotard, *The Postmodern Condition: A Report on Knowledge* (Minneapolis: University of Minnesota Press, 1984), p. 81.

29 J. Arac, 'Introduction' (ed.), *Postmodernism and Politics* (Manchester: Manchester University Press, 1986), pp. ix–x iii (p. xxi).

30 Craig Owens, 'The discourse of others: feminists and postmodernism', in Foster (ed.), op. cit., pp. 57–82.

31 Dianne Chisholm, 'French feminist writing' (unpublished paper, 1986).

32 Ownes, op. cit., p. 65.

33 Laura Mulvey, 'Visual pleasure and narrative cinema', *Screen* 16, 3 (1975), pp. 6–18.

34 Gertrud Koch, 'Exchanging the gaze: re-visioning feminist film theory', *New German Critique* 34 (1985), pp. 139–53.

35 Teresa de Lauretis, 'Aesthetic and feminist theory: rethinking women's cinema', *New German Critique* 34 (1985), pp. 154–75.

36 Pauline Johnson, 'From Virginia Woolf to the postmoderns: developments in a feminist aesthetic', *Radical Philosophy* 45 (1987), pp. 23–30 p. (29).
37 In Moi (ed.), *Kristeva Reader*.
38 Hélène Cixous and Catherine Clément, *The Newly Born Woman* (Manchester: Manchester University Press, 1986).
39 ibid., p. 166. In her postmodernist mingling of poetry, theory, and criticism Irigaray likewise joins the ranks of those who cannot unproblematically be decried as essentialist, for all are against articulating a theory as a male discourse of power. See Braidotti's rereading of Irigaray in this book, and also Whitford's, which argues that she has been misconstrued as one merely rewriting psychoanalytic theory, whereas she should rather be seen as a post-Lacanian trying to bring about a change in the symbolic order.
40 Monique Wittig, *Les Guérilliéres* (New York: Viking, 1971).
41 *Feminist Issues*, 1, 1 (1980), pp. 103–10.
42 ibid., p. 105.
43 ibid., p. 110.
44 ibid., p. 107.
45 ibid., p. 109.
46 Sandra Harding, *The Science Question in Feminism* (Ithaca and London: Cornell University Press, 1986).

Chapter Nine

'Their "symbolic" exists, it holds power – we, the sowers of disorder, know it only too well'

Morag Shiach

The title of this paper is a quotation from 'The laugh of the Medusa' by Hélène Cixous. The quotation mobilizes terms that are central both to Cixous's work over the last twenty years and to this collection on psychoanalysis and feminism. Focusing on questions of 'the symbolic', of power, and on the politics of disorder, Cixous's work suggests new sorts of solutions to the relationship between psychoanalytic theory and feminist practice. It allows us to analyse what we mean by feminist theory or feminist criticism and to consider the implications of a theoretical practice that begins with an articulated politics: 'feminism' is, after all, a political term, an interrogation of power and of the possibility of change, and not just a matter of technique.

Cixous begins by evoking the symbolic, which points us towards the discourse of psychoanalysis. But she puts it in quotation marks, and thus questions its ontological status: are we dealing with metaphor, with representation, or with some kind of real? She also describes it as 'their' symbolic. It is thus a term from which she invites women to take a certain distance, even if only rhetorically, and she implicitly offers the possibility of another symbolic, one that would be 'ours'.

The complicated nature of this invocation of the language of psychoanalysis is, as we shall see, typical of Cixous's work. Notions such as 'the imaginary', 'the symbolic', and 'lack' recur in her writing, but are constantly undermined. Having stated the problem of power and 'the symbolic', Cixous then insists that 'we are in no way obliged to deposit our lives in their banks of lack'.[1] The observation is rhetorical, and the obligation, as Cixous knows, is real enough: but that does not mean it is not open to attack. At other times, Cixous develops a critique of the language of psychoanalysis which engages with the sort of arguments made by Naomi Segal in this volume about the contingent nature of the narratives mobilized by psychoanalysis. Cixous argues that 'they've theorized their desire for reality', and that psychoanalysis 'reproduces the masculine view, of which it is one of the effects'.[2] She thus distances the political and theoretical project of feminism from the partial accounts of subjectivity and sexual identity offered by psychoanalysis.

Yet, the problem of the ways in which we, as women, are involved in the narratives of psychoanalytic theory cannot, as Cixous demonstrates, simply be wished away in a claim that 'psychoanalysis has nothing to do with us'. The problem lies in the extent to which some of the accounts offered to us by psychoanalysis do seem to engage with the experience of oppression, with the difficulty of our accession to language, with the very motor of a sexual politics. The dilemma is very similar to the one explored by Alice Jardine in relation to theories of postmodernism: these theories seem to have some purchase, to say something that is useful to the project of feminism, but, on the other hand, they are clearly not about us, and indeed not always *about* anything in particular.[3] We thus have a series of theoretical initiatives that are inescapable, but also beside the point, and sometimes just wrong.

Cixous's approach to this dilemma leads to a very complex project of theoretical and fictional writing, of strategic concessions and theoretical refusal, of writing through sets of images, and taking apart the powerful narratives of myth and legend. She is aware that the stakes are high, and that women writers and theorists are still vulnerable to the 'new old man': 'Luring them with flashy signifiers, the demon of interpretation – oblique, decked out in modernity – sells them the same old handcuffs, baubles and chains.'[4] Cixous herself, of course, is not immune from this vulnerability, and there are times when her writing seems to concede too much to the rumoured invisibility of women.

We can see then that 'the symbolic' takes us to the heart of the problems addressed in this book, but so, too, does the next term in the quotation: 'power'. Cixous has equated power, here, with the symbolic. I am not sure that this is an equation that everyone would be prepared to accept: we might want to examine other sorts of institutions and mechanisms for the expression and reinforcement of power relations. The equation is, however, central to Cixous's writing: her contention is that it is the organization of language, the dual hierarchized sets of oppositions that structure philosophical thought and narrative language, that provide the rationale for, and the means of, the oppression of women.

To this 'power', Cixous offers the possibility of refusal, of disorder. We, women, are to be the sowers of disorder, the point of difficulty in the rigid structure that would render us invisible and silent. But this raises an important question in relation to Cixous's work: does 'disorder' represent a challenge to power, or is it merely the only available space for the articulation of powerlessness?

In order to answer such a question, we have to come to the final term of the quotation: 'knowledge'. What is it that we know only too well? Through a critical account of Cixous's best known theoretical texts, *La Jeune née*, recently translated as *The Newly Born Woman*, and 'The laugh of the Medusa', I will attempt to demonstrate the extent to which Cixous interrogates the 'knowledges' that structure our identity and our social relations. I will argue that the best known 'excesses' of Cixous's position, the insistence, for example, that women, because of their proximity to the maternal, must write in 'white ink', can only be understood as part of an engagement with the representations of 'woman' which are embedded in, and perpetuated by, philosophical and fictional texts. Cixous's investigation of the theoretical and political bases that structure our 'knowledges' is continued both in her responses to the Brazilian modernist writer, Clarice Lispector, and in her plays. I will argue that these texts cannot be seen simply as evidence for a 'feminine' aesthetic, but must rather be put in the context of a set of theoretical problems about the nature of difference: problems that are most clearly articulated in the work of Jacques Derrida. Cixous tries to represent in more concrete, and more obviously political, terms, the relation between categories of thought and structures of oppression. She tries to challenge dominant definitions of 'woman' and of sexual difference, while retaining the possibility of political action by, and on behalf of, women.

Cixous adopts various strategies to subvert the certainties of a discourse that she perceives as resolutely patriarchal: she takes some representations literally and pushes them to uncomfortable conclusions, she refuses other representations entirely, still others she simply ridicules. The familiar charges of naïvety or essentialism are, I will argue, generally the result of failing to take account of the complexity of the project in which Cixous is involved, and of the extent to which she is, quite consciously, talking about representations, and available strategies for their transformation, rather than about reality. The difficulty of maintaining the metaphorical nature of Cixous's writing, particularly in relation to the bodily, returns us to a more general problem within feminist theory. Jane Gallop has written of 'a difficulty in accepting the body as metaphor, a demand that metaphors of the body be read literally', which she attributes to a reluctance to think through the extent to which the bodily, and experiences of sexuality, are always mediated by discourse.[5] I think, to some extent, she is right, but the worry is more substantial. Writing of the body, we fear appropriation at the point where, historically, we have been most vulnerable, and where we have been so ruthlessly placed.

The importance of acknowledging the metaphorical and strategic dimension of Cixous's theoretical writings becomes even more inescapable when we put them in the context of her writing as a whole: Cixous has written more than a dozen novels and several plays and short stories, as well as numerous essays and 'fictions'. Even this categorization of her work is problematic: her response to the work of Clarice Lispector appears both as theoretical essay, in the pages of the journal *Poétique*, and as fictional writing, in the book *Vivre l'orange* (*To Live the Orange*). Her writing moves between the poetic and the theoretical, and seems at times to move towards a poetics of theory. This is not said as a case of special pleading, but rather to point out the importance of considering her writing as a whole, as a political, philosophical, and literary project, rather than fixing on one or two of her 'theoretical' pronouncements as adequate to a representation of her work.

In looking now at two of Cixous's more obviously theoretical texts, my aim is to clarify the use which Cixous makes of three separate, but frequently confused terms: 'feminine', 'woman', and 'women', and to suggest ways in which the practice of writing which Cixous describes as 'feminine' relates both to our political project as women, and to the powerful cultural construct, 'woman'.

As I have said, the basis of Cixous's critique of the philosophical categories that organize our thought lies in her description of sets of binary hierarchized oppositions. Cixous describes a structured set of oppositions that serve to privilege particular terms and concepts, and to repress others. She cites the oppositions 'culture/nature', 'activity/passivity', and 'logos/pathos' and relates them to the opposition 'man/woman.'[6] It should be clear here that Cixous's argument is about representations. She suggests that 'Logocentrism subjects thought – all concepts, codes and values – to a binary system, related to "the" couple man/woman.'[7]

Her criticism is of a mode of thought that struggles to establish the 'empire of the self same': a system of thought that seeks to repress difference, where 'the same is what rules, names, defines and assigns "its" other'.[8] The position is, by now, fairly familiar: thought proceeds on the basis of sets of oppositions which break up reality, and return us to the security of recognized structure and of exchange. Yet, this security is a matter of constant struggle, it depends on difference, which it must ruthlessly repress. 'The paradox of otherness is that, of course, at no moment in History is it tolerated or possible as such. The other is there only to be reappropriated, recaptured, and destroyed as other.'[9]

Cixous examines the operation of this 'murderous' system, as the support of both patriarchy and colonialism. The argument is about forms of representation that serve to produce, and to legitimate, power relations. Returning to what she sees as *the* structuring opposition, between 'masculine' and 'feminine', Cixous argues: 'The (political) economy of the masculine and the feminine is organized by different demands, which, as they become socialized and metaphorized, produce signs, relations of power, relations of production and reproduction.'[10] A certain slippage is perhaps already clear here. Having begun with 'man' and 'woman' as culturally constructed signs, Cixous has shifted into a discussion of masculinity and femininity (with no inverted commas) as actually existing alternative economies. The slippage is repeated at various points through both these texts, and is, I think, the very source of the unease about the status of what Cixous is claiming about 'women', in relation to femininity.

Despite this occasional imprecision, however, there are important continuities in the ways in which Cixous uses the terms 'feminine', 'woman', and 'women'. The failure to distinguish between these terms has led to serious misrepresentations of Cixous's political and theoretical work. Cixous uses *the feminine* to refer to forms of writing, and of thought, that exceed the binary oppositions which have structured western thought and, she argues, supported patriarchy. The 'feminine' is what Cixous describes as excessive, as disruptive. Polemically, she grounds this concept in another account of sexuality: rejecting Freud's grounding of sexual difference in the visible ('a voyeur's theory') she locates it at the level of *jouissance*, which cannot be quantified, cannot be 'referred to the masculine economy'.[11] Cixous is quite clear that this concept of 'the feminine' is not to be equated with 'woman', or with women. Among the writers who demonstrate the possibility of a feminine economy, she cites Kleist and Genet. The 'feminine' is that which has been repressed, which returns as disruption through the mechanisms of the unconscious.

Cixous talks, in both *The Newly Born Woman* and 'The laugh of the Medusa', about *woman* as a cultural construct: a category with definable attributes, which have been massively reinforced by myth, legend, and literature. In *The Newly Born Woman*, Cixous examines the role of 'woman' in a range of literary texts. She asks 'where is woman in all the spaces he surveys, in all the scenes he stages in the literary enclosure?'.[12] Her answer, on the basis of a close reading of Greek legend and drama, of Shakespearean drama, and of Joyce's *Ulysses* is that 'woman' has been consistently relegated to the margins of narrative and of history. She has been what makes heroism possible, but she has been consistently silenced. Cixous discusses this literary history under the label of 'The dawn of phallocentrism'. She argues, 'look at the happy times of King Orestes: inheritance is transmitted through the men – patriarchy – political economy – sexual economy – it has all sorted itself out since they checkmated those great screeching females.'[13] The argument, then, is that narrative can only proceed by the construction of a particular concept of 'woman', which is then forced into the margins, and used to reflect and to validate male heroism.

Although Cixous's argument is about fictional representations, about literature, she is clear that this strategy of marginalization has more general social ramifications. Her concentration on fiction is a response to the power of legend and myth to structure our categories of thought, to offer us models of social and sexual relations: 'This is a locus where the repression of women has been perpetuated ... in a manner that's frightening since it's often hidden or adorned with the mystifying charms of fiction.'[14]

But this quotation brings us on to the third term that is addressed in Cixous's writing: *women*. As historical beings, women, we, are equivalent neither to 'the feminine' nor to 'woman', though our identity is continually negotiated in terms of these categories. What, then, does Cixous have to say about women?

She has already argued that women have a particular interest in breaking up the security of a discourse which is based on a fixed structure of oppositions. Her arguments about the repression of femininity lead her to assert the importance of articulating sexual identity, not in terms of rigid categories of 'masculinity' and 'femininity' apportioned on the basis of anatomy, but rather in terms of a fundamental bisexuality. She asserts: 'Now it happens that at present, for historico-cultural reasons, it is women who are opening up to and benefiting from this vatic bisexuality.'[15] So, while 'femininity' as an effect of writing can be produced by both men and women, it is women who have the most interest in the disturbance of language and thought that such writing produces.

Yet Cixous is aware of the difficulty of such a claim, the problem of reaching beyond the representation of 'woman' to the experience and interests of women:

> men and women are caught up in a web of age-old cultural
> determinations that are almost unanalyzable in their complexity. We can
> no more speak of 'woman' than of 'man' without being trapped within
> an ideological theater where the proliferation of representations, images,
> reflections, myths, identifications, transform, deform, constantly change
> everyone's Imaginary and invalidate in advance any conceptualization.[16]

But conceptualize she does, trying to work out the strategies of writing – for writing is where she theorizes the possibility of transformation – that will best disrupt the categories of patriarchal thought, and therefore best express, and advance, the interests of women.

Her starting point is clear: 'I write this as a woman, towards women.'[1] It is in writing, Cixous argues, 'that woman will affirm woman somewhere other than in silence, the place reserved for her in and through the Symbolic'.[18] She grounds this commitment, to a project of writing for and towards women, in her observation that: 'not only are there class enemies, colonialists, racists, bourgeois and anti-semites against me – "men" are added to them.'[19] Thus from a basis in the perception that gender is a structuring term in social and symbolic oppression, Cixous tries to develop a writing practice for, and in the interests of, women.

'The laugh of the Medusa' is an exploration of 'what women's writing *will* do': that is, it is a polemical text, exploring the possibility of a disruptive writing practice, and the interests of women in such a practice. It is not a description of how, historically, women have written, although Sandra Gilbert, in the introduction to *The Newly Born Woman*, makes an interesting case for reconsidering Emily Dickinson and Virginia Woolf in terms of Cixous's account of a feminine writing practice. Nor is it a claim that women can only write in one way – such a claim would anyway be ridiculous, given the ease with which Cixous herself moves between different forms and genres of writing. It is an exercise in the possibility, and the pleasure, of disruption: 'the thing that jams sociality.'[20]

So, 'The laugh of the Medusa' is about the production of new representations that are ruinous to authority, to the 'empire of the self-same'. The writing practice which Cixous advocates is put under the label of *voler*: to fly/steal. By this, Cixous means that writing should subvert the accepted conventions of narrative, should 'fly' above them, stealing fragments of discourse and putting them to scandalous uses. She advocates a writing that is excessive, slippery, difficult, that reproduces the pleasure of song, reintro-duces the materiality of the voice, and re-explores the body. 'The body' is not, here, intended as the grounding of an 'obvious' identity for women, but rather, once more as the return of the repressed. Cixous insists that 'the body' has been appropriated by a discourse that fears difference, has been stolen from women. In 'writing the body', women must explore the possibility of new images, new ways of representing sexuality, and materiality. What is intended here is the same sort of complex negotiation discussed by Rosi Braidotti in this volume: a negotiation between the social, the sexual, and the corporeal, as mediated by the unconscious, that is, as already caught up in representations.

'The laugh of the Medusa', then, is a particular attempt to ally the interests of women with the writing practice of femininity. It is not entirely successful, as is demonstrated by the unacknowledged slippages which I have already mentioned, between 'women' and the 'feminine'. The project is intensely personal, and at moments quite explicitly autobiographical. It makes sense in relation to Cixous's own writing practice, in her novels and her short stories. It does not, however, manage to sustain the consistent equation, even at a polemical level, between what women must do to change their political and cultural space, and the strategies of feminine writing. The strategic alliance works in parts of the text but, over all, 'the feminine' and 'women' seem to be pulling in slightly different directions. Can we really feel that a writing practice is meant just for us, when it seems to be done so much better by Genet or Kleist?

It is the seemingly contingent nature of this equation between *women's history and writing* and what Cixous has defined as *feminine writing* which is challenged by Cixous's account of the work of Clarice Lispector. Cixous has been writing about Lispector for more than ten years. She uses Lispector's work to argue for a more direct, and less contingent, relation between women's history and 'feminine' writing.

This engagement begins with Cixous's admission of feelings of isolation: that she has been involved in a project which does not have the kind of ramifi-cations, the kind of political purchase, that drove her to writing in the first place: 'I wandered ten glacial years in over-published solitude, without seeing a single human woman's face.'[21] This isolation is ended by the encounter with Lispector's writing. The connection between a particular use of language and the possibility of transforming the political and cultural position of women is, Cixous argues, perceptible in the writing of Clarice Lispector.

Cixous's interest in Lispector's writing lies in the way it uses language in non-coercive, non-categorical, and therefore emancipatory ways. Cixous argues that Lispector's writing respects the specificity of objects, goes to the source of social relations and of natural phenomena, and produces a poetics that communicates women's experience in very particular and powerful ways. In talking of the ways in which Lispector's writing respects the specificity of objects, Cixous links this to the recognition of difference, and the refusal to

159

impose false categorizations. Each element in Lispector's fiction imposes itself on the writing, rather than being subsumed by the demands of narrative.

Cixous relates Lispector's writing to the concept 'orange'. This is a concept used in earlier texts by Cixous. It is meant to suggest both a personal history: *orange* breaking down into *Oran* (Cixous's birthplace) and *je* ('I'), and a particular notion of the power and fluidity of the poetic. Lispector's writing, Cixous argues, 'lives the orange': it thus brings together the poetic, the Utopian possibility, and the proximity to detail which is typical of the experience of women. Lispector's writing is celebrated as profuse, as intimate, as unveiling, as respecting all its objects, however meagre, and as allowing the power of memory, of history, to circulate throughout her novels.

Cixous bases a whole project of politicized criticism on Lispector's writing, itself already intensely political. This project involves the mediation of Des Femmes, the publishing house which published both much of Cixous's work, and French translations of Lispector, but also, more generally, the mediation of 'women', culturally and politically conscious of themselves as a group.[22] Throughout *Vivre l'orange* the question recurs, 'What have I in common with women?'

Vivre l'orange, one of the texts in which Cixous develops her response to Lispector, is classified as a 'fiction', so we have to be wary of producing too categorical an account of the arguments developed within it. None the less, it is certainly suggestive of the sorts of relationships between forms of writing and forms of power that Cixous wants to assert. The concept of 'orange' takes Cixous to Oran and then to Iran: the text was written during the Iranian revolution. 'Iran' comes to represent, in the text, the priorities of political activism, to which Cixous feels she must answer. Cixous interrupts her text on Lispector to respond to a telephone call: 'The telephone was crying. It was Renata's anxiety.... And Iran? What were you doing? ... And Iran? You were forgetting.'[23] But Cixous refuses the polarization, arguing that 'the love of the orange is political too'.[24] She argues throughout the text that an ability to perceive clearly, to respect the integrity of different cultures, to allow things to happen slowly and complicatedly, to recognize difference, has important political implications. She advocates a different economy of political and cultural relations, expressible through the poetic. She links the struggle of women, and of Iran, through an account of Lispector's writing. Cixous also relates Lispector's particular voice, as a Jewish writer, to these struggles, thus cutting across the expected hierarchy of oppositions.

Her claims are very large: 'the survival of the orange ... is the condition of the liberation of all of humanity kept silent, hidden, hated, beneath the peoples and their histories.'[25] Gayatri Spivak has expressed her frustration at this 'tendency to offer grandiose solutions with little political specificity, couched in the strategic form of rhetorical questions'.[26] I understand this response, but I think such anxieties can be somewhat allayed by attention to the very factor in Cixous's writing to which Spivak refers: its strategic form.

Cixous's response to Lispector makes sense in terms of that sort of *impasse* I described above: between women's history and the practice of feminine writing. She uses Lispector as a means to negotiate this difficulty: to push 'women' and 'the feminine' together, and place them clearly within political struggle and within history. She is not talking about the real Clarice Lispector, a Brazilian left-wing modernist writer who died in 1977, but rather exploring the power of 'Lispector' as a symbol, and seeing the sort of connections Lispector's writing allows her to make. Cixous had found 'women' as a political problem, and 'feminine writing' as a political solution. In Lispector she tries to construct the unity of these two terms. The resulting text *Vivre l'orange*, is suggestive, but it cannot be definitive. It makes sense in terms of Cixous's writing, the theoretical problems it raises, and the images it explores, but *Vivre l'orange* has to be seen quite clearly as a fiction: an engagement with the metaphors and representations that structure our experience of social reality. It is useless to pretend that, for us, the answer is an orange.

The strategic nature of Cixous's engagement with Lispector becomes clearer when we look at an article about Lispector published by Cixous in the journal *Poétique*. Once more, the celebration is of Lispector's writing in terms of its representation of difference, its deconstruction of processes of naming. But here, the emphasis is on the extent to which Lispector's writing exceeds, surpasses, the deconstructive imaginations of male writers: 'The texts ... of Rilke, or of Heidegger, or of Derrida had been already read, transported into, and answered in the writing of C.L.'[27] Having argued that women have most interest in the deconstruction of the dual hierarchized oppositions that structure language and thought, Cixous now states, polemically, that Lispector is the writer most able to realize this project.

Cixous does not simply theorize the possibility of writing which undermines a dual hierarchized structure of oppositions; she also produces such writing. I will thus now look at Cixous's theatrical writing as an attempt to produce new forms, and new narratives, for the representation of difference. This writing constitutes part of Cixous's own engagement with a politics of the symbolic.

The problem that is explored in Cixous's theatrical texts is the possibility of representing sexual, or indeed social, difference, without returning to the dual hierarchized oppositions explored in *The Newly Born Woman*. Cixous writes about difference, but not as something given, natural, or essential. She offers us neither such security, nor such paralysis. Instead, she struggles to represent the fact of difference, as process, as structure, and as constitutive of social and sexual identities.

The theorization of difference, a difference which does not return to the implied judgements of 'different from', is perhaps best known in terms of the writing of Jacques Derrida. In *Margins of Philosophy* Derrida explains his use of the concept, or rather the process, of *différance*. He insists that difference cannot be thought in relation to a fixed structure of positive terms. *Différance* is that which allows the production of meaning. It involves a plethora of relationships across time. Meaning is always constituted by both structural differences and temporal deferrals – and this temporal element is what we have lost in our concept of 'difference'. Derrida argues that: '*différer* in this sense is to temporize, to take recourse, consciously or unconsciously, in the temporal and temporizing mediation of a detour that suspends the accomplishment or fulfilment of "desire" or "will".'[28] This *différance*, difference with no positive terms, is further described by Derrida as 'the becoming-time of space and the becoming-space of time'. The question then becomes how such a complex relation can be representable: '*Différance* as temporization, *différance* as spacing. How are they to be joined?'[29] One answer, I believe, lies in theatre, which organizes its representations explicitly along both temporal and spatial axes: thus, the attraction of the form of theatre in terms of Cixous's attempts to rewrite, to retheorize, difference.

Cixous has discussed the importance of the temporal aspect of theatre: the spectator 'moves forward [through a play] with a beating heart, not knowing what is going to happen next'.[30] Everyone is in this state of alertness to the existence of time, confronted by its opacity. No one in the theatre can have prior, or superior, knowledge. Each spectator is caught in the play of differences, and the production of meaning.

Cixous has written of her commitment to the poetic over the novelistic. Novelists are the 'allies of representationalism' who try to produce coherence, fixity, and transparency, whereas poets are committed to complexity, to the density of language, and to the power of the unconscious.[31] This commitment to the 'poetic' can also make sense of the terms in which Cixous uses the medium of the theatre: her use of gesture and of image, in order to complicate, or undermine, the stability of narrative. She uses theatre as a means to represent intertextuality, in her constant allusions to and quotations from other theatrical and mythical texts. This foregrounding of the ways in which both 'action' and 'character' are produced through a negotiation with existing texts forces a questioning of the 'natural' bases of character and identity. Cixous produces multivocal forms of theatre, where voices echo each other, contradict each other, and constitute each other. She represents, theatrically, the power of history to disturb, to question, the certainty of the present. All of these strategies can be related to her insistence that writing 'should infinitely dynamize by an incessant process of exchange from one subject to another'.[32] Theatre is speech rather than writing, or at least it is written speech, but it represents exactly such an exchange of subjectivities.

This claim that the basis of Cixous's commitment to, and use of, the form of theatre is *theoretical* should not, perhaps, come as a great surprise. 'Theatre' and 'theory' share a common linguistic origin. Both derive from the concept of 'spectacle', of 'looking', and, as we know, it is not only theatre that can be spectacular! 'Theatre' and 'theory', then, share a lot, but it is the 'something more', the 'poetic' that is offered by the theatre that explains the power of Cixous's theatrical texts. As Jane Gallop observes:

> Perhaps in a theoretical text one can never do more than say 'there is
> more, there is love and beauty' which is a necessary affirmative
> supplement to the murderous negation that theory must be. But in
> *Portrait de Dora*, in the theatrical text ... this is not a problem, the
> affirmative is interwoven in various patterns with the negative.[33]

And Cixous is always on the side of the affirmative, against the murderous.

Theatre, then, can be used to represent the process, and the possibility, of
différance. Cixous further observes the close relation between theatre and
psychoanalysis, both in terms of the theatricality of the process of
psychoanalysis (its origins in 'family dramas') and in terms of the ways in
which theatre represents the relation between, and the constitution of,
subjectivities. It is this nexus that leads Cixous to explore, theatrically,
questions of sexual difference.

This exploration is carried on in the opera *Le Nom d'Oedipe* (*The Name
of Oedipus*), whose title places it immediately at the intersection of theatre and
psychoanalysis: Oedipus' drama, after all, became one of the founding
narratives' of psychoanalysis. Cixous says that in *Le Nom d'Oedipe* she aims
to bring 'splitting', to bring sexual difference, to the stage.[34] *Le Nom d'Oedipe*
dramatizes sexual difference, explores the relation between masculine and
feminine subjectivity, and retells a myth.

Le Nom d'Oedipe speaks, and sings, in many voices, which contrast with,
harmonize with, or disturb each other. The opera explores the sexual encounter
between Oedipus and Jocasta, his mother, as observed by the bisexual and
prophetic figure of Tiresias. Jocasta struggles to relate to Oedipus, without the
use of names, or words that will reveal their relationship and make their love
impossible. Her own identity is uncertain: 'I, who was you yesterday.'[35] Jocasta
declares that 'words escape me', insists that she loves Oedipus 'with my flesh
and my soul – and without names'. Tiresias encourages her, 'don't say the
delicious old words, spit them out'. But this is too much disruption, the old
words reassert themselves, the Law is put in place and Jocasta dies. Oedipus,
however, who, as the choir suggests 'is a man, like all other men, their desire
is always the same', is left alive, but unsure of his own identity, without the
comforting mirror of devoted love: 'who am I if you don't tell me?' Oedipus,
throughout the opera, seeks to repress his name, his place in the symbolic order.
He tries to repress the existence of the Law, in order to assure his complete
possession of Jocasta: 'Promise you will never have another lover ... I alone
want to be your child, your father if you wish'. But the imposition of the Law
does not lead to Oedipus' death. He is left with speech, with language. We
are left in no doubt as to who has most interest in challenging the Law that
supports the symbolic order, but we also see that the stakes are high, that
murder is possible.

Portrait de Dora also explores the construction of sexual identities, the
drawing of portraits, and it also retells an old story. Cixous's treatment of

Freud's case history explores the relation between power and language and the silencing of Dora, the hysteric whose only power is absence and refusal. Cixous has already warned us of the way in which portraits function to produce fixity and identity, and of the complicity of psychoanalysis in this process: 'hold still, we're going to do your portrait, so that you can begin looking like it right away.'[36]

Dora is constantly being constructed within narratives, 'she is no longer a child', she 'could have taken the place of [their] mother'. She is caught in the determinations of narratives and dramas that circulate around her and through her. The staging, and the structure, of *Portrait de Dora* represent infinite mirroring, the repetition of relations that function to erase the feminine, except as 'nothingness' and silence.

This mirroring theme, so crucial to the formation of subjectivity, is reflected in the dialogue of the play. Freud tells that 'each time Dora's father was asked about her health his eyes filled with tears' and Frau K. tells Dora that 'your father cannot speak about you without tears coming into his eyes'. Language is quotation, is repetition, and identity is always precarious. As Freud says, 'Who is in whose place in this story?' Frau K. is occasionally in Freud's place. She, after all, delivers his observation from the Dora Case History about openness and frankness, 'J'appelle un chat un chat'. Frau K. and Freud are linked, as objects of Dora's love. Cixous, however, *represents* what Freud had only hinted at: Dora's love for Frau K.

The equation of women and nothingness circulates throughout the play: Dora says of her father that 'my mother is nothing for him', and quotes Herr K. as saying that 'you know my wife is nothing to me'. 'Woman' becomes an empty sign. Dora knows that within these narratives and repetitions she has only one place: that is a place within the structure of exchange of women. This is what she refuses. She undermines the transparency and immediacy of the stories she is told, and by which she is placed, when she says to Freud, 'I "knew" you would say that'. She 'knows' the basis of his certainty: she understands the ways in which she is placed by Freud's narrative.

Dora tries to take up a place within the symbolic, as a means to end the perpetual mirroring in which she is caught. She challenges Freud, who has told her that the body speaks, asking, 'Why do you turn your pen over seven times before speaking to me?' But Freud is not to be caught: 'you know perfectly well I'm an institution', 'keep to the rules'.

Cixous stages these encounters, offering us spatial and temporal representations of the dynamics of Freud's exploration of hysteria, of female sexuality. The mechanics of Freud's narratives are made explicit, the 'transparency' of his discourse is undermined by the physical presence of its object. The play represents mirroring and repetition, it stages the power relations in which Dora is caught. At the end of the play Dora walks out on Freud, she takes her revenge by choosing to go it alone. But for this action Dora pays a high price. Freud asks her to write to him (a frequent amorous ploy) but Dora replies, 'write – that's not my business' – and she's right.

Dora's refusal, her 'dismissal' of Freud, is disruptive. Freud is bereft, but it leaves the symbolic order intact – and unavailable to Dora. Within the narratives and compulsive repetitions that constitute the 'portrait' of Dora, there is no place for Dora to write, to speak, or to construct a different and less murderous identity. Nothing comes of nothing.

So, Cixous has tried to stage the process of sexual differentiation, to show the possibility of refusal, of transgression, of moving beyond the Law. In both *Le Nom d'Oedipe* and *Portrait de Dora*, we are offered exhilaration, difference, and disruption, but the rest, unfortunately, is silence. In both plays the symbolic reasserts itself, a little battered but not destroyed. In more recent plays, however, Cixous has represented the process of differentiation in more social terms, and has offered the possibility of more hopeful conclusions: the construction of new sorts of identity, which cut across 'dual *hierarchized* oppositions'. This move, from painful marginality to new sorts of unity which respect the facts of difference, is represented as possible, but as infinitely fragile. Cixous has argued that theatre is uniquely placed to construct such identities, which do not repeat the dominant hierarchical system of difference. She says that theatre offers recognition and new identification, an intersubjectivity that is elsewhere impossible.[37]

This seems to be the impetus behind the more recent plays: *La Prise de l'école de Madhubaï*, *L'Histoire terrible mais inachevée de Norodom Sihanouk, Roi du Cambodge*, and *L'Indiade ou L'Inde de leurs rêves*. *La Prise de l'école de Madhubaï* represents a society which is divided between rich and poor, between power and powerlessness, between educated and illiterate. Sakundeva, the heroine, is a guerrilla leader driven outside this structure, into armed struggle. She embodies the values of justice and sympathy, which are repressed and negated by the social hierarchy of oppositions in which India is caught. Her relationship with Pandala, her aunt, establishes the importance of women in the struggle to represent difference and thus to promote equality. Pandala, with her second sight, offers a counterpoint to the calculating logic of 'the minister'. By the end of the play, we are confronted with the possibility that the hierarchical system which is Indian society could be undone: power could be forced to listen to powerlessness, Sakundeva could bring about the building of a school at Madhubaï. We do not know, yet, whether this possibility is realizable: that, as 'the minister' says, would involve another play.

L'Histoire terrible mais inachevée de Norodom Sihanouk, Roi du Cambodge also explores the hierarchized system of oppositions that structure social and political relations. Cambodia is represented as caught in a system of conflict and of oppositions which have, in fact, nothing to do with the people or the history of Cambodia. Against American imperialism and Vietnamese expansionism, Cambodia is represented as struggling to assert a different sort of identity: a kind of independence, of neutrality, which is in fact more a question of multiple influences and determinations cancelling each other out.

The survival of Cambodia becomes a metaphor for the survival of that sort of difference which does not ground itself in fixity and in certainty. Cambodia comes to represent laughter, music, poetry, a kind of knowledge that does not seek to destroy. Sihanouk suggests that we 'give our imaginations a moment of rest, with music', and this is also what Cixous offers us: the possibility of a different sort of difference. Once more, it is fragile. We are offered two different endings to the play: neither of them triumphant. But we are left with a country still in touch with its past, through the presence of the living dead, of whom there are many, who undertake to protect Cambodia, to preserve its independence. *L'Histoire terrible mais inachevée de Norodom Sihanouk, Roi du Cambodge* stages history: the history of Cambodia and the history of the theatre (articulated in terms of quotations, particularly from Shakespearean texts). It forces us to recognize spatial and temporal relations in all their complexity, and invites us to celebrate the possibility of non-hierarchical, non-oppressive social relations, based on the principle of difference. It never allows us to forget, however, the threat such relations offer to the dominant social order.

L'Indiade continues Cixous's project of representing the history of political and cultural difference. The play deals with the Indian struggle for independence, and with the politically disastrous consequences of the partition of India. The dominant figure in Cixous's play is Gandhi, who struggles to find a language and a practice which will respect the cultural differences of India, at the same time as asserting its national unity. He is defeated, however, by the brute facts of a difference that can exist only by repressing, by murdering, its Other.

That Cixous's most successful theatrical interrogations of the dual hierarchized oppositions that structure our thought take place in relation to nation and class, rather than gender, does not affect the importance of Cixous's work for feminism. It is rather an indication of the difficulties, of which we are all aware, of rethinking the categories of sexual difference, and of the necessary relations between any such project and a rethinking of class relations and of the bases of imperialism. My aim throughout this chapter has been to make connections between the different discourses, 'feminist', 'historical', 'literary', and 'psychoanalytic', which are mobilized in Cixous's texts. The connections are powerful and inescapable: the conclusions, like the history of India, or of Cambodia, are still open to political struggle.

Notes

1 Hélène Cixous, 'The laugh of the Medusa', in Elaine Marks and Isabelle de Courtivron (eds), *New French Feminisms* (Brighton: Harvester, 1981), pp. 245–64 (p. 255).
2 ibid., p. 255.
3 See Alice Jardine, this volume.
4 ibid., p. 262.

5 Jane Gallop, '"Writing and sexual difference" the difference within', in Elizabeth Abel (ed.), *Writing and Sexual Difference*, (Brighton: Harvester, 1982), pp. 283–90 (p. 288).
6 See Hélène Cixous, 'Sorties', in Hélène Cixous and Catherine Clément, *The Newly Born Woman*, trans. Betsy Wing (Manchester: Manchester University Press, 1986), pp. 63–132.
7 ibid., p. 64.
8 ibid., p. 71.
9 ibid., p. 71.
10 ibid., pp. 80–1.
11 ibid., p. 82.
12 ibid., p. 67.
13 ibid., p. 112.
14 'Laugh of the Medusa', p. 249.
15 ibid., p. 254.
16 'Sorties', p. 83.
17 'Laugh of the Medusa', p. 245.
18 'Sorties', p. 93.
19 ibid., p. 74.
20 ibid., p. 96.
21 Hélène Cixous, *Vivre l'orange* (Paris: Editions des Femmes, 1979), p. 48.
22 For discussion of the multiple ramifications of 'des Femmes', see Jane Gallop, 'Keys to Dora', in *The Daughter's Seduction: Feminism and Psychoanalysis* (London: Macmillan, 1982), pp. 132–50 (p. 133). See also *Vivre l'orange*, p. 64.
23 *Vivre l'orange*, pp. 22–4.
24 ibid., p. 26.
25 ibid., p. 34.
26 Gayatri Chakravorty Spivak, 'French feminism in an international frame', *Yale French Studies* 62 (1981), pp. 154–84 (p. 177).
27 Hélène Cixous, 'L'approche de Clarice Lispector', *Poétique* 40 (1979), pp. 408–19 (p. 409); my translation.
28 Jacques Derrida, 'Différance', in *Margins of Philosophy*, trans. Alan Bass (Brighton: Harvester, 1982), pp. 1–27 (p. 8).
29 ibid., p. 9.
30 Hélène Cixous, 'Le chemin de légende', in *Théâtre: Portrait de Dora et La Prise de l'école de Madhubaï* (Paris: Editions des Femmes, 1986), 'La Prise', pp. 7–11 (p. 10); my translation.
31 'Laugh of the Medusa', p. 250.
32 ibid., p. 254.
33 'Keys to Dora', p. 148.
34 See text on back cover of Hélène Cixous, *Le Nom d'Œdipe: chant du corps interdit* (Paris: Editions des Femmes, 1978).
35 All translations from Cixous's plays are my own.
36 'Laugh of the Medusa', p. 263.
37 See 'Le chemin de légende'.

Chapter Ten

Echo and Narcissus

Naomi Segal

If literature is the unconscious of psychoanalysis, its *'unthought'*,[1] this is because psychoanalytic theory, like any other discourse, has something to hide. In this paper, I shall be looking at a group of fictional texts published in France between 1731 and 1863. A psychoanalytic reading of these texts bears out the Lacanian claim that castration is the price of entering the symbolic of the fathers, but if we take up the position that I have elsewhere called that of the unintended reader, it may reveal something else as well.

It is a long time since literary criticism used psychoanalysis in a biographical bid to expose the unconscious of the author; if instead it has tended to psychoanalyse the text as the symptomatic utterance of the narrator, this is not because the ontological status of the latter is any more 'real', but because any piece of language functions as a piece of evidence. I take it that the narrators in the texts I have examined act as a function of the author's desire. The narrative is a motivated fantasy, but whose fantasy it is is a question we may and perhaps must leave undetermined. This very uncertainty is endorsed by the tendency of the texts to operate by a grouping of male doubles both within the fiction in the form of male characters and outside it in the implicit meeting of men who generate and men who receive the utterance. These stable–unstable systems reproduce the negative collusion created by the son's acceptance of castration in order to speak with the fathers. I want to suggest that the transaction between oedipal father and oedipal son into which the reader is invited to enter is another piece of evidence that we can psychoanalyse. We can do that best by standing outside it, in the alternative fantasmatic position of the woman it excludes. In this third position for psychoanalytic criticism, now a feminist-psychoanalytic criticism, it may be possible to subvert the text's desire, to hear what it does not wish to say.

In the French genre of the confessional *récit*, the protagonist is a young man, mismothered, unable to love; he recounts the story of his failure to a paternal interlocutor and frame-narrator who serves him as double and invites him, through confession, to enter the patriarchal order. The stake is a female character who, in almost every case, dies (more or less by his wish), releasing him to tell the tale. Her absence is necessary for him to narrate. But, as Gide's

Michel puts it, 'at times I am afraid that what I have suppressed will take revenge'.[2] There remains in each of these texts the trace of the woman's voice, uttering her desire and her knowledge, to haunt the male couple.

Let us suppose that when men write fiction they take up in phantasy the position of the oedipal father. Bidding to be in conscious control of language, they negotiate to place the reader in the position of son. What is at stake between them is the unknowing, momentarily desired mother. As I have argued elsewhere, this can be seen most clearly in realist fiction in the transaction of irony, where the quintessential character is the woman whose *style indirect libre* is marked as stupid, uncreative, uncontrolled.[3] The reader is uncertain of 'his' gender, for by the very act of reading, 'he' is approaching the receptive role of an Emma Bovary who has read clichés and can think in nothing else. If for Flaubert a temporary identification with her ('Madame Bovary, c'est moi') is, controlled by irony, a fantasmatic mode of emancipation from his own desire, the reader must choose 'his' gender by ignoring the desire of the woman and joining the author in an ironic critique of her. Son and father agree to write the mother out of the text, for to desire her is not to have the phallus. They conspire both to rid the text of her and to entrap her in it: she is immured. A man's reading is already problematic, as I have suggested; but to read as a woman is to find oneself in the outsiderhood of the hysteric: never implied by the system, one can co-opt its fantasy by accepting the phallic law of the triad (though that makes one's own position hopeless), or risk psychosis by forming a kind of alliance with the mother-character.

The *récits* I shall refer to here are Prévost's *Manon Lescaut* (1731), Chateaubriand's *René* (1805), Constant's *Adolphe* (1816), Gautier's *Mademoiselle de Maupin* (1835–6), Musset's *La Confession d'un enfant du siècle* (1836), Mérimée's *Carmen* (1845), Nerval's *Sylvie* (1853), and Fromentin's *Dominique* (1863).[4] These texts display the following set of 'family resemblances': they are written by, of, and (by implication) to men; in the narrative of the protagonist's failed life the central woman, somewhat older than him, focuses the motifs of childbed death and incestuous desire; in almost every case she dies and he lives to tell the tale. The frame-narrator to whom the protagonist speaks chides and criticizes him but also sympathizes and listens with the express aim of bringing him into a patriarchal adulthood, even though, with the woman dead, he is in a zomboid, helpless state, as if he were the victim rather than the agent of her murder.

In nearly every one of these texts, the protagonist's mother is dead; most typically she has died giving birth to him: 'I cost my mother her life when I came into the world', Chateaubriand's René begins his confession.[5] This traumatic moment of the childbed death is the premise from which his history proceeds: the infant hero has both murdered and been abandoned by the mother, and his consequent attitude to the mother's surrogate is both resentment and guilt. The beloved functions as a substitute mother upon whom a vengeful repetition of the childbed death will be practised. But as first, incestuous substitute she is also (in *René* literally) his sister. Implicit in his sibling structure is a hint that the mother-daughter pair will not entail a childbed death: that, even if sometimes problematically, mother and daughter can coexist, forming a kind of couple that mother and son cannot. These texts are almost all haunted by a grouping of women in knowledge or desire that is the inverse of the man's own deadly relationship with the mother.

An archetypal structure for all these themes is the myth of Narcissus and Echo. I want to suggest that this myth is the 'unthought' of the Oedipus complex, just as the mystery of female sexuality both lies behind and is excluded from the Oedipus complex. Not only the desire of women but women's knowledge is written out of it: yet for the latter to exist this desire and this knowledge must first have been there. Mother and daughter alike must be unsaid in order for the men to speak.

If we look at Ovid's text on the Narcissus myth, we find that the story begins with an argument over knowledge. Jupiter, in his cups, and Juno (drunk or sober, we are not told) are having a jovial discussion about which sex gets more pleasure out of love-making; he asserts that it is the woman; she disagrees. (For here, unsurprisingly, he is playing Lacan: 'the women simply don't know what they are saying, that's the whole difference between them and me'.)[6] They call in Tiresias to arbitrate, for he once spent eight years cursed with a woman's body, and ought to know; and he sides with Jupiter. In anger, Juno strikes him blind; to compensate, her husband gives him the gift of infallible knowledge and the voice of prophecy.

The first exercise of Tiresias' skill is in his judgement on Narcissus. Asked if he will live to a ripe age, the prophet replies, '"If he ne'er know himself."'[7] The child of a nymph raped by the water-god, Narcissus is so beautiful that everyone loves him, but he loves nobody. Chief among his adorers is the nymph Echo, a skilled speaker who once kept Juno talking so that the other nymphs who had been dallying with Jupiter could get away; for this her speech was 'curtailed' and she was condemned by Juno only to repeat the last words that others spoke to her. Echo falls heatedly in love with cold Narcissus; she turns his rebuffs into her own appeals, but he is indifferent to her desire, and eventually she fades (without dying) into the dry rocks and hills of the landscape, fated always to see and repeat. So much for the mother's knowledge and the daughter's desire. Narcissus, as we all know, gets his come-uppance when, espying his own reflection in a pool, he falls in love with the one creature that cannot physically requite him. Here is the description of the pool:

> There was a clear pool with silvery bright water, to which no shepherds ever came, or she-goats feeding on the mountain-side, or any other cattle; whose smooth surface neither bird nor beast nor falling bough ever ruffled. Grass grew all around its edge, fed by the water near, and a coppice that would never suffer the sun to warm the spot. (p. 153)

This pool is not only as glassy as a mirror; its shadiness, secrecy, mysterious coolness and inaccessibility to anyone but Narcissus surely designate it as the entrance/exit of the mother's genital. His fate is to return to the uncanny repressed, seek his reflection there and find death. As for Echo, she ends up being no more than the repetition of words provided by Narcissus; yet despite this she has the gift of survival. What remains of her is somehow less vulnerable that what remains of him, a voice that haunts rather than the mark of a flower. Through her silencing a truth subsists that proves him a liar. In this, Juno and Echo are, despite their mutual enmity, brought together. The women's knowledge and desire are only disabled as long as they are silenced and kept apart. How this provisionally happens in the individual texts we shall see in a moment. The main way is by isolating the woman in the position of the protagonist's mirror.

For while, as I suggested above, the male figures in and around the text function as doubles for the protagonist, the woman is required to serve him as his mirror. We are familiar with the object-relations theory that the mother must reflect the child in order to give it first security, then a rightful emancipation from her; in Lacan, she is likewise one mirror before which the infant can practise the fiction of a self. In a remark by Kristeva we can see the consequences of this for the mother: 'we direct towards the mother not only our needs for survival but above all our earliest mimetic aspirations. She is the other subject, an object that guarantees my being as a subject.'[8] The rapidly switched juxtaposition of 'subject' and 'object' in the second sentence here shows how the mother's subjectivity is strictly constrained by the child's desire for her as mirror. This carries through to the relations of men and women in adulthood. Irigaray's 'plane mirror' is the focus in which men wish to hold women as other, to guarantee their own position as knowing subjects. Woolf argued sixty years ago that 'women have served all these centuries as looking-glasses possessing the magic and delicious power of reflecting the figure of man at twice its natural size':[9] her smallness is a measure of his stature. But the process is never stable: even the most passive mirror is always a fiction. Woolf continues, 'if she begins to tell the truth, the figure in the looking-glass shrinks'; the concave speculum or the speaking woman is the pool in which Narcissus perishes. Curiously or not, what we find in the texts is that it is when the woman seems most clearly to resemble the man that he finds her the most threatening. Like the mother and son of the childbed death, it seems, in his imagination, she cannot know or desire without damaging his knowledge and his desire.

I want to take some examples from the confessional *récit* of how the protagonist attempts to use the woman as his mirror, what he seeks to find there, and how, when he fails – or, as he suggests, she fails him – he directs towards her a destructive violence that ends by serving him ill. I shall conclude by suggesting that this whole manoeuvre enacts an epistemophilia in which his knowledge is sought at the expense of hers. In a variety of ways, what is presented in these Romantic texts as overweening desire is a penetrative impulse in which the man seeks a reflected self he can never have. The *imaginaire* invested in the woman cannot be carried into the triadic structure of adulthood. She has to die, in order for him to speak to the fathers. But her destruction, like Echo's, is never complete.

A cluster of key motifs emerges from these texts. In the first two I shall discuss, *Manon Lescaut* and *Carmen*, the woman plays the role of a *femme fatale*. Manon is first glimpsed by the worldly-wise frame-narrator, the Man of Quality, chained by the waist among a group of prostitutes bound for deportation. She immediately strikes him as different: '[her] look and face were so ill-fitting her situation that in any other state I should have taken her for a person of the noblest rank.'[10] The protagonist Des Grieux is standing close by; he has even less place in this company; yet of him the frame-narrator comments: 'he was dressed very simply, but one can distinguish a man of birth and breeding at the first glance.... I perceived, in his eyes, his face and every movement, such a refined and noble manner that I felt instinctively disposed to wish him well' (p. 13). The Man of Quality quits the scene shaking his head at 'the incomprehensible nature of women' (p. 15).

Where women are enigmatic, men are recognizable. As the story is told, it becomes clear that Manon's very unreliability is essential to Des Grieux's recognition of himself. For him to love she must fail to love. To explain his crimes to the fathers – he swindles, murders, escapes from prison, and abducts Manon – it is enough to plead that his passion and specifically the object of his passion is at fault. Manon's desires – 'she was mad about pleasure; I was mad about her' (p. 50) – are the sufficient cause of Des Grieux's profligacy. But when she works to support them both (and sleeping with rich men is the only way open to her) the boy is aghast; for here the mirror has turned from the reflector that enlarges to one that diminishes. Her skill can only suggest his inadequacy: he finds himself in the role of dependent son. The turning point of their relationship comes when Manon sends her lover a surrogate, a girl she hopes 'will cheer you up for a little while; for the faithfulness I want from you is the faithfulness of the heart' (p. 147). In front of this woman, a more malleable mirror (for he has nothing invested in her), Des Grieux learns the power of the epithet 'whore', and makes *maman* into *putain* by subsuming Manon into 'a sex that I detest' (p. 136); henceforth she is more or less silenced.

The next time they are imprisoned, Des Grieux is offered his freedom at the price of Manon's deportation; he pleads on her behalf, not because he differs from the fathers in viewing her as the guilty cause of his errors, but because he still wants her as his 'thing'. They go together into exile, where she services all his needs, avows her guilt, showers him with attentions. But he feels incomplete in private bliss; admitting to the Governor of Louisiana that he lied when he said they were married, Des Grieux asks to make an honest woman of Manon. Now the exchange of women goes into operation, and it becomes clear that Des Grieux is not yet a man. Manon may be a cypher, a thing, but she confers significance. In order to function, he will have to relinquish her, the phallus he must first concede in order to seek it in the symbolic. They run away, she dies, uttering undying devotion, and he breaks his sword and buries 'in the bosom of the earth the most perfect and lovable thing it ever bore' (p. 200). He collapses prostrate on her grave. With this voluntary castration, he earns the right to return and to speak.

By burying Manon, Des Grieux is going one stage further than when he tried to use her as his mirror. He closes his story: 'you will find this difficult to believe, but all the time I was carrying out this doleful ministry, not a tear fell from my eyes nor a sigh from my lips' (pp. 200–1). In other words, he is giving nothing away, but incorporating the *mana* that Manon gave forth as she literally expired. For what emerges from his narrative is that it is from the moment he met her that he acquired eloquence, the language he can now turn to symbolic uses. In order to be his own narrator the protagonist must consume the woman, both her skills and her utterance, and then give her forth as his text. This is the exchange upon which his transaction with the Man of Quality depends, just as it is the arrangement by which the author seeks to make us his double, the implied reader. But in a whole series of ways, Manon continues to echo in the text. By popular consent her name alone is used as its title (the original title names them both: *Histoire du Chevalier des Grieux et de Manon Lescaut*) and this suggests not just that she remains the stake among the men who read her, but also that something of her exceeds the entrapment of the structure.

In a key scene just before the turning point of the surrogate woman, Manon plays a joke on Des Grieux and his rival, an Italian prince. Persuading her lover to stay at home so that she can dress his hair in front of her looking-glass, she watches him with fascination as he is seduced by the image of himself as feminized Narcissus; then she drags him by his hair to the doorway where she holds a hand-mirror up to the prince and declares that Des Grieux is the only one she can love. This scene, a late addition, is apparently intended to show Manon in a more devoted light than elsewhere; but the mirrors tell their own tale. The woman has subverted the oedipal structure, turned the mirrors outward and laughed at the men. Des Grieux misreads her act as simply flattering and remains unconscious of the threat; but plot allows him quickly and definitively to curtail her power. When she moves on to what amounts to a proffered exchane of Des Grieux among the women, her transgression is too overt to tolerate, and she is doomed.

The *femme fatale*, then, is a woman whose very strengths are tolerated by the order that requires her to function as its mirror. Her speech and skills are co-opted as guilts that justify her lover's crimes. In *Carmen*, these crimes culminate in murder. Don José tells his story to the sympathetic frame-narrator on the eve of his execution; he has murdered the gypsy Carmen, and he recounts his confession in order to prove her the cause of her own death. The crux of this text is political. The very endogamy of the dark woman threatens to make Don José a gypsy: here we see the reverse of the consumption of woman by men. If he is to be perceived (as the frame-narrator 'recognizes' him) as essentially blond and fine, a *hidalgo* under a tanned exterior, he must kill the woman who has tolerated him in her gang. Like Manon, she works for her living, commands several languages, is a mistress of disguise, and regards her lover as a 'pretty boy' with whom she can be briefly happy. But by the end of the narrative, she is similarly speaking the language he wants of her. She consents to her murder in the terms of her own soothsaying, which now serves the narrator as fictional fatality: '"You want to kill me, I know it", she said; "it is written; but you will not make me yield."'[11] In the death-scene, by the logic of the mirror, Carmen's strength is José's weakness. He cannot win. As he strikes her, she falls 'without crying out. I can still see her large black eye staring at me; then it clouded over and closed' (p. 402).

The large black eye, emblem of the woman as uncanny and malign, will recur elsewhere. Like Des Grieux, Don José reacts to Carmen's death by collapsing: 'I remained prostrate for a whole hour before the body' (p. 402). In confessing, he must show himself the victim rather than the aggressor: only the frame-narrator can tame her into an anthropological exemplum of a wayward tribe: he closes the text with a spectacularly irrelevant excursus on Gypsy ways. In this instance, the frame allows a pause for adjusting the clothing. But Carmen as *femme fatale* retains her gleaming eye.

In *René* and *Adolphe*, the earliest nineteenth-century *récits*, the oedipal thematics emerge especially clearly. Chateaubriand's fantasm of incest as prelapsarian innocence informs his earlier fiction, *Atala*, in which the American-Indian heroine dies because her Christian mother made her vow eternal virginity; temptation in the shape of her quasi-brother Chactas proves so powerful that suicide is her only way out. In *René*, the hero suffers from a vague malaise: nothing seems to satisfy him; disembodied and objectless desire blights his universe; he travels everywhere but ends up trailing home to his sister Amélie who seems unwilling to welcome him. René's problem is descried in a preface by the author as having to do with premature reading: too many examples vicariously enjoyed makes any real *jouissance* impossible. The suggestion here is that speech never preceded writing: the triad was always already in place, René cast into it and forever seeking an origin. His own story tells things a bit differently. He is not noticeably a reader, but his origin is shrouded by the absences, angers, and guilts of the childbed death. His father favours an older brother (a staple of the family-romance structure of most Romantic narratives) and he spends an idyllic youth running free on the ancestral estate with Amélie. Only after they leave home does she begin to behave with inexplicable disloyalty: slipping away, retreating to a convent, insisting he must walk alone.

This set of reactions becomes 'Amélie's secret', and secrecy is another form of enigma. The protagonist has a right to penetrate this veil: how dare she keep something from him? What he finds, uttered from the coffin in the drastic intimacy of the convent ceremony wherein Amélie plays both the bride and the sacrifice of Christ, is the avowal that she loves him incestuously. Thus she is guilty. But as the frame-figure Père Souël observes, 'I fear that, by a horrible justice, this confession from the grave may have troubled your soul in its turn' (p. 243). There are plenty of clues that René has shared or even perhaps initiated this desire. As soon as he hears her utter the secret, he feels a sudden relief; having 'a pain that [is] not imaginary' (p. 234) provides him with a meaning at last: 'my passions, so long indeterminate, flung themselves violently upon this prey' (p. 234). The sadism of the image is not fortuitous.

The nun acts just like a *femme fatale*: Amélie's secret is the incarnate, deadly equivalent of René's malaise. Just as she serves him as oedipal mother, so she provides the body in which to bury his tabooed desire. Like the other protagonists, René lives aimlessly and passively from the time of his sister's death until he expels his story. He fails even now to admit either the desire or the guilt that is really at stake; he remains enclosed in his self-pity, sueing with the fathers Chactas and Souël for a right to manhood that they variously concede.

Adolphe as a male-authored love story has an unusual twist: it is the woman, not the protagonist, who desires in vain. But from the model of *René*, we can infer that in doing this she is carrying something for him that he cannot overtly admit. Adolphe, another brilliant boy of whom the fathers have high hopes, grows up motherless, alone with a father whose coolness and cynicism make the son seem passionate. It is only later, when his primary and embattled partnership is with Ellénore, that Adolphe sees himself (reflected in her 'domineering' desire) as cold, pitying, tied by the conscience that doth make cowards of us all. This woman, another outsider, talented linguist, a disempowered heiress living with a Count whose children she has borne but who will not marry her, is browbeaten into becoming Adolphe's mistress, whereupon he immediately tires of her. Her anxious possessiveness appears to follow him everywhere, there is nowhere in the visible world where she is not calling him home. Throughout the rest of her life, he struggles to be free, so he claims, but never succeeds in disengaging himself until she reifies his wish by a quasi-suicidal collapse.

Then, even before she is dead, Adolphe realizes that he needs her gaze in order to know he exists: 'I had crushed the one who loved me ... already I felt my isolation ... I no longer lived in the atmosphere of love that she had spread around me ... all nature seemed to be telling me that soon, for ever, I would cease to be loved.'[12] These terms anticipate (or for Adolphe, as narrator, echo) a letter from Ellénore which he reproduces at the end of his narrative. In a particularly acute form in this text, we see the blight of the triadic structure. The death of his mother is not even mentioned, yet the logic of the childbed death informs the fantasy of the narrative. With his father, Adolphe communicates by letter: distance is perceptible even in their closest encounters. While wooing Ellénore, the gap to be overcome lends energy to desire: 'I tried ... every way to fix her attention upon me' (p. 45). But as soon as they have become lovers, 'Ellénore ... was no longer an aim; she had become a tie' (p. 59). Here the woman stands as the negative link between Adolphe and his adulthood; what he does not perceive is that (Romantically) their couple preserves him in a delicious state of potentiality. Ellénore's mythically maternal demands on his time and loyalty – only once, in a liminal letter, do we glimpse her as other friends see her, charming, sociable; everywhere else her slightest and frequent initiatives are reworded by Adolphe as pathetic bids to hold him – place her as the fixed point from which his transcendence pulls. But paranoia is simply the inverse of need: when the natural universe is rid of her, there is no one to mark out his value, and no reaction-formation 'pity' to justify indecision. We see Adolphe in the frame as zomboid, lifeless, exactly as Ellénore has predicted. For the direct confrontation of the mirror was necessary to justify the triad; without it, Adolphe's occupation is gone.

Two texts published in the 1830s provide variations on the structure of the *récit*. In neither does the woman die. There is in each a stress on the protagonist's childishness, a kind of innocence that incorporates the blaséness of early corruption, always someone else's fault. The deformation of desire still burns the man but brands the woman. *Mademoiselle de Maupin* and *La Confession d'un enfant du siècle* also share a preoccupation with surface and costume in which epistemophilia is a matter of rending the clothing and penetrating to a secret nudity.

In *Mademoiselle de Maupin*, we find in narrative Gautier's aesthetic of the surface, an art-for-art's-sake fascination with the ambiguities of form. The protagonist d'Albert desires a woman he has never met but whom he can precisely describe. Restless meantime, he takes up with a hard-headed woman who keeps him amused and whom he names Rosette after the colour of her dress – and the name of his dog. D'Albert's phantasy is based in an aesthetic that can conceive of beauty only as static and female; yet there are hints that he desires it less as something to have than as something to be: 'I have never wished for anything so much as to be like the seer Tiresias and meet those serpents on the mountain that cause a change of sex.'[13] If in Rosette he finds only 'a *jouissance* of the skin' (p. 126), he imagines that with his ideal woman he will both penetrate and be penetrated. As it turns out, d'Albert meets the object of his desire while he is staying in Rosette's chateau – but to his consternation she appears to be a man. This ambiguity (in Gautier's poetry, precisely the most maddening source of beauty) horrifies the protagonist, for now the self he sees reflected is of no sex, no one.

This text is unusual both in the explicitness of the protagonist's desire for feminization and in that the woman is the most fully drawn; Madeleine de Maupin has taken on men's clothing because of a desire to know. Entrapped as a girl, she enacts her transcendence in the only way that will allow her to hear what men say to each other when no women are present. By the time she meets d'Albert, however, moved by the passion she has aroused in Rosette, she is unsettled: desiring both a woman and (in the abstract and with a certain reluctance) a man, she is blighted precisely by the costume that makes her accessible to each. She and Rosette discuss d'Albert in the most dismissive of terms, but they are both contained by the aesthetic he has voiced. Madeleine cannot undress because, if the logic insists that only surface can be desired, *jouissance* is precluded by knowledge. Since only a woman can be beautiful, for Madeleine to be the woman she is under the clothes, she has to go through a denudation that can only be loss. The image she presents d'Albert, problematic for him, becomes for her a presiding wish for androgyny: 'my dream would be to have both sexes by turn, in order to satisfy my double nature: today a man, tomorrow a woman ... thus my whole nature would produce itself and be visible, and I should be perfectly happy' (p. 394). After a certain loss of innocence, she could be what d'Albert desires.

There is a happy ending of sorts. Madeleine appears dressed as Rosalind in a closing scene from *As You like It*. The cross-dressed surface did indeed lie: Rosette turns pale and d'Albert exults 'I felt an enormous sense of well-being, as if a mountain or two [i.e. breasts?] had been lifted from my chest' (p. 294). After waiting a while, Madeleine lets him undo her *décolleté*, and we are proudly assured that his potency is satisfying and multiple. But even this performance must end in exhaustion and when d'Albert is asleep, Madeleine passes on to Rosette's room. The frame-narrator concludes: 'what she said there, what she did there, I have never been able to find out, though I have made the most conscientious researches' (p. 410). Knowledge is, finally, the secret of women.

The triumph of women at the end of this text is markedly overt. D'Albert henceforth will only be able to seek the trace of Madeleine, who departs in self-possession, upon the body of Rosette. The conclusion of the aesthetic quest remains irresolvable, but in the 'oral sexual intercourse' of women's speech and desire,[14] it is suggested, there is something beyond the surface that phallic knowledge cannot attain.

La Confession d'un enfant du siècle is best understood in conjunction with Musset's play *Lorenzaccio*, written during the liaison with George Sand that provided the model for the novel. Lorenzo, the hero, has planned the oedipal murder of his cousin Alexandre, tyrant over the mother-city Florence. For half of the play, we see this girlish boy wear a corrupt exterior, pimping for his uncle, mocking revolutionary values. Then he confesses to a paternal friend that, all along, he has been acting a role: the 'true self' awaiting the moment to strike remained within in the form of motive. The imagery of surface and depth is extremely rich. Lorenzo recognizes that from the moment he began to play the part of Alexandre's ally he was entering a 'brotherhood [*confrérie*] of vice'.[15] Here the French noun, feminine in gender and containing an additional pun on the female genital, indicates how the self as transcendent, the questing phallus, feels itself soiled by the very medium of the female body, what Sartre calls the 'viscous'. Now, at the point of confession, Lorenzo recognizes that vice has become a garment that is 'stuck to my skin' (p. 118).

177

He can no longer divest himself of it, it has become all he is, there is no 'true self' and all that remains is the phallic existential act – 'my whole life is at the tip of my dagger' (p. 120) – which must be both futile and suicidal.

If we compare Lorenzo and Madeleine de Maupin we find significant differences. She can remove the costume and her naked self is positively androgynous; he perceives himself as a part-object, the transcendent motive embodied in a separating phallus that can only castrate what it leaves behind. In carrying out his assassination, he enacts his wish to enter the symbolic, but he cannot survive the act, for the quarrel is not really with the man, as the intervening years have proved, it is with the loss of self into the woman. Like d'Albert, he wishes to 'put on' womanhood, but finds that it has entrapped him, he cannot come out again.

The protagonist of *La Confession d'un enfant du siècle*, Octave, is an innocent surrounded by bad educators. His mistress betrays him, his friend leads him into vice, his father is feeble, his mother presumably dead, and the very century is an inadequate parent. In the phase when he is following his friend into the seedy centres of Paris, we glimpse, among the skeletal prostitutes, several for whom vice is a kind of filial virtue: mother and daughters coexist here somehow while women and men can only strangle one another. The corrupt man is described thus: 'nature herself feels her divine entrails withdrawing around you ... you have played false with your mother's laws, you are no longer the brother of nurselings ... every woman you embrace takes a spark of your strength without giving you any of hers ... where a drop of your sweat falls there grows a sinister graveyard plant.'[16] Heterosexuality is a version of onanism at best, a petrifying contagion that makes a man sterile.

The woman Octave finally falls in love with is another nun-like figure, modest, nurturing, and framed in the benign world of nature. Brigitte must have a past – she is a youthful widow, retired to tend roses – but we never hear of it. It is left to Octave to be the corrupting influence; as soon as, like Ellénore, she has given in to his demands, she becomes the butt of obsessive but always objectless jealousy. Precisely the opposite of the model George Sand, Brigitte has seemingly no desires of her own, so that the jealousy is attributable only to the boy's cruel powers. Nights of passionate conflict, masks, costumes, vows, and reconciliations send them both half-mad. Then they go to Paris intending to leave for a journey, and during this interim Octave suddenly finds his suspicions vanish and his heart fill with trust. A family friend of Brigitte's, the saintly Smith, appears frequently but at this point, where the plot requires that Brigitte shall at last turn to someone else, Octave is innocent of any sense of rivalry. Virtue, in other words, must now remain intact, and the maternal woman must be prepared to sacrifice even desire in order to nurture the boy, so that he can rise to the consummate sacrifice of (father-like) 'giving her away' to Smith. When Octave considers murdering Brigitte but chooses instead to pass her on to the other man, he is opting for the mode of manliness that most effectively silences her and reaffirms his 'innocence'.

It is in *Sylvie* that the protagonist comes nearest to admitting how the woman serves him as a mirror. Diagnosing his generation of aesthetic youngsters as horrified by a real woman because the latter 'outraged our naivety [*révoltait notre ingénuité*]',[17] he suggests a mutual causation between the sense of innocence and the repulsion from a dyadic encounter. Similarly, he has avoided getting to know the actress he adores because 'I was afraid I might cloud the magic mirror that cast me back her image' (p. 590). A mirror can only cast me back my own image; the wording here indicates not only how far the woman as unreal carries the perceived reality of the man, but also how almost-consciously he understands his repulsion as *fear*. What he is afraid of he keeps at bay by ignorance. Not knowing her, he can believe in a more or less prenatal symbiosis: 'I felt myself living in her, and she lived for me alone' (p. 590).

There are three women in this text; two, Aurélie the actress and Adrienne the nun, are felt uncannily to resemble each other, almost to be one person. The protagonist (he is never given a name) only ever saw Adrienne twice, both times spotlighted in a nimbus of aristocratic sanctity and singing in a 'penetrating' voice; now he feels suddenly sure that he desires the actress simply as a double of that idealized figure. The third is the eponymous Sylvie, a childhood friend he actually knew; but, characterized as 'sweet reality' (p. 624), she too is required to sit still and play the abstract noun. In the course of the narrative, encounters with Sylvie and Aurélie show how the mirror that speaks must outsize the gazer. To each of them the head-in-air protagonist takes a tellingly venal attitude: Aurélie must by her profession be for sale, and as for Sylvie, though he has not visited her for three years, no one will have married her, she is so poor. Money as his mode of control is supposed to keep each woman in place. But when he goes back to find Sylvie, she is much changed. No longer the lace-maker he rejoiced to see 'almost' (but no more) 'a young lady' (p. 603), she now makes gloves with a nasty-looking machine, sings not folk-songs but the airs of opera, and, most disturbing of all, has started reading books. Whereas, a few years earlier, the protagonist could impress her with quotations from *La Nouvelle Héloïse*, she has since ignored the prefatory warning in the book that any girl who enters its pages will be 'a fallen woman [*perdue*]' and read on, 'trusting to my reason' (p. 611). Now the man finds himself inhibited: 'I tried to talk of what was in my heart but, I don't know why, all I could find were common expressions, or even suddenly some pompous phrase from a novel – which Sylvie might have read' (p. 617). The irruption of the woman's knowledge into a sincerity that suddenly seems derivative is darkening the mirror. He leaves hastily and goes back to Paris and the actress.

The latter proves no more amenable. After a year or more, they begin an affair, but it collapses when the protagonist tells her the story of Adrienne. She is outraged at the transference: '"you expect me to tell you that the actress is the same as the nun; you are trying to create a drama and the ending won't work. Go away, I don't believe you any more!"' (p. 623). Here too, then, the mirror refuses to comply; in her over-resemblance – for she does know how to love – she serves him ill and wants no more of him.

There is a twist at the end. If the uncanny doubling is a threat, since it proves derivation, points towards a repressed origin in the never-had mother, then the canny pairing among rivals might seem more hopeful. The protagonist sees between Adrienne and Sylvie a pairing he can control: native of the same region but divided by class, rivals for his affection, 'two halves of a single love, the one the sublime ideal, the other sweet reality' (p. 624). But at the close of the text, he reports Sylvie's reaction to his suggested likeness between the actress and the nun. She bursts out laughing at the absurdity of it, then sighs and adds: '"Poor Adrienne! She died at the Convent of Saint-S..., in 1832"' (p. 626). Here, as in *Mademoiselle de Maupin*, we once again find the protagonist and the implied reader excluded from a knowledge and alliance shared by women. We never discover how or why Adrienne died; we cannot even tell when, since the date meshes with no other date in the text; and the sigh denotes a kind of solidarity that routs the doubling of author and implied reader. The woman's death in this text is subverted by the knowledge of another woman.

Dominique, the last of my nineteenth-century *récits*, is written self-consciously as a latecomer. Maturity is its presiding pose. We are to believe the eponymous protagonist fully emancipated from his selfish youth, but as lord of the manor he has now what he always desired: utter domination over the space he surveys. The childbed death is explicit here, but the orphaned Dominique feels no bereavement until, in his early teens, he has to leave the estate, site of circumscribed Nature and locus of the father's inherited name. At school he meets the elegant Olivier and the latter's two cousins, Julie, a mere child, and Madeleine, convent-raised, described in nothing but negatives, who will become the arbitrary object of desire.[18] When, one spring, Dominique feels the sap rising, Madeleine is the first creature he sees and thenceforth every energy is devoted to forcing her to look on him.

This sadistic process takes years, for, as the intelligent Olivier points out, Madeleine is now married, probably perfectly happily, and has no more than a friendly interest in him. But the discovery of her engagement – '"Madeleine is lost [*perdue*] and I love her!"'[19] – is understood by Dominique as a challenge he cannot let go. Olivier is adored by his younger cousin Julie and feels her gaze pursue him wherever he goes; yet we see Julie love in precisely the opposite way to Dominique, masochistically and anorexically turning the man's refusal against herself. In this text, women's desire is always dangerous, at once pursuing phallus and the quicksand *vagina dentata*. Here is the description of Julie's eye:

> What a strange child she was in those days! dark, slight, nervy, with
> the impenetrable air of a young sphinx, and her gaze, sometimes ques-
> tioning, never answering, her absorbant eye! This eye, perhaps the finest and

the least seductive that I have ever seen, was the most striking feature
in the physiognomy of this over-sensitive, suffering, proud little creature.
Large, wide, with long lashes that never let a single bright point show
through, veiled in a dark shade of blue that gave it the indefinable colour of
summer nights, this enigmatic eye dilated without light, and all the rays
of life were concentrated there, never again to spring forth. (pp. 127–8)

Beautiful but unseductive, we are anxiously assured, this eye nevertheless
draws the 'rays of life' towards its colourless hole. Dark, shadowy, like the
'little creature' for which it is metonym, it is also large, wide, striking, dilates
like a penis, mirroring the object it kills. The image is both castrating and a
fearful portrayal of fatherhood: for the rays that do not emerge are an
ejaculation accepted by the female body and therefore no longer the man's.
Where the seed remains, there is a rival child. It is no wonder that Madeleine
will be condemned (unlike her biographical original) to childlessness. This is
another instance of the pool in which Narcissus drowns; what lies within it is
a mirroring unsafe to desire.

After hounding Madeleine until she utters the 'secret' that she knows he
loves her, Dominique observes with delight that he has provoked a passion
that is tearing her apart. Recalling the moment, he exults: 'Madeleine was lost
[perdue] and all I had to do now was dare' (p. 250). 'Perdue', that key feminine
epithet, has come full circle from meaning 'unavailable' to meaning 'available'.
After an interim, Dominique visits Madeleine at her estate and finds her
throwing herself at him.

The final pages are full of tension. Her frustration, expressed in grins, glares,
a fiendish horse-ride, terrify the lover who prowls by her unlocked door but
'saves himself' by choosing not to enter. On the day he is to leave, she asks
him to help fold her shawl, and falls into his arms. Here we see the limits of
his desire. At first immobile and pale as a corpse, Madeleine then opens her
eyes, reaches up, and begins to kiss him. The narrator now describes how he
flings her off, 'loosening my grip as a beast might stop biting' (p. 276). Typing
her 'the beloved victim', he abandons her out of something he calls pity, and
watches as she leaves the room backwards without taking her eyes off him,
'with a terrifying pantomime that still today fills these ancient memories with
all manner of anxieties and shame' (p. 277).

The woman's desire is the 'secret' Dominique has drawn forth; once she
has admitted she wants him, he leaves her. For consummation is precisely what
he does not wish: 'drawn in' by her gaze he might lose all he knows as himself,
finding inside the maternal body something that castrates.

The self found in the pool is surely terrifying because, as in Manon's mirror
or the effigy of Madeleine de Maupin, it is in one form or other feminized.
The reflected figure desired by Narcissus could be, rather than another male
self, a sister, that creature who evades the childbed death and can coexist with
the mother. Women's desire is the impossible reply which emerges from the

mirror. This is the meaning of the women's survival in all these texts; not only the single woman (or the single eye) but also a plurality of sisters, rivals turned allies, mothers and daughters, undermine the pairing structure of the male doubles. The exchange of women among men – cyphers hyped as unique – is broken down by a female doubling that is a communication of both desire and knowledge. This happens both horizontally – between Madeleine and Julie, Rosette and Madeleine de Maupin, Sylvie and Adrienne, Manon and her surrogate – and vertically between female character and reader.

I want now to suggest how the cluster of themes we have found in these texts can be brought together in an epistemophilia wherein the son can know only at the expense of the mother's bodily completeness. In the place where the maternal body is understood as castrated, that site of the uncanny which I have likened to Narcissus's pool, the male gaze sees a deadly threat to its phallic monopoly on knowledge. The women perhaps do know what they are saying after all.

It is a curious fact that in these texts, the doubles – generally taken, with reason, as a marker of the Gothic imagination – are not uncanny in their effect; the woman as mirror, more firmly embedded in a realistic alterity, is. It is because she is outside him that she affects the protagonist (and his double the implied male reader) as enigmatic or dangerous; the male figures are, by contrast, ambiguous but biddable projections of himself.[20] As I suggested earlier, it does not much matter whether we consider the author or the protagonist narrator as the projecting ego; for either of them the fictional doubles act as wishful surrogates. If we look at the thematics of *Lorenzaccio* we can see how this fantasy operates. By projection, a pure motivating self tries to preserve its knowledge (its 'aim') as distinct from an outer, acting self. The myth of an inner and an outer self – or, as I believe we can usefully infer, the ego and its phallic projection – depends on a certainty of separation. In other words, it is based both in narcissism and the fear of castration; what is valued can or must be lost. What is within must come forth – but if it does it is risked. D'Albert believes that both he and the woman he desires can be unclothed; in fact Madeleine de Maupin retains a complete self both acting and androgynous. The man's desire seeks to penetrate under the surface, but the danger in this is that, if the woman reveals the hole he wishes to find, the phallus sent forth to 'know' her may be forever lost to him; soiled by the desire of the woman, he may be feminized. By seeking in the maternal body the site of her castration, he risks his own. This is why the men, driving the women to death in the effort to release their 'secret', find every time that it is nothing other than their own secret, the image of a castrated self that means their death as men.

If the man is to be the knowing subject, women must seem epistemologically penetrable, but not easily so: there is no end-point to this knowledge, it must forever be restarted. In order to present a front which appears to invite but also evade epistemological penetration, women must be clothed in a seduction that is never really narcissistic.

Female narcissism revolves around surface phenomena – poses in mirrors, clothing, make-up. It is meant to create ever more elaborate surfaces for the male gaze to penetrate. It is not designed to cover up our 'lack' – for all that Freud symptomatically lists side by side women's narcissistic vanity and their humiliated urge to clothe the shame of castration – but to present it as an available picture which can be torn down, torn through. That this 'narcissism' is neither self-love nor self-knowledge is proved by the fact that none of us is ever satisfied with what she sees in the mirror. We reproduce a masculine epistemophilia that, going beyond the fictionality of the *imaginaire*, denies the physical wholeness of what we see.

A particularly interesting example of this can be found in Virginia Woolf's confessional writings.[21] The narrator has described her shame at looking in the mirror and the feeling that 'my natural love for beauty was checked by some ancestral dread' (p. 79); a few pages later we read about 'the moment of the puddle in the path; when for no reason I could discover, everything suddenly became unreal; I was suspended; I could not step across the puddle; I tried to touch something ... the whole world became unreal' (p. 90, ellipses Woolf's). In *The Waves*, this scene is developed further in the voice of Rhoda:

> I came to the puddle. I could not cross it. Identity failed me. We are
> nothing, I said, and fell. I was blown like a feather, I was wafted down
> tunnels. Then, very gingerly, I pushed my foot across. I laid my hand
> against a brick wall. I returned very painfully, drawing myself back into
> my body over the grey, cadaverous space of the puddle. This is life
> then to which I am committed. (p. 43)

Rhoda is an isolated figure – 'the world is entire, and I am outside of it' (p. 15) – whom other people see as 'authentic' (p. 78) or 'wild' (p. 167) but who hates mirrors, for what she sees in them 'is not my face ... I have no face' (pp. 29 and 150). On her first night in school she resolves to 'seek out a face, a composed, a monumental face, and will endow it with omniscience, and wear it under my dress like a talisman' (p. 23). But the face worn under the dress is the hole men look for, and the shallow, murky puddle beneath her feet, which she must leap over, is as exposing of that face as the mirrors nasty boys carry up stairs behind women teachers. To cross the puddle, for Woolf or her surrogate, is an unbearable reminder of the function of all mirrors in which we are meant to espy our beauty without 'ancestral dread'. Neither face is allowed to be omniscient.

Female narcissism, then, by definition a failure of knowledge, is a secondary phenomenon. The beauty by which we are desired is that which presents us as the other's mirror. If the woman's knowledge and desire are constrained by her function as mirror, that is because she is always placed in the position of mother. Both in psychoanalytic theory, wherein the mother supplies the frame of the imaginary, and is shut out from the symbolic at the risk of impeding the child's release into it, and in such remarks as Kristeva's, quoted above, in which the mother's subjecthood is limited by its function in producing the child as subject, there seems no place for her to know.

If knowledge is possible only within the logic of the phallus, there is no way out of this impasse. But, as the texts I have analysed suggest, the very ubiquity of failure, the men's death at the hands of their own narcissism, point towards an alternative. Reading the texts against their demand allows us to find not only a destructive attitude from the son towards the mother that overrides any oedipal parricide but the implicit alternative the texts cannot quite exclude: a communication between women in the text, the implicit coexistence of women, and the Echo who outlives Narcissus. It also allows us to subvert the proliferation of doubles standing guard over the narrative both inside and out, by reading as women, in a kind of knowledge which is not epistemological penetration.

Notes

This article largely reproduces material used in my book *Narcissus and Echo: Women in the French Récit* (Manchester: Manchester University Press, 1988). All translations from French are my own and reference is given to the original text. Further references to a cited text appear after quotations in brackets; passages without page reference are from the last-cited page.

1 See Shoshana Felman, *Literature and Psychoanalysis* (Baltimore and London: Johns Hopkins University Press, 1977, 1980), p. 10.
2 André Gide, *Romans, récits et soties; œuvres lyriques*, ed. M. Nadeau, Y. Davet, and J.-J. Thierry (Paris: Gallimard, 1958), p. 471.
3 See my '*Style indirect libre* to stream-of-consciousness: Flaubert, Joyce, Schnitzler, Woolf', in P. Collier and J. Davies (eds), *Modernism and the European Unconscious*, (Oxford: Polity Press, 1989).
4 See my *Narcissus and Echo*; the analysis concludes with a chapter on Gide's *L'Immoraliste* (1902) and *La Porte étroite* (1909). In these and such other twentieth-century texts as Alan-Fournier's *Le Grand Meaulnes*, Bernanos's *Journal d'un curé de campagne*, Camus's *L'Etranger*, Sartre's *La Nausée*, and Proust's *A la Recherche du temps perdu*, the key motif to emerge is that of undesire, directed not only towards the central woman but also towards the doubling men in whom homosexual or homosocial desire is more or less invested.
5 François-René, vicomte de Chateaubriand, *Atala. René, Les Aventures du dernier Abencérage*, ed. F. Letessier (Paris: Garnier, 1962), p. 185.
6 Jacques Lacan, *Le Séminaire XX: Encore*, ed. J.-A. Miller (Paris: Seuil, 1975), p. 68.
7 Ovid, *Metamorphoses I*, trans. F. J. Miller (London: Heinemann, 1916), p. 149.
8 Julia Kristeva, *Pouvoirs de l'horreur*, (Paris: Seuil, 1980), p. 43.
9 Virginia Woolf, *A Room of One's Own*, (London: Triad/Panther, 1977), p. 35.
10 Antoine François Prévost d'Exiles, *Histoire du Chevalier des Grieux et de Manon Lescaut*, ed. F. Deloffre and R. Picard (Paris: Garnier, 1965), pp. 11–12.

11 Prosper Mérimée, *Romans et nouvelles II*, ed. M. Parturier (Paris: Garnier, 1967), p. 401.
12 Benjamin Constant, *Adolphe*, ed. J.-H. Bornecque (Paris: Garnier, 1960), p. 139.
13 Théophile Gautier, *Mademoiselle de Maupin*, ed. M. Crouzet (Paris: Gallimard, 1973), p. 127.
14 See Neil Hertz, 'Dora's secrets, Freud's techniques', in C. Bernheimer and C. Kahane (eds), *In Dora's Case* (London: Virago, 1985), p. 235.
15 Alfred de Musset, *Lorenzaccio*, ed. D.-P. Cogny and P. Cogny (Paris: Bordas, 1976), p. 117.
16 Alfred de Musset, *La Confession d'un enfant du siècle*, ed. G. Barrier (Paris: Gallimard, 1973), pp. 133–4.
17 Gérard de Nerval, *Œuvres*, de. H. Lemaître (Paris: Garnier, 1966), p. 591.
18 Similarly in Gide's *récits*, both Marceline and Alissa are first described as having the quasi-invisibility of the very familiar. Marceline, for instance, is (within a couple of pages) known both 'very little' (p. 372) and 'too well to see her with fresh eyes' (p. 375); Alissa, like Madeleine, is described as having a beauty that other people see, but the protagonist fails to notice. Proust's Swann can only become obsessed with a woman who is 'not his type'. All these examples surely suggest a passion that is both entirely arbitrary and totally motivated: the incestuous desire for the mother. One's mother is never one's type.
19 Eugène Fromentin, *Dominique*, ed. B. Wright (Paris: Garnier, 1954), p. 120.
20 See Otto Rank, *The Double*, trans. H. Tucker (Chapel Hill: University of North Carolina Press, 1971), and my *The Unintended Reader* (Cambridge: Cambridge University Press, 1986), pp. 159–93.
21 Quotations from Woolf in this section are from *Moments of Being*, ed. J. Schulkind (St Albans: Triad/Panther, 1976), and *The Waves* (London: Triad/Panther, 1977).

Part Five

Sexual difference (1): reason and revolution

Chapter Eleven

Patriarchal thought and the drive for knowledge

Toril Moi

Feminism, science, and philosophy

Feminists have long criticized a phenomenon variously labelled 'male science', 'male theory', or 'male rationality', arguing that such forms of structured thought are inextricably linked with traditional sexualized – and sexist – categories of dominance and oppression. The subject/object division, for instance, essential to certain conceptions of objectivity, is cast as homologous with the male/female opposition. Science, philosophy, rationality – call it what you like – constantly re-enacts the Cartesian mind/body divide in its most basic methodological moves, so feminists claim. Always and everywhere the rational, active, masculine intellect operates on the passive, objectified, feminized body. To be intellectual – to think? – under patriarchy, the argument goes, is willy-nilly to take up a position marked as masculine. If one doesn't, one has no option but to embrace the other side of the tedious series of homologous patriarchal oppositions, where irrationality and thoughtlessness is equated with femininity, the body, object-being, emotionality, and so on. In this paper, I want first to examine certain problematic aspects in current feminist critiques of the subject/object and mind/body split, and then to sketch out a somewhat different approach to these problems.

The most influential arguments against 'male science' have been put forward by Evelyn Fox Keller. Drawing on Keller's critique in her own reading of Descartes, Susan Bordo extends her arguments to philosophy and the humanities in general. Keller's main enemy is the concept of 'objectivity', which she sees as the ruling ideological paradigm of the natural sciences. In her pioneering article of 1978, 'Gender and science',[1] she first outlines her critique of 'male science'. According to Keller, scientific ideology divides the world into 'two parts – the knower (mind) and the knowable (nature)',[2] and insists that the relation between 'knower and known is one of distance and separation ... that between a subject and object radically divided'.[3] Having divided the world, patriarchal ideology *genders* the two halves. Nature, object-ified and oppressed, is female, whereas knowledge is characterized as male:

The characterization of both the scientific mind and its modes of access to knowledge as masculine is indeed significant. Masculine here connotes, as it so often does, autonomy, separation and distance. It connotes a radical rejection of any commingling of subject and object, which are, it now appears, quite consistently identified as male and female.[4]

Scientific objectivity, then, may best be characterized as the result of the unflinching enforcement of such gendered distance between male knower and female known. Such ideology, Keller claims, excludes women from science by casting them as 'non-objective', as 'non-knowers'. Feminists, Keller argues, must refuse to accept this male vision of the subject/object division. Instead, Keller proposes a 'commingling' of the two, or an empathetic 'feeling' for the object, where the object is no longer reified, but respected in its integrity. Such empathy can only be achieved if *feeling* is allowed a place within science, not relegated to a space outside it.

So far, there is no reason to disagree with Keller. Her critique of dominant forms of Cartesian rationalism is inspiring; her denunciation of the logic of domination and objectification at work in the ideology of science timely. I particularly warm to the idea of undoing the split between reason and emotion: Keller is surely right to assume that such a change will make science – or intellectual work in general – more accessible and more attractive for many women. Apparently, my only doubt concerns a trivial matter of language: her decision to label the new mode of knowledge (which will include feeling) 'female'. If, as I take it, the new mode of thought is superior to traditional ways, why should we not claim it as universal – simply as *the* way to do science? Why imply that this new mode somehow is less suitable for males? Nor would I want to call traditional science 'male' – why not 'patriarchal'? Just as all women are not feminist, not all males are patriarchal.

Pondering these differences in vocabulary, however, I realize that they are not coincidental, and that Keller's predilection for the terms 'male' and 'female' is closely bound up with her espousal of Nancy Chodorow's deeply influential feminist rewriting of non-Kleinian object-relations theory in *The Reproduction of Mothering*.[5] Keller's project is, first, to analyse and criticize dominant notions of science and objectivity, and then to study the 'processes by which the capacity for scientific thought develops, and the ways in which those processes are intertwined with emotional and sexual development',[6] which for her means turning to Chodorow's account of the development of female and male personality structures. This theory is too well known to be repeated here.

Chodorow-inspired philosophy of science, however, goes something like this. First there is the original, blissful unity between mother and child. Then comes the inevitable separation which makes little boys lose touch with the maternal body forever, but luckily makes little girls more permeable, more open to merging with the world. Male science is structured on the male experience of separation and autonomy, which not only severs it from true communion with nature, but also leads it to adopt a language of conquest, power, and domination in its dealings with the world. This situation makes it harder for women to become scientists or intellectuals, since they will have to do violence to their female nature, their need for contact and communion, if they are to follow the paths of male science or male philosophy. The feminist solution is to work for a transformation of male science by demanding that the female virtues of empathy and understanding, often called 'female modes of knowing', be included in the scientific enterprise. Such an inclusion would also put an end to science as a domineering, power-mongering enterprise. True science or true philosophy recreates the lost unity between the knower and the known.

Keller's vocabulary of 'male' and 'female' signals her Chodorovian belief in fundamental sexual differences in male and female personality structures. In its consistent promotion of 'female' relatedness and 'male' separateness, Chodorow's deep-seated cultural (as opposed to biological) essentialism reintroduces age-old patriarchal beliefs in a specific female nature pitted against an equally specific male nature. Chodorow, Keller, Gilligan, Bordo, *et al.* come to stand as exponents of a psycho-social variety of 'difference feminism'. The root of their essentialism can be located in Chodorow's unproblematic use of non-Kleinian object-relations theory for feminist purposes. And this is not the only problem with such theory: in my (Freud- and Lacan-inspired) opinion non-Kleinian object-relations theory does not take the unconscious sufficiently into account, mistakenly rejects Freud's theory of drives as pure biologism, fails to theorize the difficult construction of subjectivity and sexual difference, neglects the contradictory and self-defeating nature of sexuality as theorized by Freud, and ends up idealizing the pre-oedipal mother–child relationship without being able to offer a coherent account of the role of the father, the Law, or repression in the construction of the subject.

The consequences for feminism are, among other things, an essentialist and quasi-biologist belief in fixed gender-identities (Chodorow will unproblematically discuss gender differences in the pre-oedipal period), and the failure to theorize resistance, disruption, and failure of identity, a failure which leads Chodorow to assume that ideologically suspect gender roles *always* succeed in imposing themselves on the human subject. Such theories cannot account for disruption, exceptions, or 'unsuccessful' socialization. Chodorow, for instance, simply abandons the question of women who choose *not* to 'reproduce mothering', just as Keller or Bordo can say nothing at all about male philosophers who do not conform to their idea of 'male objectivity'. But surely a series of male thinkers from Marx, Nietzsche, and Freud through Heidegger, Wittgenstein, and Derrida have suggested deeply anti-rationalist, anti-philosophical critiques of the Cartesian subject/object or body/mind division? Perhaps we are to think of them as 'female' philosophers? But if so, why are they never discussed by Keller and her followers?

But let us return to Keller's main problematics: the question of 'commingling' of subject and object,[7] which goes hand in hand with the 'interaction between emotional and cognitive experience'.[8] Unfortunately, the Chodorovian rejection of the theory of the drives deprives Keller of *any* discourse of the body. While 'affective' and 'cognitive' structures are supposed to meet, mind and body go unmentioned. Leaving the problem of the body aside, it is hard to understand exactly what kind of union of subject and object Keller has in mind. Terms such as 'mediation' and 'interaction'[9] remain vague. Susan Bordo, drawing on Keller, Gilligan, and Chodorow, writes approvingly about the 'natural foundation for knowledge, not in detachment and distance, but in closeness, connectedness, and empathy',[10] and nostalgically evokes the 'medieval sense of relatedness to the world', which she sees as the 'interpenetrations, through meanings and associations, of self and the world'.[11] Perhaps the best account of the ideal relationship between subject and object comes in Keller's outline of ideal, adult maturity: 'Ultimately, however, both sense of self and of other become sufficiently secure to permit momentary relaxation of the boundary between – without, that is, threatening the loss of either.'[12]

I take this to mean that the distance between subject and object is to be momentarily abolished, that is to say that the two are to merge or commune without losing their self-identity. But in its paradoxical insistence on a unity *containing* self-identity untransformed, Keller's vision of communion can only reassert the original subject/object division. In many ways the whole discourse of empathy is neither new nor particularly feminist, but rather an unwitting repetition of 'male' Romanticism. Romantic poets and philosophers sought precisely to overcome the subject/object division by advocating some form of communion between subject and object. Logically speaking, there are only two possible forms of such communion: either the object engulfs the subject, in which case there is nobody around to do the communing: or the subject engulfs the object, thereby radically destroying it as other. There is of course a sense in which the Chodorovian account of 'male' science presents us with a third solution: the image of a transcendental, *lost* unity (the original, symbiotic relationship between mother and child) to be *re-established* through 'female' empathy. As paradoxical and prone to fissures as any other 'unity' of different self-identities, such a strategy can be no more than a fantasy dissolution of a real problematics.

Drawing on her critique of the scientific 'objectification' of nature, Keller denounces modern science as essentially an enterprise of domination and mastery. In 'Feminism and science' she claims that science has only two options: control and domination (both expressions of 'masculine' aggression) over nature or 'ecstatic communion' with it.[13] But just as the child's attempt to impose control and order on its world cannot be equated with exploitative domination, it is singularly unhelpful to see all forms of intellectual mastery simply as aggressive control and domination. To be consistent, Keller's denunciation of all possible forms of mastery would logically have to include the rejection, not only of rapacious exploitation of natural resources, nuclear weapons, and dictatorship, but of agriculture, house-building, and bicycling as well.

For me, then, the problem with Keller's and Bordo's Chodorovian analysis of gender and science and philosophy is not only its cultural essentialism, but the fact that the solution proposed ('commingling', 'union' of subject and object) remains curiously timid and flawed. If the 'union' proposed reinforces the separate identities of subject and object, their grand vision of 'female science' promises no more than a certain elasticity of boundaries between separate, self-identical essences. There is no attempt here to question the logic that underpins patriarchal metaphysics, or to contest the very meaning of terms such as masculine/feminine, reason/emotion, and so on. Keller's and Bordo's timidity contrasts sharply with Hélène Cixous's deconstructive onslaught on the very same oppositions:

> Where is she?
> Activity/Passivity
> Sun/Moon
> Culture/Nature
> Day/Night
>
> Father/Mother
>
> Head/Heart
> Intelligible/Palpable
> Logos/Pathos
> Form, convex, step, advance, semen, progress.
> Matter, concave, ground – where steps are taken, holding and dumping ground.
>
> *Man*
> ———
> Woman
>
> . . .
>
> [All] these pairs of oppositions are couples ... Theory of culture, theory of society, symbolic systems in general – art, religion, family, language – it is all developed while bringing the same schemes to light. And the movement whereby each opposition is set up to make sense is the movement through which the couple is destroyed. A universal battlefield. Each time, a war is let loose. Death is always at work.[14]

By focusing on the inevitable struggle, the warring relationship between such hierarchical oppositions, Cixous at once signals that the battle between the sexes insinuates itself in the very structure of the sign, and that in the case of such binary oppositions the sexual struggle is bound up with the effort to deconstruct phallogocentric logic. By reversing and displacing the oppositions at stake, Cixous seeks to show that every opposition entails repression, violence, and death. The deconstructive move is not to *abolish* oppositions, or to deny that such signifiers exist, but rather to trace the way in which each signifier contaminates and subverts the meaning of the others. Such an approach *opens* the sign up, insists that its meaning is always deferred, never fully present to itself. In its questioning of the metaphysics of presence and identity, deconstruction offers a more radical solution to the problem of subject and object raised by Keller and Bordo. The problem is, of course, that deconstructive logic undermines all forms of essentialism, including the Chodorovian belief in 'self-identity' or 'female identity'. Paradoxically, then, the very psychological theory which enables Keller and Bordo to launch their research into the problem of knowledge in the first place, in the end radically prevents them from breaking out of the straitjacket of patriarchal binary thought.

The structures of knowledge: Michèle Le Doeuff

If Keller's analysis of knowledge and feminism turns out to be somewhat disappointing, it may be because it remains trapped by the categories of the scientific ideology it sets out to read. Perhaps one way around this problem is to approach the question from a slightly different angle. Examining not so much the ideology of knowledge as the way in which that ideology is produced by the very structures of knowledge, the French feminist philosopher Michèle Le Doeuff raises two questions: what is there in the structure of knowledge itself that lends itself to patriarchal ideologization?[15] And what is the alternative for feminists? In her excellent and wide-ranging essay 'Women and philosophy' (first published in 1976), she opens up the question of the relationship between feminism, femininity, and philosophy. Although Le Doeuff adheres to the term 'philosophy', her critique of philosophy may be read as a general critique of so-called 'male science' or 'male theory' as well.

Focusing on the double problem of the empirical exclusion of women and the theoretical repression of femininity in western philosophy, Le Doeuff argues that traditional western philosophy exhibits a striking contradiction at its centre. On the one hand, philosophy is an activity based on the recognition of *lack*: philosophy, in other words, exists because there is something that *remains to be thought*. On the other hand, philosophy also works from the imaginary assumption that the knowledge produced by philosophy creates completion, that its aim is to construct a flawless structure *without lack*. The paradoxical truth is that, for this school of thought, perfect philosophy would simply cease to be philosophy at all.

Confronted with the fundamental contradiction, woman is caught in a double bind and found doubly wanting. First, woman (the singular here denotes the imaginary, universal fantasy of woman entertained by philosophy) is perceived as lacking the phallus. According to the patriarchal imagination, what a woman needs is a man, not philosophy. If a woman declares that she too feels the philosophical lack, her desire for knowledge can only be a compensation for her primary sexual frustration. On this logic, then, the thinking woman necessarily becomes synonymous with the blue-stocking, the frustrated spinster of patriarchal ideology: the female lack is never *truly* a philosophical lack. In other words, the woman is always suspected of not being able to think simply because she is taken to suffer from the *wrong* lack.

On the other hand, woman is also deemed incapable of philosophy, that is to say of rational thought, because of her self-sufficient plenitude. Here there is no question of her lack or her castration, rather, she becomes the very emblem of narcissistic self-sufficiency. On this logic, women cannot think because they suffer no lack at all: they are complacent, cow-like, content, or *plant-like* as Hegel prefers to put it:

> Women may be capable of education, but they are not made for the
> more advanced sciences, for philosophy and certain forms of artistic
> production which require universality. Women may have ideas, taste, and
> elegance, but they do not have the ideal. The difference between men
> and women is like that between animals and plants; men correspond to
> animals, while women correspond to plants because they are more of a
> placid unfolding, the principle of which is the unity of feeling. When
> women hold the helm of government, the State is at once in jeopardy,
> because women regulate their actions not by the demands of
> universality, but by arbitrary inclinations and opinions.[16]

Woman is an inferior thinker, in other words, not because of her lack, but because of her lack of a lack. Whether woman is thought of as a whole or a hole, she is perceived as lacking in philosophy, that is to say as irrational.

By positing woman as the symbol of lack and negativity, western philosophy turns her into the ground of its own existence: by her very inferiority she guarantees the superiority of philosophy. In this way the idea of 'woman' as defective becomes a defence against the thinking male subject's potentially devastating insight into his own lack. Historically, such strategies have not only been used against women, but also against 'primitive tribes', 'slaves', 'blacks', 'children', 'Jews', 'Moslems', and so on.

The fact that philosophy presents woman as that which relentlessly undermines man's rational endeavours is not an ideological coincidence. It is the very structure of scientific thought which here is revealed. Le Doeuff insists that a discipline can only exist in so far as it can define itself *against* something else: in the same way, rational discourse can only know itself as rational by positing some irrational *outside* excluded from its own territory. Philosophical discourse is structurally obliged to assume that there is also a *different, non-rational knowledge*, of which it can know nothing. This illicit, mysterious, and threatening knowledge becomes a nameless undefined object of exclusion, only capable of metaphorical description. Thus, Le Doeuff claims, the 'man/woman difference is invoked or conscripted to signify the general opposition between definite and indefinite, that is to say validated/excluded'.[17] Philosophy itself creates its own inner enemy: femininity becomes the necessary support and signifier of rationality, operating within it as an eternal shadow that cannot be dialectically absorbed, neither obliterated nor fully assumed by the discipline.

Unlike some French feminists, Le Doeuff scornfully rejects this fantasmatic image of femininity:

> Women (real women) have no reason to be concerned by that femininity. We are constantly being *confronted* with that image, but we do not have to recognize ourselves in it.... As soon as we regard this femininity as a fantasy-product of conflicts *within* a field of reason that has been assimilated to masculinity, we can no longer set any store by liberating its voice. We will not talk pidgin to please the colonialists.[18]

For Le Doeuff only a philosophy aware of its own open and unfinished nature can hope to avoid being caught in the sterile dichotomy between reason and unreason, masculinity and femininity. A philosophy or a science conscious of its own lack, abandoning any hope of achieving that magic, imaginary closure, would be able to think through its own relationship to exclusion, instead of becoming its unwitting victim and perpetrator. This is not to say, of course, that such a self-reflexive inclusiveness would lead to the *end* of exclusion: as Le Doeuff shows, no structured thought is possible without it.

Knowledge as analytical dialogue

There can be no doubt, then, that even the most radical new construction of knowledge will produce new forms of closure, new boundaries, and new exclusions. The advantage of Le Doeuff's account is that it allows us to analyse and deconstruct the opposition between inside and outside which structures knowledge itself. In this respect, Le Doeuff's deconstruction of the boundaries between knowledge and non-knowledge is not only reminiscent of Derrida,[19] but of the very specific dialogic situation created by psychoanalytic practice. Perhaps the analytic situation may be seen as a different model of structuring knowledge, one that forces us steadily to reflect on the points of exclusion, repression, and blockage in our own discursive constructions?

At one level, Freudian psychoanalysis can be characterized as an effort to *open up* and *extend* the field of rational knowledge. Unlike Charcot, who chose to *exhibit* his hysterical patients in a gesture of dominance, Freud decided to *listen* to them: psychoanalysis is born in the encounter between the hysterical woman and the positivist man of science. It is in this reversal of the traditional roles of subject and object, of speaker and listener, that Freud more or less unwittingly opens the way for a new understanding of human knowledge. But the psychoanalytical situation is shot through with paradoxes and difficulty. For if Freud's (and Breuer's) act of listening represents an effort to *include* the irrational discourse of femininity in the realm of science, it also embodies their hope of *extending* their own rational understanding of psychic phenomena. *Grasping* the logic of the unconscious, they want to make it accessible to reason. In Joseph Breuer's listening to Anna O., there is at once a colonizing, rational impulse and a revolutionary effort to let female madness speak to male science.

When the colonizing impulse gains the upper hand, psychoanalysis runs the risk of obliterating the language of the irrational and the unconscious, repressing the threatening presence of the feminine in the process. There can be no doubt that such a imperialist tendency runs right through Freud's own writings, surfacing for instance in his treatment of Dora. But there is also in his texts a will to let the madwoman speak, to consider *her* discourse as one ruled by its own logic, to accept the logic of another scene. As long as this contradictory project is in place, the discourse of the hysteric continues to unsettle and disturb the smooth positivist logic of the man of science. Inscribing the madwoman's discourse into science, Freud unknowingly starts a process that will transform the very notions of scientificity that he believed in.

But if the analytical situation radically questions the split between active subject and passive object denounced by Keller, it is not simply because the doctor here turns listener (that would be a simple reversal and nothing more), but because the analytical session engages both analyst and patient in *transference* and *countertransference*. If transference in analysis can be roughly defined as the process whereby the patient transfers earlier traumas and reactions, whether real or imaginary, on to the analyst, countertransference may be characterized as the analyst's more or less unconscious reactions to the discourse of the patient, or rather to the transference of the patient. Transference and countertransference engage analyst and analysand in a complex, differential set of interactions, which may literally 'make or break' the analysis. The truth of the analysis, its power to cure, is the discursive construction of this transferential network. Transference and countertransference turn the analytic session into a space where the two participants encounter each other in the place of the Other, in language.[20]

Emphasizing and developing the methodological and theoretical implications of Freud's analytical practice, Jacques Lacan sees the Freudian discovery of the unconscious as a discovery of a new form of *participatory* reading:

[Freud's] first interest was in hysteria.... He spent a lot of time listening, and while he was listening, there resulted something paradoxical, a reading. It was while listening to hysterics that he read that there was an unconscious. That is, something he could only construct, and in which he himself was implicated; he was implicated in it in the sense that, to his great astonishment, he noticed that he could not avoid participating in what the hysteric was telling him, and that he felt affected by it.[21]

Caught in a web of transference and countertransference, the psychoanalytic reading, or the psychoanalytic construction is, as Shoshana Felman points out, 'essentially, constitutively dialogic'.[22] Such dialogue, however, is not enclosed in a simple dualism: for Lacan, the fact that analysis is constructed in language implies that analytic dialogue is essentially *triangular*:

> [It] is not a dialogue between two egos, it is not reducible to a dual relationship between *two* terms, but is constituted by a third term that is the meeting point in language ... a linguistic, signifying meeting place that is the locus of ... insight.[23]

For Lacan, Freudian reflexivity, Freudian dialogue, unsettles and undoes any clear-cut oppositions between subject and object, self and other. Felman draws out the implications of this point:

> By shifting and undercutting the clear-cut polarities between subject and object, self and other, inside and outside, analyst and analysand, consciousness and the unconscious, the new Freudian reflexivity substitutes for all traditional binary, symmetrical conceptual oppositions – that is, substitutes for the very foundations of Western metaphysics – a new mode of interfering heterogeneity. This new reflexive mode – instituted by Freud's way of listening to the discourse of the hysteric and which Lacan will call 'the inmixture of the subjects' (*Ecrits*, p. 415) – divides the subjects differently, in such a way that they are neither entirely distinguished, separate from each other, nor, correlatively, entirely totalizable but, rather, interfering from within and in one another.[24]

There is, then, in the psychoanalytic situation a model of knowledge which at once radically questions and displaces traditional notions of subject–object relationships and deconstructs the firm boundaries between knowledge and non-knowledge. As this situation of knowledge offers no firmly established binary opposites, it cannot be gendered as either masculine or feminine, thereby offering us a chance to escape the patriarchal tyranny of thought by sexual analogy. As feminists in search of new ways to think about objectivity, knowledge, and modes of intellectual activity, we can ill afford to neglect the model offered by psychoanalysis.

Epistemophilia or the drive for knowledge

If the psychoanalytic situation offers an interesting model of knowledge, it has little to say to Evelyn Fox Keller's interest in the genesis of knowledge or cognition. If I am unhappy with Keller's Chodorovian account of the origins of knowledge, it is first and foremost because it posits *separate* systems of emotion and cognition from the start.[25] But this is precisely the problem that needs to be solved. We should also bear in mind the way in which the reason/emotion (or head/heart) split is deeply bound up with the mind/body division (needless to say, both oppositions are read through the male/female paradigm). Feminism needs a theory of knowledge which undoes and displaces *both* dualisms, not one that in a mistaken fear of biologism rejects all efforts to include the body in thought. I now want to argue that the Freudian theory of *epistemophilia*, or the drive for knowledge, provides us with a first outline of such a theory.

For Freud the drive for knowledge, often manifested as curiosity, informs all forms of human knowledge production, including intellectual work. The desire to construct intellectual hypotheses, to obtain knowledge, and to engage in philosophical speculation, Freud claims, can be traced back to the little child's insatiable curiosity about sexuality. Often reacting to the unwelcome birth of a sibling, the child wants to know where babies come from. The question of sexual relations or what 'it means to be married' is associated with this quest for origins. So strong is the desire for knowledge that Freud calls it a drive (or 'instinct' as the *Standard Edition* has it):

> This instinct cannot be counted among the elementary instinctual components, nor can it be classed as exclusively belonging to sexuality. Its activity corresponds on the one hand to a sublimated manner of obtaining mastery, while on the other hand it makes use of the energy of scopophilia. Its relations to sexual life, however, are of particular importance, since we have learnt from psychoanalysis that the instinct for knowledge in children is attracted unexpectedly early and intensively to sexual problems and is in fact possibly first aroused by them.[26]

An ambiguous force, the drive for knowledge is uneasily poised on the dividing line between anal mastery, sadism and voyeurism, and sublimated cultural creativity. In a later (1913) essay on obsessional neuroses Freud emphasizes the sadistic aspect:

> We often gain an impression that the instinct for knowledge can actually take the place of sadism in the mechanism of obsessional neurosis. Indeed it is at bottom a sublimated off-shoot of the instinct of mastery exalted into something intellectual, and its repudiation in the form of doubt plays a large part in the picture of obsessional neurosis.[27]

Surfacing in the anal phase, the drive for mastery signals the child's need to dominate itself and its world (starting with its bowel movements). Sadism and masochism are, respectively, the active and passive form of this drive.[28]

Consistently emphasizing the ingenuity and perceptivity of children's theory formations, Freud is never tempted to discard them as irrational fantasies.

However muddled, they always contain a kernel of truth – they are, in other words, prototypes of adult, rational operations: 'the sexual theories of children ... are reflections of their own sexual constitution, and ... in spite of their grotesque errors the theories show more understanding of sexual processes than one would have given their creators credit for.'[29]

The inquisitive child is nevertheless always disappointed in its intellectual explorations. The truth about sexual intercourse is not to be had or cannot be properly understood by the child because of its own physical immaturity. 'There are', Freud writes, 'two elements that remain undiscovered by the sexual researches of children: the fertilizing role of semen and the existence of the female sexual orifice – the same elements, incidentally, in which the infantile organization is itself undeveloped.'[30] If this frustration is deeply felt by the child it may lead to permanent injury to the drive for knowledge. As a consequence of the unduly repressive child-rearing practices brought to bear on little girls, this tragic destiny is more often imposed on women, Freud argues in his 1908 paper '"Civilized" sexual morality and modern nervous illness':

> [Women's] upbringing forbids their concerning themselves intellectually
> with sexual problems though they nevertheless feel extremely curious
> about them, and frightens them by condemning such curiosity as
> unwomanly and as a sign of a sinful disposition. In this way they are
> scared away from *any* form of thinking, and knowledge loses its value
> for them.... I do not believe that women's 'physiological
> feeble-mindedness' is to be explained by a biological opposition between
> intellectual work and sexual activity .... I think that the undoubted
> intellectual inferiority of so many women can rather be traced back to
> the inhibition of thought necessitated by sexual suppression.[31]

This passage stands in marked contrast to Freud's own disapproval of Dora's attempts to gain sexual knowledge.[32] Strongly encouraging childish sexual theory, both the 'Three essays' and '"Civilized" morality' passage are much more reminiscent of Freud's analysis of Little Hans[33] than of Dora. If we take a closer look at the chronology of these papers, the discrepancy between Freud's treatment of Dora and that of Little Hans comes across not simply as one of sexist denial of knowledge to women, but one of a marked development *away* from an early, patriarchal disapproval of sexual curiosity in females towards a later, more liberal view. The point to notice here is that although he did not publish 'Dora' until 1905, Freud actually analysed her in 1900 or 1901, and wrote up the case story in 1901. In the period leading up to 1905 and the publication of the 'Three essays' with their positive view of epistemophilia, it seems likely that Freud fundamentally revised his views on sexual curiosity, now explicitly linking it with intellectual development. '"Civilized" morality' from 1908 and 'Little Hans' from 1909 only continue and expand on this trend, which culminates in the 1910 paper on Leonardo da Vinci.

Whatever the fate of the child's early sexual researches, Freud insists, its solitary quest for knowledge opens up a gap between it and its environment. 'The sexual researches of these early years of childhood are always carried out in solitude', Freud writes. 'They constitute a first step towards taking an independent attitude in the world, and imply a high degree of alienation of the child from the people in his environment who formerly enjoyed his complete confidence.'[34] The seeds of intellectual life are sown in the solitary brooding of a child who suspects its parents of deliberately hiding secrets of vital importance to its existence. No wonder, then, that Freud in later years compared philosophical speculation to paranoid delusions.[35]

In his 1910 essay on Leonardo de Vinci,[36] Freud argues that after the initial repression of the period of infantile sexual researches, the drive for research has 'three distinct possible vicissitudes open to it'.[37] In Freud's account, then, there is no 'normal' development and no 'deviations' from the norm: the three paths are simply possible 'turns' where none is more 'normal' than the others. In the case of the first 'vicissitude' curiosity remains inhibited for the rest of the subject's life. Such a person, presumably, will not become an intellectual. In the second case the intellect resists repression, without being able to free itself from the repressed association between thought and sexuality. In this case, Freud writes, the 'suppressed sexual activities of research return from the unconscious in the form of compulsive brooding, naturally in a distorted and unfree form, but sufficiently powerful to sexualize thinking itself and to colour intellectual operations with the pleasure and anxiety that belong to sexual processes proper'.[38] In such individuals, the frustration of the early infantile explorations is repeated in endless brooding over problems that remain permanently unresolved: the orgasmic solution never comes.

Finally, there is the case of the fully sublimated intellectual drive, where the libido is not repressed but simply diverted to a new aim. The diversion of libido means that for the truly sublimated intellectual research becomes to a large extent a substitute for sexual satisfaction. Given the absence of repression, his or her compulsive epistemophilic drive remains free of neurosis and therefore 'operate[s] freely in the service of intellectual interest', as Freud puts it.[39] Obviously destined to bolster his own ego as well as to explain Leonardo da Vinci's life and work, Freud's powerful idealization of intellectual life nevertheless has the merit of including childhood sexuality as an element in the highest intellectual endeavours.

Knowledge, sublimation, the body, and the drives

But what exactly does it mean to say that intellectual pursuits are sublimations? And what are the implications of linking the production of theory to childhood sexuality? Is this not just another wildly reductive view of knowledge? Whatever else it may be, sublimation is *not* the same thing as repression. Notoriously vague and undertheorized, the concept of sublimation is normally defined as a diversion of sexual energy to new, culturally acceptable aims. This new aim is no longer sexual, Freud claims, but 'psychically related to the first aim'.[40]

It remains unclear whether the new aim is *anaclitic* (metonymically linked) to the first (as seems to be the case in the Leonardo essay), or whether there is some other relationship between them. The first of these relationships would be analogous to that between the body and the drives.

But what exactly is the role of the drives in Freud's theory of epistemophilia? First of all, the drive for knowledge, or the capacity for intellectual speculation, is set in motion by the child's frustration at the arrival of a new baby (or other frustrations of its narcissistic fantasies of omnipotence). The intellectual activity itself sets the child apart from its surroundings, emphasizing for the first time its loneliness and its incapacity to understand the world into which it has been thrown. If rational thought is the result of the child's effort to *overcome* frustration, rational enquiry only succeeds in the end in producing an even more overwhelming – and alienating – sense of impotence and disenchantment. So deep is the frustration created by the exercise of the child's intellectual faculties that it threatens to obliterate curiosity for ever. Intellectual labour, then, is not only the *result* of frustration: in its very powerlessness it is also the *source* of its own frustration. The desire for rational knowledge, or indeed the pursuit of philosophy, is a self-defeating drive for imaginary satisfaction.

Like sexuality, then, rationality is its own frustration. In his 1912 paper on 'The universal tendency to debasement in the sphere of love' Freud explicitly formulates the idea that 'something in the nature of the sexual instinct itself is unfavourable to the realization of complete satisfaction'.[41] In the same way, something in the nature of human rationality is unfavourable to its own unfolding. This 'something', in both cases, is the human body.

For Freud, the drives take the human body as their point of departure: oral, anal, and genital drives develop because of the physical functions of these parts of the human body. This is not to say that the drive is *identical* to the original biological need, or that it can be *reduced* back to them. Freud explains that the drive is 'anaclitic' to the body, a spin-off from the physical function, neither identical with nor reducible to the biological need that set it in motion in the first place. The Freudian body is perceived as the limiting *horizon* of our thought and our discourse, not as its inherent identity or essential meaning. In this way, Freudianism is a materialism but not, as is often argued, a form of biologism.[42] The body limits and frustrates the drives: the desire for total sexual satisfaction or for complete epistemological mastery can be no more than a fantasy of the Imaginary. The human body, whether male or female, is constructed under the sign of castration: it is always suffering, always already mutilated.

This is not to deny the fact that the full, 'oedipal' castration complex posits the subjects differently in relation to the phallus, and thus also constructs sexual difference. It is, however, to indicate that for Freud the roots of rationality are to be found in the first narcissistic wound, one that is situated in the pre-oedipal space where sexual difference does not yet apply. (A full examination of sexual difference and the construction of knowledge, and of the psychoanalytic deconstruction of the 'subject supposed to know', would require a separate paper.) Intellectual labour, then, is the spin-off of our original effort to understand how this incomplete and limited body came to be, our defence against the narcissistic wound imposed by the arrival of other bodies on our scene. The presence of the body produces the drag in our discourse and the muddle in our thoughts. And this meddling body is always already libidinal.

Self-defeating, always frustrated by the limitations of the body, the Freudian drive for knowledge is structurally incapable of achieving total insight or perfect mastery: the philosopher's dream of self-contained plenitude is here unmasked as the imaginary fantasy it is. Freudian theory posits the drive for knowledge (epistemophilia) as crucially bound to the body and sexuality. If reason is always already shot through with the energy of the drives, the body, and desire, to be intellectual can no longer be theorized simply as the 'opposite' of being emotional or passionate. Evelyn Fox Keller is right to turn to psychoanalysis for valuable inspiration for her battle against patriarchal ideology in science, and much work remains to be done in the field pioneered, however differently, by Keller and Le Doeuff. I see my own contribution simply as an effort to indicate that an anti-essentialist feminist philosophy of science stands to gain rather more from Freud and Lacan than from Winnicott and American ego-psychology.

Notes

I am grateful to Parveen Adams, Teresa Brennan, and Jane Tompkins for their comments on earlier versions of this paper, and to Vigdis Songe Møller for philosophical inspiration and feminist solidarity.
All references to Freud are to both the Pelican Freud Library (PFL), 15 vols (Harmondsworth: Penguin, 1976–86), and to *The Standard Edition of the Complete Psychological Works of Sigmund Freud* (*SE*), ed. J. Strachey, (London: Hogarth, 1951). Essays by Freud are listed by date.

1 Evelyn Fox Keller, 'Gender and science', reprinted in Sandra Harding and Merill B. Hintikka (eds), *Discovering Reality: Feminist Perspectives on Epistemology, Metaphysics, Methodology and Philosophy of Science* (Dordrecht, Boston, and London: Reidel, 1983), pp. 187–205.
2 ibid., p. 190.
3 ibid., p. 191.
4 ibid.
5 Nancy Chodorow, *The Reproduction of Mothering* (Berkeley: University of California Press, 1978). Although Chodorow notes that object-relations theory has been less popular in the US than in Europe, it is significant that the theories of the object-relations school she uses overlap with those of the American ego-psychology school. Despite manifest differences (the ego-psychologists are biologistic, Chodorow is not) both schools stress adaption as an aim of psychoanalysis, privilege external reality, and neglect psychical

reality. Both discount Klein's theory because it is not based on external reality.

6 Keller, 'Gender and science', pp. 190–1.

7 ibid., p. 191.

8 Evelyn Fox Keller, *Reflections on Gender and Science* (New Haven: Yale University Press, 1985), p. 116.

9 Evelyn Fox Keller, 'Feminism and science', reprinted in Harding and Hintikka (eds), op. cit., pp. 238 and 242.

10 Susan Bordo, 'The Cartesian masculinization of thought', reprinted in Sandra Harding and Jean F. O'Barr (eds), *Sex and Scientific Inquiry* (Chicago: University of Chicago Press, 1987), p. 263. See also Carol Gilligan, *In a Different Voice* (Cambridge, Mass.: Harvard University Press, 1982).

11 ibid., p. 257.

12 Keller, 'Gender and science', p. 194.

13 Keller, 'Feminism and science', p. 242.

14 Hélène Cixous, 'Sorties', in Hélène Cixous and Catherine Clément, *The Newly Born Woman*, trans. Betsy Wing (Manchester: Manchester University Press, 1986), pp. 63–4.

15 Unfortunately, Michèle Le Doeuff's work is not sufficiently well known in English-speaking countries. Her collection of philosophical essays, *L'Imaginaire philosophique* (Paris: Payot, 1980), in which 'Women and philosophy' originally appeared, is now being translated.

16 Hegel, *Philosophy of Right*, para. 166, Zusatz, trans. Knox (modified by Le Doeuff), pp. 263–4; quoted in Michèle Le Doeuff, 'Women and philosophy', reprinted in Toril Moi (ed.) *French Feminist Thought* (Oxford: Blackwell, 1987), p. 190.

17 Le Doeuff, op. cit., p. 196.

18 ibid.

19 I am not implying that Le Doeuff is directly influenced by Derrida. Le Doeuff herself emphasizes that her theoretical inspiration on this point comes from her intensive study of the plays of Bertolt Brecht.

20 For further information on transference and countertransference see Jean Laplanche and J.-B. Pontalis, *The Language of Psychoanalysis* (London: Hogarth, 1980). For a brilliant discussion of transference as rhetorical trope and/or knowledge, see Cynthia Chase, '"Transference" as trope and persuasion', in Shlomith Rimmon-Kenan (ed.), *Discourse in Psychoanalysis and Literature* (London: Methuen, 1987), pp. 211–32.

21 Transcribed from a recording of a talk by Lacan at the Kanzer seminar, Yale University, 24 November 1975, translated by Barbara Johnson, quoted by Shoshana Felman in *Jacques Lacan and the Adventure of Insight: Psychoanalysis in Contemporary Culture* (Cambridge, Mass.: Harvard University Press, 1987), pp. 22–3.

22 ibid., p. 23.

23 ibid., p. 56.

24 ibid., p. 61.

25 See Keller, 'Gender and science', pp. 192, 193, 195, 197, and 203.

26 Sigmund Freud, 'Three essays on the theory of sexuality', 1905, PFL, 7. pp. 112–13; *SE*, 7, p. 194.

27 Freud, PFL, 10, p. 143; *SE*, 12, p. 324.

28 For an outstanding discussion of Freud's endless hesitations over what comes first, sadism *or* masochism, see Jean Laplanche, *Life and Death in Psychoanalysis* (Baltimore: Johns Hopkins University Press, 1976). On psychoanalytic theories of masochism, see Adams, this volume.

29 Freud, 1905, PFL, 7, p. 115; *SE*, 7, p. 196.
30 ibid.
31 Freud, '"Civilized" sexual morality and modern nervous illness', 1908, PFL, 12, pp. 50–1; *SE*, 9, pp. 198–9.
32 Freud, 1905, PFL, 8; *SE*, 7.
33 Freud, 1909, PFL, 8; *SE*, 10.
34 Freud, 1905, PFL, 7, p. 115; *SE*, 7, p. 197.
35 See, for instance, 'Totem and taboo', 1913, PFL, 13, p. 130; *SE*, 13, p. 73.
36 PFL, 14, pp. 145–231; *SE*, 11, pp. 63–137.
37 Freud, 1910, PFL, 14, p. 169; *SE*, 11, p. 79.
38 PFL, 14, p. 170; *SE*, 11, p. 80.
39 ibid.
40 '"Civilized" sexual morality', PFL, 12, p. 39; *SE*, 9, p. 187.
41 PFL, 7, p. 258; *SE*, 11, pp. 188–9.
42 For an excellent account of the 'anaclitic' relationship between the drives and the body, see Jean Laplanche, op. cit.

Chapter Twelve

Feminism and deconstruction, again: negotiating with unacknowledged masculinism

Gayatri Chakravorty Spivak

Argument. It is not just that deconstruction cannot found a politics, while other ways of thinking can. It is that deconstruction can make founded political programs more useful by making their in-built problems more visible. To act is therefore not to ignore deconstruction, but actively to transgress it without giving it up. (A slightly tougher formulation which clarity-fetishists can ignore: deconstruction does not aim at *praxis* or theoretical practice but lives in the persistent crisis or unease of the moment of *techne* or crafting.) Feminism has a special situation here because, among the many names that Derrida gives to the problem/solution of founded programs, one is 'woman'. I explain in the essay why feminism should keep to the critical ways of deconstruction but give up its attachment to that specific name for the problem/solution of founded programs ([*psfp*], also named 'writing'. I put it so awkwardly because so-called 'political' academics will still insist that writing is only script and make the blindingly brilliant critique that Derrida ignores mothers speaking to infants!).

This is a more charitable position on the usefulness of deconstruction for feminism than I have supported in the past. It is a negotiation and an acknowledgement of complicity. This is a result of my recent teaching stint in India, which persuaded me that the indigenous elite must come to terms with its unacknowledged complicity with the culture of imperialism. Patriarchy/feminist theory is standing in for imperialism/post-coloniality here. I write more directly on the latter topic in my forthcoming book *Riding on the Hyphen*.

The paper that follows is written in the musing style of speaking to one's 'school-mates', the occasion being Teresa Brennan's invitation to speak to feminists generally sympathetic to poststructuralism and psychoanalysis in the seminar series on which this book is based.

GCS

I first conceived of the line of thought pursued in the following pages immediately after six months of teaching in Delhi and Calcutta. Teaching for the first time in the country of my citizenship, and occasionally in my native language, was an unsettling and ambivalent experience. The measure of my unease will be sensed when I point out that I found a resonance in Thomas Nagel's reflections on the Vietnam years:

the United States was engaged in a criminal war, criminally conducted. This produced a heightened sense of the absurdity of my theoretical pursuits. Citizenship is a surprisingly strong bond, even for those of us whose patriotic feelings are weak. We read the newspaper every day with rage and horror, and it was different from reading about the crimes of another country. Those feelings led to the growth in the late 1960s of serious professional work by philosophers on public issues.[1]

Rajiv Gandhi and his centralized power-structure were attempting to redefine India as the habitation of the tiny percentage of the taxpaying upper crust. That is my class alliance, which I felt much more strongly than my class-position as an academic in a trivial discipline in the United States. Those were also the months of the crisis of the Bofors arms scandal, not much publicized in the international press but certainly disturbing to a critic who regularly theorized the 'epistemic violence' of imperialism. It did not help that that particular crisis was later managed by the Indian intervention in the Sri Lankan Civil War.

The position of academic feminism in the elite universities in the two Indian cities where I worked was not strikingly different from the United States, where I habitually teach. And I am not given to unquestioning benevolence towards that dubious category – 'Third World women'. Yet, there was produced in me, not infrequently during my time in India, 'a heightened sense of the absurdity of my theoretical pursuits'. When I spoke in Cambridge in response to Teresa Brennan's invitation, immediately after leaving India, I found myself reconsidering the relationship between feminism and deconstruction in terms of that sense of absurdity.

Before I could embark on such a chastening project, it seemed necessary to situate a sympathetic misrepresentation of the connection between the two movements. In that spirit I offered a reading of a few pages from a book then recently out, Jacqueline Rose's *Sexuality in the Field of Vision*.[2]

At the end of Rose's introduction to her book, there is a dismissal of Derrida as a certain kind of subjectivist essentialist. Unlike Elaine Showalter's or, more recently, Margaret Homans's dismissals of deconstruction, Rose's text is based on a *reading* of Derrida.[3] When I deal with this dismissal, you see me defending a sort-of-Derrida against Rose defending a sort-of-Lacan. This is yet another instance of 'the [necessary] absurdity of my theoretical pursuits'. Those six months in India, spent as a diasporic Indian and a working academic, gave me a sense of how peculiarly uneasy people were about the cultural legacy of imperialism. This was certainly true in my own class but was also pervasive, however inarticulately, across the classes. The unease straddled the genders, and, in its context, varieties of elite nativism seemed defunct and self-protective. The practical effects of this legacy remain to be fully negotiated and theorized.[4] As a reminder of this unease, and in response to Brennan's specific invitation, I felt I must reckon with the legacy of patriarchy which, like the culture of imperialism, is a dubious gift that we can only transform if we acknowledge it. My entire discussion of Rose must be read as framed by this absurdity.

I agree with Rose that 'to understand subjectivity, sexual difference and fantasy, in a way that neither entrenches the terms nor denies them' remains a crucial task for today.[5] On these terms, in fact, there is not much difference between how she understands Lacan and how I understand deconstruction. For Rose, 'only the concept of a subjectivity at odds with itself gives back to women the right to an impasse at the point of sexual identity, with no nostalgia whatsoever for its possible or future integration into a norm'.[6] This desire for an impasse is not unlike the desire for the abyss or infinite regression for which deconstruction must perpetually account. I do, of course declare myself bound by that desire. The difference between Rose and myself here is that what she feels is a right to be claimed, I am obliged to recognize as a bind to be watched.[7] I think the difference between us in this context comes from Rose's understanding of deconstruction as *only* a narrative of the fully dispersed and decentered subject. I am not myself suggesting a strict opposition between structure and narrative, or morphology and narrative. But I do want to insist that when it is understood only as a narrative, deconstruction is only the picture of an impossibility that cannot help *any* political position. Or perhaps it can, only too easily. (I am thinking here of other arguments, relying on a trivialized description of deconstruction as a narrative, arguments which suggest, for example, that since women are naturally decentered, deconstruction is good for feminism and vice versa.)

In her introduction to *Sexuality in the Field of Vision*, Rose is by no means a trivializer, but seems still to understand deconstruction only as a narrative. One way of showing this is to bring a different understanding of deconstruction to bear on Jacqueline Rose's general presentation of psychoanalysis as a project.

It seems to me that, for Rose, the psychoanalytic project is a kind of epistemological project, through which women and men understand their ontology in terms of (or at least not excluding) sexual difference:

> Feminism must depend on psychoanalysis because the issue of how
> individuals recognize themselves as male or female, the demand that
> they do so, seems to stand in such fundamental relation to the forms of
> inequality and subordination which it is feminism's objective to change.[8]

This sentence is, I think, about male and female subjects construing themselves as knowable objects, especially if I am right in thinking that the word 'recognize' is doing duty here for the more critical 'cognize'. Now the anti-sexist project of feminism bases itself upon the conviction that distinctions arising in social practice out of the declaration of a fundamental ontic difference are, more often than not, incorrect, because, like most declarations of difference, these involve a dissimulated ranking. The range of such social practices runs from sociobiology to corporate (civil) and familial (domestic) practice. Rose's new epistemological itinerary will allow us to correct this. It will use the epistemology of sexual difference as an answer to the ontological question: what am I (woman)? and then to an accounting of that epistemology: how do I recognize myself (woman)?

It is, however, the next step, contained in the last part of the sentence from Rose quoted above which gives me trouble. That step covers the quick shift from epistemology/ontology to the axiological project. The subject recognizing herself (woman) seems in Rose's reading to do so in order to act in the interests of psycho-social justice: in a 'fundamental relation to the forms of inequality and subordination which it is feminism's objective to change'. Rose's position is of course sufficiently subtle. She is aware that 'femininity [the formula for this ontic secret that we discover through the epistemological itinerary of the divided subject – woman] in psychoanalysis, is neither simply achieved nor is it ever complete'. It none the less involves that unacknowledged shift I have described between epistemology/ontology on the one hand and axiology on the other. If, as Rose suggests, it is crucial to admit the division in the subject, it seems to me no less crucial to admit the irreducible difference between the subject (woman) of that epistemology, and the subject (feminist) of this axiology.[9] Perhaps I am doing nothing more than theorizing here the division between the women's movement and feminist theory.

If one looks at the deconstructive *morphology* (rather than simply reading it as the narrative of the decentered subject), then one is obliged to notice that deconstruction has always been about the limits of epistemology. It sees the ontological impetus as a programme implicated in the writing of the name of Man.[10]

Let me emphasize this by reopening *Spurs*, where Derrida comments on Heidegger and his reading of Nietzsche.[11] Simplifying Derrida's argument a little, we could read it as follows: there is a question which is precomprehended even by the careful subtlety of the Heideggerian articulation of the onticoontological difference. Simplifying that Heideggerian subtlety, we might summarize it as follows: Heidegger suggests that *Dasein* is ontically programmed to ask the ontological question, *and* not to be able to answer it. This is undoubtedly a corrective for any account which assumes that when we work for an epistemological itinerary to cleanse the ontological account of ourselves, this might contribute or, indeed, lead to correct psycho-sexual political action. (One may argue that 'correct' epistemologies can be the basis of 'correct' public policy – but that seems not to be Rose's argument.)

Even this Heideggerian corrective is critiqued by Derrida because it does not attend to the naming of woman.

For not having posed the sexual question, or at least for having subsumed it in the general question of truth, Heidegger's reading of Nietzsche has been idling offshore ever since it missed the woman in the *affabulation* of truth.[12]

Spurs gives an account of how one can read Nietzsche's master concept-metaphors. The most interesting one for Derrida is 'woman'. Like all concept-metaphors, 'woman' is here used in such a way that one cannot locate an adequate literal referent for it. There *is* something special about it, however, for the question of sexual difference in Nietzsche is not 'a regional question in a larger order which would subordinate it first to the domain of a general ontology, subsequently to that of a fundamental ontology, and finally to the question of the truth of being itself'.[13]

Derrida rescues this reading of the concept-metaphor 'woman' in Nietzsche, and also suggests that Nietzsche's own *analysis* of sexual difference is caught within a historical or narrative understanding/misunderstanding of 'propriation'.

(This notion, of the originary and therefore structurally inaccessible auto-position of the subject, is a fairly common one in generally non-foundationalist 'marxist' philosophers such as Louis Althusser or Theodor Adorno. Althusser's ill-fated remark about the 'apparently paradoxical proposition which I shall express in the following forms: *ideology has no history*' belongs to this family of notions; as does Adorno's carefully articulated statement, 'the subject is appearance in its self-positing and at the same time something historically altogether real'.[14] Derrida places the question of sexual difference, at least, as he sees it in Nietzsche, in this space. (For Althusser, by contrast, sexual difference is one of the ideologies (rather than Ideology), which are within history: 'it is in this implacable and more or less pathological ... structure of the familial ideological configuration that the former subject-to-be will have to ..."become" the sexual subject (boy or girl) which it already is in advance.'[15] For Adorno the question of sexual difference cannot be entertained on this level.)

In Derrida's reading, Nietzsche is able to sketch sexual difference as pre-ontological propriation perhaps *because* he is bound by and gives his assent to significations and values that define sexual difference in terms of the eternal war between the sexes, and the mortal hatred of the sexes in love, eroticism, etc. Thus propriation in Nietzsche may at first glance seem to have nothing but a series of restricted meanings: appropriation, expropriation, taking possession, gift and barter, mastering, servitude.[16] You have, then, on the one side, Heidegger with his extraordinarily subtle account of the ontological difference, *not* posing the sexual question, at least in this context. You have, on the other, Nietzsche, using or having to use the concept-metaphor 'woman' to point at pre-ontological difference, using it, none the less, inside male-dominated historical narratives of propriation.

Jacqueline Rose, when she writes about propriation in a couple of sentences in her introduction, is obliged to keep within the Nietzschean historical assumptions about propriation, without the emancipating moment of the emergence of woman as 'catachresis', as a metaphor without a literal referent standing in for a concept that is the condition of conceptuality. Any programme which assumes continuity between the subject of epistemology/ontology and that of axiology must also assume that the latter is a referent for the former.

The distinction between the narrow sense and the general sense of a catachresis is never clear-cut in deconstruction, although the difference is always acknowledged. According to Derrida, if one looks at propriation in the general sense in Nietzsche, one sees a question that is 'more powerful than the question, "what is?"', more powerful than 'the veil of truth or the meaning of being',[17] because before one can even say that *there is being*, there must be a decision that being can be proper to itself to the extent of being part of that proposition. (In German, before the gift of being in *Es gibt Sein*, one has to think the propriety to itself of the *Es*.) Outside of all philosophical game-playing, the irreducible predicament pointed at here is that the ontological question cannot be asked in terms of a cleansed epistemology, for propriation organizes the totality of 'language's process and symbolic exchange in general'.[18]

I believe that in 'Displacement and the discourse of woman', I missed the fact that in Derrida's reading of Nietzsche in *Spurs*, there is an insistence that 'woman' in that text was a concept-metaphor that was also a *name* marking the pre-ontological as propriation in sexual difference.[19]

When one of us defends Derrida against the other of us defending Lacan, we are moving away from the suggestion in deconstruction (indeed European post-Hegelian theory in general) that a thinker does not make a point on the full steam of his sovereign subjectivity. Nietzsche, even as he depends upon propriation in the patriarchal, restricted, or narrow sense, reaches the general sense of propriation by putting the *name* of woman on it through the conduct of his text. And Derrida, grasping his reach as reader, does it not to trump Nietzsche but to make his text more useful for us. I hope the rest of this chapter will make clear how crucial it is not to ignore the powerful currents of European anti-humanist thought that influence us, yet not to excuse them of their masculism while using them. This is what I am calling 'negotiation'.

Thus we can read Nietzsche's text in a way that suggests that the name of woman makes the question of propriation indeterminate. Let us look at the sentence: 'there is no truth of woman, but because of that abyssal self-apartness of truth, this non-truth is "truth".'[20] If one takes the crucial term 'woman' out of the sentence, it would be possible to suggest that this is what Nietzsche thinks is new about his philosophy of truth, that the nature of truth is such that it is always abyssally (in a structure of repeated indefinite mirroring) apart from what one propriates as the truth in terms of which one can act. This non-truth is 'truth'. The quotation marks indicate a catachrestical setting apart. 'Truth' here is something for which there is no *adequate* literal referent.

Because, in Nietzsche's understanding of propriation in the narrow sense, woman is seen as the custodian of irreducibly inadequate literal referents, she is also seen as a model. In other words, when Nietzsche suggests there is no truth of woman in his historical understanding, a certain *kind* of woman is a model for the 'no truth'. Woman is thus 'one name for that non-truth of truth':[21] one *name* for that non-truth of truth.

My previous position on this essay of Derrida's was polemical. I suggested that it was not correct to see the figure of woman as a sign for indeterminacy. Reading my analysis of appropriation in this polemic, Jacqueline Rose gives me the benefit of the doubt by claiming solidarity on this particular position.[22] And, within its own context, I accept this gesture. But today, negotiating, I want to give the assent for the moment to Derrida's argument. Affirmative deconstruction says 'yes' to a text twice, sees complicity when it could rather easily be oppositional. At Cerisy in 1980, Derrida described his first phase as 'guarding the question', 'keeping the question alive'. (*Let us say, the question of the difference between the epistemological/ontological, and the axiological, in Rose.*)[23] He described the second phase as calling to the absolutely other. (If sexual difference is indeed pre-comprehended by the ontological question then, miming Derrida's Nietzsche, *we* might think 'philosophers', by way of the same historical narrative that gave Nietzsche 'woman', as *our* wholly other. And thus we 'women' might indicate, or even figure forth and thus efface, that call to the wholly other as *taking the risk of saying 'yes' to Heidegger, Nietzsche, Derrida.*)

How does this shift from the first phase to the second translate into a strategy of reading, a strategy of giving assent? Let us look at Derrida's relatively recent study on Nietzsche, *The Ear of the Other*, a discourse on the politics of reading.[24] He suggests there that the reader should not excuse the texts of Nietzsche for their use by the Nazis. There is no reason to say that that was a mere misreading. On the contrary, the reader should note that there is something in Nietzsche's text which leads exactly to that kind of appropriation. This is one paradoxical way of saying 'yes' to the text, but it entails understanding from within, as it were, so that the moments that lend themselves to the so-called misappropriation are understood in the text's own terms. It is then that one can begin to develop a politics of reading, which will open up a text towards an as yet unknown horizon so that it can be of use without excuse. Let us now call this: negotiating with structures of violence. It is in that spirit of negotiation that I propose to give assent to Derrida's text about woman as a name for the non-truth of truth.

Affirmative deconstruction of this kind was already signalled in *Of Grammatology*.

> The movements of deconstruction do not destroy structures from the outside. They are not possible and effective, nor can they take active aim, except by inhabiting those structures. Inhabiting them *in a certain way*, because one always inhabits, *and all the more when one does not*

suspect it. Operating necessarily from the inside, borrowing all the strategic and economic resources of subversion from the old structure, borrowing them structurally, that is to say without being able to isolate their elements and atoms, the enterprise of deconstruction always *in a certain way* falls prey to its own work.[25]

How many times have I quoted this passage? It is this particular attitude that presages the crucial difference between the first and the second phases. The second attitude towards that which is critiqued, the giving of assent without excuse, so much that one inhabits its discourse – a short word for this might be 'love'.[26]

Deconstruction is not an exposure of error, nor a tabulation of error; logocentrism is not a pathology, nor is the metaphysical closure a prison to overthrow by violent means. Looking for irreducibles, realizing the theoretical absurdity of my position, it is with that 'love' that I am reading texts already read, and questioning the usefulness of reading deconstruction merely as the narrative of the decentered subject, of the fully dispersed subject. This is where I began, with the suggestion that Rose's case against deconstruction was based on such a reading.

Let us look in more detail at why it is unsatisfactory to reduce deconstruction to a narrative.

The main focus of deconstruction as a morphology is the graphematic structure. In this brief compass, I will present the morphology also as a narrative (perhaps this is inescapable) – the narrative of a narrative if you like – and contrast it to the narrative of a decentered subject which deconstruction offers not only to Jacqueline Rose, but to readers such as Jürgen Habermas and Fredric Jameson.

One focus, then, of deconstruction is the graphematic structure. The adjective 'graphematic' comes from Derrida's analysis that writing is historically the structure that is supposed necessarily to operate in the presumed absence of its origin, the sender.

Any act must assume unified terms to get started. The implicit mechanics by which these assumptions are established or taken for granted spell out a structure of repetition, which cannot be posited as reproducing something existing as prior. These mechanics are generally found to be suppressed or finessed, so that beginnings do not seem problematic. Nearly all of Derrida's writing has been a discussion of such gestures – sometimes even self-conscious gestures of dismissal as difficulties or counter-examples – performed in different ways in different discourses. Let us decide to call this the suppression of a graphematic structure. This decision cannot be fully endorsed by deconstructive theory. The graphematic structure that seems to orchestrate the inauguration of all acts (including acts of thought) is a structure *like* writing, it is not writing commonly conceived, it is not, that is, necessarily the mark of an absent presence. This unendorsable naming of the discovery of the repetition at the origin as graphematic, by way of writing as a catachresis, is the double bind that founds all deconstructive *praxis*.

By this reasoning, human beings think themselves unified also by finessing the assumption of a repressed graphematic structure. There is no way to get hold of a subject before this two-step. This is the narrative of the famous decentered subject. In early work such as 'Structure, sign, and play' and the first chapter of *Of Grammatology*, Derrida does invoke 'our epoch', meaning specifically, an 'epoch' that privileges language and thinks (impossibly) to have got rid of centrisms.[27] To turn this critique – of a claim to have decentered method, by pointing out that the subject can only ever be posited by the finessing of a graphematic structure at the origin – into merely the story of the individual becoming decentered with late capitalism (Jameson), the passing of the pre-Socratics (Heidegger), the inception of modernity (Habermas via Weber), or Derrida's bolstering of Eurocentric patriarchy (Rose), is a plausible but unexamined move.

The useful part of deconstruction is in the suggestion that the subject is always centered. Deconstruction persistently notices that this centering is an effect-structure with indeterminable boundaries that can only be deciphered as determining. No politics can occupy itself with only this enabling epistemological double bind. But when a political analysis or program forgets this it runs the risk of declaring ruptures where there is also a repetition – a risk that can result in varieties of fundamentalism, of which the onto/epistemo/axiological confusion is a characteristic symptom.[28]

Différance is one of the names for the necessity to obliterate the graphematic structure, *and* the necessity to misname it 'graphematic', since there is no other way one can call it. This double bind – the double session of 'difering' – is at the origin of practice.[29]

Rose suggests, and she is not alone, that there is in Derrida a desire to suppress sexual difference in the interest of *différance*, and a privileging of *différance* as *the* name. (It seems to go unnoticed that, in his later work, the word is hardly ever used.)

Différance is, and it cannot be repeated often enough, only *one* name for the irreducible double bind that allows the very possibility of difference(s). We are obliged to assume a pre-originary space without differences in the interest of suppressing that 'graphematic' structure at the inauguration of our texts; and *différance* is only *one* name for that necessity. There is no harm in admitting that it's not just the production of *sexual* difference that's being framed here, but the possibility of thinking difference itself.

I invite you to consider again that, in the discourse of this critic of phallogocentrism, 'woman' is another name for this irreducible double bind. This is a difficult consideration when we want to claim deconstruction for or against feminism, but I now see no way around it. Here *différance* as the ungraspable ground of propriation *is* (but the copula is a supplement) sexual difference.[30] The *name* (of) woman occupies this site in Derrida. *Différance* and 'woman' are two names on a chain of nominal displacements where, as unmotivated names, neither can claim priority. We are rather far away from the 'subject' of feminist axiology. In fact, we are still looking at the (im)possibility of broaching the epistemo/ontological.[31]

If *différance* (or 'woman', as well as the other names) opens up the question of symbolic possibility in general, it is not, as Rose writes, by suppression of thoughts of cultural form. The thought of cultural forms, which implies the differentiation of one culture from another, or of sexual difference, and indeed all other kinds of difference, difference between being and non-being, if you like the ontico-ontological difference in this particular understanding, our desire to have an impasse which can only be between two things, our desire even for the undecidable, is limited by the possibility that at the beginning is a suppression which we cannot get a handle on. That's all it is, it's no big deal, but it's *not* a story-line which dismisses these differences as culturally unacceptable. We are still circling around the possibility of story-lines, even the story-lines that put one 'culture' over against another. (I have learned this all the better in terms of the politics of the post colonial clamor for cultural difference in those six months of teaching.) If all this seems too ethereal, remember we wouldn't have to do this if 'deconstruction' had not been diagnosed in the first place as a story-line suppressing sexual and cultural difference in the interest of *différance*. As you will, I hope, see in the end, I prefer a more pragmatic line of reasoning (by way of a persistent active and only immediately forgetful transgression of theory) myself when I am thinking/doing as a feminist.[32]

'Woman', then, is a name that is the non-truth of truth in Derrida reading Nietzsche. To emphasize the status of a *name* in thinkers of this type, I quote a celebrated passage by Foucault on power: '[Power] is the *name* that one attributes to a complex strategical situation in a particular society.'[33] This particular species of nominalism, an obsession with names that are necessarily mis-names, names that are necessarily catachreses, 'writing', '*différance*', 'power' – 'woman' in this case – names that have no adequate literal referent, characterizes poststructuralism in general, in spite of local differences. It is important to remember that each of these names is determined by their historical burden in the most empirical way. (Derrida calls this 'paleonymy'.) I hope it is by now clear that Nietzsche uses a name such as 'woman' because he has inherited it, and thus he uses all the contemporary allegorical, sociological, historical, and dismissive stereotypes about woman. On the other hand, since Nietzsche also wants to welcome this name as a name for his own practice – 'my truths' – what one sees in his text is the site of a conflict or a negotiation. Nietzsche, or Derrida, or for that matter Lacan, is here fully complicit with masculism (quite as Nietzsche is with the possibility of the grafting of Nazism onto his text), yet it is also possible to see, and Derrida is asking us to see this in Nietzsche because if we do this we can make the text useful, that within this itinerary there is that peculiar affirmation. This is the model Nietzsche wants

– woman in that sense is *twice* model (modelling the non-truth of truth, and being as unlike the dogmatic philosopher of truth as possible by way of some of the dubious historical stereotypes). It might be useful for us to *accuse* the text responsibly, and then lift this lever and *use* the text, rather than not use it at all. Derrida himself is also bound (as is Lacan, and as are we in our taste for a pragmatic feminism that claims to be theoretical even as it forgets the difference between the subjects of onto/epistemology and axiology) by a certain set of historical presuppositions.

Derrida gives proof of this bind when at the end of *The Ear of the Other*, speaking still about his politics of reading, he sounds a theme that has been sounded by him before: the patronymic (the father's name), because through it the man can continue to survive after death, is a kiss of death. By contrast, the nameless feminine is the name of living. And it is this peculiar *livingness* of the feminine that is in some ways contaminated or betrayed by what Derrida perhaps understands as 'feminism':

> No woman or trace of woman. And I do not make this remark in order to benefit from that supplement of seduction which today enters into all courtships or courtrooms. This vulgar procedure is what I propose to call 'gynegogy'.[34]

It must be acknowledged that this perspective, constituted by the historico-legal tradition of the patronymic in patriarchy, exists in Derrida's text just as much as a perspective constituted by *his* historical legacy exists in Nietzsche's catachrestical use of 'woman' as name. Thus, because of the necessity of the historical determination of the name 'woman' for the double bind at the origin of the production of 'truth(s)', there is no sense in talking about the relationship between deconstruction and feminism as if women were naturally decentered.[35]

Yet the name of woman as the non-truth of truth *can* have a significant message for us if we, refusing fully to honor the historically bound catachresis, give the name of woman to that *disenfranchised* woman who is *historically* different from ourselves, the subjects of feminist theory, and yet acknowledge that she has the right to the construction of a subject-effect of sovereignty in the narrow sense. Then we, as those by now largely self-enfranchised subjects, will share and understand the philosophers' anxiety about the nasty historical determinations which allow this name to exist. Since these philosophers are not essentialists, they have a real anxiety about the loss of the name 'woman' because it survives on these precariously sketched, basically essentialist historical generalizations. This is what is reflected in the kind of masculist noises we noticed at the conclusion of *The Ear of the Other*.[36]

There is a passage in Lacan's 'Love letter', an essay translated by Jacqueline Rose in *Feminine Sexuality*, where he talks about the understanding of the place of woman beyond the question of sex, in soul-making and in naming God, which I think can be put together with Nietzsche's longing for affirming the name of woman as the non-truth of truth, and Derrida's anxiety about not compromising the living feminine in the interest of a gynegogy which would sell itself to the death-story of the patronymic.[37] This, to my mind, marks the moment of the need for taking the name of woman in the interest of a *new* philosophical practice. It is, in fact, no more and indeed no less than that, a need for a name. It is easier to grasp this if we look at the way in which Derrida writes about *différance*. In 'Différance', the essay by that name, he repeats tediously that *différance* is neither a concept nor a metaphor, nor indeed a word, and yet, in the end, the entire essay is argued in terms of the conceptuality and metaphoricity of the term. This particular tactic, of marking the anxiety by keeping the name intact against all disavowals unreadable without the name of that graphematic structure which can only be misnamed, makes the work open to traditional masculism, in the case of the name of 'woman', as it makes it open to traditional modes of language use in the case of *différance*.

What can we do about this? I've already mentioned that I welcome the idea of the embattled love of the text that's given to us by deconstruction. Yet we cannot err too long on that path. Deconstruction is not androgyny, phallocentrism is not a pathology. After we have repeated these lessons, we must still insist on the project of anti-sexism, because sexism *is* also a pathology.[38] In that perspective, women can no longer be names for 'writing', or the non-truth of *différance*. We cannot claim both the desire to identify with the oppression of woman in terms of an ontological deception, and the desire for the right to an impasse, to a deconstructive feminism which would take woman as a name for the graphematic structure and the non-truth of truth. We have to give up the one or the other. I would propose that we should not share this anxiety for the name, we should not identify the guarding of the question with *this* particular name. This would allow us to use the ontological and epistemological critiques found in deconstruction (and indeed psychoanalysis) and appreciate poststructuralist 'nominalism'. We must remember that *this particular name*, the name of 'woman', misfires for feminism. Yet, a feminism that takes the traditionalist line *against* deconstruction falls into a historical determinism where 'history' becomes a gender-fetish.

Guarding this particular name for the graphematic structure is perhaps the most essentialist move of all — this turning of deconstruction into a narrative whether in praise or dispraise. If we lose the 'name' of woman for writing, there is no cause for lament.

It is *in the interest of* diagnosing the ontological ruse, on the basis of which there is oppression of woman, that we have to bring our understanding of the relationship between the name 'woman' and deconstruction into crisis. If we do not take the time to understand this in our zeal to be 'political', then I fear we act out the kind of play that Nietzsche figured out in *The Genealogy of Morals*: in the interest of giving an alibi to his desire to punish, which is written into his way of being, in other words in the interest of a survival game, man produces an alibi which is called justice. And in the interest of that alibi, man has to define and articulate, over and over again, the name of man. It seems to me that if *we* forget that *we* cannot have a deconstructive feminism which decides to transform the usefulness of the name 'woman', itself based on a certain kind of historical anxiety for the graphematic structure, into a narrative, and thus take up arms against what we sometimes call essentialism, *then* we might be acting out this particular scenario, adequately contradicting and thus legitimizing it – by devising newer names of woman – in the interest of giving the desire to punish the alibi of justice. And if you ask me whether the disenfranchised can think this critique, I would say yes. It is the disenfranchised who teaches us most often by saying: I do not recognize myself in the object of your benevolence, I do not recognize my share in your naming. Although the vocabulary is not that of high theory, she tells us if we *care* to hear (without identifying our onto/epistemological subjectivity with *her* anxiety for the subjectship of the axiological, the subjectship of ethics) that she is not the literal referent for our frenzied naming of woman in the scramble for legitimacy in the house of theory. She reminds us that the name of 'woman', however political, is, like any other name, a catachresis.

(I am not being ethereal here. I know the kind of woman I am thinking about. And I also know that this person is not imaginable by most friends reading these words. I cannot enter into the immense and complicated logic of why this is so. Let this remain a lost parenthesis.)

The claim to deconstructive feminism (and deconstructive anti-sexism – the political claim of deconstructive feminists) cannot be sustained in the name of 'woman'. Like class consciousness, which justifies its own production so that classes can be destroyed, 'woman' as the name of writing must be erased in so far as it is a necessarily historical catachresis.

The name of woman cannot be the 'reality' of writing or of the necessary graphematic structure unless you turn the theory into nonsense. Let us say, speaking from within, that we have to deconstruct our desire for the impasse, neutralize the name of 'woman' *for deconstruction* and be deconstructive feminists in that sense. If we want to make political claims that are more useful all round than the general bourgeois academic feminist toothsome euphoria, this seems now to be the only way.

This point is not quite identical with the other note I have been sounding on and off: the object that is known to us through the epistemic project, the cleansed object that knows the itinerary of its recognition of itself as male or female, cannot be identical with the constituency of anti-sexism, the subject of axiology. I will bring the two together by way of a consideration of Foucault's double-play with 'power' and power, and compare it to ours with 'woman' and woman: the name and, as it were, the thing, the phenomenal essence. It should be a lesson to us that *if* we do not watch out for the historical determinations for the name of woman as catachresis in deconstruction, and merely seek to delegitimize the name of man, we legitimize what is diagnosed by Nietzsche and acted out by Foucault.

'Objective' precedes the famous chapter on 'Method' in *History of Sexuality I*. By the end of this section, everything happens as if the lessons learned from Nietzsche, precisely the alibi for the ontological compulsion to articulate an epistemology (name of man as subject of justice as alibi for the ontological need to punish), could be undone by an act of will. Thus Foucault is able to say, 'We must at the same time conceive of sex without the law, and power without the king.'[39] This sentence leads into the section entitled 'Method'. Arrived here, the *name* 'power' is systematically sold short for the 'thing' power, and we are able to get a method because we know the objective, now reduced to an act of willed thought. (The best way to deconstruct this is through Foucault's own notion of the 'referential' in the *Archaeology of Knowledge*.)[40]

This is comparable to the way that we would naturalize the *name* 'woman' if we transformed it into the central character in that narrative of woman's recognition within sexuality, however deferred. Foucault's naturalizing of the *name* 'power' allows the coding of the phenomenality of power as something like an arithmetical system of equivalences: 'And it is doubtless the strategic codification of these points of resistance that makes a revolution possible, somewhat similar to the way in which the state relies on the institutional integration of power relationships.'[41] We see here a case of Foucault's desire to get beyond the ontological/epistemological bind, comparable to our equation of the subject of onto-epistemology and axiology.

I have warned against an abuse of theory, because we cannot stop where the analytic philosopher can stop, with 'the heritage of Socrates' behind him.[42] I quote the following words, continuing my very first quotation in this essay, not in mockery, but recognizing how self-critical they are. 'Moral judgement', Nagel writes, 'and moral theories certainly apply to public questions, but they are notably ineffective.' What I have been arguing so far about the relationship between feminism and deconstructive feminism, feminism and the confusion between the object of the epistemic project and the constituency of anti-sexism might translate to what is being said here.

> Moral judgement and moral theory certainly apply to public questions, but they are notably ineffective. When powerful interests are involved it is very difficult to change anything by arguments, however cogent, which appeal to decency, humanity, compassion and fairness. These considerations also have to compete with the more primitive moral sentiments of honour and retribution and respect for strength. The conditions under which moral argument can have an influence are rather special, and not very well understood by me. They need to be investigated through the history and psychology of morals, important but under-developed subjects much neglected by philosophers since Nietzsche. It certainly is not enough that the injustice of a practice of the wrongness

of policy should be made glaringly evident. People have to be ready to listen, and that is not determined by argument.[43]

In the end Nagel says, in a kind of melancholy self-distancing from Marx's Eleventh Thesis on Feuerbach: 'I do not know whether it is important to change the world or to understand it, but philosophy is best judged by its contribution to understanding, not to the course of events.'[44] If, in fact, we do not acknowledge that the object of the epistemic search and the constituency of anti-sexist work are not identical, and we simply finesse the fact that the feminist challenge must combine method and act, we might be able to echo the nobility of these sentiments. I myself think we cannot stop here, because we have not had an acknowledged code of 'honour and retribution and respect for strength' except as victim/supporters. I will, then, repeat my modest solution.

Incanting to ourselves all the perils of transforming a 'name' to a referent – making a catechism, in other words, of catachresis – let us none the less name (as) 'woman' that disenfranchised woman whom we strictly, historically, geo-politically *cannot imagine*, as literal referent. Let us divide the name of woman so that we see ourselves as naming, not merely named. Let us acknowledge that we must change a morphology to a story-line, acknowledge that we participated in obliterating the traces of her production, stage the scene of the effacing of the graphematic – her biography – in the crudest possible way. The anxiety of this naming will be that, if we must think a relationship between the subject of onto/epistemology (ourselves, roughly, in this room at Cambridge, or Elaine Showalter at Princeton) and the object of onto/axiology (that disenfranchised woman, not even graduated into that subject, whose historicity we cannot imagine beyond the regulation 'women's union' human interest anecdote), the hope behind the political desire will be that the possibility for the name will be finally erased. Today, here, what I call the 'gendered subaltern', especially in decolonized space, has become the name 'woman' for me.[45] In search of irreducibles, after the chastening experience of coming close to the person who provides that imagined name, I want to be able not to lament when the material possibility for the name disappears.

Notes

1 Thomas Nagel, *Mortal Questions* (Cambridge: Cambridge University Press, 1979), p. xii.
2 Jacqueline Rose, *Sexuality in the Field of Vision* (London: Verso, 1986).
3 Quoted by Elizabeth Skolbert, 'Literary feminism comes of age', *New York Times Sunday Magazine*, 6 December 1987, p. 112.
4 See Ashis Nandy, *The Intimate Enemy: Loss and Recovery of Self Under Colonialism* (Oxford: Oxford University Press, 1983); and Partha Chatterjee, *Nationalist Thought and the Colonial World: A Derivative Discourse* (London: Zed, 1986).
5 Rose, op. cit., p. 23.

6 ibid., p. 15.
7 I had commented on this as early as the Preface to J. Derrida, *Of Grammatology*, trans. Spivak (Baltimore: Johns Hopkins University Press, 1976), p. lxxvii. When in *In Other Worlds: Essays in Cultural Politics* (New York: Methuen, 1987), pp. 263 and 308 n. 83, I somewhat tendentiously remark that affirmative deconstruction 'is not the rhapsodic high artistic language of elite feminist literary experimentation', I have something in mind like the difference between the desire for an impasse and negotiating with an enabling double bind. This ignoring of the double bind in non-foundationalist philosophy is now affecting Euramerican Marxism as well: a 'justification of Marxian theory on the grounds of its social context and consequences amounts to warranting a theory by means of the self-same theory ... we are not bothered by the nature of [the alternative anti-essentialist] infinite regress of meaning-production, by this complete rejection of a referent that is independent of these "independent terms" and that can serve as an ultimate ground of truth for these meanings' (Stephen A. Resnick and Richard D. Wolff, *Knowledge and Class: A Marxian Critique of Political Economy* (Chicago: University of Chicago Press, 1987), p. 28.
8 Rose, op. cit., p. 5.
9 It would be to belabor the obvious to point out that there is rather a straight and self-conscious line here between Kant and Freud. See, for example, Sigmund Freud, *The Standard Edition of the Complete Psychological Works* (London: Hogarth, 1964), vol. 22, pp. 61 and 163.
   The relationship between the knowing and acting subject is a rupture rather than a continuous progression. It is surely one of the gifts of structuralist and poststructuralist psychoanalysis to make us productively uneasy about that relationship. (I use 'productive' where I should perhaps say 'potentially productive'. I mean that the unease can be less intransigent than a mere privileging of either theory or practice, or the assumption of achievable continuity between them.)
10 Again, this is rather a prominent cornerstone of the critique of humanism. The lines here fall unevenly between Nietzsche, Heidegger, Foucault, and Derrida. Foucault, having decided to name the problem itself the empirico-transcendental discursive mark of the modern, went off in other interesting directions. Derrida has kept patiently producing its implications. He stated the problem simply in 1963 (in a sentence that I often quote) with special reference to the anthropologizing of philosophy, a project in which the later Rose as a feminist (Derrida is speaking of Sartre as a humanist) is perhaps also engaged: 'Everything occurs as if the sign (man) has no origin, no historical, cultural, or linguistic limit' (*Margins of Philosophy*, trans. Alan Bass (Chicago: University of Chicago Press, 1982), p. 116.
11 Jacques Derrida, *Spurs*, trans. Barbara Harlow (Chicago: University of Chicago Press, 1978). I have modified all translations when necessary.
12 ibid., p. 109. The essay 'Geschlecht: sexual difference, ontological difference', in *Psyche: Inventions de l'autre* (Paris: Galilée, 1987) should be considered if one wants to engage Derrida specifically on the issue of the place of sexual duality in Heidegger's thought. It has little to do with our argument here.
13 Derrida, *Spurs*, p. 109.
14 Louis Althusser, 'Ideology and ideological state apparatuses (notes towards an investigation)', in *Lenin and Philosophy and Other Essays*, trans. Ben Brewster (New York: Monthly Review Press, 1971), p. 159. Theodor Adorno, 'Subject and object', in *The Essential Frankfurt School Reader*, trans. Andrew Orato and Eike Gebhardt (New York: Urizen, 1978), p. 508.

15 Althusser, op. cit., p. 176.
16 Derrida, *Spurs*, p. 110.
17 ibid., p. 111.
18 ibid., p. 110.
19 G. C. Spivak, 'Displacement and the discourse of woman', in Mark Krupnick (ed.), *Displacement: Derrida and After* (Bloomington: Indiana University Press, 1983). I do mention the fact of the 'name', but do not seem to grasp its import.
20 Derrida, *Spurs*, p. 51.
21 ibid.
22 Rose, op. cit., p. 21 n.38.
23 This phase in Derrida begins as early as his deconstructive reading of the philosophy of Emmanual Levinas in 'Violence and metaphysics', published in 1964 (and trans. Alan Bass in *Writing and Difference* (Chicago: University of Chicago Press, 1978)). Levinas argues there that Husserl and Heidegger, both within the Greek tradition, ultimately write philosophies of oppression. Neutralizing the other, fundamental ontology and phenomenology perform the same structural operation as philosophies of knowledge, appropriating the other as object. By contrast, Levinas suggests, the gaze toward the other must always be open, an open question, the possibility of the ethical. '"Before the ontological level, the ethical level"' (p. 98). Derrida reads Levinas critically, suggesting that he too is complicit with philosophy in the Greek. But about the openness of the question, the prior claim of responsibility to the trace of the other (which will be for him the possibility of 'the non-ethical opening of ethics': *Of Grammatology*, p. 140), he is in agreement.
24 Jacques Derrida, *The Ear of the Other: Otobiography, Transference, Translation*, trans. Peggy Kamuf (New York: Schocken, 1985).
25 Derrida, *Of Grammatology*, p. 24; emphasis mine.
26 The paleonymic burden of the word 'love' for a feminist is to be distinguished rigorously from the gentlemanly or belle-lettristic attitude of 'love for the text'.
27 'Structure, sign, and play in the discourse of the human sciences', in *Writing and Difference*.
28 The last three paragraphs are from my book, provisionally entitled *Riding on the Hyphen: Deconstruction in the Service of Reading*, forthcoming from Columbia University Press.
29 Part of the idea behind spelling 'differance' with an 'a' was that it would be a neographism, be visible, not audible. To keep the word in English and to pronounce it in the French way has foiled that project. Since another part of the idea was to include both 'differ' and 'defer' and indicate that this was the spacing/time structure of the inevitable break between, among other things, theory and method (epistemo/ontology and axiology, too, of course), I propose 'difering' (or 'deffering') in English. I will do nothing to give this translation currency.
30 'The supplement of copula: philosophy before linguistics' in *Margins of Philosophy*, trans. Alan Bass (Chicago: University of Chicago Press, 1982). The 'supplement' – both adding and filling a pre-existing whole – is something like the 'difering' that every 'is' pretends or professes it isn't doing.
31 As I have pointed out abundantly elsewhere, the '(im)' in such a formulation marks the enabling double bind at the inauguration of practice that, literalizing a catachresis, allows the possibility of practice as craft.
32 I add this parenthesis because, when I gave a version of this paper at the University of Virginia, so clear a thinker as Richard Rorty thought that my message was that feminism must 'ignore' deconstruction altogether in order to

act. To spell it out this way sounds bizarre. In the doing it is something like a reflex, the 'faith' (habit?) that Gramsci refers to in 'The formation of intellectuals' (Antonio Gramsci, *Selections From the Prison Notebooks*, trans. Quintin Hoare and Geoffrey Nowell Smith (New York: International Publishers, 1971), p. 339). I think, although it does not matter to me very much, that Derrida himself is aware of this at all times, and that it is because of this that, in the introduction to his 1987 collection *Psyche*, he calls the unifying theme in his writings of the last decade a *theorie distraite* – the best English translation of which would be, in my judgement, 'an inattentive theory' (*Psyche*, p. 9).

33 Michel Foucault, *The History of Sexuality*, trans. Robert Hurley (New York: Vintage Books, 1980), p. 93.

34 Derrida, *The Ear of the Other*, pp. 16–17, 38.

35 It is interesting to see that Derrida falls back on the most 'orthodox' model of deconstructive method – reversal and displacement – when he makes a somewhat similar point and does not, of course, refer to his own position within patriarchal presuppositions: Derrida, 'Women in the beehive', in Paul Smith and Alice Jardine (eds), *Men in Feminism* (New York: Methuen, 1987), p. 194–5. It is these presuppositions of the name 'woman', rather than the morphology of 'différance' that will not allow for the acknowledgment of class and race specifically in women – radical heterogeneity in another guise – that I go on to discuss in my text.

36 Foucault fabulates this anxiety poignantly in the adult male Greek's anxiety about the loss of the boyhood of the boy as erotic object in *The Use of Pleasure: The History of Sexuality*, trans. Robert Hurley, vol. 2 (New York: Vintage, 1986).

37 Lacan, 'God and the *jouissance* of woman, a love letter', in *Feminine Sexuality*, trans. Jacqueline Rose (London: Macmillan, 1982), p. 155f.

38 An interested insistence of this sort, not absolutely justified by theory, is, of course, pervasively crucial to deconstructive method. The two articulations that I still find most useful are *Of Grammatology*, p. 162, and 'The double session', in *Disseminations*, trans. Barbara Johnson (Chicago: University of Chicago Press, 1981), p. 235.

39 Foucault, op. cit., p. 91.

40 Michel Foucault, *The Archaeology of Knowledge and the Discourse on Language*, trans. A. M. Sheridan Smith (New York: Pantheon, 1972).

41 ibid., p. 96.

42 For this particular bonding, see Richard Rorty, 'Solidarity or objectivity?', in Cornel West and John Rachjman (eds), *Post-Analytical Philosophy* (New York: Columbia University Press, 1985).

43 Nagel, op. cit., p. xiii.

44 ibid.

45 I have discussed the literary representations of such a figure in '"Draupadi" by Mahasweta Devi' and 'A literary representation of the subaltern: "The breast-giver"', both in *In Other Worlds*; and in 'Narratives of nation' (forthcoming).

Part Six

Sexual difference (2):
the psychical in the social

Chapter Thirteen

Cutting up

Joan Copjec

In contemporary analyses of the relation of psychoanalysis to politics, the real
has no place; the psychical and the social are conceived as a realtight unit
ruled by a principle of pleasure. I propose to show that *it is the real that unites
the psychic to the social*, that this relation is ruled by the death drive. Taking
seriously those formulations by which the subject and the unconscious are
termed the *effect* of the social order, I will describe this relation as a causal
one. But, reader, please beware: a definition of cause that depends on and is
produced through a definition of the death drive will certainly not be
familiar.

First, the real. How has it been evicted from current discussions? Within
psychoanalysis the status of the real is problematic from the beginning. Once
it is observed that pleasure is the goal of all psychic mechanisms and that the
psyche is able to obtain pleasure by means of its own internal processes – i.e.,
by producing a hallucinatory pleasure   the subject appears to be 'independent
of' what Freud calls 'Fate',[1] and what we will call the real. Psychical reality
can indefinitely defer, and thus replace, the reality of brute fact. 'Happiness'
is therefore defined in *Civilization and Its Discontents* as 'essentially
subjective'. This means that even if we were to imagine the most unhappy
historical situations – 'a peasant during the Thirty Years War, a victim of the
Holy Inquisition, a Jew awaiting the pogrom'[2] – it would be impossible to
assume from the objective facts alone how, or even that, the victims suffered
as a consequence of their situations. One would also have to recall that there
is a whole range of psychic operations (to which we do not have direct access),
which, by numbing, blunting, or distorting the harmful sensations, might shield
the victim from pain.

It is nevertheless wrong to think that this Freudian description of the
pleasure principle neatly separates psychical and social reality. The reality with
which the reality principle puts us in touch is not simply a perceptual object,
which can test the adequacy of the object of hallucination produced by the
pleasure principle. That this is so is clear from the fact that Freud does not set
social reality – civilization – *against* the pleasure principle, but rather defines the
former as a product of the latter. Civilization does not test, but realizes our

fantasies; it does not put us in touch with Fate (the real), but protects us from it. The social subject is thus pictured as 'a kind of prosthetic God',[3] whose fantastic, artificial limbs substitute for the inferior, natural ones Fate bestows. Civilization endows the subject with a fantasmatic body and fairytale-like powers. The subjects of modern cultures have telescopes, microscopes, cameras for eyes; microphones, radios, telephones for mouths; ships, trains, cars, and planes for legs; and all of these instruments-that-extend-our-grasp for arms.

For Freud, this definition of civilization does not, of course, end the question of the real; the real is not thereby banished from civilized existence, which brings discontent as well as pleasure. Although the real which is associated with discontent can no longer be conceived simply as that which opposes itself to the imaginary or the psychical, Freud retains the reference to the real.

For much of contemporary theory, however, the question *is* closed. Since the real is conceived as radically outside our ken, inaccessible to us, it is therefore thought to have no bearing on us. Between the subject and the real, civilization – the social order – is interposed. This order is now conceived not only as that which, in equipping the subject with a fantasmatic body, satisfies its desires, but more, as that which produces the desires it satisfies. Happiness is thus defined as objective. For all the mirrors, cameras, telephones, microphones, planes, passenger lists, and statistics can be seen as so much social paraphernalia of surveillance by which alone the subject is made visible – even to itself. If we cannot judge immediately what measure of pain or pleasure belonged to a historical individual, this is not because happiness is subjective and that we cannot project ourselves into her private mental sphere, but rather because we cannot so easily project ourselves into her objective *social* sphere in order to discern the categories of thought that constructed her expectations, narcotized her against disappointment, made her obtuse to her own suffering.

Consider, for example, certain analyses of the hystericization of women's bodies, of the 'invention of hysteria'. According to these, an investigation of turn-of-the-century medical practices, codes of photography, discourses of the Church and of psychoanalysis, and so on will tell us not how hysteria was studied, but, more accurately, how it was constructed as a historical entity. From the point of view of the hysteric, however, how does this argument work? By assuming – implicitly or explicitly – that it is her 'desire' which these practices construct. Her complicity and even her pleasure are secured as she looks at and constructs herself through the categories provided by these discourses.

Consider also the example of contemporary film theory. The concept of the gaze elaborated there is founded on assumptions similar to those just named. The gaze is conceived as a point constructed by the textual system of the film from which the subject is obliged to look; it is the condition of the possibility of the viewer's vision. The gaze acts as a kind of keyhole,[4] the only opening onto the visual pleasure the film affords. One sees and desires to see what it is given to see and desire; one assumes with pleasure – even if masochistic[5] – her own subjective position.

In these examples, the social system of representation is conceived as lawful, regulatory, and on this account the cause of the subject, which the former subsumes as one of its effects. The subject is assumed to be already virtually there in the social and to come into being by actually wanting what social laws want it to want. The construction of the subject depends, then, on the subject's taking social representations as images of its own ideal being, on the subject's deriving a 'narcissistic pleasure' from these representations. This notion of pleasure, however vaguely invoked, is what makes the argument for construction stick, it 'cements' or 'glues' the realm of the psychic to that of the social. (Hume described cause as the 'cement of the universe' – the metaphor helps to determine a certain conception of cause.) The point of insertion of the subject into society thus becomes a point of resemblance, convergence, attachment.

This is the understanding – by which the subject is thought to recognize itself in representations – that I intend to counter. I will begin by opposing to it two images meant to indicate the complexities that are currently erased. The first, taken from *Civilization and Its Discontents*, follows the description of the fairytale-like prostheses that define the contours of the modern bodily ego. 'Man', Freud writes, first appeared on earth 'as a feeble animal organism', and no matter how far the society into which he is born has succeeded in making this earth serviceable to him, 'each individual of the species must once more make its entry ("oh, inch of nature!") as a helpless suckling.'[6] It is the parenthetical phrase, 'oh, inch of nature!', which interests us particularly. This fraction is literally fractious, an oxymoron. For the very segmentation and measurement of nature denatures it; an inch of nature is itself unnatural, found not in nature, but in the rods and rules by which culture calculates. It is perhaps this very unruliness of the image that *resists* the interpretation that it provides the measure of the little man, who would thus be defined absolutely by the yardstick of the society into which he enters. In offering its resistance, the image refuses to offer itself as the *equivalent* of the man, that little piece of nature which *is* man. Rather, the 'inch of nature' is that which is *not* incorporated into society that which is sacrificed upon entry into the social.

The second image is opposed specifically to film theory's concept of the gaze, which asks us to assume the perfect functioning of apparatuses of surveillance. The image, taken from Samuel Beckett's *Watt*, describes the functioning of a five-man examining committee:

> They then began to look at one another and much time passed before
> they succeeded in doing so. Not that they looked at each other long; no,
> they had more sense than that. But when five men look at one another,
> though in theory only twenty looks are necessary, every man looking
> four times, yet in practice this number is seldom sufficient.[7]

And then it seems that several more pages describing the twistings, turnings, and other manoeuvrings of the five men is still not sufficient to establish that exchange of looks by which the committee would succeed in looking at itself. For some look always goes unreciprocated, spoiling indefinitely the perfect exchange.

Beckett's description is presented here as no mere anecdote; it is offered quite seriously as the means of rethinking the significance of the recalcitrant 'inch of nature'.

The death drive: Freud and Bergson

No one ever accused Freud of being a cutup,[8] except Fliess, as you will remember, who pointed out a resemblance between *The Interpretation of Dreams* and a book of jokes. Freud took Fliess's observation one step further by writing *Jokes and Their Relation to the Unconscious* in which he noted some more specific resemblances between his theory and that presented in Henri Bergson's 'Laughter', published in the same year as *The Interpretation of Dreams*. Freud cites Bergson's essay several times, indicating always that he finds it both charming and canny. To support his own, economic view of pleasure, he quotes the following sentence from Bergson: 'What is living should never, according to our expectation, be repeated exactly the same. When we find such a repetition, we always suspect some mechanism lying behind the living thing.'[9] The constantly changing nature of life, Freud argues, demands a perpetual expenditure of energy by our understanding: repetition, then, the rediscovery of something already familiar, is pleasurable because it economises energy. Laughter is the discharge of the excess of energy called up by our expectations of the new and made superfluous by the recognition of the same. In addition to this specific reference, we find more general references and broader gestures of approval of Bergson's 'plausible train of thought from automatism to automata', as Freud, like Bergson, considers the relation of jokes to the games of children.

Bergson's basic argument is that laughter is elicited by a perception of the mechanical encrusted on the living, of the 'mechanization of life'.[10] Where life is defined essentially by its 'organic elasticity', as a ceaselessly changing, irreversible process of pure time and perpetual novelty, the mechanical is defined by its machine-like intractability, manifest in three different operations: repetition, inversion, and the reciprocal interference of series. These operations are illustrated by children's toys, automata, like Jacks-in-the-box, puppets, a game of ninepins in which the ball rolls forward, upsetting the pins, and backwards, restoring the pins to their upright position. Laughter is thought to serve a social function, not as in Freud by providing a potentially healing respite from the expenditure of energy, but rather by issuing a rebuke to every inelasticity of character, thought, and action. Laughter thus acts to restore us to social life and its constant demands for our alert attention and complete presence of mind.

The essay on laughter is supported by Bergson's larger metaphysical project: the assimilation of Darwin's theory of evolution to a non-mechanistic theory of mind.[11] The creative energy of the human mind, he maintains, is irreducible to the material conditions which triggered the mechanisms of selection. As part of this project, Bergson unfavorably contrasts the intellect (which relies on abstract concepts formed by language) with intuition (a kind of 'auscultation', a sympathetic listening to the 'throbbing of [life's] soul').[12] Intuition grasps the supple flow of life directly, while the intellect, distanced by its reliance on rigid and discontinuous spatial concepts, is doomed to let mobile reality slip forever through its categories.

The polemical force of this theory is aimed at the Eleatic philosophers, most notably Zeno. By Bergson's account, Zeno's paradox could be described as comic. This paradox is based on the inchmeal contemplation of an arrow in flight; the trajectory of the arrow is broken down into an infinite number of points in space and the result is offered as proof of motion's impossibility. Since the arrow's flight is composed of these points, the arrow, which occupies one of them at any given moment, must always be at rest. To this analysis Bergson responds with a laugh: it is not motion which is impossible, but the comprehension of motion, of life, by the intellect. The simple lifting of one's arm becomes grotesquely comic when contemplated by the intellect, which can only cut up movement, like a film, into hundreds of discrete moments. It is only the perception of motion from the *inside*, by intuition, that allows us to observe the former's completeness.

(In a way, Bergson's theory of laughter seems tailor-made to account for the humorous, Tayloresque description of the five-man examining committee: it is the division of the completed look into a number of discrete glances that renders its accomplishment impossible.)

The similarities between Bergson and Freud turn out, however, to be superficial when we look more closely at the whole of Freud's work – especially its later development. We turn, then, to *Beyond the Pleasure Principle*, in which Freud returns to the subject of the relations among pleasure, repetition, and the games of children. At this point there can be no mistaking the differences between the two theorists of laughter. In his 1920 essay, Freud, still viewing children's games in the terms he did earlier, now sees adumbrated there the workings of the death drive, a principle beyond pleasure. The surprising turn of the argument hinges precisely on the term *organic elasticity*, the term used by Bergson to name the defining characteristic of the *animate*, of life. Freud, on the contrary, finds in this 'organic elasticity' a pressure to return to an earlier, *inanimate* state. This is what he says: '*a [drive] is an urge inherent in organic life to restore an earlier state of things ... it is a kind of organic elasticity, or, to put it another way, the expression of the inertia inherent in organic life.*'[13] Allow me to state the obvious: there is simply no way to understand *organic elasticity* and *inertia* as synonymous as long as we hold to the Bergsonian model. Nor would we be able to understand why Freud, far from contrasting repetition with life, interprets repetition as the invariable characteristic of the drives that fuel life. The being of the drives, he claims, *is* the compulsion to repeat. The aim of life is not evolution, but regression, or, in its most seemingly contradictory form, the aim of life is death.

The seeming contradictions of *Beyond the Pleasure Principle* can only be unravelled if we take it not as the biologistic myth it is often accused of being, but as, in fact, a charge against such myths, including the one formulated by Bergson.[14] Freud's text is incomprehensible if one confounds instinct with drive, or – in a distinction made by Lacan, who finds it latent in Freud's work – if one confounds the first and the second death.[15] The first is the real death of the biological body, after which there is usually another, the second, exemplified by the various rituals of mourning that take place in the symbolic. It is with this second death that we are concerned when we speak of the Freudian concept of the death drive. This distinction between the two deaths separates the vital order of biological evolution – the order to which 'process' or 'evolutionary' philosophers, like Bergson, refer[16] – where events can be said to move only progressively forward, taking place once and for all time, from the order of the signifier, the symbolic, in which the text of human history is inscribed. In this second order, the past is *not* immortal. Since the signifier always receives its signification retroactively, what was done can always be undone; the past can, therefore, have no permanent existence. According to Bergson, the novelty of the present is assured only by the total survival of the past, novelty being defined as the moment's unique difference from its complete antecedent context. The persistence of the past in its entirety is thus necessary if the possibility of a recurrence of events is to be excluded. The death drive, then, which recognizes the possibility of the past's destruction, is inextricably linked to repetition. The death drive and the compulsion to repeat are thus the inevitable corollaries of *symbolic* life.

Cause: Lacan and Aristotle

In his elaboration of Freud's concept of the death drive, Lacan does not, however, make explicit reference to Bergson, but rather to Aristotle. The connections between these last two are nevertheless clear: starting with the fact that they articulate their arguments in opposition to the same theoretical foes. Aristotle, too, took the Eleatics – metaphysical materialists who asserted that Being is immutable and change impossible – as his primary philosophical enemy. Contrary to the Eleatic position, Aristotle, like Bergson, based his philosophy on the primacy of change, of a becoming which is not divisible into parts exterior to each other. One of their major differences is their positions with respect to teleology. Aristotle argued for the validity of teleological explanation, while Bergson argued most adamantly against it on the grounds that the concept of an internal finalism destroyed time and annihilated novelty. But Aristotle, for his part, was careful to distinguish his position from the idealist one in which form is thought to be given at the outset and to guide from an ideal space; form in Aristotle is always the terminus of change in the natural world. And time for him, as for Bergson, is what retards, it hinders everything's being given in advance, all at once. The teleological argument was advanced in an attempt at a *non-mechanical* explanation of change.

This is merely to say that when Lacan, in his explanation of Freud's death drive, names the signifying network that is its domain, *automaton*, he mounts an argument which answers Bergson as well as Aristotle, even though it is to the latter's use of the word that we are referred. In *The Physics* and elsewhere in Aristotle, the term 'automaton' appears as part of an attempt to define cause. His basic position is that natural, living substance (as opposed to the inanimate) has an internal principle of change. Yet because Aristotle must coherently argue that there is a diversity as well as an eternity of change, he is led to suppose that a natural substance changes according to its own nature *and* that it depends on something else for the realization of change. This something else is, of course, the well-known Prime Mover.

Automaton, the general category of chance or coincidence, occurs, by contrast, not through some inner principle of change, but as a result of the collision of separate events each with its own independent cause. None of the events occurs because of the other and there is no cause, no connected cause or explanation, for their simultaneity. Their conjunction is therefore not, properly speaking, an event. One example given is that of the man who goes to the market to buy something and happens to meet there a debtor who repays his loan. Aristotle argues that since the first man did not go to the market for the sake of recovering his money, but rather for some other reason, the meeting with the debtor demonstrates a certain *failure* of final cause as explanatory principle: that which results occurs not for some purpose, but *in vain*.[17] It is this notion of failure which Lacan will systematically explore, linking it to Aristotle's general assertion that accidental causes are indeterminate. In *The Four Fundamental Concepts*, Lacan says clearly: 'cause is to be distinguished from that which is determinate in a chain,' and a bit later 'whenever we speak of cause ... there is always something indefinite'.[18]

Before we can understand Lacan's intervention, we must recall again the difficulties of Aristotle's argument. As we have said, what must be maintained is both the diversity of finite change and the eternity of change in general. The universe cannot be thought to stop and start without sacrificing this last requirement. We have also said that this dictates the solution of the doubling, in effect, of the cause of change. It also dictates the distinction between an underlying substance and its attributes, or properties. The substance is that which continues, remains the same, while the attributes register change by coming to be or falling away. The sentence 'the uncultured man became a cultured man'[19] serves as illustration. Man, we see, is constantly present throughout the transformation in which the attribute of culture comes to replace its absence. The parts of natural substance must always be of this order; they must be qualities rather than mechanical parts, if the *per se* unity of the substance is to be safeguarded. (I need not add, I think, that the concept of underlying substance is the point of Lacan's attack.)

And yet at points, especially in the *De Motu Animalium*, when Aristotle attempts to detail a simple process of locomotion, this unity seems to break down, as the movement in a film breaks down when the projection is slowed. In order to make room for the Prime Mover (who must himself be unmoved), the description of physical movement is forced to take on a remarkably mechanistic tenor:

> the origin of movement, qua origin, always remains at rest when the lower part of a limb is moved; for example, the elbow joint, when the forearm is moved, and the shoulder, when the whole arm; the knee when the tibia is moved, and the hip when the whole leg.[20]

Things grow still worse when Aristotle places an instrument, specifically a stick, in the hand whose movement he contemplates. Seeking the 'true original' of the stick's movement, the analysis makes its way up the arm joint by joint rejecting each with the declaration that it is something 'higher up' which can always initiate the motion even if each joint were to stiffen and thus each section of arm go rigid as the stick. The arm itself is in this way turned into an instrument.

It is to this passage, or some similar, in which Aristotle determines the necessity of the Prime Mover on the basis of the corporeal experience of raising one's arm (the same experience which Bergson claims can only be grasped by intuition) that Lacan refers in his seminar on anxiety[21] when he summarizes the classical philosophical position on the question of cause: seeing myself as self-moving (as *automaté*), I focus my attention on some appendage, my arm, say, which I can move at will. But once I have isolated my arm by considering it the intermediary between my wish and my act, it becomes necessary to modify the fact that, if it is an instrument, it is not free. It is necessary to insure myself against the fact not of my arm's amputation immediately, but of my losing control of it, of its coming under the power of another, or of my simply forgetting it – as if it were some common umbrella – in the metro. Paradoxically, I reassure myself that I maintain control over myself through one form of determinism or another. I hold to the belief that even in the absence of my conscious attention, my arm will move automatically, according to a whole system of involuntary reflexes or to an ultimate guiding presence.

In other words, the whole sum of the body functions, the entire corporeal presence is assumed in order to maintain Man's freedom of thought and will. But ironically this sum depends for its existence on our supposing the intervention of some supernatural power, some power beyond us: Aristotle's Prime Mover, Bergson's Spirit.

In opposition to this, Lacan argues that we think not as a consequence of our engagement with the totality of our bodily presence, but rather as a consequence of the fact that 'a structure carves up [Man's] body.... Witness the hysteric.'[22] Now, this plain hortatory may, I fear, prove misleading. For one thinks first of all of the vivid, visible symptoms of hysteria – the hystericization by which the body and its movements become an erotic spectacle: the passionate attitudes, the arcs of circle, the pregnancies. And by now, with the help of the theory of psychoanalysis, one recognizes 'hysterogenic zones' as symptoms inscribed by language. The body is written, it is constructed by language and not pregiven; all the work on the 'technologies of the body' have repeated this often enough. Lacan would not deny this – in fact, it is largely his theory which enables this position to be taken. Yet, I would suggest that when Lacan tells us that language carves up the body, '*Witness the hysteric*', he is speaking of a more unkind cut than that which merely carves *out* (or defines) a body image through which the subject will assume its being. The cut to which Lacan refers instead carves *up* (divides) the body image and thus drives the subject to seek its being beyond that which the image presents to it; it causes the subject to find in its image something lacking. Lacan is asking us to witness the paralyses and anaesthesias of the hysteric, those blind spots in consciousness, those spaces of an omitted attention which mark the point where something is missing in the hysteric's image of herself. The fact that she is constructed by society's language means *to the hysteric* that part of her body will *not* be visible, or present to her. The inert limb or the facial paralysis of the hysteric bears the testimony of a cut too often ignored by those who would turn Lacan's theory into a linguistic or cultural determinism. Those who speak of the 'invention of hysteria' as the pure imposition on the subject of an identity formed by the social neglect to consider that hysteria is conceived by psychoanalysis as a challenge to the subject's social identity: hysteria is the first analyzed instance of the subject's essential division.

We are now in a position to reconsider the matter of the *failure* of identity. Earlier, we cited the example of Beckett's five-man examining committee that fails infinitely in the exchange of looks which would establish its identity. Immediately we turned to Bergson's theory of laughter, which would account for the impossibility of the look's completion by its limitless segmentation. Indeed, the almost complete degeneration of movement in Beckett's fiction in general seems to result from its division into endless inventories of its exact spatial possibilities. The humor seems to result from the overly analytic attempt to grasp movement. Yet, at the outset of the Beckettian hero's trajectory, a desire is expressed which can be seen to impel the whole narrative machine. This desire gives us an entirely different understanding of the fiction's relation to failure. This desire is expressed by Murphy, who yearns, it is revealed, to participate in the bliss he imagines to be the hysteric's own:

> And it would not surprise me if the great classic paralyses were to offer unspeakable satisfactions. To be literally incapable of motion at last, that must be something! And mute into the bargain! And just enough brain intact to allow you to exult![23]

It is this identification with the hysteric, more specifically with her paralyses, which yields the succession of heroes not an identity, but precisely the long trail of its undoing. While to us it offers the means of considering Zeno's paradox in its proper, psychoanalytic perspective. The immutable being in which Zeno believes is not, as Bergson maintains, the consequence of the illusion that our being is only equal to the 'practical' or 'abstract' definitions that language imposes on it. It is the consequence, rather, of the illusion that part of our being resides beyond language's limits. For Lacan it is the being beyond not the being within language which is perceived as immutable, as the inert pound of flesh, the 'inch of nature', which the blank in memory or sight signals as missing from our own self-image. The subject constructed by language finds itself detached from a part of itself. And it is this primary detachment which renders fruitless all the subject's efforts for a reunion with its complete being. The arc of its strivings appearing to the subject as Zeno's arrow – an endlessly interrupted flight that can only asymptotically approach its goal. It is the cutting off of the subject from a part of itself, this part being the object-cause of its desire, which accounts for the cutting up of the subject's movements and the *reductio ad surdum*, i.e., the reduction to infinite series of its replaceable objects. While Bergson argues that the Eleatic tradition errs by making the future, all time, present at once and thus by abolishing time, change, and succession, Lacanian psychoanalysis shows that, on the contrary, it is the non-presence of the subject to its whole self which determines the formulation of the Eleatic paradoxes.

Bergson and Lacan are in agreement, however, on one point at least: they both oppose the logico-implicative notion of language. But while Bergson understands language according to this notion and thus attacks language for its tenselessness, for being able to derive consequence only as something already contained in a premise, Lacan takes the logico-implicative as a *mistaken* notion of language. His task becomes, then, the clarification of the way consequence *is*, in fact, derived from language. He will thus define the subject not as an effect contained within language, but as an effect of that which it cuts off, that which language makes disappear. Lacan will say, in short, that it is this missing part – nothing – which causes the subject: the subject is created *ex nihilo*.

This position could not be more directly opposed to that of Bergson, for whom, recall, duration (*durée*, the name Bergson gives to his progressive temporality) is thought to 'grow' out of all that precedes it. The process he describes is one of 'intususception', in which the present is conceived not as something added to the past, but as incorporated into it. The present, and all that comes into being depends absolutely on the existence of everything that comes before it. Nothing comes from nothing. For Bergson, nothing is simply a meaningless concept. There is no difference, he maintains, between thinking of something and thinking of it as existing. He believed, as many have, that existence is an attribute of all that can be thought. It is this assumption which must be discredited if one is to imagine creation *ex nihilo*.

Lacan, as we know, believed in the priority of social discourses, of language, over the subject. In referring to the signifying chain as *automaton*, he declares this belief in the fact that language 'produces effects ... in the absence of intention; [that] no intentions intervene to animate and fill up speech'.[24] As Derrida has written, the classical *condemnation* of the machine is a denial of this fact. Now, to say that language exceeds the intentions of the subject is to say that signifiers are opaque to intentions. But this opacity prohibits not only their being used for the communication of intentions, it also prohibits their reflection of an exterior reality. We have returned, then, to the place where we began, with the observation that a certain definition of the social being of language seems only to founder on this impasse, to trap us wholly in a socially constructed reality in which and with which we are bound to be happy. Or perhaps more simply, in which we are bound. For if we begin by assuming that the subject is the effect of a particular social organization in the sense of being a *realization* or *fulfilment* of its demand, then pleasure becomes a redundant concept and the need to theorize it is largely extinguished. It becomes merely the subjective synonym of the objective fact of the subject's construction. An exclusive reliance on the pleasure principle as the only available form of the subject's relation to the social ends in the elimination of the need for pleasure.

It is at this point that *delay* – that which prevents everything's being given at once – becomes a crucial concept in Lacan's argument, much as it was in Aristotle's and Bergson's. But whereas in Bergson delay is called on to refute the claims of language, to overturn it in favor of duration, in Lacan (following Freud) it is understood as prolonging the pleasures of language; it introduces the reality principle, which psychoanalysis defines as that which delays the pleasure principle, or which maintains desire beyond the threats of extinction presented by satisfaction. The death drive does not negate the pleasure principle, it extends it.

We have said that the opacity of signifiers means that language does not reveal a reality or truth behind them. This logic must now be extended to take note of the fact that this very opacity also guarantees that whatever reality or meaning is produced by them will never be able to convince us of its truth or completeness. *Since signifiers are not transparent, they cannot demonstrate that they are not hiding something behind what they say – they cannot prove that they do not lie.* Language can only seem to the subject a veil which cuts off from view a reality that is other than what we are allowed to see. Because of its *organic elasticity* – recall the point on which Freud turned the Bergsonian argument against itself – language stretches beyond, or delays, determinate meaning, it produces always something more, something indeterminate, some question of meaning's reliability. It is this question that suspends the automatic attribution of existence to everything that is thought and instead raises the possibility of conceiving non-existence: nothing. Signification gives rise inevitably to doubt, to the possibility of its own negation; it enables us to think the annihilation, the full-scale destruction of our entire signified reality.

When, therefore, Lacan says that the subject is created *ex nihilo*, he acknowledges the fact that any statement prepares the possibility of its own negation, the fact that the pleasure principle (the subject's independence from fate) leads inexorably beyond itself, outstrips itself by producing doubt, which in turn produces the belief that there is a reality lying behind language.[25] The subject can only question whether what it has been given to enjoy is truly what there is. Whether there isn't something missing in what has been offered. Desire is produced not as a striving for something, but only for something else or something more. It stems from the feeling of our having been duped by language, cheated of something, not from our having been presented with a determinate object or goal for which we can aim. Desire has no content – it is for nothing – because language can deliver to us no incontrovertible truth, no positive goal.

The Lacanian aphorism – desire is the desire of the Other – is often taken to mean that the subject fashions itself in the image of the Other's desire. It is this which I have been taking as a problematic political position, but my particular interest is in the problem this position presents for feminism. For when this assumption is combined with the uncovering of a masculinist bias in the ordering of social relations, then woman can only be comprehended as a realization of male desires, she can only be seen to see herself through the perspective of a male gaze. Lacan's answer to this mistaken interpretation of his formula is simply that we have no image of the Other's desire (it remains indeterminate), and it is this very lack which causes our desire. It is first of all an *unsatisfied* desire that initiates our own, one that is not filled up with meaning, or has no signified. That desire is *unsatisfiable* is a secondary truth resulting from this primary condition.

To all those who describe the subject as a fiction of extravagant prostheses, a prosthetic god manufactured by (and in the image of the desire of) a cultural order, we must now issue a reply. It is not the long arm of the law that determines the shape and reach of every subject, but rather something that escapes the law and its determination, something we can't manage to put our finger on. One cannot argue that the subject is constructed by language and then overlook the essential fact of language's duplicity, that is, the fact that whatever it says can be denied. This duplicity insures that the subject will *not* come into being as language's determinate meaning. An incitement to discourse is not an incitement to being. What is aroused instead is the desire for non-being, for an *in*determinate something which is perceived as *extra*discursive. This indeterminate something (referred to by Lacan as object a) that causes the subject has historical specificity (it is the product of a specific discursive order), but no historical content. The subject is the product of history without being the fulfilment of a historical demand.

Zenophilia

We have so far been concerned with defining the Lacanian position through its opposition to certain foes of Zeno [Zeno-foebs]: Aristotle and Bergson. But it is also necessary to distinguish Lacan's position from a current Zenophilia, a current love, or at least privileging of difference. To this end, we now turn to a very finely argued essay by Samuel Weber, 'Closure and exclusion', which underscores the relevance of Zeno's paradoxes for any semiotically-based theory of the subject.[26] Weber's essay is concerned with the fact that the acceptance of the Saussurian dictum (in language there are no positive terms, only differences) forces us to confront the specter of Zeno and the problem of infinite regress. Once one breaks up the signifying chain, the statement, into an infinite series of diacritical marks – one signifier referring to another, which refers to another, and so on, and on – once the play of difference is no longer grounded in some external reality, we are obliged to wonder how it is possible to produce any reference or any statement at all. Weber relates the way Charles Sanders Peirce – who believed, too, that a sign is not the representation of an object, but something which addresses itself to another sign – was plagued throughout his life by Zeno's paradox of Achilles and the tortoise.

Peirce obtained a solution to this paradox by joining his pragmatic theory to his semiotic investigation, that is, he came eventually to see that the other 'sign' to which a sign addresses itself is 'not entirely or simply some other *thought*', but entails as well 'practical bearings', 'effects that engage behavior'. Pragmatic fact, then, leapfrogs over semiotic division, just as Achilles, despite the infinite, geometric division of his movements, does, in fact, overtake the tortoise. At first Peirce conceived of these behavioral effects of language as 'habit', but finally, feeling that an emphasis on habit would bring to a standstill the whole *process* which he took semiotics to be and would reduce thought to a kind of *automatism* ('something like Freud's repetition compulsion', Weber adds),[27] he settled instead on 'habit-change' as the only possible ultimate sign and the only solution to Zeno's paradox.

Weber is quite right to note the similarities between this notion of habit change and Derrida's notion of iteration, the continuous alteration and difference in which repetition results. What should also be clear, however, from this discussion and the emphases we have given it, is how dangerously similar habit-change and iteration can seem to be to those notions of self-change and perpetual novelty which found the 'creative' subject and, in the end, eliminate repetition. This similarity does not escape the notice of Weber, who carefully tries to dissociate the subject of self-*division* implied by Peirce and Derrida from the self-present, self-*changing* subject of Bergson and Aristotle. But the dangerous similarities remain a threat, even if recognized here. The infiltration of Bergsonianism into modern thought has been so thorough that many of our supposedly 'postmodern' ideas are still shaped by it. All too often is the Derridean notion of difference used to support an apolitical (naïve) optimism of eternal change: nothing can ever appear twice the same because the context which determines meaning is always different from the context of the moment before. The 'subject-in-process' is often accorded this sense of a perpetual and progressive self-changingness which gives the slip to the rigidifying structures of the social order.

The problem, however, is not *simply* a lack of vigilance, or a misuse of Derrida's theory. One can locate already in Derrida and his followers a certain leap in their argument. A leap which becomes necessary to their solution of Zeno's paradoxes – once their psychoanalytic point has been gone unobserved:

> Does the absolute singularity of signature as event ever occur? Are there signatures? Yes, of course, every day.[28]

> Having established a certain structural instability in the most powerful attempts to provide models of structuration, it was probably inevitable that Derrida should then begin to explore the other side of the coin, the fact that, *undecidability notwithstanding*, decisions are *in fact* taken, power *in fact* exercised, traces *in fact* instituted.[29]

The fact or effect (the signature effect, institution effect) is held, then, in the face of and against ('the other side of the coin') the delay installed by semiotic difference, but the mechanism by which these effects take effect is not made clear.

In retrospect it seems that Weber's description of Peirce's theoretical trajectory is more accurately a description of the argument made by Derrida and accepted by Weber. All the arguments for difference yield in the final moment (like a Sidneyan sonnet's unprepared-for fourteenth line) to an argument for language's illocutionary force. And so while Derrida will offer a lengthy critique of Austin's definition of the performative – its dependence on a determinable context – he will, nevertheless, safeguard, in the end, Austin's major premise: words do (and do not merely describe) things. They construct subjects (the subject effect), for example. Yes, but *how*? Having thoroughly and legitimately critiqued Austin's explanation, Derrida, surprisingly, offers no other in its stead. He simply asserts that they do have a performative function.

And so we are left to imagine a kind of binding operation by which differences are somehow bundled into a unity, an identity or effect. But this binding is not completely successful; its force is not strong enough to eliminate the initial differences and this results in a failure, a dispersal of identity. Difference 'leaks out from', or 'ruptures' the narrow bounds of a carved out identity. In the end, then, a system of pure signifying difference effects a subject of pure difference – and some nominal identity.

This vague scenario of failure (which underwrites a great deal of contemporary theory) has assumed a place in feminist analyses that locate the possibility of political change in the fact that originary difference triumphs over constructed identity, which fails to take hold completely. Here, again, my quarrel: there is, for the most part, no attempt to give this failure any psychical explanation; it seems an ill-conceived and unpsychoanalytic matter of forces which manage more or less well or badly to constrict the subject.

Recently, in an attempt to evade the impasses that have resulted from positing the gaze as the single point of entry into the film system, feminists have begun to analyse film as a fantasy structure.[30] The reasons for this are unquestionably sound. For too long the psychic mechanisms of the viewing subject have been assumed by film theory only to be ignored by concrete analyses. Though considered necessary, the psychical apparatus has so far served no function other than that of being generally available as the site of the cementing of subject to social structures. This, as we have said from the beginning, has resulted in the reduction of the subject to a mere – yet tenaciously unassailable – point. Attention to the structures of fantasy restores the subject to fuller view, since the fantasy displays the subject's desire.

And yet there is something troubling in the way the consideration of fantasy has tended often to limit itself to the polemical observation that, in the fantasy scenario, the subject takes up and shifts between different and even contradictory positions, here a female position, there a male one. Certainly it is important to be reminded of the psychoanalytic claim that the sexed positions one occupies in fantasy and other discourses are not determined by one's anatomy. But it is unclear where this emphasis on the multiplicity of shifting positions can lead us. Above all, we must not allow it to confuse the limitlessness of the replaceable objects of the subject's desire with a limitlessness of the subject. *The subject of desire is finite, limited.* Fantasy defines these limits, not the subject's infinite dispersal. What must be observed in fantasy is not simply the range of positions assumed, but how these different positions are structured so as to circumscribe and thus define an absence at the fantasy's center. This absence or 'kernel of nonsense'[31] holds the fantasy and the subject in place, limits the subject. The location of this kernel is the aim of psychoanalysis and should be, I propose, the aim of feminism and other political theory as well. It provides the link between the subject and social discourses.

When psychoanalysis speaks of the hysteric's failure of identity, it accounts for this failure not by a model of energetics, of strong and weak forces, but by means of the materiality of language, which always cuts the subject off from a complete identity. Yet the necessary failure of social discourses in their representations of the subject is not taken by psychoanalysis – as it is by Derrida and Weber – as the subversion of the subject's identity. Rather this failure, the very *impossibility* of representing the subject to the subject, is conceived as that which *founds* the subject's identity. *The failure of representation produces rather than disrupts identity.* That missing part which representation, in failing to inscribe, cuts off is the absence around which the subject weaves its fantasies, its self-image, not in imitation of any ideal vision, but in response to the very impossibility of ever making visible this missing part.

We are constructed, then, not in conformity to social laws, but in response to our inability to conform to or see ourselves as defined by social limits. Though we are defined and limited *historically*, the absence of the real, which founds these limits, is not *historicizable*.[32] It is only this distinction which informs the Lacanian definition of cause that allows us to think the construction of the subject without being thereby obliged to reduce her *to* the images social discourses construct *of* her.

Cause and the law

Although Lacan's position must be differentiated from others with which it has been confused, it should not be seen as simply idiosyncratic, for it shares many insights with other current theories of cause.

The dominant philosophical position, held for some time, was that cause is implied by invariable sequence or the constant conjunction of events ruled by a covering law. Causal explanations were thought to establish a formally determinable, deductive relation between statements describing the effect to be explained, the initial (i.e., causal) conditions, and a law allowing the deduction of the former from the latter. It is to this position that Lacan refers in *The Four Fundamental Concepts of Psycho-Analysis* when he says that his concept of cause is to be distinguished from that which sees it as *law*. He gives as an example of that to which his theory is opposed the invariable sequence, or constant conjunction of action and reaction, whose covering law, as we know, was set out by Newton.[33]

In recent years much effort has gone into contesting the covering-law theory of cause. Some of the most fruitful efforts have, ironically, been inspired by Aristotle. For although Aristotle maintained that a substance's nature was revealed only through specific, or typical sorts of change, he did acknowledge that atypical changes could be described. These were thought to be due to a mere interference with the natural course of things and to give, therefore, no information about the substance's nature. Nevertheless, Aristotle does spend considerable attention on these interferences and, in fact, ends up defining voluntary movement – say, once again, the lifting of one's arm – *negatively*, in terms of the absence of interference or of 'excusing circumstances'. He thus devotes much space to the examination and full description of the context of an event and the excuses which contribute to the *failure* of natural change to be exhibited by cause. Remember, too, that this attention to context was also entailed by his initial division of cause into four primary kinds. From the beginning, then, a definition of cause demanded an investigation of context in order to determine which kind of cause was appropriate.

In 1956 J. L. Austin was able to create a philosophical stir by writing ceremoniously and approvingly of this fascination with failure for which Aristotle had so long been chided.[34] A few years later, two of Austin's colleagues at Oxford, H. L. A. Hart and A. M. Honoré published *Causation in the Law*,[35] a work which has, through its detailed attention to context and failure, proved extremely influential in the development of theories of causality that connect cause not to law but to failure. The book offers very convincing arguments against 'the doctrine that the generalizations or laws which it is the business of experimental sciences to discover, constitute the very essence of the notion of causation'. It also offers an indictment (though by no means centrally or extensively considered) of the bodily metaphor – of the experience of exerting bodily pressure or force on an object in order to move it – which Hart and Honoré assume to underlie the notion of cause that their book repudiates. It is because of this underlying and unanalyzed metaphor, they argue, that cause comes to be conceived as a positive force, and non-events, accidents, and failures are eliminated from consideration as possible causes.

Causation in the Law makes a basic distinction between conditions or occasions, the normal and inconspicuous factors surrounding effects, and cause itself, conceived as a deviation from normal circumstances, as something that goes wrong and thus stands in need of explanation. Hart and Honoré offer by way of illustration the example of a fire breaking out.[36] Normally one would refuse to attribute the cause of the fire to the presence of oxygen, though certainly no fire can occur without it. One looks for the cause, rather, in some abnormal circumstance, in something that has gone wrong.

Even this summary description of their argument should be sufficient to suggest ways in which Lacan can be seen to share and improve on the insights of Hart and Honoré.

1   Lacan also focuses on the bodily metaphor that underlies a
    particular conception of cause, but he makes this metaphor more
    central to his theory and demonstrates why it is invalid.
2   Lacan makes failure independent of the static and problematic
    norm/deviation distinction.
3   By making the question that requires us to seek after cause arise
    not from the subject, but from the materiality of language, Lacan
    eliminates the psychologism that plagues all (including Hart and
    Honoré's) conflations of cause and explanation.

As the philosophical question of cause opens out thus before us, some humility is, of course, in order. We are accustomed to associating this question with *the* grand metaphysical project that has always been active and promises never to end. We think of cause as a perennial question. It is not – although it would take a long and difficult analysis to reveal the shifts in the concept of cause and the questions that have constructed it. Cause is a concept that must be forged anew if we are to build some understanding of the relation between the social order and psychical existence. Humility is still advisable, though we assume it not in the face of the long history of philosophy, but rather in the face of our own recently constructed theoretical difficulties in articulating the relation between psychoanalysis and politics, particularly a feminist politics. Too often these difficulties entail either the elimination of psychical reality, its virtual absorption by the social, or the elimination of social reality, which is conceived merely as a realization of a given psychical relation between men and women. Each alternative foredooms feminist analysis, which depends on the existence of a psychical semi-independence from patriarchal structures. It is out of a dedication to the very real cause of feminism that I have undertaken this preliminary analysis of the real *as* cause.

Notes

1 Sigmund Freud, *The Standard Edition of the Complete Psychological Works of Sigmund Freud* (*SE*), trans. James and Alix Strachey, (London: Hogarth and the Institute of Psychoanalysis), vol. 21, p. 82. Also in the Pelican Freud Library (PFL).
2 ibid., p. 89.
3 ibid., p. 92.
4 Judith Mayne, for example, in 'The woman at the keyhole', *Revision: Essays in Feminist Film Criticism* (Los Angeles: American Film Institute, 1984) discusses various feminist films in which the voyeuristic relation of men watching women is inverted and women are allowed to position themselves at the keyhole (i.e., as subjects of the gaze). The notion, however, that the gaze is a single cognitive position from which it is not only possible, but necessary, to look, is a commonplace of film theory, supported partially by a misreading of Lacan.
5 See especially Mary Ann Doane's important *The Desire to Desire* (Bloomington: Indiana University Press, 1987) in which Doane shows how the 'woman's film' of the 1940s and 1950s made the female spectator's pleasure simultaneous with a masochistic viewing position. Her historically specific argument is subtle and convincing. I object not to this kind of argument, but rather to a general alignment of female pleasure and masochism which is common to analyses that focus on the principle of pleasure and neglect the complications and contradictions introduced by the principle of reality. See, for example, the work of Raymond Bellour.
6 Freud, op. cit., p. 91.
7 Samuel Beckett, *Watt* (New York: Grove, 1972), p. 175.
8 A cutup is, in American slang, a jokester or prankster.
9 Freud, *SE*, vol. 8, p. 209.
10 Henri Bergson, 'Laughter', in *Comedy* (New York: Doubleday, 1956).
11 Bergson's theories also had a tremendous impact on literary and artistic modernism. For Bergson, the artist was one who was free of the necessity to view the world in terms of its practical utility and thus capable, through the unique qualities of his or her perception, to 'create', i.e. to modify phenomenal reality through the active engagement of mind. Art, then, was thought to occupy an aesthetic realm separate from that of the everyday. The 'postmodern'

attention of art and literature to the textual practices of everyday life and the erasure of absolute boundaries between the 'scientific' and the 'artistic' text, signal, in this respect at least, a waning of the influence of Bergsonianism. The writings of T. E. Hulme are useful in making clear this relation of Bergson to modernism.

12 Bergson, *An Introduction to Metaphysics*, trans. T. E. Hulme (New York: Bobbs-Merrill, 1955), p. 37.

13 Freud, *SE*, vol. 18, p. 36.

14 Within psychoanalysis itself, the concept of the death drive has been repeatedly questioned and rejected. In response to one such repudiation, made this time by Rudolph Loewenstein, Lacan wrote: 'It is certain that man distinguishes himself in the biological domain, in that he is the only being who commits suicide, who has a superego' (quoted in Elisabeth Roudinesco, *La Bataille de cent ans*, vol. 2 (Paris: Seuil, 1986), p. 136). Man (sic) distinguishes himself also as the only being who speaks and it is due to *this* distinction that he attains the other.

15 Lacan, in *L'Ethique de la psychanalyse* (Paris: Seuil, 1986), clearly constructs this distinction; in doing so he states straightforwardly that the death drive is 'a function of the signifying chain', and thus 'situated in the historical domain', (p. 250).

16 Samuel Alexander is another 'evolutionary' philosopher; he is cited by Louis S. Sass in 'Introspection, schizophrenia, and the fragmentation of self' (*Representations* 19 (Summer 1987)) in support of a definition of schizophrenia that runs directly counter to current Lacanian-influenced literary definitions. A historical analysis of the refutation of Bergsonian/Janetist, i.e., 'evolutionary' psychiatry by the structural psychoanalysis of Clerambault/Lacan would reveal the problems inherent in Sass's definition.

17 Aristotle also speculates etymologically that the term *automaton* may be derived from *matèn*, 'in vain'.

18 Jacques Lacan, *The Four Fundamental Concepts of Psycho-Analysis*, trans. Alan Sheridan (London: Hogarth and the Institute of Psychoanalysis, 1977), p. 23.

19 Aristotle, *Physics*, I. 7, 189b.

20 Aristotle, *De Motu Animalium*, 7.

21 Lacan, 'L'Angoisse', unpublished seminar, 8 May 1963.

22 Lacan, 'Television', trans. Denis Hollier, Rosalind Krauss, and Annette Michelson, *October* 40 (Spring 1987), p. 10.

23 Samuel Beckett, *Murphy* (New York: Grove, 1959), p. 180.

24 Jacques Derrida, 'Economimesis', *Diacritics* 2 (Summer 1986), p. 18.

25 Lacan's fullest discussion of the creation *ex nihilo* of the subject is to be found in *L'ethique de la psychanalyse* (Paris: Seuil, 1986).

26 Samuel Weber, 'Closure and exclusion', *Diacritics*, 2 (Summer 1986).

27 ibid., p. 44.

28 Derrida, 'Signature event context', *Glyph* 1 (1977), p. 194. This essay, an extended critique and celebration of J. L. Austin's theory of speech acts, is followed by another – 'Limited, Inc.', *Glyph* 2 (1977) – which makes many of the same points as the first, this time in response to John Searle's clumsy defence of Austin.

29 Weber, 'Introduction', *Demarcating the Disciplines* (Minneapolis: University of Minnesota Press, 1986), p. ix.

30 See Elisabeth Lyon, 'The cinema of Lol V. Stein', *Camera Obscura* 6 (Fall 1980); Janet Bergstrom, 'Enunciation and sexual difference', *Camera Obscura* 3–4 (1979); Constance Penley, 'Feminism, film theory and the bachelor machines', *m/f* (1985); and Elizabeth Cowie, 'Fantasia', *m/f* 9 (1984). Bergstrom

and Penley merely argue for the multiplicity of identificatory positions provided by fantasy; their essays are polemical *rather than* analytical. Lyon and Cowrie analyse particular films *as* fantasies and thus are more sugestive than the polemic alone would allow them to be.

Here as elsewhere in this chapter, however, the assumptions I am critiquing are not limited to the works I cite, but are contained in a wide range of works – including some of my own.

31 Lacan takes the phrase from Freud, particularly from his analysis of the Wolf Man. My preoccupation with the importance of the concept contained in the phrase – and its relative neglect in most analyses of the construction, or 'performance' of the subject – began with the writing of my 'Seduction, sedition, and the dictionary', *m/f* 8 (1983).

32 I borrow the terms of this distinction from Slavoj Zizek's unpublished paper, 'Walter Benjamin: la dialectique en suspens', where they are employed to describe the object a.

33 Lacan, *The Four Fundamental Concepts*, p. 22. A sentence quoted earlier in this chapter can now be completed: 'Cause is to be distinguished from that which is determinate in a chain, in other words the *law*.' Once again – cause is not a discursive law, but that which escapes it.

34 J. L. Austin, 'A plea for excuses', *Proceedings of the Aristotelian Society* 57 (1956–7). Austin demonstrates in this paper an interest in context and failure similar to that revealed in his work on speech-act theory.

35 H. L. A. Hart and A. M. Honoré, *Causation in the Law* (Oxford: Clarendon, 1959).

36 It seems likely that Lacan's analysis of the burning child dream owes something to the tradition of philosophy which makes of fire an almost emblematic example of an effect requiring explanation.

Chapter Fourteen

Of female bondage

[handwritten marginal note: In comparing people (or seeking psychiatric aid ⌀ turn-of-the-century males to her female contemporaries who declare themselves satisfied w/their sexuality, she stacks the decks against the ♂ M.]

Parveen Adams

Social science students are often set essays on sex and gender which they dutifully deliver in terms of the naturalness of sex and the constructed nature of gender. The biological and the sociological present little difficulty for social science students; they know what's what. Sex can be thought of in biological terms; gender can be thought of in sociological terms. To introduce psycho-analytic theory is to complicate things because we have to make room for one more reality, this time psychical reality. If psychoanalysis is dealing with quite another reality, it is not surprising that psychoanalysis seems to have nothing to say about sex and gender. What psychoanalysis speaks about is sexuality. Sexuality can indeed be thought of in biological or sociological terms but in neither case does it coincide with Freud's concept. For Freud sexuality is a drive which inhabits and determines the space of a psychical reality. There is a chasm between this and the concept of sexuality either as instinct or as something determined by the environment.

Nevertheless, I want to make something quite clear: there *is* a sense, and this is important for the thesis of my paper, in which Freud's theory of sexuality is inextricably bound up with both biological sex and sociological gender. It is important because I want to show later what a separation of sexuality and gender might look like. I am of course talking about genital sexuality. In Freudian theory while sexuality pervades infancy, infantile sexuality does not know sexual difference. It is genital sexuality, fundamentally altered by what comes before it, that is closely tied to sex and gender in Freudian theory. Sex, sexuality, and gender form a knot from which sexuality cannot be easily extricated.

Now these knots that sex, sexuality, and gender form; let us say that sometimes these are slip knots and that sometimes they are tie knots and that they correspond to the knots that form women and the knots that form men. Of course these knots have their variations, but the generic difference remains. And while men may sometimes be said to be feminine, the knots remain tie knots; and while women may sometimes be said to be masculine, the knots remain slip knots.

In order to see the generic difference more clearly consider the Oedipus complex, the moment of the differentiation into masculinity and femininity. The Oedipus complex and its resolution turn around the question of castration, a lack represented by the phallic signifier, a castration that presupposes the phallus as reference point. Both the boy and the girl have to submit to castration to allow the emergence of desire, that investment of the object with erotic value which makes the object relation possible. To demonstrate the intrication of sexuality and gender it is crucial to make quite explicit how this works. The whole economy of desire is rooted in the phallus *and* this phallus is attributed to the father. Moustapha Safouan is quite clear on this when explaining the move from narcissistic choice to object choice: 'In fact, the function of the ideal [a model with which the subject identifies at first], insofar as it penetrates the whole economy of desire, is rooted in the promotion of the *phallus* i.e., precisely, of that whose insufficiency is discovered for the boy and its non-existence for the girl, at an early age in an attribute of the father.'[1]

So if desire is the investing of the object with erotic value, this investment is not made in relation to difference as such, but in relation to a gendered difference. The object's erotic value is dependent on the question of whether the man or the woman has the phallus. Desire is *engendered* by difference.

In practice the boy and the girl will have a different relation to the phallus because of the anatomical difference between the sexes. Now a gendered difference would not matter were it not for the fact that the girl's sex and gender work to obstruct her entry into desire. In the girl's case the Oedipus complex admits of no solution; everything that looks like a solution is secretly wrecked by the havoc of *penisneid*.

Let us first see how the boy treads the path to desire. For the boy, the Oedipus complex leads to the castration complex and, with the sword of Damocles hanging over his genitals, the boy has to make up his mind in a hurry. Usually he does so, giving up his love for his mother, indeed also giving up his love for his father and identifying with him instead; with the proviso that he recognizes himself as *unlike* the father in so far as the essentials are concerned The identification holds a promise for the future in lieu of symbolic castration.

For girls, the castration complex precedes the Oedipus complex. Once she is safely within the latter Freud gives her three options – retreat from sexuality, or femininity, or masculinity. It is Catherine Millot, a Lacanian analyst who spells out what these options mean for the girl's entry into desire. In her article on the feminine super-ego she discusses these in a most telling way.[2] Fundamentally the choice is one of remaining within the Oedipus complex and not acceding to desire (retreat from sexuality, and penis envy which is one mode of the masculinity complex) or of an exit from the Oedipus complex which none the less remains marked by the desire for the paternal phallus, a problematic entry into desire (femininity and the masculinity complex).

To understand this layout of female sexualities we can imagine a group of post-castration-complex girls lounging about within that haven of refuge, the

Oedipus complex. Actually, to be more precise, some of the girls aren't so comfortable; the castration has been a trauma, they know that they will never have a male genital again and they are utterly despondent (read: retreat from sexuality). Some distance away is the exit to the Oedipus complex, the gateway to desire. These girls are oblivious of its existence; they stare vacantly in another direction. Another group of girls face their fathers; they are not resigned to their loss and they noisily demand what they want (read: *penisneid*). These girls also do not see the sign saying 'Exit from the Oedipus Complex'. But there are some who do and they discover one of two ways out. Some see that a baby would be a good substitute for what they want (read: femininity) and some, realizing that the father won't give them the male genital, decide to give up loving him and to give up demanding his love. They go for him in another way; they identify with him (read: masculinity complex). This means they yield up their demands and can exit. Of course they do emerge on the other side in the domain of desire – but with a paternal super-ego. Sure, these girls accede to desire, but something is wrong. Each now enjoys the fantasy that she possesses the male organ, thanks to which she will now suffer from a castration anxiety of some magnitude. Joan Rivière's patient is the classic example.[3] An example, as Catherine Millot puts it, of a woman who regards herself as a man, who passes for a woman. Whenever this woman successfully displayed her considerable intellectual gifts in public she was compelled to reverse this performance by ogling and coquetting with father figures who had witnessed the performance. This was a way of allaying the anxiety and fear of retaliation produced by the fantasy that she possessed the male organ.

Since the Oedipus complex has to do with the promotion of the paternal phallus it looks as though the girl is going to lose out. Her sexuality, feminine or masculine, is going to be out of line. For her there is no ideal exit from the Oedipus complex; the Oedipus complex neuroticizes the girl. It is one thing to say that the Oedipus complex is the source of all neurosis; it is quite another to recognize that the Oedipus complex pathologizes femininity and feminine sexuality.

Catherine Millot goes further: within the domain of the paternal function the woman does not exist – a good old Lacanian proposition that Millot understands as the impossibility of a post-Oedipal feminine identification. Woman does not exist because there is no ideal exit from the Oedipus complex for the girl. Neither can the woman come into existence by copying the man's entry into desire; it just doesn't work. In the effort to not let her evaporate altogether we are offered the notion of a feminine *jouissance*. In all the moves that women make Lacan sees a *jouissance* that tries to but of course cannot realize itself within the phallic domain and it is posited as a *jouissance* beyond the phallus.[4] But does this help?

Given a boy with a penis and a girl without, a father with the phallus and a mother most probably without, the stage is set for all the posturings of the characters, for their envies and anxieties, for the masquerade of womanliness,

249

for the faithlessness of manliness, for mutual deceit, and for all the boys who act as girls who dress up as boys.

All this does nothing but reproduce the social and familial order, the order in which the phallus coincides with the father, in which the links between sex, sexuality, reproduction, and gender find a material support. I do believe that Freudian psychoanalysis has discovered the human psyche – the necessity of a relation to the phallus and the necessity of unconscious representations which articulate the space between drive and desire. The theoretical issue is this: could these unconscious representations be different? What relation could an unconscious representation have to reality? Does the unconscious simply borrow whatever is most appropriate and ready to hand; in which case the bits of reality which are appropriated in a representation are but possible and predictable materializations of unconscious life? Or do aspects of reality press forward and make possible a change in the balance of unconscious life; in which case reality produces a possible but unpredictable materialization of unconscious life?

To say that the unconscious representations could be different is to say that sexuality could be organized in a different relation to the phallus, that there could be new sexualities. Perhaps these new sexualities would be divorced from gender positions. In this article I want to show how new sexualities can be identified and explained using psychoanalytic concepts. I hope to contribute some new arguments to the debates on sexual politics by showing that psychoanalysis can theorize new phenomena without transforming itself into sociology or psychology.

Disavowal, fetishism, masochism

What I have described so far are a set of sexual relations and their inherent difficulty, in particular a difficulty of the assumption of femininity, though masculinity is far from straightforward either. What is clear however is that the split between femininity and masculinity which is necessitated by the father's phallic attribute is quite different for the little girl than it is for the little boy. But what if the phallus is not attributed to the father? Then we are in the domain of the perversions, those sexual positions whose essence is fetishism. Now in the case of masochism, which is the subject of this chapter, Freud does not make this connection explicitly. Instead, in his 1919 paper 'A child is being beaten',[5] Freud defines the masochistic position through the grid of neurosis. The fantasy 'a child is being beaten' is analysed in standard Oedipal terms; it concerns a child, either male or female, with an incestuous desire for the father. I have commented more fully on Freud's argument elsewhere.[6] Here it suffices to point out that later writers, psychoanalysts and others, have recognized in masochism that element which is so crucial to the perversions, disavowal and the construction of a fetish. Of course it is Freud himself who gave us in two papers, 'Fetishism' and 'The splitting of the ego in the process of defence',[7] the definition of fetishism that is being used here. But he does not anywhere explain masochism in relation to disavowal and fetishism. However it is just this that is stressed by three writers I will draw on, Gilles Deleuze, Joyce McDougall, and Jean Clavreul, three quite distinct figures, philosopher, psychoanalyst of the International Psychoanalytical Association, and Lacanian.[8]

So, what are the perversions, psychoanalytically speaking? Traditionally the perverse figures are the figures of the fetishist, the sadomasochist, and the male homosexual. But the fetishism that produces the fetishist is also at the root of the other perversions. Fetishism is of the essence of the perversions. There, there is always fetishism and fetishism always concerns disavowal. This disavowal is the refusal to recognize that the mother does not have a penis. He who refuses to recognize the absence of the mother's penis may then avow its material existence in some other part of the body or in some object. This material element that thus consecrates the disavowal is the fetish. Notice that the fetish is the means of denying that there is a sexual difference between the mother and the father.

In our earlier account of the Oedipus complex we did not have occasion to speak of disavowal precisely because the Oedipus complex is the means of sexual division. There may be problems, as we saw; none the less, the problems are organized in a particular way. Since it is the recognition of the mother's castration that necessitates sexual division, none of the girl's Oedipal difficulties concern disavowal. The Oedipal account of sexual difference concerns the 'normal' and the neurotic; the disavowal of sexual difference and the fetish concern the perverse.

The phallus is equally important both in the neuroses and in the perversions but it is used very differently. It shores up the familial and social order in the former, but it is the occasion of transgression in the latter. None of this is new; I have merely set out what I am referring to when I speak of different relations to the phallus. This difference is basically marked out by the neuroses on the one hand and the perversions on the other.

Of course the perversions are not a homogeneous field. Pure fetishism differs from (male) homosexuality and both are different from masochism. But I am not arguing that these differences constitute different relations to the phallus. It is more important for my argument that masochism itself is not a homogeneous field. In my view the sexual formations of masochism have to be distinguished into at least three groups: that of the self-flagellating man of religion, that of the traditional sexual pervert, and that of contemporary lesbian sadomasochism. I doubt whether fetishism is of the essence of the first group but I will argue that it is crucial to the other two groups. Notwithstanding the disavowal in these cases, the mark of perversion as it were, I will argue that the reconstruction of sexual difference in the two cases differs in its significance and in its success.

In order to distinguish the three groups of masochists from a psychoanalytic point of view I have to start from the only group which has been studied both clinically and theoretically, the masochist as sexual pervert. The classic picture of masochism is to be found in Theodor Reik's *Masochism in Modern Man* published in 1941.[9] Reik specifies four characteristics of the masochistic scene, two of which, fantasy and the factor of suspense, concern us. The first characteristic is of great importance since the preparatory fantasy is essential. Masochistic performances are the dramatized, ritualized acting out of these fantasies, their staging. The second characteristic, suspense, involves a delay, a waiting; it is a state with no definite end-point; it is an endless postponement of gratification. Actually being suspended, being hung, is the most transparent sign of this dimension.

Deleuze gives Reik full credit for isolating what he calls the formal characteristics of masochism. But he shows that they derive from disavowal. The disavowal of reality is transposed into fantasy and the disavowal also extends to sexual pleasure itself which is postponed through waiting and suspense. Since fetishism also derives from disavowal it takes little more to add fetishism to the list of characteristics. Masochism involves fetishism, fantasy, and suspense. Deleuze describes a masochistic fantasy in which the elements of suspense and fetishism are quite clear.

> Consider the following masochistic fantasy; a woman in shorts is pedalling energetically on a stationary bicycle; the subject is lying under the bicycle, the whirring pedals almost brushing him, his palms pressed against the woman's calves. All the elements are conjoined in this image, from the fetishism of the woman's calf to the twofold waiting represented by the motion of the pedals and the immobility of the bicycle.[10]

Suspense then is the mark of disavowal within the masochistic scene. The qualities of suspense can be seen in the bicycle fantasy and also in the photograph-like scenes of Masoch's *Venus in Furs*: the woman torturer takes on the poses of a statue, a painting, a photograph – she breaks off and holds the gestures of bringing down a whip or taking off the furs or turning to look at herself in a mirror. The photograph and the painting capture the gesture mid-way and this is the moment of suspense. Now the fetish itself has the qualities of suspense, the frozen, arrested quality of a photograph, the something fixed to which the subject constantly returns 'to exorcize the dangerous consequences of movement'.

If we accept disavowal as central to masochism we have an explanation not only of fantasy and suspense, but also an explanation of how masochism constitutes transgression. Here I follow Jean Clavreul in his article on 'The perverse couple'.[11] Masochism is a transgression of the Law. Not in the sense that it offends against laws on the statute book, but in its setting aside of Oedipal Law. We have already seen how the Oedipus complex leads to the prohibition on incest through the reference to the paternal phallus. This whole operation depends on distinguishing between the father who has a penis and the mother who turns out to be without one. If there is disavowal this distinction is not made; the Oedipus complex is no longer the moment of sexual difference as is usual. Disavowal means that the child refuses to recognize that the mother he had always imagined to be endowed with the phallus is without it. Disavowal means that the child refuses to recognize the sexual difference of the parents. So the pervert has the puzzle of inventing sexual difference, a puzzle that he has to solve with his own wits. But he can construct and maintain a viable sexual difference only if someone colludes with his disavowal. This someone is the mother who remains blind to the disavowal; at first, it is the mother's look that lets itself be seduced and fascinated.

If we accompany Clavreul as far as this we can see what is transgressive about the pervert's sexuality. For in so far as the mother's look also refers to the father through whom the relationship to the Law is founded, the seduction of the mother's look challenges the social and familial order, indeed, we could say, perverts it. Think of the masochist in particular; though he may appear as victim he is in fact in charge. He is the stage manager in charge of the scenery, the costumes, and the roles.

Putting together some writings on masochism has led us to the disavowal at the heart of masochism, the disavowal which explains fantasy, suspense, and the transgression of the Oedipal order. How does the first of our three groups of masochists compare with this masochist as sexual pervert? What can be said of the self-flagellation of the man of religion? It is Reik again who comments on this in a chapter on the martyr and the masochist. It must be made clear that Reik does not hold that religious martyrdom is a form of sexual masochism. 'Both do approximately the same thing', he writes, 'but it does not mean the same thing, as it is performed under different psychic suppositions.... The thorn driven in the flesh has here the function of atonement, there the function to create excitement.'[12]

None the less, while noting the differences in the 'more limited sexual sense' between martyr and masochist, Reik wishes to make a comparison between the two in a broader sense, comparing sexual masochism with what he calls social masochism. Here, he resorts to the three fundamental characteristics again; the special significance of fantasy, the suspense factor, and the demonstrative feature. He finds these characteristics at the level of the organization of martyrdom. There is a collective fantasy through which the individual identifies with the divine figure and longs for the pains of martyrdom in his name. The suspense factor is marked not only by the postponement of pleasure until the next world, but also in the way in which the suffering is detailed and drawn out. Finally, there is the demonstrative feature and what more apt than the figure of Simeon Stylites on his pillar to represent it?

Certainly the fundamental characteristics describe some aspects of the organization of martyrdom. But why should we call this any kind of masochism? Reik saw very clearly that the similarities in behaviour were not equivalent; and he drew back from linking martyr and masochist at the narrow sexual level. But the narrow sexual level is the level which concerns disavowal, fetishism, and hence the relation to the phallus which defines the masochistic position. It seems, then, that the similarities at the broader level cannot have some common signification either. Even here the differences are more striking than the similarities. Reik quotes Cyprian: 'He conquers once who suffers once, but he who continues always battling with punishments and is not overcome with suffering is daily crowned', and Flaubert's Saint Anthony: 'Martyrs who have been beheaded, pinched with tongs or burned, perhaps have less merits than I, because my life is an incessant martyrdom.' [13] Clearly this competitive insistence on incessant suffering is not what the sexual pervert aims at. One can only heed Reik's own initial warning against holding martyrdom to be a form of sexual masochism: 'Both do approximately the same things, but it does not mean the same thing.'

There are two definitive points of contrast to be made at the narrow sexual level. (It should be obvious that there can be no comparison at a broader level which is not derived from the narrower one.) First, the disavowal of sexual difference is crucial to the masochist; the martyr, however has heterosexual fantasies and temptations. Second, the disavowal of the masochist is also a disavowal of the father, an abolition of the father from the symbolic and the pervert attempts to pervert the course of the Law. Suffice it to ask how the martyr could be said to abolish the father from the symbolic. This comparison should teach us to identify and avoid the temptations of behavioural similarity! The organization of martyrdom enables the psychic production of martyrs; if the martyr occupied a different sexual position from others of his time then we could say that something of reality, the organization of martyrdom, is essential to the establishing of a new sexuality. But we know nothing of this.

We do, however, know something about the fantasies and practices of our third group of masochists, the lesbian sadomasochists. These practices do indeed seem to be organized around disavowal and to be transgressive, but I will show that while they are indeed masochistic, nevertheless they constitute a new sexuality. Before this argument can be made, however, it is necessary to look more closely at what is involved in fetishism. The important question concerns the subject's relation to the phallus and the extent to which this reference point limits the pervert's success in placing himself within a different psychical order of sexual relations.

There is disavowal and disavowal

What we have not noted so far and what Freud made abundantly clear is that fetishism is crucially about a splitting of the ego. Which is to say that it concerns not only the disavowal of the absence of the penis in the mother, but also, contradictorily, the recognition that the mother does not have the penis after all. Indeed, when the child disavows what he has seen he doesn't do this directly; he doesn't have the nerve to say that he has actually seen a penis.

Instead, he avows the existence of the penis in some other part of the body or in some other object. Thus the fetish is a 'memorial' to castration; it is 'a token of triumph over the threat of castration and a protection against it'.[14] So two contradictory attitudes can coexist and Freud points out that there are fetishists with the same fear of castration as is found in non-fetishists.

The ratio between the two attitudes varies considerably so that in some cases a fetish does not preclude a considerable amount of normal sexual behaviour and Freud even speaks of the case where fetishism may be 'limited to a mere hint' (*An Outline of Psychoanalysis*).[15] It is worth noting that this is to say that sexual difference is simultaneously and contradictorily disavowed and avowed. This hint of fetishism suffices to bring about a splitting of the ego. But Freud also identifies a splitting of the ego in neurosis where there is no question of fetishism. The formation of a fetish is not necessary for splitting; all that is required is both a disavowal and at the same time an avowal of that which is disavowed. In his inimitable fashion Freud universalizes disavowal.

We can see what this means by looking at Octave Mannoni's article 'Je sais bien ... mais quand même'.[16] Mannoni analyses the workings of disavowal outside of cases of fetishism. The two examples I use from this article show how disavowal can have consequences for the subject's relation to the paternal phallus. However, whether the paternal phallus is readily or reluctantly accepted, it is important to note that it remains the structuring principle.

The first example shows how the splitting occasioned by disavowal is actually used to put the phallus in place in the initiation ceremonies through which the Hopi child enters the familial and social order. By analysing part of Talayseva's *Sun Chief, The Autobiography of a Hopi Indian*, Mannoni looks at the way in which beliefs essential to Hopi religion are produced. The initiate's original belief is transformed into the religious belief (in such a way that the original belief is also maintained). What Mannoni shows is that the adults are using the structure of the coexistence of contradictory beliefs to guide the initiate into the belief which is essential to Hopi religion.

Katcina are Hopi masks. The Hopi child has a firm belief that the Katcina are terrifying figures who are interested in eating children. They appear once a year and the mothers have to buy back their children with morsels of meat. The Katcina then give the children red maize *piki* to eat. When the Hopi child is 10 years old initiation ceremonies directly evoking castration take place and now the belief in Katcina is rudely shattered. The 'fathers' and 'uncles' reveal themselves as the Katcina; the reality is that the Katcina are not spirits. Yet the child is initiated into a new belief in the Katcina. The child is told that the *real* Katcina once came to dance, but no longer come as of yore (*comme autrefois*); now they only come in an invisible form and inhabit the mask in a mystic manner. The Hopi can then say: '*Je sais bien* that the Katcina are not spirits, they are my fathers and uncles, *mais quand même* the Katcina are there when my fathers and uncles dance with their masks on.'[17]

The splitting occasioned by castration is the prototype for *je sais bien... mais quand même'*. Mannoni's example shows that the splitting is actually *required* for the normalizing rites of initiation among the Hopi. They take advantage of the splitting of the ego to put the phallus in place.

The second example from Mannoni concerns a more troublesome disavowal which leads to a relation to the phallus that is both defiant and submissive. It concerns the play of disavowal in Casanova. He may believe that everyone including his mother has the phallus, yet he knows that he can lose his own organ. Here disavowal, still at the level of belief, not yet materialized in the fetish, is clearly linked to a system of protection against castration. Mannoni shows how the protective structure of Casanova's beliefs is easily threatened, leaving him at the mercy of the reality of the castration he wished to deny. Belief in the paternal phallus is not so easily abandoned.

Casanova cannot resist profiting from finding two dupes. The first possesses a knife which he believes is the one with which Saint Peter cut off Malchus's ear; the other is a peasant who imagines he has treasure in his cave. Casanova convinces them that with the knife for which he has provided a magical sheath, the gnomes will bring the treasure to the surface. The pleasure lies in one fool helping another to find treasure that doesn't exist. Casanova writes that he is longing to play the role of magician which he loves to distraction; Mannoni glosses: I know full well that there is no treasure but all the same it is tremendous.

Now the peasant has a daughter, Javotte, and Casanova decides that conquering her will be part of his triumph as magician. But for the moment he declares her virginity essential to the success of the undertaking. So Casanova makes himself some magic robes by making an enormous circle of paper with cabbalistic signs on it. And at night he dons this garment and goes outside. A storm breaks, the dupes fail to show up, and Casanova is in total panic. I knew the operation would fail, he says; to Mannoni this implies a *mais quand même*. Although he knows that the storm is natural (*je sais bien*), he begins to be afraid (*mais quand même*). He persuades himself that the lightning won't strike him if he continues to stand in his paper circle; so he stands all night without moving. The circle is magical after all.

What has happened? Casanova had denied his belief in magic and it was firmly lodged with the dupes. When the storm breaks and the dupes stay away, their absence provokes a reversal in Casanova. Casanova had wanted to be a magician in their eyes; now he is the one who believes in magic.

This 'hero of anti-castration' is made impotent with the reversal. On returning he feels frightened of Javotte, who 'no longer appeared to be of a sex different from mine, because I no longer found mine different from hers'.[18] He has been magically castrated. For Casanova magic (a way of disavowing castration) took the place of the fetish when he offloaded belief onto the dupe. By doing this he possessed the phallus not through magic but through imposture. Of course the impostor is the magician *quand même*, and when the magician fails, when the impostor takes back on himself the belief in magic, he comes under the threat of magical castration.

In both of the examples discussed, though in very different ways, the disavowal of the lack of the maternal phallus and the splitting that ensues appear to be inextricably intertwined with the valorization of the phallus, the paternal phallus. Does this remain true when an actual fetish is constructed? To answer this question we need to know something more about this construction of the fetish. Now Mannoni sees that Freud's account of the origin of the fetish object is merely an account of the constitution of screen memories. But Mannoni himself can go no further than noting that while disavowal opens onto the field of belief, with an actual fetish in place it is no longer a question of *belief*. The fetish no longer appears to relate to a belief in the phallus. Where does this leave the fetishist in relation to the phallus?

There is fetishism and fetishism

The question of the fetishist's relation to the phallus is re-posed by Leo Bersani and Ulysse Dutoit[19] as the question of whether the fetish is a phallic symbol at all. It is obvious that the fetish does not necessarily resemble the penis. But these writers claim that the success of the fetish actually depends on its being seen as authentically different from the missing penis. In his paper on fetishism Freud had written, 'Yes, in his mind the woman *has* got a penis, in spite of everything; but this penis is no longer the same as it was before.' Bersani and Dutoit argue that the fetishist knows that the fetish is not a penis, doesn't want it to be that alone, and knows that there is a lack (to which he is resigned) which nothing can replace. 'The fetishist can see the woman as she is, without a penis, because he loves her with a penis somewhere else.'[20] This penis somewhere else, this fetish that he loves her with, is itself the sexual object and it is quite different both from the penis and from the maternal phallus. The fetish as sexual object is a displacement from one object onto another; it is not a replacement of an internalized absent object.

Bersani and Dutoit proceed to outline these two models of the sexual object. The first model has a founding object of desire (a model they characterize as 'fetishistic' because it repudiates the absence of the object). We have already seen that for the Freudian child everyone has a fantasy phallus. The sight of the anatomical difference between the sexes is crucial for sexual division in that this fantasy can be seen to be realized in relation to the father while at the same time the mother is seen as lacking in relation to it. This is the foundation for the dimension of illusion, the dimension in which the child will substitute an object for the absent phallus.

But Bersani and Dutoit's young fetishist relates to the anatomical distinction in a different way. We should note that the neurotic may well have the fantasy that the mother has the phallus. But the young fetishist does not do this either.

One could say that the fetishist does not know whether the mother has the penis or not, or one could say that the fetishist knows that she does not have the real organ and can only ever have the 'penis [which] is no longer the same as it was before'.[21] This penis, no longer the same, is the fetish, that which the fetishist now desires. Since the mother has not got the penis which signifies the phallus she has nothing that links her with the fantasy phallus. Since the mediating substitute is missing, desire is 'cut off' from the phallus; henceforth anything can come to be the object of desire.

If indeed the gap between desire and its first object is recognized and accepted, fetishism implies a quite sufficient castration of an order different from the neurotic's. For the neurotic the penis continues to symbolize the phallus and desire remains tied to its first object. But the irreducible difference between the fetish and the first object demonstrates that desire itself might be cut off from its object and may therefore travel to other objects. Bersani and Dutoit conclude: 'Thus the very terror of castration can initiate us into those psychic severances which guarantee the diversification of desire.'

To speak of desire being detached from the phallus does not mean that the phallus ceases to have any function in the organization of sexuality. Without its function as a third term there would be psychosis. The point is rather that the desire is detached from the paternal phallus; there is a phallus, but it is not the paternal one. We might say that the pervert recognizes that no one has the phallus. He knows full well that the mother does not have it. Of course he disavows this but this disavowal merely puts her on a par with the father. Whatever it is that they both have or don't have won't suffice to symbolize the phallus. Which is to say that the pervert refuses to distinguish between them in so far as having the penis/phallus is concerned. So the difference necessary for sexuality and sanity has to be constructed on some other basis. The axis of this difference will come to be represented by all sorts of other differences. This is one way of coming to terms with the fact of the lack of the phallus. If we can continue to say that the phallus is the signifier of desire, albeit in a somewhat different sense, it is because it is not replaced by some other signifier which substitutes as a fixed point of reference for the construction of some fixed sexual difference. The entry into desire is necessarily through castration and it is in the perversions that we see the possibility that the form desire takes will be freed from the penile representation of the phallus and freed into a mobility of representations.

This is my understanding of Bersani and Dutoit's claim that desire can be detached from the phallus and thus be rendered mobile. Of course they are aware that the claim for the mobility of desires contrasts oddly with the rigidity with which the clinical fetishist holds on to his fetish. He has not fully accepted his castration and detached himself from the phallus; he has not been freed into a mobility of desires. The clinical fetishist still believes in the paternal phallus. The disavowal of the lack of the maternal phallus is not necessarily followed by a disavowal of the paternal phallus. Logically it should be so, but when did psychical processes ever follow the dictates of logic? So, contrary to his own expectations, the pervert finds himself in the company of the paternal phallus, an unwelcome companion which reminds him that some people have penises and others do not; penises are disposable. Paradoxically, then, the pervert who has disavowed castration suffers at the same time from castration anxiety. The paternal phallus exacts its price. In spite of the construction of the fetish the pervert, like, Casanova, has retained his fearful position in relation to the domination of the paternal phallus.

The castration anxiety of the fetishist had not escaped Freud's notice; nor was he the only one. Here, a quotation from McDougall on the forms of castration anxiety will suffice:

the script of the sado-masochist with his concentration on pain... or the fetishist who reduces the game of castration to beaten buttocks and bodily constriction (the important bodily marks that symbolise castration but are so readily effaced) or the transvestite ... or again the homosexual – in every instance the plot is the same: castration does not hurt and in fact is the very condition of erotic arousal and pleasure. When anxiety appears nevertheless (and it is rarely absent) it is in turn eroticised and becomes a new condition of sexual excitement.[22]

The clinical fetishist, then, is engaged in a constant struggle to avoid the reality of sexual difference. He is engaged in the continuous and repetitive task of maintaining the fabric of the illusion that sustains him. Clavreul talks of the tightrope act that the pervert must maintain, and McDougall writes that 'the pervert is facing a losing battle with reality. Like trying to repair a crumbling wall with scotch tape, it has to be redone every day.[23]

Now if the fetishist succeeds in maintaining his illusion, this is achieved at the price of the mobility inherent in the structure of the fetish. The pervert's objects and acts are marked by a rigidity, a repetition, a compulsion that cannot fail to bring to mind Casanova standing all night in the pouring rain with bolts of lightning around him. He subjects himself to constraints as a means of control, as a means of ensuring that he does not find himself in unexpected situations, situations in which the threat of castration might suddenly surprise him. One could say that the pervert is all right so long as things go according to plan. The trouble is that he finds his own plans compelling and has little ability to change them.

There is masochism and masochism

Of course a certain rigidity, repetition, and compulsion mark all sexual positions; there are always conditions of satisfaction. But a compulsive sexuality of the order just described raises the question of pathology. To this must be added the lack of potency which is such a frequent theme in the clinical literature on masochism; such a dysfunction can be taken as another sign of

259

pathology. What exactly constitutes the pathological is a complex matter but I am assuming that there would be some general agreement on the characteristics I have called pathological.

The question then is what explains these characteristics. Now in Freudian theory pathology in the adult is consequent on deviations from a genitally organized relation to the opposite sex. In masochism there is a regression from genitality to anality which is evident enough in the beating of buttocks and in urination and defecation within the sexual scenario. Since the fact that the mother and the father copulated is disavowed, genital sex must be replaced and sexual pleasure must come about in other ways. McDougall specifies this task as the reinvention of the primal scene and suggests one way in which the regression to anality leads to a lack of potency: 'the primal scene, divested of its genital significance, becomes an anal-narcissistic struggle. Orgasm is then equivalent to a *loss of control*, and must frequently be retarded or even warded off altogether.'[24]

Is Freud right, then, on the pathological consequences of deviation from a genitally organized relation to the opposite sex, or is his theory normative? There is no easy straightforward answer to this question. As we will see, Freud's claim about such deviations does not appear to fit the case of lesbian sadomasochism. On the other hand, clinical masochism is a case that appears to fit. The clinical masochist seems to embody a deviation from a heterosexual genital relation in the sense that he has maintained a reference to the norm at the same time that he partakes of the pleasures of perverse sexuality. As we saw, the clinical masochist has to deny actively and constantly the relation between the sexes which is constituted by the Oedipal Law. The Oedipal order is a threat to him. Gender remains a threat to his sexuality.

I think this is clear when we look at what the heterosexuality of the clinical masochist means, for the traditional masochistic couple is indeed a heterosexual pair. Freud had argued that the masochist escapes the homosexual position both by regression to the anal-sadistic and by retaining the opposition of the sexes in the beating fantasy. Whatever we may think of this general argument, the fact remains that others have also documented this avoidance of any taint of homosexuality on the masochist's part. McDougall writes of a patient who paid prostitutes to whip him and stamp on his genitals. This man became highly anxious when another client claimed some similarity with him because he, too, paid to be whipped on the genitals, though in his case he was whipped by boys. McDougall quotes the patient, 'but that man's crazy. We have absolutely nothing in common. Why, he's a homosexual!'

But of course the clinical masochist is no ordinary heterosexual. He is heterosexual in so far as he cannot afford to transgress the demarcations of gender even for the sake of his sexuality. His sexuality is constituted via the women who will distance him from the father and from men who can serve neither as objects of desire nor as objects of identification. His female partner colludes with him in denying the reality of the woman's castration and in seducing her he undermines the place of the woman in the Oedipal order. The invented primal scene has to have a woman in it and if the clinical masochist likes to be whipped it is clear that not just anybody can administer this whipping. Where Severin, the hero of Sacher-Masoch's *Venus in Furs*, is whipped by the Greek sexual reality breaks in. It is too much. Indeed this thorough thrashing cures Severin of his masochism. Once again we see how very precarious the perverse position is. And once again it is because the rejection of the sexual reality of the Oedipal order is so precarious.

I would say that the heterosexuality of the clinical masochist is itself a mark of pathology. It is a pathological consequence of deviation from a genitally organized relation to the opposite sex. But there is a paradox here; this heterosexuality is pathological because the clinical masochist *remains* on the edge of the Oedipal order.

The question then is whether all human sexuality is Oedipally organized and whether the perversions which are not so organized are indissociable in principle from pathology. Which is to ask whether the psychoanalytic model is correct in assuming that the disavowal of the truth of sexual difference at the heart of all perversion entails pathology.

But we cannot answer the question about the link between perversion and pathology without noting that in this formulation the idea of perversion is not problematized. When is a perversion a perversion? We could speak of perversion when it is possible to identify processes stemming from disavowal and fetishism. But while psychoanalysis teaches us how to do this, it at the same time conceptualizes the perversions as pathological. Which is to say that it treats fetishism, homosexuality, and masochism as syndromes. At certain times and in certain places this may well be so, but to link psychical processes to syndromes leaves no room for fetishisms, homosexualities, and masochisms that may be perverse but are not pathological. Such new sexualities will not be the same entities that Freud investigated. If we can show that there are entities which are perverse but not pathological we will have demonstrated that psychical processes do not of themselves *determine* sexualities and their 'normal' or pathological status.[25] I asked at the beginning whether 'aspects of reality press forward and make possible a change in the balance of unconscious life' which would produce 'a possible but unpredictable materialization of unconscious life'. I now ask whether lesbian sadomasochism is such a materialization.

Can lesbian sadomasochism be considered a case of a predominantly perverse organization of sexuality and, if so, must it be considered pathological? I think the first attempt to answer this question must be at the factual level. While the lesbian sadomasochistic literature[26] describes practices that fit the descriptions of the masochistic scenarios I have outlined, there are important differences between the lesbian sadomasochist and the clinical masochist. These differences suggest that although we are dealing with perversion we are not dealing with pathology.

261

What precisely are the similarities and the differences between the lesbian sadomasochistic woman and the traditional heterosexual masochistic man? They can be summed up in a sentence: the similarities lie in the scenarios which involve fetishes, whipping, bondage, all that goes with the factor of fantasy and suspense; the differences are that lesbian sadomasochism appears not to be compulsive, can just as easily be genital as not, and is an affair of women.

What is similar is what flows from disavowal and leads to a degenitalization of sexuality, and yet the lesbian sadomasochist has the capacity for genital pleasure. We might ask whether if genital pleasure remains available we are dealing only with an unusual set of fore-pleasures. If that were the case, the absence of the compulsive element would be accounted for. But that is too simple. Fore-pleasures are foreshadowed by the satisfaction of pre-genital organizations of sexuality. The pleasure of kissing harks back to oral gratification. The fetish, the whip, the gag, suspense, and delay do not bear the same relation to any pre-genital gratification. Where do they come from? Is it possible to treat these forms of satisfaction as mere behaviours, randomly put in place? Psychoanalytically speaking all behaviours conducive to sexual satisfaction have a psychical significance; we are dealing with the marks of disavowal which signal perversion. Certainly there is a hint of the process of disavowal in us all, but not everyone constructs a fetish. Mannoni's distinction between the domain of belief and the actual fetish means that we can distinguish between the disavowal of the neurotic who holds two contradictory beliefs and the disavowal of the pervert who actually constructs a fetish. Technically, when disavowal leads to fetishism and beyond that to sadomasochism, we *have* to speak of perversion. The sexual scenarios of lesbian sadomasochism have to be recognized as perverse scenarios.

If the similarities demonstrate perversion, what of the differences? The enigma of compulsion, a necessary heterosexuality, and a disturbance of genitality, are absent. Instead, there is choice and mobility, an experimentation with the sexual yield of consensual constraint; there is the construction of a sexuality between women; there is genital satisfaction as one among many pleasures of the body. I have shown how some features of clinical masochism fit into a pathological structure and it is just these features that are absent from lesbian sadomasochism.

If the clinical masochist failed to take advantage of the inherent possibilities of fetishism outlined by Bersani and Dutoit, it seems that the lesbian sadomasochist takes full advantage of these possibilities. For the clinical pervert things have to be just so. The fetishist is immobilized by his fetish, the masochist plays and replays the scene that is essential to him. The rigidity and repetition constitute the compulsion and the enigma of the masochist's sexuality. For the lesbian sadomasochist, on the other hand, there is an erotic plasticity and movement: she constructs fetishes and substitutes them, one for another; she multiplies fantasies and tries them on like costumes. All this is done quite explicitly as an incitement of the senses, a proliferation of bodily

262

pleasures, a transgressive excitement; a play with identity and a play with genitality. It is a perverse intensification of pleasure.

Now if this illustrates quite precisely what Bersani and Dutoit mean when they talk of a mobility of desires, can we assume the detachment from the phallus on which this mobility of desires was predicated? Has the lesbian sadomasochist succeeded in detaching herself from the paternal phallus without falling into a sickness? Here the psychoanalyst is likely to be constrained by his presuppositions. For as usual it is the question of the paternal phallus as the north pole of the compass of desire and the pathological consequences of orienting oneself outside its magnetic field. Mannoni's text shows how the disavowal of the Hopi Indian is used for both his phallic and his cultural orientation. But it suggests a tinge of pathology in Casanova's case where the reference to the paternal phallus is accompanied by a more developed disavowal. I have shown that the clinical pervert also has retained this reference in spite of the disavowal of sexual difference and has perhaps done this at the price of pathology. Could we say that it is this contradiction that determines the presence of pathology?

If so, the absence of pathology in the lesbian sadomasochist would suggest the absence of the contradiction; which is to say that she has succeeded in detaching herself from the phallic reference and in orienting her sexuality outside the phallic field; which in turn suggests that the question of sexuality has finally been divorced from the question of gender.

This takes us back to the beginning of this essay. There I showed how the girl's sex and gender work to obstruct her entry into desire. This is her difficulty: that she recognizes sexual difference. We could almost say that she *therefore* has difficulty with the question of her own sexuality and gender. Desire is a problem precisely because sexuality is linked to gender. We then saw that what happens in the perversions is very different. So what happens for the lesbian sadomasochist is very different.

What then does the homosexuality of the lesbian sadomasochist signify? It is crucial to recognize that it is a homosexuality which is quite differently organized from that of the lesbian who is not a pervert. (In the traditional account female homosexuality is not a perversion even though male homosexuality is.) The traditional homosexual woman is fundamentally similar to the traditional heterosexual woman in that she also bears the burden of maintaining a reference point which cannot give her her bearings. For both these women the paternal phallus is the signifier of desire and nothing changes this. In the feminine heterosexual position the woman finds the signifier of her desire in the body of the man; within the masculinity complex the heterosexual woman who has made a virile identification with the father wants the man to recognize her virility and the homosexual woman is in the same way enabled to offer that which she does not have. But the woman is not simply a man; so we find Lacan talking of a specifically feminine *jouissance*. It seems that the problem of the entry into desire has to be understood as the attempt to realize a specifically feminine *jouissance*. This attempt is doomed to fail within the Oedipal drama. Hence the question of a feminine *jouissance* beyond the phallus.

But if the lesbian sadomasochist has solved the problem of her entry into desire it is not through the realization of anything we could call feminine *jouissance*. She has refused the forms of womanly pathology organized within the phallic field; she does not find the signifier of her desire in the body of the man nor, since she makes no virile identification, does she offer that which she does not have. Since the lesbian sadomasochist has refused to operate within the space of masculine and feminine choices, it would be meaningless to call this a *feminine jouissance* beyond the phallus. The lesbian sadomasochist has separated sexuality from gender and is able to enact differences in the theatre where roles freely circulate.

This is a sexuality which is not centred around the paternal phallus and which thereby remains outside the social and familial order. But paradoxically such a transgressive sexuality can only accede to a psychical reality in a complex relation with some fledgling piece of external reality.

Notes

1 M. Safouan, 'L'Oedipe est-il universel?', ch. 8 of *Etudes sur L'Oedipe* (Paris: Seuil, 1974); trans. B. Brewster in *m/f* 5/6 (1981).

2 C. Millot, 'Le Surmoi féminin', *Ornicar?* 29 (Summer 1984); trans. B. Brewster, together with a discussion following its presentation at an *m/f* conference in London, in *m/f* 10 (1985).

3 J. Rivière, 'Womanliness as a masquerade', *International Journal of Psychoanalysis* 10 (1929).

4 J. Lacan 'Propos directifs pour un congrès sur la sexualité féminine', *Ecrits* (Paris: Seuil, 1966); 'Dieu et la jouissance de la femme', 'Séminaire XX', *Encore* (1972–3); both trans. J. Rose in J. Mitchell and J. Rose (eds), *Feminine Sexuality: Jacques Lacan and the Ecole Freudienne* (London: Macmillan, 1982). The question of feminine *jouissance* is also addressed in M. Montrelay, 'Recherches sur la femininité', in *L'Ombre et le nom* (Paris: Minuit, 1977); trans. P. Adams in *m/f* 1 (1978).

5 S. Freud, '"A child is being beaten": a contribution to the study of the origin of sexual perversions' (1919), *The Standard Edition of the Complete Works of Sigmund Freud*, ed. J. Strachey, trans. J. Strachey *et al.* (hereafter *SE*), 17.

6 P. Adams, 'Per os(cillation)', in J. Donald (ed.), *Thresholds: Psychoanalysis and Cultural Theory* (London: Macmillan, 1989).

7 S. Freud, 'Fetishism' (1927), *SE*, 21; 'The splitting of the ego in the process of defence' (1940), *SE*, 23.

8 G. Deleuze, 'Masochism: an interpretation of coldness and cruelty', introduction to L. von Sacher-Masoch, *Venus in Furs* (New York: Braziller, 1971); J. McDougall, *A Plea for a Measure of Abnormality*, (New York: International Universities Press, 1980); J. Clavreul, 'The perverse couple', in S. Schneiderman (ed.), *Returning to Freud: Clinical Psychoanalysis in the School of Lacan*, (New Haven: Yale University Press, 1980).

9 T. Reik, *Masochism in Modern Man* (New York: Grove Press, 1941).
10 Deleuze, op. cit.
11 Clavreul, op. cit.
12 Reik, op. cit.
13 ibid.
14 Freud, 'Fetishism', op. cit.
15 S. Freud, *An Outline of Psychoanalysis* (1940), *SE*, 23; PFL,
16 O. Mannoni '"Je sais bien...mais quand même" la croyance', *Les Temps Modernes* 212 (1964) (my trans.).
17 ibid.
18 ibid.
19 L. Bersani and U. Dutoit, *The Forms of Violence* (New York: Schocken, 1985).
20 ibid.
21 ibid. Bersani and Dutoit are quoting Freud 'Fetishism', op. cit.
22 MacDougall, op. cit.
23 ibid.
24 ibid.
25 Entities may be differentiated in different ways. The homosexualities that are traditionally held to be the same from the Greeks to modern times can be differentiated psychoanalytically because it can be argued that Greek 'homosexuality' is not a perversion. Without making the particular theoretical point that I am emphasizing, Georges Devereux, the well-known anthropologist and psychoanalytic psychotherapist, has argued just this. See G. Devereux, 'Greek pseudo-homosexuality and the "Greek miracle"', *Symbolae Osloenses* 42 (1967).
26 P. Califia, 'Feminism and sadomasochism', *Heresies* 3, no. 4, issue 12, (1981); Samois (ed.), *Coming to Power* (Boston, Mass.: Alyson, 2nd edn, 1982); P. Califia, *Sapphistry: The Book of Lesbian Sexuality* (Tallahassee, Fla: Naiad Press, 2nd edn, 1983).

Notes on the contributors

PARVEEN ADAMS lectures in psychology at Brunel. She co-founded and co-edited the feminist journal, *m/f*. She is the editor of *Language in Thinking* and has published numerous articles on feminism.

RACHEL BOWLBY is a lecturer in English at the University of Sussex, and author of many articles and books. Her most recent book is *Virginia Woolf: Feminist Destinations*.

ROSI BRAIDOTTI is Professor of Women's Studies at the University of Utrecht. She is the author of *Patterns of Dissonance*, and many articles and translations.

TERESA BRENNAN studied psychoanalysis at the Tavistock Clinic. She has published articles on feminism, history, and political economy, as well as psychoanalysis. Her *History After Lacan* will be published by Routledge next year.

JOAN COPJEC is an editor of *October* magazine, based in New York. She has published widely on feminism, psychoanalysis, and film. Her forthcoming book is *Apparatus and Umbra: A Feminist Critique of Film Theory*.

JANE GALLOP is Professor of Humanities at Rice University in Texas. She is the author of *Intersections: A Reading of Sade with Bataille, Blanchot, and Klossowski*, of *Feminism and Psychoanalysis: The Daughter's Seduction*, and of *Reading Lacan*. Her most recent book is *Thinking Through the Body*.

LUCE IRIGARAY is the author of more than ten books, including *Speculum: Of the Other Woman* and *The Ethic of Sexual Differance*. These and others of her books have been (or are being) translated. Luce Irigaray is also a practising psychoanalyst, and divides her time between her practice and the CNRS, where she is a director of research.

ALICE JARDINE is Professor of Romance Languages and Literatures at Harvard. She is the author of *Gynesis*, and co-editor of *The Future of Difference* and *Men in Feminism*.

LISA JARDINE is a fellow of Jesus College, Cambridge. She is the author of articles and books on topics ranging from the philosophy of science to women and literature. She is currently working on a book *Reading Shakespeare Historically* and is also editing *Testaments of Women 1200–1550*.

TORIL MOI is the author of *Sexual/Textual Politics: Feminist Literary Theory*, editor of *The Kristeva Reader* and of *French Feminist Thought*, and is currently working on a book on Simone de Beauvoir. She divides her time between Norway, where she is adjunct Professor in the Department of Comparative Literature, and Duke University, North Carolina, where she is a Professor in Literature. She lives in Oxford.

NAOMI SEGAL teaches Modern Languages at St John's College, Cambridge. She is co-editor of a collection of papers on *Freud in Exile* and author of three books: *The Banal Object: Theme and Thematics in Proust, Rilke, Hofmannsthal and Sartre*; *The*

Unintended Reader: Feminism and Manon Lescaut; and *Narcissus and Echo: Women in the French Recit.*

MORAG SHIACH is a lecturer in English at Queen Mary College, London. She is the author of *Discourse on Popular Culture: Class, Gender and History in Cultural Analysis, 1730 to the Present Popular Culture.* She is writing her next book on Hélène Cixous.

GAYATRI CHAKRAVORTY SPIVAK has published extensively in feminism, deconstruction, and on critiques of imperialism, and is Derrida's best known translator. She is Mellon Professor of English at the University of Pittsburgh, and has also taught in New Delhi at the Centre for Historical Studies, Jawaharlal Nehru University. Her most recent book is *In Other Worlds.*

MARGARET WHITFORD lectures in French at Queen Mary College, London. Her publications include *Merleau-Ponty's Critique of Sartre's Philosophy* and she is co-editor (with Morweena Griffiths) of *Feminist Perspectives in Philosophy.*

ELIZABETH WRIGHT is lecturer and fellow in German, Girton College, Cambridge. She is the author of *Psychoanalytic Criticism: Theory and Practice* and *Postmodern Brecht: A Re-presentation.*

Index